THE DISCONTINUOUS TRADITION

THE DISCONTINUOUS TRADITION

*Studies in German Literature
in honour of*
ERNEST LUDWIG STAHL

Edited by P. F. GANZ

OXFORD
AT THE CLARENDON PRESS
1971

Oxford University Press, Ely House, London W. 1

GLASGOW NEW YORK TORONTO MELBOURNE WELLINGTON
CAPE TOWN SALISBURY IBADAN NAIROBI DAR ES SALAAM LUSAKA ADDIS ABABA
BOMBAY CALCUTTA MADRAS KARACHI LAHORE DACCA
KUALA LUMPUR SINGAPORE HONG KONG TOKYO

© OXFORD UNIVERSITY PRESS 1971

PRINTED IN GREAT BRITAIN

ERNEST!

Academics more than other people need the shelter which a sense of tradition can give, for the dialectic of their studies can develop only against a background of continuity in method and subject. Germanists have no such security. The discontinuity in German political and cultural history is a central feature of our subject and, indeed, of the German situation itself. The rejection of the Enlightenment in Germany; the misinterpretation of the German medieval heritage; the retreat into an idyllic, pre-industrial world; the idealization of the spirit of Weimar as the basis of an apolitical, self-sufficient culture of the private personality: they all pose questions which we must try to answer.

German literary history does not know a firm established canon of classical writers, and even the place of Goethe is not secure. Neither does there exist an unbroken tradition of critical writing in Germany, where Germanistik itself has become suspect. Hugo von Hofmannsthal put this sadly and succinctly in his essay 'Das Schrifttum als geistiger Raum der Nation', where he compared the role of tradition in France with its complete absence in Germany: 'Kein Zusammenhang in der Ebene der Gleichzeitigkeit, kein Zusammenhang in der Tiefe der Geschlechterfolge.'

This discontinuity—and the attempts to overcome it—is the problem which we face whenever we try to see German literature in perspective, and it seems an apt theme for this volume, prepared by friends and colleagues in this country and abroad who are linked by a common concern for our subject and a sense of friendship for you.

All contributors and all your friends and pupils in Oxford and elsewhere join me in the wish:

DA SPATIUM VITÆ, MULTOS DA, IUPPITER, ANNOS

The names of Matthijs Jolles and Eudo Mason were to have been on the list of collaborators, but they died suddenly before their articles were completed.

Ernest Ludwig Stahl

ERNEST LUDWIG STAHL was born on 10 December 1902 in Senekal, his father, Philip Stahl, a burgher of the Orange Free State, having become a British citizen after the Boer War. He was a pupil at Senekal Secondary School and then studied at Capetown University, where he took a B.A. with distinction in English, German, and History, and an M.A. with distinction in English. In 1925 he came to Oxford as a Porter scholar at Wadham College. In Oxford it was Marshall Montgomery who exerted the most lasting influence and first introduced him to Hölderlin's poetry. Between 1927, when he took a First in German, and 1930 he studied in Cologne, Berlin, Frankfurt, and Heidelberg, and then spent two years as Lektor in Berne where he took his Ph.D. under Fritz Strich with a thesis on *Die religiöse und die humanitätsphilosophische Bildungsidee und die Entstehung des deutschen Bildungsromans im 18. Jahrhundert*, which was published in 1934. Among his teachers in Germany and Switzerland were Paul Hankamer, Friedrich von der Leyen, Friedrich Gundolf, Karl Jaspers, and Helmut de Boor. In 1932 he returned to England, and taught as Assistant Lecturer in Birmingham until 1935 when he moved back to Oxford as a Lecturer. He was in demand as a tutor and very popular with the successive generations of undergraduates who had the good fortune to be taught by him. In 1945 he became Reader in German Literature and was also elected a Student of Christ Church. On his appointment in 1959 as Taylor Professor of the German Language and Literature he moved to the Queen's College, but Christ Church preserved its link with him by electing him a Student Emeritus. In 1942 he married Kathleen Mary Hudson, who, as an African historian and a scholar in her own right, has taken an affectionate interest in Oxford German studies.

During his years in Oxford as Lecturer, Reader, and Professor, his interests grew out of his early concern with the age of Goethe. His study, *Hölderlin's Symbolism* (1944), set the tone of his scholarship, which is distinguished by heuristic acuity untrammelled by preconceptions. This work, consciously brief in its scope and modest in its aims, nevertheless remains one of the best characterizations of Hölderlin's use of symbols. It was followed by *Heinrich von Kleist's Dramas* (1948, revised edition 1961), which has become a standard work in England, and *Friedrich Schiller's Drama* (1952), a study of Schiller's unique fusion of aesthetic theory and dramatic genius. Ernest Stahl's ability to give clear and illuminating interpretations of major literary works became known to a wider audience through his editions of *Werther* (1942), *Emilia Galotti* (1946), *Torquato Tasso* (1962), and a commentary on *Iphigenie* (1961). His inaugural lecture, devoted to *Creativity, a Theme from the Duino Elegies and Faust* (1961), is indicative of his breadth of interest and was followed by an edition of the *Duino Elegies* (1965) which accomplished the difficult task of presenting a hermetic work to English students.

He always regretted the difficulties young scholars find in getting articles and dissertations published, and it was to help them that, together with L. W. Forster and A. T. Hatto, he founded *Anglica Germanica*, a series of monographs devoted to literary studies. The periodical publication *Oxford German Studies* pursues the same aim and, while not confining itself to articles by Oxford colleagues and students, seeks to give them special encouragement.

Ernest Stahl has watched the growth of German studies in Oxford from the time when there was only one College Fellow in the School to the present day when it numbers more than twenty teachers, and he has helped to establish the reputation of his subject in this country, and in Oxford in particular, through his contacts with scholars in Europe and in the United States.

His influence on students and colleagues was exercised not only through his writings but through his teaching and personality. Those who know him will remember his impressive and lucid expositions of the history of German thought. He possesses two qualities which are essential in a good teacher: humanity and a sense of humour. It was because he combines a genuinely sympathetic approach to the work of his students with a determined upholding of critical standards that he was able to impress the members of his seminar groups, who realized that behind his exceptional modesty, patience, and charity there was an acute intellect which made students aware of the weaknesses in their arguments and the bluntness of their critical sense. He is deeply committed to his subject, with all its problems, and feels strongly that due recognition should be given to all aspects of German studies: oral proficiency, linguistics, medieval literature, history of ideas and of art as well as of literature.

Ernest Stahl is a man of a kind that Oxford, and indeed any university, has need of: his arrival in any group heightens the sense of sociability through his real concern, at once lively and considerate, for the opinions of others. His hospitality has been extended to a remarkably wide circle of friends in academic life, the London literary world, and post-colonial personalities whom he knew through his wife's work and his own South African origin and liberal convictions. He was a friend of Louis MacNeice, whom he met during their common phase at Birmingham and with whom he collaborated in producing the translation of Goethe's *Faust* which was broadcast by the B.B.C. on the occasion of the Goethe bicentenary in 1949 and published in their joint names.

Three decades of service to German studies were rewarded when Ernest Stahl received the Gold Medal of the 'Goethe-Institut' for 'hervorragende Verdienste um die Pflege der deutschen Sprache im Ausland', an honour which gave him great pleasure.

At the end of his tenure of the Oxford Chair he leaves behind a harmonious group of teachers and a school which owes much of its distinctive character to his guidance and example.

Contents

ERNEST L. STAHL. Photogaph by Ramsey & Muspratt, Oxford. *Frontispiece*

R. HINTON THOMAS (*Warwick*) Tradition and the Germanisten   1

F. J. LAMPORT (*Oxford*) Lessing and the 'Bürgerliches Trauerspiel'   14

E. A. BLACKALL (*Cornell*) Goethe and the Chinese Novel   29

L. W. FORSTER (*Cambridge*) Faust and the Sin of Sloth   54

R. PEACOCK (*London*) T. S. Eliot on Goethe   67

W. MÜLLER-SEIDEL (*Munich*) Die Idee des neuen Lebens. Eine Betrachtung über Schillers *Wallenstein*   79

G. W. MCKAY (*Oxford*) Three Scenes from *Wilhelm Tell*   99

W. RASCH (*Münster*) Blume und Stein. Zur Deutung von Ludwig Tiecks Erzählung *Der Runenberg*   113

F. J. STOPP (*Cambridge*) Keller's *Der grüne Heinrich*: the Pattern of the Labyrinth   129

MALCOLM PASLEY (*Oxford*) Nietzsche and Klinger   146

T. J. REED (*Oxford*) Thomas Mann and Tradition. Some Clarifications   158

J. C. MIDDLETON (*Texas*) The Rise of Primitivism and its Relevance to the Poetry of Expressionism and Dada   182

S. S. PRAWER (*Oxford*) Dada Dances. Hugo Ball's *Tenderenda der Phantast*   204

H. HENEL (*Yale*) Kafka's *Der Bau* or, How to Escape from a Maze   224

C. DAVID (*Paris*) Zu Franz Kafkas Erzählung *Elf Söhne*   247

V. LANGE (*Princeton*) Language as the Topic of Modern Fiction   260

A Select List of the Published Writings of E. L. Stahl   273

Index   275

Tradition and the Germanisten

R. HINTON THOMAS

IN their conflict with the Moderns, the Ancients took their stand on precedents, but they did not appeal to tradition. To do so was still not a habit of mind familiar to the eighteenth century. The nineteenth century, however, became familiar with the idea of tradition, associated often with the notion of continuity. The way for this was, in the case of Germany, prepared and facilitated by the interplay of the doctrine of the organic growth of culture, initiated by Herder, and nineteenth-century historicism. By the end of the nineteenth century tradition had come to be seen in the main as something to be defended, and this, significantly enough, at a time when doubts were also being raised about its validity, by Nietzsche, for instance, and Rilke ('Ist es möglich, dass die ganze Weltgeschichte missverstanden worden ist? Ist es möglich, dass die Vergangenheit falsch ist . . . ?'[1]). One defends something because it is felt to be of value; one is most moved to do so when it is felt to be endangered. By about the turn of the century powerful and distinguished voices were making themselves heard as champions of tradition, of the need to be mindful 'auch der Grösse unserer Verpflichtung gegen die Vergangenheit als ein geistiges Continuum, welches mit zu unserem höchsten geistigen Besitz gehört': 'Alles, was im entferntesten zu dieser Kunde dienen kann, muss mit aller Anstrengung und Aufwand gesammelt werden, bis wir zur Rekonstruktion ganzer vergangener Geisteshorizonte gelangen.' Thus, one example among many, Burckhardt in the *Weltgeschichtliche Betrachtungen*.[2]

To the doubts about tradition, and to the urge to insist on its importance, a number of different factors contributed. The most fundamental, to which all others were in their various ways related, was brought about by advanced industrialization, with all its economic, social, and intellectual consequences. The changes ensuing from this radical transformation were analysed with pioneering insight by Simmel, whose essay, *Die Grossstädte*

---

[1] *Die Aufzeichnungen des Malte Laurids Brigge*, Deutscher Taschenbuch-Verlag, Munich 1962, p. 20. [2] Berne 1941, p. 50.

und das Geistesleben (1903),[1] remains indispensable for the understanding of this period. Urbanization was for him characterized by a new 'objektive Kultur', deriving its substance 'aus unpersönlichen Inhalten und Darbietungen'.[2] This offered the individual freedom, opportunity, and mobility, but raised difficulties. 'Dass die Persönlichkeit sich sozusagen dagegen nicht halten kann'[3] was among the aspects that caused him concern. In his discussion the question of continuity and the problem of the self belonged together, because 'wir die Kontinuität des Geschehens unmittelbar in einer nicht aussprechbaren Weise als unsere eigene Daseinsform erleben'.[4] This led him to distinguish between *Geschichte* and *Geschehen*, the one denoting a sequence of historical events in the form of 'Diskontinuität der "Ereignisse"', the other their 'kontinuierliche Realität' mediated by 'ein von dem konkreten historischen Inhalt zurücktretender, abstrakt reflektierender Gedanke'.[5] Hence the fascination for him of ideas associated with the current *Lebensphilosophie*, the German equivalent of Bergson's rejection of 'separate states' for 'creative evolution', and from this Bergson, too, derived reassurance about the self. 'We are creating ourselves continually', Bergson rejoiced to note; 'our personality shoots, grows and ripens without ceasing', 'to mature is to go on creating oneself endlessly'.[6] In historicism the same conjunction is evident, of individuality and personality sustained and reassured by the sense of involvement in the past, viewed as process and continuity. Meinecke, the disciple of Ranke, expressed this very clearly, in metaphysical terms. 'Sich zu entwickeln', he wrote, 'ist das Charisma des einzelnen Menschen. Er fühlt sich dabei... wohltätig geleitet sowohl vom eigenen Lebensgesetze wie von unzähligen, ihm überkommenen Lebensgesetzen der Vergangenheit.... Er findet sich selbst und seine eigene Art ... vergrössert und gesteigert in der Weltgeschichte wieder...' When the individual 'wahrhaft weltgeschichtlich denken lernt, dann überströmt ihn das Gefühl, einer höheren... allschöpferischen Macht, einem Urquell aller Individualität in Geschichte und eigenem Leben verpflichtet und entsprossen zu sein'.[7]

[1] Reprinted in *Brücke und Tor*, Stuttgart 1957.   [2] Ibid., p. 241.
[3] Ibid., p. 241.   [4] Ibid., p. 55.   [5] Ibid., pp. 53–4.
[6] *Creative Evolution*, London 1911, pp. 6, 8.
[7] Quoted in W. Hofer, *Geschichtsschreibung und Weltanschauung. Betrachtungen zum Werk Friedrich Meineckes*, Munich 1950, pp. 537–8.

Tradition and the Germanisten 3

The perspective thus established is very relevant to the question of the past as it comes to present itself in important sectors of Germanistik. A passage from Böckmann's *Formgeschichte der deutschen Dichtung* will illustrate what is meant. He is talking about the 'allgemeine Krisensituation des modernen Daseins und Bewusstseins', by which he means 'das überall sichtbare, hilflose Hineingerissenwerden des Einzelnen in einen technisierten und dadurch nur übermächtigeren Staats- und Gesellschaftsapparat'. This has rendered 'den Menschen als solchen verdächtig', a point he takes in conjunction with a reference to man's 'Unsicherheit der eigenen Herkunft gegenüber', and from which results a 'beunruhigende Formlosigkeit des privaten wie des öffentlichen Daseins'. What is necessary, therefore, is 'die Überlieferung in einem radikaleren und echteren Sinn zum Sprechen zu bringen'.[1] Consider also Bieber's comments concerning the end of the nineteenth and the early twentieth century, his remarks about the 'veränderte Stellung des Individuums zur Allgemeinheit'. In this connection he mentions the 'Verschwinden des einzelnen innerhalb einer wachsenden, unbekannten und Anonymität ausbreitenden Masse', the 'abnehmende Durchsichtigkeit der Lebensbeziehungen', and the 'Beeinflussbarkeit' of the individual 'durch Stimmungen und Ideen, die ausserhalb seines eigenen Lebenskreises entstehen'. Experience of these facts, he goes on, 'hat das Selbstgefühl des einzelnen erschüttert und ihm seinen Abstand von der Natur, der Wahrheit, von den Instanzen des geschichtlichen Prozesses, in den er selbst verwickelt ist, aufgezeigt'. The title of the book from which these quotations are taken is *Der Kampf um die Tradition*.[2]

The situation here described is more or less what Tönnies would have seen as the decay of what he subsumed under the concept of *Gemeinschaft*. This we can paraphrase as all forms of relationship predominantly characterized by 'social cohesion', 'emotional depth', 'fusion of thought and feeling', 'continuity in time',[3] and a 'tight set of values'.[4] Tönnies himself referred to it as 'ein lebendiger Organismus', to *Gesellschaft* by contrast as 'ein mechanischer Aggregat und Artefact'.[5] For the individual,

[1] Hamburg 1949, i. 3–4.   [2] Stuttgart 1928, pp. 2–3.
[3] R. A. Nisbet, *The Sociological Tradition*, London 1967, p. 47.
[4] D. Riesman, *The Lonely Crowd*, abridged edition, New Haven and London 1968, p. 13.
[5] *Gemeinschaft und Gesellschaft*, 2nd edn., Berlin 1912, p. 5.

4   Tradition and the Germanisten

thus at home in a reality 'vertraut' and 'heimlich', the problem of identity, in terms of self-awareness or in relation to his past, does not arise, and tradition, naturally at home, needs no particular stimulus or encouragement. To this sense of integration corresponds a response to oneself and to others of an essentially emotional, unifying order, rather than one that analyses and dissects, an emphasis, as Simmel said of small-town life in contrast to large-scale urbanization, 'auf das Gemüt und gefühlsmässige Bedingungen'.[1] *Gemeinschaft*, Tönnies said, 'wird von jedem empfunden', and he attached importance to the close bond of language. The 'wahres Organ des Verständnisses' is 'die Sprache selber'.[2]

It was, in fact, on the unifying idea of the community of the *Volk*—'der Inbegriff von Menschen, welche dieselbe Sprache reden'[3]—that, at the institutional beginnings of Germanistik at the Frankfurt Germanistenversammlung of 1846, Jacob Grimm based the subject, and Germanistik quickly came to be seen as characterized by the concept of a natural, organic unity: 'Um die Dichtungsgeschichte als ihr Zentrum lagern sich religions-, sitten- und rechtsgeschichtliche Agfuabenbereiche, deren Erträge insgesamt dem Ziel einer Wesensbestimmung von einem imaginären Ursprung her unveränderlichen deutschen Volksgeistes dienen.'[4] The important feature is the primacy of *Dichtung* and its relation to the concept of history and the *Volksgeist*. Poetry was thought of by the founder-fathers of Germanistik as 'die eigentliche Stifterin des Nationalgeistes'; and Grimm himself identified *Germanist* and *Dichter*.[5] For if in the organic mode of historicist thinking and feeling, dominated as it was by the sense of the mysterious bonds linking the generations, it fell to the historian to reveal these in their process of growth, it was, on this view, for the Germanist to uncover them in their quintessential manifestations in the voice of the poet.

Thus by the circumstances of its origins Germanistik was not well placed, when the time came, to adjust itself, except in terms

[1] Op. cit., p. 228.   [2] Op. cit., p. 4.
[3] *Verhandlungen der Germanisten zu Frankfurt am Main am 24., 25. und 26. September 1846*, Frankfurt am Main 1847, p. 11. The discussions on this occasion are analysed in some detail in my book *Liberalism, Nationalism, and the German Intellectuals 1822–47*, Cambridge 1951, pp. 81 f.
[4] E. Lämmert, in the title essay of *Germanistik — eine deutsche Wissenschaft*, Frankfurt am Main 1967, p. 24.
[5] Cf. ibid., p. 24.

of a hostile response, to Germany's abrupt experience, towards the end of the century, of advanced industrialization. Its efforts to do so had notoriously their discreditable aspects. Faced with historicism's problem of the relativization of values, and the challenge of what on the original assumptions it could only regard as materialism and the victory of destructive reason, its reaction around the turn of the century was to assert against the forces of change ideals of unity and integration glamourized with a *völkisch* mystique. But Germanisten were not alone in doing this, and in any case we need not now lose any sleep about nationalistic excesses of this kind. The problem nowadays is of rather a different, but ultimately perhaps not unrelated, kind.

The idea of unity has never ceased to preoccupy Germanistik in various ways. As Lämmert has stressed, it has to the present day tenaciously clung to the concept of its own inherent unity as a subject, a principle explicitly insisted on in recent years. In its view of literature, unity has come to be the quality most respected and admired. The work of literature, if it is worth anything, is the 'einheitliche Gestaltung einer eigenen Welt',[1] despite the fact that what is here singled out is, to say the least, not very obvious in German literature before the later eighteenth century brought in the ideal of *Persönlichkeit*, nor in the time of the disintegration of *Persönlichkeit* when, structurally speaking, literature has moved very obviously in the direction of fragmentation and incongruity. Germanistik seems often to resent this, and in its canon this criterion of literature and a corresponding view of the individual support each other. The unified work presupposes the unified creator, the 'dichterische Persönlichkeit', as the phrase goes. 'Jedes Kunstwerk', declares the *Sachwörterbuch der Deutschkunde*, 'das nicht nur formales Spiel ist ... wächst organisch und gesetzmässig aus dem ein für allemal gegebenen Naturgrunde einer Persönlichkeit heraus, die nichts anderes kann als ein solches Werk schaffen.'[2] More recently the implications have been elaborated in the Fischer *Literatur-Lexikon*. The poetic work is 'Einheit in mehrfachem Sinn ... Einheit von Mensch und Welt im sprachlichen Kosmos'. In everyday experience—and, we might add, in a great deal of important modern literature—'das Aussen und das Innen, die

[1] W. Kayser, *Die Vortragsreise*, Berne 1958, p. 58.
[2] Leipzig and Berlin 1930, i. 248.

Teile und das Ganze, das Sinnliche und das Geistige' fail to synthesize. In contrast stands 'die dichterische Einheit', 'sie entfaltet sich aus ihnen'.[1] The most rigorous and influential protagonist of the doctrine of unity as applied to literature is Staiger, in whose gospel the consistency of all the parts within the whole, in the writer and in the work, becomes the governing criterion of excellence: 'Schön aber muss nun ein Kunstwerk heissen, das stilistisch einstimmig ist. Stilistische Einstimmigkeit besagt, dass alles Verschiedene in das eine Gültige, das ist die Welt des Künstlers, aufgehoben wird.'[2] What, in the final analysis, this view presupposes is articulated in the *Meisterwerke deutscher Sprache*, to whose 'festeste Überzeugungen' belongs belief in the 'Einheit des menschlichen Wesens', revealed through study of its 'einzelne Erscheinungen'.[3] There follows an exclusive view of literature, which qualifies as such only what renders (or by the 'kunstgerechte Auslegung, die alles mit allem zusammenhält'[4] can be made to seem to render) this totality apparent. Particular poems or works chosen to suit these presuppositions will naturally seem to confirm them. If they do not, as Müller-Seidel has pointed out,[5] the evidence may have to be touched up.

In any case, what is here really at issue is not a merely literary theory. Fritz Strich, though his methodological approach was declaredly different from that now represented by Staiger, happens to illustrate this very clearly in his *Kunst und Leben*. He defined *Dichtung* as 'eine unteilbare Einheit und Ganzheit, welche ... die menschliche Einheit und Ganzheit, die noch im Dichter lebt, zum Ausdruck bringen'. What disposed him to this view was the feeling that 'das Leben der Welt heute in Gefahr [ist], sich atomistisch aufzulösen'.[6] Here historicism still colours the idealization of the poet as the voice of wholeness and essence, but it is seen to be abdicating as a philosophy of change —the conservative inversion of Troeltsch's more dialectic kind of historicism, 'Geschichte durch Geschichte überwinden'.[7]

[1] *Das Fischer Lexikon (Literatur II, Erster Teil*, ed. W.-H. Friedrich and W. Killy), Frankfurt am Main 1965, p. 140.
[2] 'Versuch über den Begriff des Schönen', in *Trivium*, 3 (1945), 192.
[3] 2nd edn., Zürich 1948, p. 10.   [4] *Trivium*, 3 (1945), 192.
[5] *Probleme der literarischen Wertung*, Stuttgart 1965.
[6] Berne and Munich 1960, p. 8.
[7] *Gesammelte Schriften*, iii, Tübingen 1922, p. 772.

Tradition and the Germanisten

The outcome may be impressive in its erudition, but when stated, the principles sound quaintly naïve. In his *Geist der Goethezeit* Korff's aim was an 'Intensivierung unseres historischen Wissens': 'Gemäss dem Faustwort strebt es nicht nach dem äusseren Erwerb *neuen*, sondern nach dem inneren Erwerben *alten* Besitzes, indem es ein tieferes Verständnis für die als solche wohlbekannten Schätze der deutschen Dichtung zu erwecken sucht.'[1] In *Die deutsche Literatur von Goethes Tod bis in die Gegenwart* Walzel expressed the hope that, with existence now 'zu wenig gefestigt', there might reawaken 'das Zutrauen zur Dauer des Bestehenden'.[2] Böckmann's hope was 'im Rückgang auf die geschichtliche Überlieferung Mass und Möglichkeit des Menschen deutlicher zu begreifen', and to combat the 'Ohnmacht all jener Versuche . . . durch dogmatische Setzungen und schematische Auslegungen mit der Geschichte fertig zu werden oder gar ein Neues in Gang zu bringen'.[3] It may be necessary, Staiger recognizes, 'immer wieder an Unerhörtes zu glauben', but he is sure that, 'sofern ihm Dauer beschieden ist', this reveals itself 'als Spielart des hocherhabenen Einerlei . . . das über den Menschen waltet und seine Anmassungen und seine Schwächen früher oder später sühnt'. So in literature the important thing is 'das alte Wahre anzufassen', 'es neu sich anzueignen'.[4] Hence his praise for Grillparzer's 'seltene Kraft der Verehrung', as a writer who 'sich . . . zum Segen der Tradition bekennt', and thereby 'einer im Gefühl des Ungenügens mehr zu eitler Unrast versuchten Zeit den Weg zum Brunnen des Heils erschliesst'.[5] The image is similar to Benno von Wiese's about Mörike, from whose 'stille Quelle' flow 'die heilenden Kräfte.'[6]

These more or less random examples, extreme but not untypical, illustrate only too well how Germanistik can, in defiance of all the facts of modern experience, persist in idealizing the *Aussöhnung* of existence. This is just what we find in many a reader of the kind often used in German schools, and such as

[1] i, Leipzig 1923, p. vi.
[2] 5th edn., Berlin 1929, p. 176.
[3] Op. cit., pp. 3-4.
[4] *Tradition und Ursprünglichkeit*, ed. W. Kohlschmidt and H. Meyer, Berne 1966, p. 38.
[5] *Meisterwerke deutscher Sprache*, p. 187.
[6] *Eduard Mörike*, Tübingen and Stuttgart 1950, Vorwort.

Minder has analysed with proper scorn: 'ein Stilleben von Riesenausmass! Agrarliteratur im durchorganisierten Industriestaat!'[1] Indeed, images of 'Brunnen' and 'Quelle', in the above quotations, may not be as fortuitous as might appear. If they evoke pre-industrial impressions of village and country life, this would correspond to the social world to which this kind of thinking so often seems to point. To the question 'was ist ein vollendeter Geist?' Staiger answers, 'Vollendet ist eine Individualität, deren Sinnen und Trachten, Kopf und Herz sich mit den Gesetzen, die Ordnung und Ruhe verbürgen, einverstanden erklären',[2] and writers portraying 'gemeingefährliche Existenzen' earn his contempt. His ideal is touchingly simple: 'Gibt es denn heute etwa keine Würde und keinen Anstand mehr, nicht den Hochsinn eines selbstlos tätigen Mannes, einer Mutter, die Tag für Tag im stillen wirkt, das Wagnis einer grossen Liebe oder die stumme Treue von Freunden?'[3] Idealizing away conflict-situations, in the interests of the peace and quiet of the intact community, is the principle involved. So it is too as regards the features high-lighted, with obvious sympathy, by Benno von Wiese in *Die deutsche Tragödie von Lessing bis Hebbel*, in connection with the early nineteenth century. Singled out here is the 'Bedürfnis nach Sicherheit, Aussöhnung, Ruhe und Gehäuse', as the 'Gegenseite zu der immer stärker werdenden Unsicherheit des Lebensgefühles, das an die Konstruktionen der Vernunft nicht mehr zu glauben vermag, in der Wirklichkeit aber noch keinen festen Boden gefunden hat ... und den Boden unter den Füssen verliert'.[4] The subjective force of this kind of language becomes the more apparent if one recalls the way he talks about Mörike, whose merit it was 'mit der Traumkraft der Seele den Weg in das Sein zurückzufinden' and who 'dem von Heimatlosigkeit bedrohten Menschen die Wirklichkeit in der Gestalt des Schönen noch einmal zu schenken vermochte'.[5] Böckmann's reason for wanting 'die Überlieferung in einem radikaleren und echteren Sinn zum Sprechen zu bringen' is in order 'das heimische Dasein mit ihr auszusöhnen

[1] *Kultur und Literatur in Deutschland und Frankreich*, Frankfurt am Main 1962, p. 33.
[2] 'Literatur und Öffentlichkeit', in *Sprache im technischen Zeitalter*, 2 (1967), 92.
[3] Ibid., p. 95.
[4] Hamburg 1948, p. 19.
[5] *Eduard Mörike*, p. 39.

Tradition and the Germanisten

und die Erinnerung an den geschichtlichen Weg des eigenen Volkes wieder in eine formende Kraft zu verwandeln'.[1]

The history of Germanistik thus embraces on the one hand the historicist idea of the inherent essence of culture and institutions at the particular moment in the process of growth. Images of 'Blüten' of culture which 'sich entfalten' are a familiar part of its vocabulary. Hettner in his time was praised for demonstrating precisely this.[2] 'Blütezeit' is entrenched among the subject's stock clichés. On the other hand, the complementary aspect of historicism, namely transience and decay, is resisted. Historicism hardens into an ahistorical traditionalism, which incidentally does nothing to further the relevance of Germanistik beyond its own in-group, and, as if to confirm the German New Left's caricature of the 'Grosskritiker',[3] concern with values is all too often revealed as an inflexible conservatism. Ridiculous this may be, but, one must hasten to add (since at this stage the discussion comes within the orbit of a debate in which ideological extremes are played off against each other), it is no more so than the now familiar opposite, an ahistorical involvement in the immediate present, as if this merely supersedes the past and makes it immaterial. Faced with this, obstinate traditionalism is self-defeating and unconstructive. It only helps to nourish this depressing form of modern philistinism by making the alternative seem so ludicrous. It is certainly no exaggeration to call it philistinism, and unless a major role of education in the humanities is to make the past appear as more than immaterial, it is difficult to know what it is about.

This philistinism, however, is not lightly to be dismissed as accidental and ephemeral. For one cannot any longer evade the fact that in modern industrial society the 'pre-industrial sense of continuity with the past' has, in the awareness of many and especially of the younger generation, been 'contracted into a narrow present'. Time 'has become a commodity', but 'only present time'. The past 'is useless, the future of interest only as a potentially better present'.[4] The quotations are from a discussion

---

[1] Op. cit., p. 4.
[2] Cf. Nachwort to Hettner's *Geschichte der deutschen Literatur im 18. Jahrhundert*, Leipzig 1928.
[3] Cf. *Kritik — von wem/für wen/wie . . . Eine Selbstdarstellung deutscher Kritiker*, ed. P. Hamm, Munich 1968, pp. 20 f.
[4] J. T. Fraser (ed.), *The Voices of Time*, London 1968, p. 137.

of the situation in the United States, but the implications extend to modern industrial society in general. What they include is indicated, in an extreme and maybe in some respects oversimplified form, by Marcuse in his prognosis of 'one-dimensional man' in a society subject to the consequences of the 'progressing rationality' of industrial production. Remembrance, he argues,[1] may 'give rise to dangerous insights, and the established society seems to be apprehensive of the subversive contents of memory'. If not preserved in history, memory 'succumbs to the totalitarian power of the behavioural universe', and modern industrial society 'tends to liquidate, as an "irrational rest", the disturbing elements of Time and Memory'. So his argument becomes a demand for recognition of our relation to the past as something that 'counteracts the functionalization of thought by and in the established reality'. Searching 'in the real history of man for the criteria of truth and falsehood, progress and regression', it is historical consciousness that has the power to 'break open a closed universe of discourse and its petrified structure'. The danger, however, is that the 'language which tries to recall and preserve the original truth succumbs to its ritualization', rigidly retaining the past, not mediating it with the present. One opposes, that is to say, 'the concepts which comprehended a historical situation without developing them into the present situation—one blocks their dialectic'. The critical function of historical consciousness in relation to the present is then disabled. Marcuse takes the example of communist society, but, nearer home, Germanistik needs just as much to get the dialectic moving.

What, in this case, should the dialectic amount to, and how should it affect the self-awareness of Germanistik as a subject? I must repeat what I have argued elsewhere,[2] that (as some of the above points help to explain) we have moved into—and, barring the destruction of advanced industrial society, will not in the foreseeable future move out of—a situation in which contemporary experience will more and more provide the effective stimuli. This is not necessarily a bad thing, and there is no need to waste our energies lamenting about it. If this assumption

[1] *One-Dimensional Man. Studies in the Ideology of Advanced Industrial Society*, London 1964, pp. 98f.
[2] *The Commitment of German Studies*, University of Birmingham 1965.

about contemporary experience is correct, and there is plenty of evidence that it is, it would be a good reason for Germanistik to reconsider the order of its priorities. It is axiomatic in Germanistik that one cannot know the present without the past. Much less easily acceptable for the subject is that one cannot know the past without the present. There is the conventional argument that, when we come to study the present, the necessary distance is lacking for proper critical assessment. Especially in Germany, the choice of subjects of doctoral theses, for example, is limited accordingly. This always seems to me a very ineffective argument, but the point to be made now is that it is double-edged. For distance is a factor not just of time, but also of attitude, and to feel too easily and naturally at home in the past is, as far as the study of it is concerned, to forfeit the advantages of alienation as an incentive to critical energy and insight. So if Germanistik should now hasten to commit itself to the contemporary, it should do so, amongst other things, in the interests of improving its understanding of the past. It is not just a question of bringing its syllabus a bit more up to date. To tack on a course or two on the twentieth century does not necessarily change anything very much.

A much more radical readjustment is needed, and what this should involve has been analysed by Reinhard Baumart,[1] who has authority to speak on this matter as one who, involved in contemporary culture as a creative writer, is also a qualified (and *habilitiert*) Germanist. I am glad meanwhile to find that I now have his support for the view that the 'Ausgangs- und Bezugspunkt' of Germanistik has to be, if it is not to be merely 'museal', 'ein zeitgenössisches Bewusstsein'; that it will only become genuinely productive again 'wenn sie von der Gegenwart aus Vergangenheit reflektiert'. In a sense, but not in the sense intended, it might be said that this is what Germanistik has been doing, disillusion with the present motivating the idealization of tradition. But then the choice is too simple, and the procedure hopelessly undialectic. It would be just as undialectic if the formulation implied, which it does not, uncritical and unreflecting acceptance of what the present throws up, whether as direct experience of the immediate reality or in the form of what are offered to us as creeds of belief claiming our

[1] 'Was soll Germanistik heute?' in *Die Zeit*, 18 Oct. 1968, p. 24.

assent, as if these too were not to be made concurrently the object of critical inquiry. It means the relativization all the time of the past by the present, and of the present by an awareness that is critical because it is also historical. Thus, on the one hand, the older texts as 'Gegenstände gegenwärtiger Reflexion', on the other, 'das Historischmachen der neuen und der neuesten Texte, ihre Behandlung als Gegenstände gegenwärtiger *Reflexion*'.

The search in the culture of the past for values, patterns, and relationships goes on—now, as ever, a central function of scholarship in the humanities. But what emerges will be seen as an intellectual construction, and so all the time hypothetical, and—like contemporary awareness itself through the complementary aspect of the dialectic—by virtue of this unremittingly subject to correction. Thus demythologized, tradition appears as a set of relative and provisional surmises and possibilities. So too, on the basis of a great deal of psychological and literary evidence, does the individual in modern consciousness. Max Weber reflected this in his ironic comment in 1919 about 'Persönlichkeit', as one of the 'Götzen, deren Kult wir heute an allen Strassenecken und in allen Zeitschriften sich breit machen finden'. 'Auf wissenschaftlichem Gebiet', he remarked, it should be seen now in a cooler and more objective light.[1] What Max Weber says about the cult of personality has its bearing on the cult of tradition. In the larger context, how one sees the past depends ultimately on how one sees oneself. The problems of the identity of tradition and of the identity of the ego appear as related and interpenetrating aspects. An illustration is provided by Konrad Bayer's 'Porträt in Prosa', *Der Kopf des Vitus Bering*,[2] where the object of the narration is both the narrating ego itself, fragmented and diversified, with all its 'Ausdehnungsmöglichkeiten', its 'Irritationen und Verstörungen', and also the 'Aktionen des Bewusstseins' operating on the past.[3] 'Was aber bedeuten hier Fakten; als was verwendet der Text Geschichte?' asks Jürgen Becker, Bayer's most sympathetic and perceptive interpreter. 'Er meint in keinem Fall Vorgänge, die ein für allemal fixiert und abgeschlossen, übersehbar und verständlich sind. Von sich aus sagt Geschichte nichts und erklärt sie nichts. Sie

[1] *Gesammelte Aufsätze zur Wissenschaftslehre*, Tübingen 1951, p. 575.
[2] Olten and Freiburg 1965. [3] Ibid., Nachwort, p. 62.

Tradition and the Germanisten

hinterlässt ihre Geschehnisse und Daten. Und stiftet damit Vorschläge, Möglichkeiten erst, vergangene Wirklichkeiten herzustellen und zu definieren. Wie das geschieht, darüber entscheidet die aktuelle Erfahrung. Der Blick aufs Vergangene wird von dem bestimmt, was dieser Blick heute wahrgenommen hat. Geschichte entsteht im Bewusstsein der Gegenwart.'[1] This is an extreme example, but it is none the worse for that. Like Becker's own *Felder*, for that matter, it gives radical expression to a problem the implications and consequences of which Germanistik might very usefully ponder in the interests of its own salvation.

[1] Ibid., p. 61.

Lessing and the 'Bürgerliches Trauerspiel'

F. J. LAMPORT

Die Personen so eingeführet sind fast zu nidrig vor ein Traur-Spiel ...
GRYPHIUS, Preface to *Cardenio und Celinde*

THE tradition of the modern German literary drama names Lessing as its founder; and one reason for this is that he himself rejected the major traditional form of serious drama of his own day, and made a revolutionary innovation. He turned away from classical tragedy in the French manner, as advocated and practised by Gottsched and his school, and introduced into Germany the middle-class domestic tragedy or 'bürgerliches Trauerspiel'. In his *Theatralische Bibliothek* of 1754 Lessing gives a brief definition of the new genre: 'Hier hielt man es für unbillig, dass nur Regenten und hohe Standespersonen in uns Schrecken und Mitleiden erwecken sollten; man suchte sich also aus dem Mittelstande Helden, und schnallte ihnen den tragischen Stiefel an, in dem man sie sonst, nur ihn lächerlich zu machen, gesehen hatte.'[1] However stylized and artificial the speech of *Miss Sara Sampson* may seem to us today, and however remote from Lessing's demonstrable intentions may be the social criticism which the modern reader tends to find implicit in *Emilia Galotti*, these two plays did represent in their own day a revolutionary move in the direction of contemporary realism and of the serious portrayal of the concerns and problems of everyday life. This was a major contribution on Lessing's part to the revival and future development of the German drama. So, on the other hand, was his theoretical advocacy of Shakespeare, another deliberate and violent break with Gottschedian neo-classicism. The two impulses move in opposite directions. But they have a common origin in the desire to establish a new

[1] Introduction to *Abhandlungen von dem weinerlichen oder rührenden Lustspiele*. Cf. *Lessings sämtliche Schriften*, ed. Lachmann/Muncker [LM], vi. 6.

Lessing and the 'Bürgerliches Trauerspiel'

form of serious drama and to escape from the false tradition of neo-classicism; and this community of impulse is recognized in the words with which J. A. Ebert greeted *Emilia Galotti*, 'O Shakespeare-Lessing!'[1] Yet an examination of the subject of Lessing and the 'bürgerliches Trauerspiel' will show that he himself was sceptical of his own innovation. Although he undoubtedly desired to find a new form of tragedy, he was by no means convinced of the rightness of the 'bürgerliches Trauerspiel' as the solution to this problem: he would have preferred something more closely resembling the traditional tragic norm.

Evidence for this assertion will be found in his numerous unfinished experiments in tragedy, and in his critical and theoretical writings; but also in his two completed full-length tragedies themselves. Both *Miss Sara Sampson* and *Emilia Galotti* are 'bürgerliche Trauerspiele', although only the former was so designated by Lessing himself. But each is in origin a modernization of a tragic prototype taken from classical antiquity; and in each of them Lessing finds it necessary to remind us of this fact. It is as if he sought thus to legitimize his own dramatic procedure, and reassure the spectator that, despite the contemporary realistic middle-class setting, he was still watching a 'real' tragedy.

In Act II, scene 7 of *Miss Sara Sampson* Marwood, who in attempting to regain her hold on Mellefont does not shun the foulest means, threatens to avenge his desertion of her upon their child. She utters this threat not directly, but by identifying herself with a figure of mythical antiquity who did take such vengeance upon a husband who had deserted her for another woman: 'Sieh in mir eine neue Medea!' It seems out of place in the genteel eighteenth-century English setting—all the more so since Marwood herself has just told Mellefont, at the beginning of this very scene, 'Drücken Sie sich ohne so gelehrte Anspielungen aus!' But, of course, she is not really talking to him, but to us. That is, while the substance of the threat is addressed to Mellefont, the manner of its delivery constitutes a signal directed at the audience. Marwood is establishing herself, as Emil Staiger puts it, as one of the 'einfach-grossen mythischen

---

[1] Letter to Lessing, 14 Mar. 1772, LM, xx. 150 f.

16 *Lessing and the 'Bürgerliches Trauerspiel'*

Urgestalten der πάθη'.[1] And through her, by this means, Lessing is expressing the claims of ordinary, unheroic eighteenth-century upper-middle-class people to act as tragic protagonists. For he is indicating that what seems merely, like Lillo's *London Merchant*, 'a Tale of private woe',[2] is really a re-enactment of an ancient, archetypal tragic plot: *Miss Sara Sampson* is a modernized *Medea*.[3]

Lessing has treated the subject in accordance with the theory of modernization adumbrated in another essay in the *Theatralische Bibliothek*, that on Senecan tragedy.[4] Although on this occasion he discusses only two of the ten tragedies attributed to Seneca, there is no reason to doubt that he knew and intended to discuss them all, including Seneca's *Medea*, which had already served as the source for Corneille's *Médée*. The Seneca essay, despite its scrappy nature, is an important and neglected work. It is concerned precisely with the problem, and the necessity, of adapting traditional tragic subject-matter to suit the characteristic aesthetic and moral sensibilities of different ages. In *Miss Sara Sampson* Lessing has shifted the centre of tragic gravity to the character with whom a mid-eighteenth-century audience could most readily sympathize: that is, from the vengeful and violent Medea to the virtuous and passive Creusa. But this shift of focus causes serious difficulties. It is most significant that of all the characters in the play it is the villain, the 'rasendes Weib',[5] the typical 'politischer Mensch der vorbürgerlichen Zeit',[6] the 'figure of outré flamboyance [who] thrashes about in this tepid setting like a sea monster in a lily pond',[7] in short the odd one out in some sense, however one may choose to define it, who can most convincingly, or at any rate least unconvincingly, identify herself with a grand archetypal tragic figure.

[1] E. Staiger, *Grundbegriffe der Poetik*[2], Zürich 1951, p. 160. Cf. also his *Stilwandel*, Zürich 1963, p. 49.
[2] George Lillo, *The London Merchant* (1731), Prologue.
[3] Cf. Erich Schmidt, *Lessing*[2], Berlin 1899, i. 278 ff.
[4] *Von den lateinischen Trauerspielen, welche unter dem Namen des Seneca bekannt sind*, LM, vi. 167 ff.
[5] Cf. E. Staiger, 'Rasende Weiber in der deutschen Tragödie des achtzehnten Jahrhunderts', *Stilwandel*, op. cit., pp. 25 ff., especially p. 44: 'Rasende Weiber sind nun eigentlich nur noch als Nebenfiguren berechtigt . . .'
[6] Fritz Brüggemann, 'Lessings Bürgerdramen und der Subjektivismus als Problem', *Jahrbuch des Freien Deutschen Hochstifts*, 1926, p. 70.
[7] R. R. Heitner, *German Tragedy in the Age of Enlightenment*, Berkeley 1963, pp. 176 f.

Lessing and the 'Bürgerliches Trauerspiel'

The eponymous heroine and moral protagonist of the play cannot do so. In the Medea tragedies of Seneca and Corneille, King Creon's daughter is only a minor character; and indeed in Euripides' *Medea* she does not appear in person at all.[1] *Emilia Galotti* is the result of an exactly similar procedure. On 21 January 1758 Lessing wrote to Nicolai that he was working on 'eine bürgerliche Virginia, der er den Titel Emilia Galotti gegeben'. Of the completed play of 1772 he no longer uses the word 'bürgerlich', but it is with the same implications that he describes the play to his brother Karl as 'eine modernisierte, von allem Staatsinteresse befreite Virginia', and commends it to the Duke of Brunswick-Wolfenbüttel as 'weiter nichts, als die alte Römische Geschichte der Virginia in einer modernen Einkleidung'.[2] Once again, the play is a modernization of an antique prototype, this time from Roman history instead of Greek legend; once again, it contains a deliberate allusion to that prototype, this time in the penultimate scene where Emilia provokes her father to the fatal stroke by her citation of the example of Virginius; and once again, although Lessing has not this time turned the play upside down, as it were, in quite the same way as in *Miss Sara Sampson*, difficulties result. The play is such an enormous technical advance on *Sara*, the dialogue, the creation of character, atmosphere, and tension are so successful that the spectator can allow himself to be convinced and moved by what happens. But when he attempts to interpret

---

[1] Otto Mann notes the basic parallel with the Medea story and observes that the action can be focused in different ways: 'Man kann die Tragödie "Marwood" nennen, um die Medeatragödie zu sehen, oder "Mellefont", um Goethes Weislingen oder seinen Fernando in der "Stella" zu sehen ...' (O. Mann, *Lessing, Sein und Leistung*, Hamburg 1948, p. 234. The point is not so clearly made in the revised edition (Hamburg 1961), but cf. pp. 233, 236). He then goes on to argue for the legitimacy of Lessing's choice of perspective, that is his decision to present the action from the point of view of Sara as the foremost and most innocent in suffering. But, in Mann's own words (1948 edn., p. 241): 'Die eine überragende Wirklichkeit in der Tragödie selbst ist die Erscheinung des zu Fürchtenden, und auch auf die Charaktere gehend sehen wir nur, dass sie unter der Macht des zu Fürchtenden stehen ... Der Grad der moralischen Veranlassung in uns wird gleichgültig gegenüber dem Grundverhältnis zwischen dieser Macht und unserer Endlichkeit.' And the proper conclusion to draw from this is not Mann's, that 'Sara wird hiervon ebenso ereilt wie Mellefont und Marwood', but rather the reverse: to focus the action from the point of view of Sara is, precisely because of her passivity, to see the other protagonists merely as the instigators of *her* suffering and accordingly to attach moral blame to them, Marwood in particular.

[2] Letters of March 1772, LM, xviii. 20–3.

Lessing's meaning, he is forced to construct some explanatory hypothesis of the kind which so many critics have devised.[1] Moreover, this would seem to be exactly what Lessing found himself obliged to do. He has chosen a subject which he recognizes as tragic, and has then tried to find or invent a meaning for it. This is in accordance with the theory of the Seneca essay of 1754, where Lessing points out that the ancients did not follow the procedure recommended by Gottsched, of first deciding on the moral and then finding a story to fit it, because they knew 'dass bei jeder Begebenheit unzählige Wahrheiten anzubringen wären'.[2] It also reflects the further refinement of the theory of psychological motivation expounded in No. 32 of the *Hamburgische Dramaturgie*, in criticism of Corneille's *Rodogune*:

> Der Poet findet in der Geschichte eine Frau, die Mann und Söhne mordet; eine solche Tat kann Schrecken und Mitleid erwecken, und er nimmt sich vor, sie in einer Tragödie zu behandeln. Aber die Geschichte sagt ihm weiter nichts, als das blosse Faktum, und dieses ist ebenso grässlich als ausserordentlich . . . so wird er vor allen Dingen bedacht sein, eine Reihe von Ursachen und Wirkungen zu erfinden, nach welcher jene unwahrscheinliche Verbrechen nicht wohl anders, als geschehen müssen.

Most significant, in this passage, is the coexistence of the recognition that a certain event belongs to the category of tragedy— 'kann Schrecken und Mitleid erwecken'—with the apprehension of it as in itself meaningless and morally repugnant—'das blosse Faktum . . . ist ebenso grässlich als ausserordentlich'. Now it might be argued that the tragic dramatist is concerned precisely with the conferring of order and shape, and hence of meaning, upon events which are inherently meaningless. This, however, would open up metaphysical perspectives which were, I think, largely if not wholly closed to Lessing and his contemporaries. What matters here is to note Lessing's recognition of tragedy as a *purely formal* category. Lessing of course succeeded, at least to his own satisfaction, in devising an ethical vindication of tragedy, based upon his theory of pity. But side by side with this, tragedy persists in Lessing's mind as a purely formal, abstract, aesthetic category, its rules laid down by Aristotle for

[1] For my own, see my article, 'Eine bürgerliche Virginia', *GLL* N.S. 17 (1964), 304 ff.
[2] *LM*, vi. 197.

Lessing and the 'Bürgerliches Trauerspiel'   19

all time. It is for this reason that, for example, at a time when Gerstenberg was already demanding 'Weg mit der Klassifikation des Drama!'[1] Lessing in Nos. 74 ff. of the *Hamburgische Dramaturgie* was going to great lengths to establish that Weisse's *Richard der Dritte*, although undeniably an effective piece of dramatic writing of some kind or other, could not be accorded the title of tragedy because it failed to satisfy certain allegedly Aristotelian criteria. The explanation of this is that Lessing was seeking, as Gottsched had done before him, to create modern German tragedy as a literary status-symbol, a means of enhancing the cultural prestige of the German nation. This could not be done without establishing a firm and evident link with the tradition of European drama going back to classical antiquity. At the same time, however, he realized, as Gottsched had not, the need to create a form of drama specifically appropriate to the requirements of a modern German audience, and he rejected the French style of neo-classic drama by this criterion. Lessing's experiments in tragedy—including the two completed 'bürgerliche Trauerspiele'—suggest that he himself realized that his two aims were doubtfully compatible with one another: that modern drama demanded realism whereas tragedy demanded *éloignement*.

The term 'bürgerliches Trauerspiel' is unfortunately not susceptible of precise definition. If we are to believe Lothar Pikulik, it has no necessary social implications whatever;[2] but Lessing's definition in the *Theatralische Bibliothek*, which has already been quoted, plainly states that the new genre chooses 'Helden aus dem Mittelstande'. This definition was of course written before *Miss Sara Sampson* had been composed or even thought of; Lessing was at this time in no way committed to the 'bürgerliches Trauerspiel'—the definition may not be without a touch of irony—and his own practice, which was to set the standard for the type in Germany, does not necessarily conform to this particular precept. The English term, 'domestic tragedy', is slightly less misleading. The reason for the popularity of 'domestic' subjects in eighteenth-century tragedy may well have been not so much bourgeois class pride as a turning away from public

[1] *Briefe über Merkwürdigkeiten der Literatur*, No. 14 (1766). Cf. *Sturm und Drang: Kritische Schriften*, ed. Loewenthal and Schneider, Heidelberg n.d., p. 14.
[2] L. Pikulik, *Bürgerliches Trauerspiel und Empfindsamkeit*, Köln/Graz 1966.

and political affairs altogether. Thus in Germany the public could not be satisfied by the aristocratic mode of tragedy advocated and practised by Gottsched and his school, not so much because it was aristocratic or 'feudal' in its ideology whereas the public wanted something 'democratic' or 'progressive', but because it was political in content whereas the public wanted something unpolitical and private. As Lessing writes in No. 14 of the *Hamburgische Dramaturgie*: 'Unsere Sympathie erfordert einen einzeln Gegenstand, und ein Staat ist ein viel zu abstrakter Begriff für unsre Empfindungen.' Or as Johnson put it: 'The passions rise higher at domestic than imperial tragedies.'[1] The 'domestic tragedy' is not *necessarily* middle-class in setting. Yet the stress placed upon private relationships, the ideal of the family, the emotional religiosity and largely passive moral values characteristic of these works can meaningfully be called typically middle-class; and in his characterization of the reading public of the 'moralische Wochenschriften', those periodicals which did so much to create the characteristic tone of early- and mid-eighteenth-century literature, Wolfgang Martens goes so far as to speak of 'ein gleichsam unpolitisches bürgerliches Selbstbewusstsein'.[2] Friedrich Nicolai, in his *Abhandlung vom Trauerspiele* of 1756, gives an implied definition of the 'bürgerliches Trauerspiel' which illustrates the ambiguity of the term. He classifies tragedies according to the emotions they seek to arouse: 'rührende Trauerspiele' seek to arouse pity and fear, 'heroische Trauerspiele' admiration. The former category includes 'sowohl alle *bürgerliche* Trauerspiele, als diejenigen, worinnen ein bloss bürgerliches Interesse herrschet, z. B. *Medea, Thyest, Merope, Zaire*'.[3] One would seem after all to be justified in defining the 'bürgerliches Trauerspiel' in terms not only of the private, domestic, unpolitical nature of the action portrayed, but also of the social class of its characters. These need not actually be bourgeois, but the very highest ranks of society—kings and princes—are normally excluded. So are mythical personages. The 'bürgerliches Trauerspiel' portrays events in the lives of characters drawn from contemporary real life. Some

[1] Letter to Mrs. Thrale, 11 July 1770, *Letters*, ed. Hill, Oxford 1892, i. 162.
[2] W. Martens, *Die Botschaft der Tugend. Die Aufklärung im Spiegel der Moralischen Wochenschriften*, Stuttgart 1968, p. 342.
[3] Reprinted by R. Petsch in *Lessings Briefwechsel mit Mendelssohn und Nicolai über das Trauerspiel* (Philosophische Bibliothek, Bd. 121), Hamburg 1910, p. 19.

measure of realism in presentation is the natural corollary of this: the 'bürgerliches Trauerspiel' is characteristically written in prose. Lessing shared the taste of his contemporaries for 'domestic' rather than 'imperial' tragedies. He felt private misfortunes to be more truly tragic than impersonal political issues or disasters on a heroic scale, and he felt the pity evoked by the former to be a more genuinely tragic emotion than the admiration aroused by the latter. Though modified considerably in detail, his theory of the tragic emotions remains, from the correspondence with Mendelssohn and Nicolai in 1856–7 to the *Hamburgische Dramaturgie* of ten years later, firmly based on pity, other emotions such as fear and admiration being in effect explained away as constituents or phases of pity or as ancillary to it.[1] In his dramatic practice too we find that he characteristically chooses 'domestic' subjects. Fathers, daughters, sons, husbands, and wives are the tragic protagonists not only of *Miss Sara Sampson* and *Emilia Galotti*, but also of *Philotas*, *Kleonnis*, *Der Horoskop*, and *Fatime*.[2] But all these 'tales of private woe' are enacted in remote and elevated milieux. *Miss Sara Sampson* is set in England and *Emilia Galotti* in Italy; and the fragment *Tonsine*, the only other work which we know to have been designated 'bürgerliches Trauerspiel' by Lessing himself, is set in Spain.[3] The nearest Lessing ever came to a German setting for tragedy is in *Samuel Henzi*, which takes place in Switzerland—and whose subject-matter is not merely contemporary, but of urgent topicality. But *Henzi* is, as the unknown author of the *Theorie des bürgerlichen Trauerspiels* of 1756 (perhaps Pfeil, the author of *Lucie Woodvil*) rightly concludes, a heroic and not a domestic tragedy, for it is about affairs of state,[4] and it is in formal alexandrine verse. Some of the later tragic experiments employ a setting of classical antiquity, namely *Philotas* (the only one to be completed), *Das befreite*

---

[1] Cf. P. Michelsen, 'Die Erregung des Mitleids durch die Tragödie. Zu Lessings Ansichten über das Trauerspiel im Briefwechsel mit Mendelssohn und Nicolai', *DVJS* 40 (1966), 548 ff.
[2] Lessing's uncompleted tragic projects will be found in the *Theatralischer Nachlass* (LM, iii), with the solitary exception of *Tonsine*, for which see the next footnote.
[3] Cf. H. Butzmann, 'Lessings bürgerliches Trauerspiel "Tonsine"', *Jahrbuch des Freien Deutschen Hochstifts*, 1966, pp. 109 ff.
[4] Quoted by J. Krueger, 'Zur Frühgeschichte der Theorie des bürgerlichen Trauerspiels', in G. Erdmann and A. Eichstaedt (eds.), *Worte und Werte. Bruno Markwardt zum 60. Geburtstag*, Berlin 1961, pp. 177 ff.

Rom, Kodrus, Kleonnis, Alcibiades, and *Spartacus. Kleonnis* and *Spartacus* were to have been written in blank verse, and Lessing approved of Gleim's versification of *Philotas,* writing to Gleim on 31 March 1759 that the play in its original form lacked 'eine edle tragische Sprache'. *Philotas* is a heroic play with an unheroic, indeed anti-heroic message, and this contradiction between form and content is the reason for its failure. The hero's self-sacrifice is just the kind of deed which heroic tragedy traditionally portrays as noble and admirable; but here Lessing characterizes it through the mouth of his moral spokesman Aridäus as an act of 'wütende Schwermut', just as in *Miss Sara Sampson* the tragic revenge of Medea becomes the merely criminal revenge of Marwood, and in *Emilia Galotti* the tragically admirable deed of the determined Virginius becomes the pathetic deed of the distraught and helpless Odoardo Galotti. One might therefore say that *Philotas* is 'verbürgerlicht' in content while retaining the trappings of classical antiquity, that it is a compromise between the classical and the 'bürgerlich'; and *Kleonnis* appears to be similar in intent. *Der Horoskop* and *Fatime* are both 'domestic tragedies' with characters of elevated rank, in blank verse (two versions of the opening scenes of *Fatime* survive, one in prose and one in verse), and with exotic, that is remote but non-classical, settings. *Der Horoskop* is, like one of its possible sources, Calderón's *La vida es sueño,* set in Poland (still, at the time of the action, subject to Tartar depredations) and *Fatime* is set in Turkey or Arabia. The use which Lessing makes of the blank verse medium in these two fragments is of great interest. The effect is not that of the classical grand style, but of a wide range of tone capable of registering great psychological subtlety. In this connection the contrast between the two versions of *Fatime* is especially remarkable: the prose version is serious and pathetic, that in verse animated and capricious, admirably reflecting the wilful character of the heroine. Although a stylized form of speech, the verse is in fact more realistic than the prose of the other version. In *Fatime* and *Der Horoskop* Lessing seems to me to be trying to create a tragic style which maintains the *éloignement* necessary to the traditional formal category of tragedy, while at the same time avoiding the classical grand style with its inescapable associations of the heroic and 'admirable', which he had rejected, and making

Lessing and the 'Bürgerliches Trauerspiel'   23

room for the greater subtleties of characterization and presentation, the increased realism, which the modern age demanded. But he failed to complete either of these most interesting and promising-looking experiments, and when they did at last bear fruit it was in *Nathan der Weise*—which is not a tragedy. Here again we find an exotic setting and a curiously de-stylized blank verse, an 'Anti-Vers' as Peter Demetz has called it,[1] as in *Der Horoskop* and *Fatime*; and here the experiment succeeds triumphantly because Lessing is no longer frustrating himself by trying to conform to the abstract category of tragedy. But in *Spartacus*, his last attempt at tragedy before *Emilia Galotti*, Lessing appears to have reverted to the full-blown classical manner. It is antique, political, and heroic: 'meine antityrannische Tragödie' he called it, in a letter to Ramler of 24 December 1770. Spartacus is, of course, a lower-class hero, but the piece is neither domestic nor contemporary nor realistic. It was apparently to have been in blank verse, which here would presumably have meant the grand manner, given the nature of the subject and the sentiments. It is in fact about as far from 'bürgerliches Trauerspiel' as any of Lessing's tragic projects.

One other of these must be mentioned which is something of a special case. On 19 November 1755 Moses Mendelssohn wrote to Lessing: 'Wo sind Sie, liebster Lessing, mit Ihrem bürgerlichen Trauerspiel? Ich möchte es nicht gern bei dem Namen nennen, denn ich zweifle, ob Sie ihm den Namen *Faust* lassen werden. Eine einzige Exklamation: O Faustus! Faustus! könnte das ganze Parterre lachen machen.' But if Lessing intended his *D. Faust* to be a 'bürgerliches Trauerspiel', then he must have meant by this application of the term something rather different from what is implied by his practice in *Sara*, and it is difficult to see how *D. Faust* would have fulfilled his own characteristic requirements for tragedy. Faust is of course not a king or a prince or a mythical hero—at least, not an antique one; the play would have been in prose, and a concern for realism seems

[1] P. Demetz (ed.), *Nathan der Weise* (Dichtung und Wirklichkeit, Bd. 25), Frankfurt 1966, p. 131. The affinity of the two exotic fragments to *Nathan* has been noted by critics. In his editorial introduction to the *Theatralischer Nachlass* in the Petersen/Olshausen edition of Lessing's works (vol. x, p. 13) W. Oehlke draws attention to the 'an den Nathan erinnernde dialogische Feinheit' of the versified *Fatime* fragment. On *Der Horoskop* see C. Enders, 'Der geistesgeschichtliche Standort von Lessings "Horoskop"', *Euphorion* 50 (1956), 208 ff.

to be indicated, at least in the case of the version of which Gebler wrote to Nicolai on 9 December 1775, a version 'ohne alle Teufelei, wo ein Erzbösewicht gegen einen Unschuldigen die Rolle des schwarzen Verführers vertritt'. Perhaps Lessing intended a literal modernization of the figure of Faust, an anticipation of Thomas Mann's treatment of the theme: something of the kind may be implied in Mendelssohn's remark. Yet in the seventeenth *Literaturbrief* of 1759, the appeal of a Faust drama is stated to lie precisely in its un-modern, traditional, demonic elements, 'das Grosse, das Schreckliche, das Melancholische'; and it is hard to see how either a modernized or a traditional Faust could be made to evoke the pity unmixed with wonder or admiration which Lessing consistently held to be the cardinal tragic emotion. It must also be remembered that Lessing's *D. Faust* was not going to end tragically: the accounts of Blankenburg and Engel agree that Faust was ultimately to be saved—evidence of Lessing's willingness to make untraditional innovations in what he would have regarded as inessentials, the really important thing being to recreate the *character* of Faust and what he stood for. If the term 'bürgerliches Trauerspiel' was applied to *D. Faust* by Lessing himself, then perhaps he meant by it no more than a *serious* play with characters not of the highest rank —in fact something like Diderot's *genre sérieux*. But this was even further removed from the canon of classical tragedy than *Miss Sara Sampson*, and so even further from providing that enhancement of national literary prestige which only tragedy could supply.[1]

Lessing's various experiments in tragedy were all attempts to discover a form which, although fulfilling what he saw as the characteristic modern requirements for tragedy—tending to be, in Nicolai's terminology, 'rührend' rather than 'heroisch', and employing characters whom the audience was not asked to admire but with whom the spectator could more readily identify himself, and who to this end should be presented in a rounded, realistic manner—could nevertheless exhibit a better dramatic pedigree than the mongrel genre represented by *Miss*

---

[1] H. Meyer-Benfey ('Lessings Faustpläne', *GRM* 12 (1924), 78 ff.) suggests that the idea of writing 'ein ernstes Drama mit gutem Ausgange' belongs to a later phase of Lessing's work on the Faust subject than that to which the designation 'Trauerspiel' appropriately refers.

Sara Sampson.[1] This view finds support in the remarkable infrequency with which the term 'bürgerliches Trauerspiel' actually occurs in his critical and theoretical writings.[2] On 20 July 1756 Lessing promised Nicolai 'eine Menge unordentlicher Gedanken über das bürgerliche Trauerspiel', but this seems never to have materialized. There is no mention of 'bürgerliches Trauerspiel' in the *Literaturbriefe* of 1759 and in the *Hamburgische Dramaturgie* the term occurs only in No. 14, which is specifically concerned with *Miss Sara Sampson*. There are, however, a number of other passages in this work which again suggest the need for tragedy to be brought nearer to the modern audience. No. 42, for example, recalls the arguments of the Seneca essay:

> Als Literator hat er [Voltaire in *Mérope*] zu viel Achtung für die Simplizität der alten griechischen Sitten und für das Kostüm bezeigt, mit welchem wir sie bei dem Homer und Euripides geschildert finden, das aber allerdings um etwas, ich will nicht sagen veredelt, sondern unserm Kostüme näher gebracht werden muss, wenn es der Rührung im Trauerspiele nicht mehr schädlich als zuträglich sein soll.

No. 75 attributes to Aristotle the view that the tragic hero should be portrayed 'mit uns von gleichem Schrot und Korne', though this appears in its context to refer above all to moral character. In Nos. 84 ff. Lessing quotes with approval the passage from *Les Bijoux indiscrets* in which Diderot attacks the artificiality and remoteness of the French classical drama and pleads for simplicity and psychological realism. And in No. 97 Lessing suggests, in passing, that the tragic poet, like the comic poet, should portray 'einheimische Sitten':

> Einheimische Sitten also erleichtern ihm die Arbeit und befördern bei dem Zuschauer die Illusion. Warum sollte nun der tragische Dichter sich dieses wichtigen doppelten Vorteils begeben? ... Die Griechen haben wenigstens nie andere als ihre eigene Sitten, nicht bloss in der Komödie, sondern auch in der Tragödie, zum Grunde gelegt.

Yet we have seen that in fact all Lessing's attempts at tragedy

---

[1] H. Rempel in his valuable study, *Tragödie und Komödie im dramatischen Schaffen Lessings*, Berlin 1935, sees Lessing's tragic experiments as attempts to escape from his dependence on the forms and techniques of comedy.
[2] Cf. Alois Wierlacher, 'Zum Gebrauch der Begriffe "Bürger" und "bürgerlich" bei Lessing', *Neophilologus* 51 (1967), 147 ff.

preserve *éloignement*. There seems to be an inconsistency here—if Lessing really was the convinced advocate of 'bürgerliches Trauerspiel' as the form of tragedy most suited to the requirements of his own age. But if he was, then it is surprising that he does not proclaim his advocacy more plainly. Perhaps he was beginning to realize that the real solution to the problem of modern drama lay in comedy and the non-tragic *genre sérieux*, where indeed he himself most satisfactorily solved the problem in practical example.

After the failure of the Hamburg 'Nationaltheater', Lessing lost interest in the drama. In Wolfenbüttel he devoted himself with enthusiasm to theology, and on 14 November 1771 wrote to his brother: 'Das Theater überhaupt wird mir von Tage zu Tage gleichgültiger.' And yet in 1770 he had begun work on *Spartacus*; and when it became evident to him that he was not going to be able to complete this work, he wrote *Emilia Galotti* instead. One wonders why he did this. The obvious, and I believe correct, inference is that he had some specific purpose in view, and that the abandonment of *Spartacus* for *Emilia Galotti* represents a change of means to achieve the same end. But I do not believe that the end was expressive—that *Emilia Galotti* was completed thanks to the pressure of some specific 'Erlebnisgehalt', as Hans Rempel believed,[1] or that it replaced *Spartacus* in the specific quality of 'antityrannische Tragödie', as Paul Rilla has maintained.[2] I have already suggested that Lessing recognized the abstract, formal category of tragedy as existing independently of any necessary content of meaning or message: his aim, first in *Spartacus* and then in *Emilia Galotti*, was once again, purely and simply, *to write a tragedy*, and the reason why this task had in 1770-2 suddenly taken on an urgency which it had not possessed before was that he had promised Voss, his publisher, that he would. On 5 January 1770 he had written to Voss proposing a new edition of his works, and Voss agreed. The new edition was to contain a complete volume of tragedies. But this meant writing a new one; and Lessing was notorious for not fulfilling promises of this kind. On 25 October 1757, for example, in reply to Lessing's declaration that he could improve

---

[1] H. Rempel, op. cit., p. 100.
[2] P. Rilla, 'Emilia Galotti', in *Feschrift zum 225. Geburtstage von Gotthold Ephraim Lessing*, Berlin 1954, pp. 6 ff.

Lessing and the 'Bürgerliches Trauerspiel' 27

upon Cronegk's *Codrus*, Moses Mendelssohn had observed: 'Jedoch, was haben Sie nicht schon für die Bibliothek gesprochen, und nicht gehalten? . . . Ich weiss es schon, dass Sie nicht eher arbeiten, als wenn der Druckerjunge in der Stube sitzt, und darauf wartet.' It looks as though Voss expressed similar doubts as to the likelihood of completion, for in a letter of 1 December 1771 we find Lessing assuring him 'dass es mir mit dem Bande Tragödien Ernst ist'. *Spartacus*, the 'antityrannische Tragödie', was intended to be the new tragedy which would fill up the volume. Lessing was working in emulation of a literary model, for he had asked Voss to send him a copy of the French dramatist J. B. Saurin's *Spartacus* of 1760,[1] upon which he thought he could improve and from which he borrowed a few ideas for the articulation of the plot. The sentiments expressed in the play, however, were a matter of comparative indifference. Indeed, it may well be that Lessing could not get on with *Spartacus* precisely because the subject was essentially political and not domestic. At last, when Voss was literally waiting to print the sheets as soon as they were written, Lessing abandoned his final attempt to write a tragedy in a manner other than that of the 'bürgerliches Trauerspiel' as represented by *Miss Sara Sampson*. Instead he reverted to the exact type of that work: a contemporary, domestic, but still geographically *éloigné* modernization of a classical story, containing a direct reference to that classical story as a reassurance of its legitimacy as a tragedy. The project for 'eine bürgerliche Virginia' had already been announced in 1758. The functional similarity of a number of the characters to those of *Miss Sara Sampson*—father, daughter, seducer, seducer's abandoned mistress—no doubt facilitated speedy completion, and it may well have been this basic similarity that sent him back to *Emilia Galotti* rather than to any other of the abandoned tragic plans and projects which he had made since writing *Sara*. (Also, by an odd coincidence, the heroine of Saurin's *Spartacus* is named Émilie.) Lessing's technical mastery, his skill in dialogue and characterization, had increased beyond recognition since 1755; the rich human complexity of *Minna von Barnhelm* had replaced the sentimentality and moral schematization of *Sara*. But despite this, *Emilia Galotti* is still in essentials a repetition of the experiment which

[1] Cf. Karl Lessing's letter to his brother, 24 Dec. 1770, LM, xix. 430.

Lessing had made in the earlier 'bürgerliches Trauerspiel': an experiment, that is, in a genre of whose aesthetic validity Lessing had been and remained ultimately unconvinced. In 1755 he had written for the *Berlinische privilegierte Zeitung* an announcement of the volume of his *Schriften* which was to contain *Miss Sara Sampson*. 'Ein bürgerliches Trauerspiel!' he wrote, with an irony which was surely two-edged: 'Findet man in Gottscheds Kritischer Dichtkunst ein Wort von so einem Dinge?'

Goethe and the Chinese Novel

ERIC A. BLACKALL

ON 31 January 1827 Goethe reported to Eckermann that he had been reading a Chinese novel, and with the greatest interest. To Eckermann's suggestion that such a work would surely appear very strange, Goethe replied as follows:

> Nicht so sehr, als man glauben sollte.... Die Menschen denken, handeln und empfinden fast ebenso wie wir, und man fühlt sich sehr bald als ihresgleichen, nur dass bei ihnen alles klarer, reinlicher und sittlicher zugeht. Es ist bei ihnen alles verständig, bürgerlich, ohne grosse Leidenschaft und poetischen Schwung und hat dadurch viele Ähnlichkeit mit meinem Hermann und Dorothea, so wie mit den englischen Romanen des Richardson. Es unterscheidet sich aber wieder dadurch, dass bei ihnen die äussere Natur neben den menschlichen Figuren immer mitlebt. Die Goldfische in den Teichen hört man immer plätschern, die Vögel auf den Zweigen singen immerfort, der Tag ist immer heiter und sonnig, die Nacht immer klar; vom Mond ist viel die Rede, allein er verändert die Landschaft nicht, sein Schein ist so helle gedacht wie der Tag selber. Und das Innere der Häuser so nett und zierlich wie ihre Bilder. Zum Beispiel: 'Ich hörte die lieblichen Mädchen lachen, und als ich sie zu Gesichte bekam, sassen sie auf feinen Rohrstühlen.' Da haben Sie gleich die allerliebste Situation, denn Rohrstühle kann man sich gar nicht ohne die grösste Leichtigkeit und Zierlichkeit denken. Und nun eine Unzahl von Legenden, die immer in der Erzählung nebenher gehen und gleichsam sprichwörtlich angewendet werden. Zum Beispiel von einem Mädchen, das so leicht und zierlich von Füssen war, dass sie auf einer Blume balancieren konnte, ohne die Blume zu knicken. Und von einem jungen Manne, der sich so sittlich und brav hielt, dass er in seinem dreissigsten Jahre die Ehre hatte, mit dem Kaiser zu reden. Und ferner von Liebespaaren, die in einem langen Umgange sich so enthaltsam bewiesen, dass, als sie einst genötigt waren, eine Nacht in einem Zimmer miteinander zuzubringen, sie in Gesprächen die Stunden durchwachten ohne sich zu berühren. Und so unzählige von Legenden, die alle auf das Sittliche und Schickliche gehen. Aber eben durch diese strenge Mässigung in allem hat sich denn auch das chinesische Reich seit Jahrtausenden

erhalten und wird dadurch ferner bestehen. (Artemis Ausgabe, xxiv. 227-8.)

What a world of difference there is, says Goethe, between this and the immoral subjects of the songs of Béranger, made acceptable only by the talented treatment. He continues: 'Aber sagen Sie selbst, ist es nicht höchst merkwürdig, dass die Stoffe des chinesischen Dichters so durchaus sittlich und diejenigen des jetzigen ersten Dichters von Frankreich ganz das Gegenteil sind?' Eckermann suggests that Béranger would not know what to do with a moral subject, and Goethe agrees, adding that Béranger reveals and develops his better nature on the very perversities of the times.[1]

It is clear from a reference in the diary for 3 February 1827, three days after this conversation, that what Goethe had been reading was a work entitled *Chinese Courtship. In Verse* by Peter Perring Thoms, first published in London in 1824, a translation of the Chinese tale entitled *Hua Chien Chi*.[2] In the preface the translator expresses his opinion 'that those who are fond of rural poetry, cannot but be pleased with the Chinese description of a garden, and their frequent allusion to the flowers, that occur in the course of the work. The distress and reciprocal feelings of the lovers—the pleasing and artful address of the servants—with the virtue and constancy of the young ladies, are not only entertaining portions of the poem, but appear calculated to excite the softer feelings of compassion: while the gallantry and bravery of Leang, and the disinterested friendship of Heaou, added to the interest the Emperor took in the marriage of the former, seem to claim for the poem, an attention which it might

[1] The contrast with Béranger takes up a topic which Goethe had been discussing with Soret just two days before. Eckermann reports him as saying on this occasion: 'Diese Lieder sind vollkommen und als das Beste in ihrer Art anzusehen, besonders wenn man sich das Gejodel des Refrains hinzudenkt, denn sonst sind sie als Lieder fast zu ernst, zu geistreich, zu epigrammatisch. Ich werde durch Béranger immer an den Horaz und Hafis erinnert, die beide auch über ihrer Zeit standen und die Sittenverderbnis spottend und spielend zur Sprache brachten. Béranger hat zu seiner Umgebung dieselbige Stellung. Weil er aber aus niederem Stande heraufgekommen, so ist ihm das Liederliche und Gemeine nicht allzu verhasst, und er behandelt es noch mit einer gewissen Neigung' (Artemis Ausgabe, xxiv. 222).

[2] The book was printed in Macao at the 'Honorable East India Company's Press', and is full of glaring misprints which I have corrected in my quotations. I used the copy in the British Museum. Page references are given after each quotation.

not otherwise demand' (vi–vii). In his praise of the morality of the work and of the part played in it by external nature, especially gardens, Goethe is therefore expanding on these words of Thoms. The novel, for such it is in the true sense of the word, tells of a talented young man named Leang, ambitious of becoming a scholar, who goes to Chang-chow to attend school there and falls in love with a beauteous maiden Yaou-sëen, the daughter of General Yang. He sees her playing chess while he is walking through a moonlit garden full of singing birds, sportive fish, plum-trees, peach-trees, almond groves, willows, roses, and many wild flowers. Everything is precisely depicted:

... a railed path that led to the white lily pond.
The white stork, on seeing man, retires with a light step to the moon,
And the bending willow causes, by the wind, a ripple on the stream. (14)

Yaou-sëen, having retired to her chamber, chides her maid Yun-heang for allowing the unknown man to approach unannounced while she was unveiled, and sends her forth to fetch the chess-board. In doing this Yun-heang encounters Leang who tries to engage her to carry a letter to her lady, whose identity he wishes to establish:

On seeing you advance, Miss, I know you are disposed,
To aid me, in imitating the conduct of the sovereign of Tsoo,
Whose daughter is the lady, that I saw in white?
She certainly is the goddess Chang-go from the palace in the moon. (22)

Two footnotes explain the reference: [1] 'It is said of Tsoo-seang, the sovereign of the state Tsoo, that while at Woo-shan, in Kaou-tang, he passed the night with a genius, who on leaving him, called herself The morning cloud and evening dews', and [2] 'Chang-go, in ancient story, was the wife of How-seïh, who begged of the goddess Wang-moo a medicine that confers immortality. Chang-go without the knowledge of her husband, ate it, and was instantly translated to a supposed palace in the moon. She is now considered the Venus of China.' These footnotes exemplify that proverb-like use of legends which Goethe refers to, though these two particular legends do not seem to be associated with 'das Sittliche und Schickliche'. A bantering conversation ensues between Yun-Heang and Leang; but she gives him no hope of success, for, says she, the lady Taou-sëen and her friends 'have been taught to remain unsullied as icicles'. Her parting advice is:

> Cease therefore to think of possessing the celestial pearly peach,
> Or being in love with the red almond by the side of the sun.
> Hasten home, and seize with speed the massive weapon,
> And slay those feelings which cause you to love. (23)

To appreciate this fully the reader is required to know that the goddess Wang-Moo (see above the note on Chang-go) planted a peach in the western hemisphere, which bore fruit of a beautiful carnation colour. But, basically, the situation is that of lovesick youth, idealized and remote lady, and teasing soubrette, with nothing 'foreign' about it. Goethe is right, except that the nature and tone of this particular situation seem closer to Western comedy than to *Hermann und Dorothea* or the novels of Richardson. The difference does indeed lie in the living participation in the situation of legend and landscape, both representing archetypes of phases and patterns of human existence. Leang is unable to sleep for thoughts of his lady:

> In the midst of the flowers, he stood as one benumbed,
> Enraged because he could not fly to her side . . . (26)

It is not mere prettiness that he should first have seen her amidst a garden of flowers: the external landscape mirrors the emotional landscape of his mind. Unaware of what has already happened, his aunt recommends that he take walks in the garden as a relaxation from studying. For her too the garden represents the place where the feelings can indulge themselves. But, as Goethe had implied in his remarks to Eckermann, this is no mere pathetic fallacy; for this nature lives its own life independent of the human characters, a life which, as we have seen, is described in precise detail. The characters are aware of this: the flowers have something intoxicating and perhaps dangerous about them: to preserve balance one must shut out the garden. Thus Yaou-sëen, not impervious to the charms of Leang, but anxious not to lose her head, declares:

> I will drop the screen, to screen myself from the influence of the
> flowers and moon,

Goethe and the Chinese Novel

And prevent the butterflies, on ascending the eastern wall, from
  entering my room. (38)

I am no sinologist. I cannot read Chinese. I am not concerned here with the implications this imagery would or should have for someone versed in Chinese culture, but with how Goethe might have read them. Obviously the passage just quoted can be read as a real and as a symbolic statement. It is not difficult to understand how such a treatment of reality would have appealed to the mature Goethe. And such treatment, as it would undoubtedly appear to Western eyes, persists throughout the novel. Leang meets Yaou-sëen's father, General Yang, who is quite willing to promote a meeting between the two young people, for a poem has demonstrated Leang's creative gifts and the General decides he would like him as son-in-law. So Leang again urges Yun-heang to convey his feelings to her lady, and in these terms:

If the virtuous lady has no compassion on the disconsolate,
The deceived youth will perish in the presence of the flowers. (62)

Again recalling legend, he declares:

Being deceived, I am determined to die by the side of the celestial
  peach. (64)

Yaou-sëen for her part seems inclined to have inquiries made 'previous to marriage', for 'Why should grief prevent the lovely moon from attaining her full?' (70) (a note [79] explains that 'the idea conveyed of the full moon, is, that as the moon wanes and waxes, so does man; he is never at his full, at the height of happiness, till married'). Somewhat anxiously she goes to meet Leang in the garden where they swear vows of constancy to each other; but the necessary preliminary forms have to be gone through, meaning the consent of parents and the assurance of the approval of Heaven, before they can marry. However, when Leang returns to his home, he finds that his father is arranging for him a marriage with Yuh-king, and feels therefore that his union with Yaou-sëen was not 'decreed' and that their 'oath amidst the flowers' is of no avail. So he decides to remain single. Yaou-sëen, thinking that Leang is unprincipled, throws aside her cosmetics and ornaments, vows to write no more odes nor play chess again, and to remain single too. At this time her father is appointed Lieutenant-General and sent to the frontiers to quell an insurrection. Meanwhile Leang has passed all his examinations with flying colours, but, hearing that General Yang and his forces are surrounded by the enemy, he leaves for the frontier to rescue him or die in the attempt, after a sorrowful parting from Yaou-sëen beneath the willows. He and his men are surrounded, and a false report of his death reaches Yaou-sëen, who calls on Leang to wait patiently in 'Hades' until she can join him. Meanwhile Yuh-king, the girl that Leang's parents wanted him to marry, having also received this report, attempts to drown herself but is rescued, though without her parents' knowledge. Leang is, however, not dead, and he helps General Yang's forces to break the siege, and both return victoriously to Peking, where they are ennobled by the Emperor. Leang reproaches himself for being the cause of Yuh-king's death. The Emperor decrees that a monument be raised to Yuh-king, and that Yaou-sëen shall marry Leang. Leang complies; but when it is revealed that Yuh-king is not dead, the Emperor decrees that Leang make a second marriage and consider the two wives as one. This occurs, and all ends happily:

The wives of Duke Leang, being happy, dwelt in harmony together,
And endeavoured to excel each other in kind attention.
When disposed to lift the cup, they repaired beneath the bright moon,
And when enjoying the cool breeze, they alternately recited verses.
It would be difficult to detail all the pleasures they enjoyed,
For their mirth and gaiety if transmitted, would alone form a volume. (247)

In this brief and simplified account of *Chinese Courtship* I have tried to convey the tone as well as the content of the work. Despite the anguish which it depicts, it is bright in general mood, and the double marriage at the end is an amusing but divine asseveration of pure love persisting through disappointments and decorous patience. The world of this novel is an ordered universe not unlike that of *Daphnis and Chloë*, with the same respect for forms and virtues despite the totally different cultural setting. In another conversation with Eckermann (20 March 1831) Goethe asserted that *Daphnis and Chloë* contained a whole world within its 'Abgeschlossenheit', admired its brightness, the clearly depicted landscapes, its taste and delicacy, the fact that 'Chloe gegen den beiderseitigen Willen der Liebenden, die nichts Besseres kennen, als nackt nebeneinander zu ruhen, durch den ganzen Roman bis ans Ende ihre Jungfrauschaft behält' (Artemis Ausgabe, xxiv. 484). Both novels present the ultimate triumph of a simple, moral principle; both portray fundamentally chaste characters who react to passion by self-control; both suggest a relationship between human lives and the patterns of development in organic nature at large. Both novels are simply but skilfully constructed, with physical violence (here the war, there the invaders) as a force which delays fruition but cannot prevent it because of the pure devotion of the lovers to each other. In both *Chinese Courtship* and *Daphnis and Chloë* there is the same over-all brightness, the same definitely depicted world, the same universality of relevance within specific limited confines, the same telling use of the motifs of romance, the same subordination of violence to beauty, and the same purity. There is, however, one important difference. In the Chinese novel the ultimate authority and judge of conduct, the moral absolute, lies within the world, in the person of the Emperor. What is represented therefore is a totally ordered world in which the focal point of the morality which determines order is the apogee of the social structure.

The conversation with Eckermann on *Chinese Courtship* continues with the famous passage on *Weltliteratur*, and is but one example of Goethe's interest during his later life in the novel as a form and in novels of all kinds and all nations. But what is the resemblance between *Chinese Courtship* and the novels of Richardson? One can more easily understand the comparison with *Hermann und Dorothea*: above all in the containing of passion within social conventions, different as these conventions are in each of the two novels. But Richardson? This has puzzled one writer who has expressed the view that Goethe was here talking not about *Chinese Courtship*, but about a different Chinese novel. namely *Hau Kiou Choaan*.[1] Another writer has pointed out that the situation of two lovers forced to spend the night in the same room but spending it in conversation does not occur in *Chinese*

[1] Chuan Chen, *Die chinesische schöne Literatur im deutschen Schrifttum*, Diss. Kiel 1933, p. 8. I have been unable to see Dr. Chen's article 'Goethe und die chinesische Erzählungsliteratur' in *Litterae Orientales*, Leipzig 1932.

36 Goethe and the Chinese Novel

Courtship but might well be a reference to *Hau Kiou Choaan*.[1] What then is *Hau Kiou Choaan*? This was one of the first Chinese novels, perhaps even the very first, to be translated into Western languages. It appeared first in an English translation in 1761 under the title *Hau Kiou Choaan or the Pleasing History*. It was translated into French in 1766, and into German by Christoph Gottlieb von Murr under the title *Haoh Kjo'h Tschwen, das ist die angenehme Geschichte des Haoh Kjo'h*. Both the English and the German translators misunderstood the title which, according to a Chinese scholar, would better be rendered 'Geschichte einer trefflichen Gefährtin'.[2] The German translation was made from the English, so it would seem, and as I have not been able to see the German version, my account of the novel is based on the English 'original'.[3]

One of the important elements of the process of wooing in *Chinese Courtship* was the exchange of poems between the lovers. The ability to write poetry is a sign both of culture and of desirability as a mate. It obviously indicates, in the stylized world of these novels, refinement of feeling, ability to communicate, and attunement to external nature. In *Hau Kiou Choaan* both hero and heroine are gifted poets. The plot of this novel is structurally akin to the romance of adventures, and particularly to the heroic novel of western Europe—a tissue of complicated intrigue through which pure love finally emerges triumphant. In broad outline the story is as follows. Our hero is a student named Tieh-chung-u, very handsome but also rough-tempered; just,

[1] Ursula Aurich, *China im Spiegel der deutschen Literatur des achtzehnten Jahrhunderts*, Berlin 1935, pp. 97–8. Further treatment of Goethe's acquaintance with Chinese literature is to be found in the following works: Erich Jenisch, 'Goethe und der ferne Osten', *DVJS* 1 (1923), 309–38; Richard Wilhelm, 'Goethe und die chinesische Kultur', *Jb. des Freien Deutschen Hochstifts*, 1927, 301–16; Otto Franke, 'Goethe und China', *Forschungen und Fortschritte* 8 (1932), 105–6; Woldemar Freiherr von Biedermann, *Goethe-Forschungen*, 3 vols., Leipzig 1886–99, various articles; Ernst Beutler's article entitled 'Goethe und die chinesische Literatur' in *Buch-Ausstellung*, China Institut, Frankfurt am Main 1928, was not available to me. There is a very brief treatment of the subject in Fritz Strich, *Goethe und die Weltliteratur*[2], Berne 1957, and a useful factual article by Wolfgang Vulpius in the new edition of the *Goethe-Handbuch*. There are several notable pages on this general topic in Strich's article 'Goethe der West-Östliche' (104–8) in *Dichtung und Zivilisation*, Munich 1928.

[2] Chuan Chen, op. cit., p. 11.

[3] I quote from the original edition (copy in the Cornell University Library). The work is in four volumes. Volume and page numbers follow each of my quotations.

humane, and noble. His father wants to marry him off, but he insists on waiting until he has found exactly the right woman. He leaves for the Court, and on his way there becomes involved in an adventure in which he rescues a young woman and her parents from the palace of a lustful mandarin where they are imprisoned, and thereby acquires a reputation for wisdom and courage. Then we turn to Shuey-ping-sin, the beautiful and crafty daughter of the mandarin Shuey-kew-yeh. Her uncle, Shuey-guwin, an illiterate boor with a daughter and three sons who are 'as ignorant and illiberal as himself' (i. 72), wants to get his niece married so that she will not inherit his brother's money which will then fall to him as next male in line. He encourages Kwo-khé-tzu, the son of a powerful mandarin, in this direction, but Shuey-ping-sin will have none of him, though she plays along for the sake of propriety and of her father who is banished to Tartary. But each time that Kwo-khé-tzu thinks he has got her, she outwits him, escaping time and time again from the most compromising and dangerous situations. Finally she is rescued from a particularly tight squeeze by a young man on the street to whom, from a closed chair in which she is being transported by force, she is able to communicate her distress. He is none other than Tieh-chung-u. After this rescue Tieh-chung-u is conducted to a pagoda to recover, where Kwo-khé-tzu gives him poison through the agency of the bonze. Shuey-ping-sin, hearing of his increasing 'sickness' and suspecting the truth, finally manages to get him away from the pagoda to her house. To have an unmarried man staying in her house is, of course, a serious breach of propriety. So the two, although by now very much in love, live separately and dine at separate tables divided by a curtain, through which she can see him but not he her. All this is reported by spies of a magistrate friendly to Kwo-khé-tzu who has been trying to work up a 'case'. He remarks: 'All this is surely incredible! Is it possible for a young lady, beautiful and blooming as a rose, and a youth shining as crystal, to be together in one house; to converse together, and drink wine; both obliged to each other; both witty and ingenious; and yet in all their conversation not to let fall one word of love: but instead thereof to preserve all the sanctity of hermits and holy men?' (ii. 102). But he suggests to Kwo-khé-tzu that he should look elsewhere for a bride. Meanwhile Shuey-ping-sin begs Tieh-chung-u to pardon her oppressors and advises him to cease travelling and return to his home and his studies. He agrees that so far he has been 'too much the sport of passion: too little under the guidance of reason' (ii. 87). The girl's uncle now decides to try to persuade his niece to marry Tieh-chung-u. 'If she accepts of him I shall still come into possession of her effects' (ii. 110). She replies that she cannot marry the man she had in her house since people would then think that there had been something between them. The young man is equally offended by the idea and for the same reasons. He decides to devote himself wholeheartedly to passing his examinations. Meanwhile Kwo-khé-tzu tries to force the Grand Visitor to decree that Shuey-ping-sin shall marry him, but she wins over the Grand Visitor and gets from him an order forbidding anyone to molest her. For this is no mean woman. Her uncle says of her at one point: 'She hath a tongue, and knows how to use it. She hath a mouth, whose words are keener than the edge of a pen-knife or razor. I had scarce uttered one word, when she immediately answered with arguments fetched from ancient and modern authors, and backed with a multitude of reasons; insomuch that I could not open my mouth' (ii. 61). She also has her moral standards: to Tieh-chung-u she says: 'Consider, Sir, the degeneracy of the times. There are only two words in our days by which both the people and Mandarins regulate their conduct, and those are RICHES and POWER' (ii. 85). There is something middle-class about these words: they could indeed be uttered by a Richardson heroine.

So far we have only reached the end of the second volume of this four-volume novel. Shuey-ping-sin had sent a petition to the Emperor complaining of the behaviour of the Grand Visitor before he came over to her side. Once she has won him over she asks him to send messengers after her servant to revoke her petition to the Emperor, but her servant has already chanced to meet Tieh-chung-u on the road and has told him what the petition contains, whereupon Tieh-chung-u agrees to help the servant deliver it. The servant, however, never appears at the gates of the Court, having in the meantime been overtaken by the Grand Visitor's messenger and persuaded to return, whereupon Tieh-chung-u retraces his steps in order to confront the Grand Visitor. (This succession of events, involving as it does the strong admixture of coincidence, is typical of the movement of the plot of this novel.) Having arrived back in the town, he soon learns of the Grand Visitor's change of heart. Meanwhile the girl's uncle and Kwo-khé-tzu try to trap him into an assignation with Shuey-ping-sin; but he smells a rat and declines on the grounds that the lady would never suggest anything so indecorous. The uncle's plan is to involve the two in the suspicion of an illicit relationship. He then tries to get the young man drunk and have him beaten up. But Tieh-chung-u is tough, survives, and presents a complaint to the Grand Visitor who issues a severe warning to the Uncle, to Kwo-khé-tzu, and his fellow ruffians. Then, by curious circumstances which we do not need to go into here, Tieh-chung-u is able to effect the return to favour of Shuey-ping-sin's father who considers the lad a good match for his daughter, not knowing about what has happened between them hitherto. Tieh-chung-u tells him there are reasons which prevent him from marrying the girl but, with a true sense of decorum, does not reveal what they are. Both fathers are in favour of this marriage. The stumbling-block is the sense of propriety of the young people and this has now to be overcome.

The fourth volume deals with further plots by Kwo-khé-tzu, who is persistent if nothing else. Meanwhile Tieh-chung-u has passed his examinations, is created Doctor of Law, 'and put foremost on the list' (iv. 17). He is also appointed by the Emperor to be one of the tutors to his son. In order to ward off the plots of Kwo-khé-tzu and a dastardly eunuch, the couple are formally married but continue to live as single persons, though in the same house, her father's. Intrigues continue. Finally a memorial reaches the Emperor himself, together with various statements from all parties. The Emperor interviews Tieh-chung-u and praises him to his face: 'A sincere and just man ... may sometimes be met with, but one like you it is difficult to find' (iv. 139) To the girl he says: 'Young lady, if you have all along kept yourself pure and spotless as at the first, there are not to be found a pair equal to you from the most remote antiquity unto the present hour. You in particular ought to be celebrated through all parts of the world, as a saint' (iv. 143). The Emperor promotes Tieh-chung-u to first Minister of State, and elevates Shuey-ping-sin to be a 'dutchess' (iv. 153), gives them handsome presents, and gets them properly married with himself as 'mediator or bridesman' (iv. 153). The wicked ones are punished, and the young couple live happily.

There are certain aspects of this novel which would certainly seem to relate more specifically than does *Chinese Courtship* to the points made by Goethe in his conversation with Eckermann of 31 January 1827 which we quoted at the beginning of this article. This is apparent, in particular, in the motif of the lovers spending their time in conversation out of respect for the decorum demanded by the unusual situation, and the interview of the young hero with the Emperor. And the twists and turns of the plot of this novel, with its various assaults on the heroine, all evaded by her native wit, have more in common with *Pamela*, the attempted abduction more with the beginning of *Sir Charles Grandison*, than anything in *Chinese Courtship*. The figure of the persistent evil wooer and his various immoral companions together with the general theme of the conflict of power and riches with virtue—all this is more like Richardson than anything in the other novel, except perhaps a fragile parallel between Sir Charles Grandison and his two women at the end of that novel and the conclusion of *Chinese Courtship*. On the other hand Goethe's emphasis on nature living its own life alongside the characters and his reference to the interweaving of legends into the novel apply better to *Chinese Courtship*, for they have little or no part in *Hau Kiou Choaan*. We have fairly definite evidence that Goethe read *Hau Kiou Choaan*. He may well have read it as early as 1796. There is a diary entry for 12 January of that year which reads: 'kam der chinesische Roman zur Sprache', without further identification. Then, on 24 January of that same year, Schiller in a letter to Goethe refers to the latter as being occupied with 'zwei weitläuftigen Erzählungen aus Indien und China'. We know that Schiller himself was interested in the work and that in 1800 he proposed to the publisher Unger that he himself prepare an abridged version of the work, of which he only completed the beginning.[1] Then, on 14 October 1815

[1] Schiller to J. F. Unger, 29 Aug. 1800: 'Es existirt ein Chinesischer Roman unter dem Nahmen Hao Kiöh Tschuen oder Haoh Kiöhs angenehme Geschichte, der anno. 1766 von H. v. Murr in Nürnberg aus dem Englischen ins Deutsche übersezt worden. Die Uebersetzung ist, wie Sie leicht denken können, veraltet und das Buch vergessen. Es hat aber so viel Vortrefliiches und ist ein so einziges Produkt in seiner Art, dass es verdient wieder aufzuleben und gewiss eine Zierde Ihres Romanen-Journals werden wird. Wörtlich übersezt würde es zwar gegen 25 oder

Goethe and the Chinese Novel

Wilhelm Grimm writes to his brother Jacob that Goethe was reading and commenting on ('liest und erklärt') *Hau Kiou Choaan*.[1] Since the title is here given as 'Haoh Kiöh Tschwen' it would seem likely that Goethe was reading it, at least in 1815, in the German version. One does not know whether he ever saw the English original. If he did, he could have read in the dedication of the work to the Countess of Sussex the following passage which certainly suggests an affinity of the moral tone of the work with that of Richardson: 'Madam, I should not intreat your LADYSHIP's acceptance of the following sheets, if they had not a moral tendency: if they were not designed to countenance virtue and to discourage vice. At a time when this nation swarms with fictitious narratives of the most licentious and immoral turn, it may have some good effect to show what strict regard to virtue and decorum is paid by writers amongst the Chinese, notwithstanding the deplorable ignorance they labour under of those sublime and noble truths, which we enjoy to so little purpose.' The writer is none other than Bishop Percy (of the *Reliques*). The translator had been a certain James Wilkinson, an English merchant who had lived many years in Canton and who in 1719 had translated the first three parts of the novel into English. These were found amongst his papers, together with the fourth part of the novel in Portuguese, but in another hand.

26 Bogen des Rom. Journals betragen; ich getraue mir aber den Geist des Werks auf 15 Bogen zusammen zu drängen und ihm durch diese zweckmässige Abkürzung ein höheres Interesse zu geben, weil die Erzählung zuweilen gedehnt ist. Ich selbst habe Lust zu dieser Arbeit, davon auch schon der Anfang gemacht ist und wenn Sie das Werk für das Journal der Romane glauben brauchen zu können, so steht es Ihnen zu Diensten. Wenn ich die Mühe, die es mir etwa machen dürfte, überschlage, so glaube ich den gedruckten Bogen um 2 Carolin liefern zu können. Sobald ich von Ihnen Nachricht erhalte, kann der Anfang der Erzählung zum Druck abgeschickt werden und noch vor dem neuen Jahr soll das Ganze in Ihren Händen seyn' (Jonas, vi. 192–3). Cf. Schiller to Unger, 7 (?) Apr. 1801: 'Die Chinesische Geschichte soll auch noch geliefert werden: den Zeitpunkt kann ich nicht genau bestimmen' (Jonas, vi. 267). The book was sent by Murr himself to Schiller who thanked him for it on 5 May 1795 (Jonas, iv. 168). Nothing, however, seems to have come of Schiller's project for a 'revised' edition of it, although his version of the beginning has been preserved (Nationalausgabe, xvi. 361–3).

[1] *Goethe-Jahrbuch* i (1880), 339. On 23 May 1827 Jean-Jacques Ampère wrote to Mme Récamier that Goethe had spoken to him 'avec beaucoup de finesse et cette légère ironie qui lui va si bien, des mœurs de mes Chinois, à propos du roman de M. Abel Rémusat [see below, pp. 42 ff.]; racontant d'autres romans chinois qu'il a lus il y a un demi-siècle, et dont les incidents lui sont présents' (André-Marie Ampère et Jean-Jacques Ampère, *Correspondance et souvenirs (de 1803 à 1864)*, recueillis par madame H. C., Paris [1875], i. 449–50).

Percy claims to have revised and edited the first three parts and to have himself translated the fourth part into English.

But this is not the end of our story. On 7 May 1827 Goethe writes to Frau von Pogwisch, sending two thalers as his subscription to her *Lesezirkel* and asks her to send him 'den Roman Ju Kiao Li' (W.A. iv. 42, 175). Two days later there is a diary entry: 'Der chinesische Roman übersetzt von Rémusat', and on 14 May he notes 'Den chinesischen Roman weiter gelesen'. The work referred to here is *Iu-Kiao-Li ou les deux cousines*, translated by Abel-Rémusat (4 vols., Paris 1826). This is another novel of complicated intrigue, and again one concerned with a hero and a heroine, both of whom are poets. The action, in general outline, is as follows.[1]

Pe, a literary man and magistrate, has an only daughter Houngiu who is also devoted to poetry. Having consciously detached himself from the world of affairs he lives for wine, poetry, and good company. At a drinking party at his house with his brother-in-law Dr. Gou and the Inspector-General Sse, which is invaded, much to his disgust, by the powerful politician Inspector-General Yang, he is saved from embarrassment by his daughter who composes a poem when he is too drunk to do so. This poem so delights Yang that he decides to marry his son to Houngiu. But the son, Yang-Fang, makes a stupid impression, and Pe will have none of him. After this Yang uses his influence to have Pe sent on a dangerous political mission to Tartary. While he is away, Dr. Gou accepts Houngiu as his daughter for her protection and removes himself from the city to escape the machinations of Yang. Dr. Gou himself has a daughter Wouyan (meaning 'sans beauté'). The two girls are now to be known as sisters. At a poetry festival to celebrate the plum-blossoms Dr. Gou meets a young poet of great gifts called Sse Yeoupe, handsome, an orphaned student, and poor. Gou immediately decides that this is the man for Houngiu. An intermediary is sent. Sse Yeoupe wants to see the girl, and is told that he can see her without being seen (and thereby not offend against decorum), but, owing to one of the numerous misunder-

---

[1] I quote from the original edition in four volumes (copy in the Cornell University Library). Volume and page numbers follow each quotation. Abel-Rémusat was a distinguished orientalist of the time who also published an edition of the Chinese text of this novel (Paris 1829).

standings and coincidences which occur in this book, it is Wouyan that he sees. He is not impressed and refuses the offer, much to Dr. Gou's amazement. Meanwhile, having come out top of the list in his examination, Sse Yeoupe is much sought after as a husband, but declares he will only marry perfection. Dr. Gou gets him struck from the top of the examination list on the grounds of stubborn character (character as well as intellectual achievement plays its part in these Chinese examinations); but Houngiu's father, returned safely from his mission and promoted to high office, has Sse Yeoupe reinstated on the list because of what he considers his 'firm' character. Then Sse Yeoupe's uncle (the Inspector-General of the first chapter), being rich, childless, and old, invites him to come and live with him. On the way he is able to help a man locate his abducted wife, and learns of a hermit with prophetic powers whom he then visits. From this hermit he hears of the beauty and intelligence of Houngiu, the daughter of Pe, whom he therefore does not connect with Dr. Gou. He then falls in with two young poets who also praise Houngiu and offer to take him to her. But one of these steals some of Sse Yeoupe's poems and presents them as his own as part of his wooing of Houngiu, for all suitors must submit verses to Pe and Houngiu if they wish to be considered seriously. This man, Tchangfanjou by name, impresses them by his poetry, which is in fact Sse Yeoupe's, but not by his appearance. They decide to test Tchangfanjou by inviting him to stay in the house and constantly giving him new subjects to compose poems on, but somehow he always manages to get Sse Yeoupe to write them for him, for this latter is a rather naïve young man. Finally the true state of affairs is unravelled by Houngiu's maid. Houngiu then gives a particularly difficult subject to Sse Yeoupe to be composed in an extremely complex form. The result is so magnificent that Houngiu is completely won over. The question now is how to get rid of Tchangfanjou. It is decided that Sse Yeoupe shall go to the capital and explain the situation to Dr. Gou and get him to act as marriage intermediary. He starts out but falls in with an old student comrade called Sse Yeoute to whom he, very unwisely, confesses his love for Houngiu and his plan of campaign. Sse Yeoute gets to Dr. Gou first and posing as Sse Yeoupe's brother elicits a letter to Pe in which the wooer is simply referred to as 'Sse' without any second name. With this he goes to Pe's house and presents it as referring to himself. Since neither Pe nor his daughter have ever seen Sse Yeoupe they think this is he. Tchangfanjou, who is still there, knows, however, that it is not. A poetry contest between Tchangfanjou and Sse Yeoute is now arranged by Pe in which both are unmasked as impostors. Meanwhile Sse Yeoupe is robbed and wounded, taken to the house of Chancellor Li, where he earns praise by verses he composes for pictures on a silk screen which Li wants to present to a judge, and encounters a dazzlingly handsome young man named Lo Mengli who lives next door and tries to interest Sse Yeoupe in marrying his sister. Sse Yeoupe in another outburst of indiscretion tells him about his love for Houngiu. Lo Mengli knows all about her, for Pe is his maternal uncle, although he does not reveal this fact to Sse Yeoupe. And so, realizing that no one can compete with Houngiu in qualities either of mind or of body, he suggests that his sister be Sse Yeoupe's second wife, but tells him that he must first marry Houngiu. And so Sse Yeoupe, who all this time has been trying to proceed on his journey but unable to do so because of the demands of politeness towards his host Li, departs. Purely by chance, he encounters his uncle (to whom he was supposed to be going before he encountered the hermit), who turns out to be the very judge for whom Li intended the silk screen. He tells his uncle that he is the author of the verses on the screen, explaining the coincidence by which he encountered Li, and also tells of his love for Houngiu. His uncle advises him to improve his marital qualifications by taking the next highest examination, because Pe is such a severe judge of men. He does so, and then proceeds to the doctorate, whereupon he is appointed magistrate. On his way to take up his new duties he returns to the house of Lo Mengli, finds it closed up, and is told that Madame Lo with her two children, a daughter of seventeen and a *son of five*, has gone to stay with her brother Pe. Houngiu and Lo Mengli (who is, of course, a girl), being both extremely gifted poets, become close friends: and Pe goes off to another poetry congress, now troubled with having to find two prospective husbands.

The idea of a double marriage with Sse Yeoupe appeals to the girls. But where is he? He is trying to find Pe who himself is seeking two good-looking poets of sterling character on the 'lac occidental'. Meanwhile Governor Wang, casting eyes on Sse Yeoupe as husband for his daughter, enlists the help of the rejected Tchangfanjou, who is all too delighted to deceive Sse Yeoupe into believing that Houngiu has died:

> Elle se livrait à des émotions funestes [he tells him], elle avait d'ailleurs rencontré un père intraitable et opiniâtre: occupé du choix d'un gendre, tantôt d'un côté, tantôt de l'autre, il ne songeait pas à mettre un terme aux ennuis du célibat de sa fille. Elle a fini par tomber malade, et son état a dégénéré en une langueur dont elle ne s'est plus relevée. Tous les médecins ont dit que c'était une sorte de consomption; mais, autant que j'en puis juger, c'est le moral qui l'a fait périr. (iv. 102-3)

Let us note this passage, for I wish to return to it later in my argument.

Sse Yeoupe refuses to consider Wang's daughter, whereupon Wang begins to use his power against him and he resigns his office and leaves. He encounters the hermit again who now tells him that he will marry two beautiful girls and regain his official position. Then, purely by chance, Sse Yeoupe and Pe meet in a monastery, each under an assumed name and therefore unaware of the true identity of the other. Sse Yeoupe asks Pe about Pe, and Pe asks Sse Yeoupe about Sse Yeoupe. Struck by his new acquaintance Pe offers him his daughter and niece. Sse Yeoupe says that owing to the death of his chosen one he is not free to accept either. Nevertheless Pe invites him to visit him at his home.

An imperial rescript elevates Sse Yeoupe to an even higher position and Tchangfanjou, seeing the way things are going, now confesses to Sse Yeoupe that the report of Houngiu's death was false and merely a ruse to get him to marry Wang's daughter. The intrigue now thickens into an immensely complicated comedy of misunderstandings. When he gets home Pe finds two letters, one from Dr. Gou and one from Sse Yeoupe's uncle, both recommending Sse Yeoupe, but he now feels bound by his promise to the young man he has met in the monastery, for this young man now tells him that the girl he had thought dead is not dead and the one he wanted for his second wife has disappeared. The climax of the book is perhaps to be found in Pe's remark: 'Ceci est encore une singulière aventure. . . . Y eut-il jamais dans aucune affaire autant de retours et de contretemps?' (iv. 189). But, in a final chapter entitled 'Broderies sur broderies: satisfaction générale', everything is cleared up and Sse Yeoupe marries both girls. He spends the first night with Houngiu and the second with Lo Mengli. And so: '... De ce moment, les trois époux virent augmenter l'estime et l'affection réciproque dont ils étaient animés. La plus parfaite harmonie régnait entr'eux' (iv. 235).

Although Goethe seems not to have read this particular novel until after the conversation with Eckermann with which we began, he knew about it earlier from a lengthy review of it in *Le Globe*. This review makes several points which are echoed in Goethe's words to Eckermann, and therefore deserves our attention. The review extends over three separate articles, the first of which, dated 23 December 1826, begins with the words: 'Il y a donc des romans à la Chine, et des romans qui peuvent soutenir le parallèle avec ceux de l'Europe!' Reference is then made to *Hau Kiou Choaan* as having lost much of its Chinese character in the French translation because this was made from the English which in turn was made from the Portuguese. The writer then asserts that *Iu Kiao Li* will mediate between the opinion that China is a palace of wise men and the view of it as a den of rogues. 'Écrit à une époque de civilisation avancée, où le talent de l'observation sociale a toute sa force, ce livre reproduit, avec les nuances les plus fines, ce mélange de bien et de mal, de talent et de ridicules, de vertu et de dépravation, qui, de Paris à Pékin, constitue notre faible humanité. C'est tout-à-fait, comme l'a dit M. Rémusat, la manière de Fielding et de miss Burney.' The last sentence refers to Rémusat's long preface to his translation which we will come to in a minute. The article goes on to note Rémusat's description of *Iu Kiao Li* as a *roman de mœurs*, and to comment on the respect for 'les bienséances et les rites' in this Chinese society around 1450:[1] 'On devient amoureux et l'on se marie sans s'être vu. De plus, on peut épouser deux femmes, ce qui est fort commode, au moins pour les romanciers, dont les dénouements deviennent infiniment plus faciles . . .' Love is not merely physical but intellectual in this world: 'Ce sentiment, dont l'unité constitue chez

---

[1] According to Chuan Chen (op. cit.) all three of these novels were written in the Ming period (1368–1644). The society in *Iu Kiao Li* is more precisely datable because of the specific historical events referred to in the novel.

nous l'essence, peut se partager à la Chine entre deux objets sans rien perdre de sa force, nous avons presque dit de son unité. Voilà certes un étrange mystère, et une nouvelle Scudéry serait bien nécessaire ici pour nous l'expliquer.' These Chinese girls are so restrained that 'près [d'elles], il faut le dire, nos Paméla et nos Clarisse risqueraient de paraître immodestes'. The general tenor of this review is therefore somewhat paradoxical: in praising the book's portrayal of the individual character of Chinese society it also frequently shows its similarity to our own. In the second article, dated 27 January 1827, comparisons are made between Yang's son as an unsuccessful suitor and Molière's Thomas Diafoirus (in *Le Malade imaginaire*), and it is asserted that the character of Pe, 'ferme et toujours serein', has some affinities with that of the Vicar of Wakefield. But not only are the characters shown as not so very different from our own, the general structure is compared with that of the romance:

> Il paraît que les Chinois, à l'époque où fut écrit le livre qui nous occupe, faisaient comme nous de la curiosité le pivot principal de leurs compositions romanesques. *Iu-Kiao-Li*, sous le rapport de l'intrigue et la science de l'imbroglio, semble une production toute moderne de notre Occident. Les couleurs sont différentes, mais les procédés de l'art sont les mêmes. L'auteur chinois trace les caractères, dispose les scènes intéressantes ou comiques, amène les descriptions de sites, noue et dénoue les fils de la narration, par des moyens absolument semblables à ceux qu'emploient nos romanciers.

These points are then elaborated in the third article, dated 22 February 1827. As in *Sir Charles Grandison*, we are told, the four main figures move in the midst of a crowd of vicious or ridiculous characters. The contrast of the serious and the gay which marks the two *cousines* also distinguishes Clarissa from Miss Howe, and Claire from Julie (in *La Nouvelle Héloïse*). The old Buddhist is a character like Dr. Primrose. Sse-Yeoupe is like a Spanish hero. As for the whole spectrum of characters in this novel:

> C'est là proprement le génie comique qui se voue à la peinture des caractères et ne fait qu'effleurer celle des passions. C'est la manière de *Gilblas* [sic] et de *Tom Jones*, auxquels il ne faut point demander les émotions profondes et les développements simples et passionnés de la *Nouvelle Héloïse* ou d'*Atala*. Il y a bien peu d'ouvrages qui réunissent la perfection de ces deux genres et qui offrent ainsi une

vue complète de l'humanité. Moins satirique que Le Sage, moins dramatique que Fielding, l'auteur chinois pourrait former la transition entre les deux romanciers européens...

This review takes up several points made by Rémusat himself in his lengthy preface to his translation of the novel. The authors of Chinese *romans de mœurs*, he says, 's'adressent plus souvent à la raison qu'à l'imagination, et semblent moins animés du désir d'émouvoir leurs lecteurs par des conceptions hardies ou des aventures singulières, qu'occupés du soin de leur offrir des sujets de réflexions et les moyens de devancer les tardives leçons de l'expérience' (8). This is, in essence, Goethe's point about the lack of 'grosse Leidenschaft und poetischen Schwung'. These novels, says Rémusat, are 'renfermées dans la sphère des objets réels, et l'imagination des auteurs s'y contient, si j'ose m'exprimer ainsi, dans les limites du monde sensible'. He continues:

> Les personnages sont des hommes et des femmes, agissant naturellement dans le cercle de leurs passions et de leurs intérêts, l'amour et l'ambition, le désintéressement et la cupidité. La bonne foi s'y débat avec l'intrigue, et d'honnêtes gens y sont aux prises avec des fripons. Aux noms près, ces inventions pourraient passer chez nous pour des réalités, et rien ne ressemble plus que Nanking ou Canton à Paris ou à Westminster. (10)

These novels are often critical of Chinese life, but not as satirical as *Gil Blas* or '*Gulliver*'. They should be compared rather

> aux bons romans anglais, dans lesquels le moraliste observateur sait déguiser son but, en forçant l'attention de ses lecteurs de se porter sur les circonstances d'une action naïvement représentée. C'est dans la peinture des détails qu'excellent les romanciers chinois, et c'est encore en cela qu'on peut les rapprocher de Richardson, de Fielding, ou tout au moins du docteur Smolett [*sic*] et de mademoiselle Burney. (14)

As with 'l'interminable drame de Clarisse' one finds the pace slow at first but regrets afterwards that it has been so rapid. The personages are mostly 'des personnes de moyen état et des rangs intermédiaires de la société' (21). In most such novels 'tout est renfermé entre les bornes du possible et même du vraisemblable' (28). *Iu Kiao Li* is, for Rémusat, a simple, well-conceived story with clearly presented characters. Too much verse, perhaps, for some readers: but the novel is about *lettrés*, and 'c'est l'idéal de la société du pays, ce sont les amusements de la bonne compagnie qu'on y trouve représentés; on y reconnaît déjà l'empreinte de ces institutions qui ont fait de la littérature la principale occupation d'une nation savante et policée' (46)—a fact that may well have appealed to Goethe, we may add. As for the general contours of the plot, Rémusat says the following:

> Il n'est ici question ni de ces vengeances atroces heureusement assez rares dans le monde, ni de ces actes d'un dévouement sublime, lesquels n'y sont pas non plus très-communs. On n'y verra ni les rencontres imprévues de l'abbé Prevost [*sic*], ni les apparitions de madame Radcliffe, ni les oubliettes de *Kenilworth*. Il ne meurt pas une seule personne dans tout le roman; et quoiqu'à la conclusion les personnages vertueux reçoivent leur récompense, les acteurs vicieux ne sont pas punis: disposition bien contraire à la moralité romanesque, et qui, de la part de l'auteur, est sans doute un sacrifice fait à la vraisemblance. (47)

It is clear that Rémusat is justifying the novel by French ideals of taste such as *vraisemblance*, *bienséance*, and *fidélité*, and even though one can hardly go along with his assertion of the lack of coincidental encounters, the general picture that emerges from his description is that of a lack of passionate extremes and an ordering according to generous morality. It seems clear that Goethe had read this preface thoughtfully.

This becomes even clearer when Rémusat comes to discuss the denouement of the novel, in a very interesting and significant passage:

> Il n'est qu'un point où le génie de l'Asie laisse apercevoir son infériorité, et c'est par malheur un point essentiel, puisqu'il tient au fond même du roman, qu'il est indiqué dès le titre, et qu'il constitue le dénouement. L'idée qu'on y découvre s'est présentée à quelques Occidentaux, et M. Goëthe, dans sa jeunesse, en a fait le sujet de son drame de Stella; mais contenu par la rigueur des mœurs européennes, il s'est borné à quelques indications, en s'abstenant de développements qui auraient pu devenir choquants, et le *Wir sind dein* de la fin est le seul mot un peu hasardé de cette singulière composition. Ici, au contraire, des sentiments qui n'ont rien que de légitime prennent un libre essor sous l'influence des habitudes nationales et des idées du pays, sans blesser aucunement la pudeur et la bienséance. Le héros, puisqu'il faut le dire, étend aux *deux Cousines* des vœux et des sentiments qui sont regardés chez nous comme exclusifs de leur nature. Il devient épris de l'une sans cesser pour cela d'adorer

l'autre. Deux femmes vertueuses se partagent les affections d'un homme délicat, et celui-ci ne croit pas manquer d'amour, pour en accorder à deux objets qui en sont également dignes: *Je n'ai qu'un cœur,* dit-il à l'une d'elles, ce qui ne signifie pas, comme on pourrait le supposer, *je vous serai éternellement fidèle,* mais au contraire, *si je trouvais une seconde femme aussi aimable que vous, comment ferais-je pour ne pas l'aimer?* Bien plus: la double union à laquelle il aspire est aussi le but où tendent les vues secrètes des deux cousines, et si elle ne s'effectuait pas, on voit qu'il manquerait quelque chose à leur bonheur. Toutes deux se défendent de l'accusation de jalousie, comme on se justifierait ailleurs d'un penchant condamnable ou d'une inclination illégitime. Non-seulement la découverte qu'elles font d'un attachement porté sur un même objet n'altère en rien leur bonne intelligence; mais c'est pour elles un motif de plus de s'estimer et de se chérir. Où l'on trouverait en Europe un sujet de discorde et de désespoir, d'aimables Chinoises voient l'effet de la plus heureuse sympathie et le gage d'une félicité parfaite. On est véritablement transporté dans un autre monde. . . . (49–51)

One can also consider the matter purely from the standpoint of the novelist:

Mais à considérer la chose en romancier, plutôt qu'en moraliste ou en philosophe, contentons-nous d'observer quelles ressources un écrivain peut tirer d'un pareil système: il lui fournit un moyen facile de contenter tout le monde à la fin du récit, sans recourir à ces maladies de langueur, à ces consomptions funestes, tristes effets d'une passion malheureuse et inutilement combattue, et seul recours de nos écrivains, quand, de compte fait, il se trouve une héroïne de trop qui les embarrasse au moment de la conclusion, et à qui la délicatesse ne permet ni de vivre, ni de changer. Le procédé chinois aurait épargné bien des larmes à Corinne, à la Clémentine de Richardson, et sauvé de vifs regrets à l'indécis Oswald, et peut-être au vertueux Grandisson [*sic*] lui-même. (53)

To these words of Rémusat we may add a comment. The 'consomptions funestes' that he refers to occur in this novel only in the *false* report of Houngiu's death made by Tchangfanjou to Sse Yeoupe: they belong therefore to fiction, to the *romanesque* or novelistic, and conflict with reality, as does Tchangfanjou's assertion in this same report that, although the doctors said she died of consumption, he himself thinks it was her morality that killed her. For in the world of this novel no one could die from morality.

Goethe and the Chinese Novel

It would seem clear from our investigations that in the statement to Eckermann with which we began Goethe is speaking primarily of *Chinese Courtship* but is also recalling *Hau Kiou Choaan*. Although referring specifically to one Chinese novel, the statement is therefore a composite of his impressions of two such novels and his absorption of the account of a third in *Le Globe*. There is further evidence for this in the conversation itself. For to Eckermann's question 'Ist denn dieser chinesische Roman vielleicht einer ihrer vorzüglichsten?' Goethe replied: 'Keineswegs, die Chinesen haben deren zu Tausenden und hatten ihrer schon, als unsere Vorfahren noch in den Wäldern lebten' (Artemis Ausgabe, xxiv. 228). There are also some details in Goethe's statement which would seem to have come from his reading of Chinese poetry rather than from Chinese novels. Woldemar Freiherr von Biedermann asserts that these statements of Goethe 'sich nicht bloss auf "Chinese Courtship" sondern anscheinend auch auf die "Chinesischen Dichterinnen" bezogen'.[1] He draws attention to the fact that on 5 February 1827 (a week after the conversation with Eckermann) Goethe dictated to John the essay entitled *Chinesisches. Gedichte schöner Frauen* (for *Über Kunst und Alterthum*) which, Goethe claimed, represented 'Notizen und Gedichtchen' culled from 'einem chrestomatisch-biographischen Werke' called *Gedichte hundert schöner Frauen* and gives convincing proof 'dass es sich, trotz aller Beschränkungen, in diesem sonderbar-merkwürdigen Reiche noch immer leben, lieben und dichten lasse' (Artemis Ausgabe, xiv. 722). One of the manuscript drafts for this essay begins with the sentence (later excised): 'Ein Roman Ju Kiao Li und ein grosses Gedicht: Chinesische Werbschaft (Chinese Courtship), jener französisch, durch Abel Remusat, dieses englisch, durch Peter Perring Thoms, setzten uns in den Stand, abermals tiefer und schärfer in das so streng bewachte Land hinein zu blicken' (W.A. i. 42 (i), 232–3). The first poem cited in this essay deals with the light-footedness of Miss See-Yaou-Hing who could dance on water-lilies, her foot itself with its little shoe being like such a lily, so much so that the other women bound their feet. Goethe then points out that delicate feet in golden shoes were called by these poets 'golden lilies', which led to the generalization of the custom of

---

[1] Woldemar Freiherr von Biedermann, 'Chinesisch-deutsche Jahres- und Tageszeiten', in *Goethe-Forschungen*, N. F., Leipzig 1886, p. 428.

binding feet. This is a good example of what Goethe means by 'die äussere Natur neben den menschlichen Figuren immer mitlebt'. The water-lilies on which this girl danced are no more an image than the eggs between which Mignon danced. Both exist as realities. But the water-lilies live their own life independent, though not remote, from man. There are lilies, and there are feet. So that what seems like a conceit is not always so in this poetry, although there are conceits in some of the other poems which Goethe cites. The theme of constancy in love and the figure of the Emperor as moral authority are found here too. The imagery is delicate, the content often akin to legends. And, as we have seen, Nature is no mere referent or backcloth, but an equal partner.

The essential framework of ideas contained in the statement to Eckermann is essentially that of Rémusat's preface. And if Goethe did not read this until May 1827, he was nevertheless familiar with its main points from the review in *Le Globe* a few months earlier. Both in this review and in Rémusat's preface there is a dichotomy. *Iu Kiao Li*, and Chinese novels in general, are presented both as something quite foreign to us and as having much in common with our own world in moral values and with our own novels in character-types and plot-configuration. The dissimilarity appealed to the *europamüde* Goethe, the similarities to the exponent of *Weltliteratur*. One of the striking facts about Goethe's literary interests was his increasing occupation with the novel as a form, from about 1795 (when he composed the famous passage in the *Lehrjahre* on the delimitation of drama from novel) onwards. Two features above all characterize his view of the novel. First: in the depiction of reality mere realism is not enough, the novel (like all art) must achieve (to use Schiller's terms) that transformation of empiric into aesthetic forms which involves elevation above the actual and yet remains within the real, a poeticization of the prosaic to be achieved by organization of material according to a controlling idea which should be felt rather than expressed. Hence—to give a few examples—his admiration for the moralness of *The Vicar of Wakefield* and *Daphnis and Chloë*, his recognition of a 'secret ethical thread' in Jean Paul's works, his appreciation of the firm moral basis to Sterne (but not to Voltaire), and his disapproval of Victor Hugo's doctrine of the grotesque as organizing principle in *Notre-Dame de Paris* because it was a gimmick rather than an idea, whereas the organizing principle of *Paul et Virginie* was a serious idea. Secondly: Goethe believed that the novel could and should express the indisputable fact of chance in human experience, whereas the logic of drama could not and should not try to. This was the essence of what he variously termed 'das Romanhafte', 'das Romaneske'—the novelistic. He did not dismiss coincidences, surprises, and sensational elements as 'reines Erzählen', as many eighteenth-century critics did. Indeed 'reines Erzählen' would, if Goethe had used that term, probably have meant something very positive to him. After all he did have that 'Lust zu fabulieren'. This he found in plenty in these Chinese novels; but together with it the organizing principle of a code of decorum and morality in which ethical and social values coalesce.[1] The motif of the double marriage in *Chinese Courtship* appears as *deus ex machina*, but embodies both of those aspects of the novel as a form which particularly interested Goethe. It is a morally grounded novelistic motif, being both moral focus and sensational turn of the plot. It may, however, seem sensational only to Western readers, for *Iu Kiao Li* develops gradually towards such a solution which is in no wise unexpected but carefully prepared. It is credible because of the world from which it springs. How interested Goethe must have been in that reference to *Stella* in Rémusat's preface! It just showed that a novelistic motif, however surprising, must emerge credibly from an organized whole.

I wish to express my gratitude to Mr. Richard C. Howard, Curator of the Wason Collection (of Chinese and other oriental books) in the Cornell University Library, for his help on the bibliographical background of this article.

[1] It has been pointed out by various scholars that all three of these novels are Confucian in spirit, and that morality defines itself in them in the five-fold duty to Emperor, father, brothers, wife, and friends, and expresses itself in actions rather than in homilies. It is indeed therefore 'verständig, bürgerlich' from the standpoint of eighteenth-century Western values.

Faust and the Sin of Sloth
Mephistopheles and the Sin of Pride

LEONARD FORSTER

IN *Faust* Goethe adapts a sixteenth-century legend about a man who, in order to achieve forbidden knowledge, magical power, and sensual pleasure, sells his soul to the Devil. The Devil serves him for an appointed span of years, but fetches him in the end in an appalling scene of violence and destruction. The fate of Faust is shown as a terrible example of what happens to those who forsake the true way. The chief elements in this story are: knowledge, power, and lust; and it is through pursuing these that Faust comes to his end. The pact with the Devil is made for a term of years, and when the time is up his perdition is inescapable. No heavenly host can save him, for he has signed away his soul, and the uses to which he has put his powers are purely selfish.

Goethe takes up the basic themes—the desire for knowledge, sensual experience, and power—and several important episodes —the pact with the Devil, the conjuring of the spirits of the past, and the appearance at the Emperor's court—but he gives them a very different slant. His drama is not about the final destruction of a lost soul, but about the ultimate redemption of an earnestly striving, though necessarily erring, human being. The sixteenth-century Faust is measured against an absolute—the imitation of Christ in the Christian life—and his initial choice is in favour of an absolute—evil instead of good. Goethe, on the other hand, works with a series of delicate gradations: his Devil is not an absolute; Faust's activity is not entirely selfish; he operates within a framework of free will in which he can use magic for good purpose and eventually be saved. The story of the sixteenth-century Faust consists of a series of astonishing events without inner development, terminating inevitably in the hero's death and perdition. Goethe's *Faust* is intended to show the development of a character from an initial traumatic experience to final redemption. The development is not uniform and it does not proceed in a straight line, but it is an essential theme of the poem. The exploration of the development of the human personality was one of the great subjects of eighteenth-century writing, and Goethe himself had led the way. It had usually taken the form of studying the development of young people towards maturity, as in *Wilhelm Meisters Lehrjahre*. In *Faust* Goethe follows the later years, from maturity to death at the symbolic age of one hundred. The keynote of this development is activity, the avoidance of the sin of sloth, the most insidious of the seven deadly sins. In the Prologue in Heaven the Lord himself says:

> Des Menschen Tätigkeit kann allzuleicht erschlaffen,
> Er liebt sich bald die unbedingte Ruh;
> Drum geb ich gern ihm den Gesellen zu.
> Der reizt und wirkt und muss als Teufel schaffen.

But there are different kinds of activity and different kinds of sloth, and it is part of the function of the drama to explore them. The pact with Mephistopheles depends on this: if Faust succumbs to sloth, then he is forfeit to the Devil. The Lord speaks of '*unbedingte* Ruh', Faust in the pact scene of holding fast the fleeting moment: 'Verweile doch, du bist so schön.' Both come ultimately to mean the same thing: a slackening of idealism. Earlier theologians had defined the sin of sloth as 'aversion to spiritual and divine things'; in the secularized language of the eighteenth century it becomes equivalent to an absence of the desire to strive for something higher, or the loss of that desire. It may result on the one hand in pointless activity, on the other in sheer idleness, disinclination for physical or mental effort of any kind, and thus finally in apathy. There are thus two sorts of sloth, as there are two sorts of activity. Mephistopheles sees the, to him, pointless striving of Faust as a symptom of one kind of sloth and thinks that he will be able to reduce him to the other kind of sloth by drugging him with material pleasures. The temptations proceed in ascending order: drink, sex, and power. Knowledge has been superseded; Faust's desire to discover 'was die Welt Im Innersten zusammenhält' does not persist after his meeting with Mephisto, and this is an indication that the temptation is taking effect.

The recognition of sloth as a sin,[1] and a cardinal one to boot,

[1] See Siegfried Wenzel, *The Sin of Sloth: 'acedia' in Medieval Thought and Literature*, University of North Carolina Press, Chapel Hill 1967. It will be clear that I am greatly indebted to Wenzel's illuminating work throughout this paper.

derives from the Desert Fathers, pious hermits who settled in the Egyptian desert in the fourth century to live an ascetic life of Christian meditation and devotion remote from the world. Like all ascetics they experienced difficulties and trials, which distracted their minds from meditation. One of these they called ἀκηδία or *acedia*; medieval theologians called it *accidie*. It was a fatigue or depression which made itself felt particularly at noon; this is the time when in the desert the heat is fiercest and the body weakest, so that concentration in prayer or meditation most easily slackens. For this reason some fathers maintained that *acedia* was the 'daemonium meridianum' spoken of in the 90th Psalm in the Vulgate (A.V., Ps. 91 : 6, renders: 'the destruction that wasteth at noonday'). The remedy generally advocated was on the one hand increased attention to spiritual exercises, varying them as requisite, and on the other some kind of manual work. Both are forms of 'Tätigkeit'.

John Cassian, writing in the fifth century, describes in some detail the symptoms of *acedia* in chapters 2 and 3 of Book X of his *Institutes of the Coenobia*:[1]

2. *A description of accidie, and the way in which it creeps over the heart of a monk, and the injury it inflicts on the soul*

And when this has taken possession of some unhappy soul, it produces (*a*) dislike of the place, disgust with the cell, and (*b*) disdain and contempt of the brethren who dwell with him or at a little distance, as if they were careless or unspiritual. It also makes the man (*c*) lazy and sluggish about all manner of work which has to be done within the enclosure of his dormitory. It does not suffer him to stay in his cell, or to take any pains about reading, and he often groans because (*d*) he can do no good while he stays there, and complains and sighs because (*e*) he can bear no spiritual fruit so long as he is joined to that society; and he complains that he is cut off from spiritual gain, and is of no use in the place, as if he were one who, though he could govern others and be useful to a great number of people, (*f*) yet was edifying none, nor profiting anyone by his teaching and doctrine. He (*g*) cries up distant monasteries and those which

[1] Latin text: *PL* 49, 365 ff. The translation quoted here is that of the works of Cassian by Edgar C. S. Gibson in the *Select Library of Nicene and Post-Nicene Fathers*, 2nd ser., vol. xi, Oxford 1894, pp. 266 ff. The italic letters in brackets are not in the text, but have been inserted for ease of reference. In what follows Cassian's works are referred to as *Inst.* for the *Instituta* and *Coll.* for the *Collationes*. The most recent general work on Cassian is W. O. Chadwick, *John Cassian*, 2nd edn., Cambridge 1968.

Faust and the Sin of Sloth

are a long way off, and describes such places as more profitable and better suited for salvation; and besides this he paints the intercourse with the brethren there as sweet and full of spiritual life. On the other hand, he (*h*) says that everything about him is rough, and not only that there is nothing edifying among the brethren who are stopping there, but also that even food for the body cannot be procured without great difficulty. Lastly (*i*) he fancies that he will never be well while he stays in that place, unless he leaves his cell (in which he is sure to die if he stops in it any longer) and takes himself off from thence as quickly as possible. Then the fifth or sixth hour brings him such bodily weariness and longing for food that he seems to himself worn out and wearied as if with a long journey, or some very heavy work, or as if he had put off taking food during a fast of two or three days. Then besides this he looks about anxiously this way and that, and sighs (*j*) that none of the brethren come to see him, and often goes in and out of his cell, and frequently gazes up at the sun, as if it was too slow in setting, and so (*k*) a kind of unreasonable confusion of mind takes possession of him like some foul darkness, and makes him idle and useless for every spiritual work, so that he imagines that no cure for so terrible an attack can be found in anything except visiting some one of the brethren, or in the solace of sleep alone. Then the disease suggests (*l*) that he ought to show courteous and friendly hospitalities to the brethren, and pay visits to the sick, whether near at hand or far off. He talks too about some dutiful and religious offices; that those kinsfolk ought to be inquired after, and that he ought to go and see them oftener; that it would be a real work of piety to go more frequently to visit that religious woman, devoted to the service of God, who is deprived of all support of kindred; and that it would be a most excellent thing to get what is needful for her who is neglected and despised by her own kinsfolk; and that he ought piously to devote his time to these things instead of staying uselessly and with no profit in his cell.

3. *Of the different ways in which accidie overcomes a monk*

And so the wretched soul, embarrassed by such contrivances of the enemy, is disturbed, until, worn out by the spirit of accidie, as by some strong battering ram, it either learns to sink into slumber, or, driven out from the confinement of its cell, accustoms itself to seek for consolation under these attacks in visiting some brother, only to be afterwards weakened the more by this remedy which it seeks for the present. For more frequently and more severely will the enemy attack one who, when the battle is joined, will as he well knows immediately turn his back, and whom he sees to look for safety neither in victory nor in fighting but in flight; until (*m*) little by little he is drawn away from his cell, and begins to forget the object of his profession, which is nothing but meditation and contemplation of that divine purity which excels all things, and which can only be gained by silence and continually remaining in the cell, and by meditation, and so the soldier of Christ becomes a runaway from His service, and a deserter, and 'entangles himself in secular business', without at all pleasing Him to whom he engaged himself.

With this in mind, we may look at Goethe's text more closely. Sloth manifests itself in an inability to concentrate, which in its turn expresses itself in distaste for the cell, and leads to restlessness and aimless wandering about and, eventually, to spiritual apathy. When the Lord mentions Faust in the Prologue in Heaven, Mephistopheles, who is naturally an expert in the matter of sins, recognizes the symptoms at once:

> Ihn treibt die Gärung in die Ferne,
> Er ist sich seiner Tollheit halb bewusst;
> Vom Himmel fordert er die schönsten Sterne
> Und von der Erde jede höchste Lust,
> Und alle Näh' und alle Ferne
> Befriedigt nicht die tiefbewegte Brust.

The passage falls into two parts; the present tense is used throughout, but with differing force. The first two lines state what is actually happening: Faust is already restless—'ihn treibt die Gärung in die Ferne'; he experiences the urge to wander about, but has not yet left his cell—*ihn treibt*, not *ihn hat getrieben*—for he is at least half-aware of the foolishness of this undertaking. As Cassian points out in another passage (*Inst.* x. 25) 'a fit of accidie should not be evaded by running away from it, but overcome by resisting it'. In the lines after the semi-colon the present is used with future force: Mephistopheles is describing where this *will* lead if Faust succumbs, as Mephistopheles thinks he will, the more so as he is only '*halb* bewusst'. Dissatisfaction with the cell will eventually lead to dissatisfaction with everything:

> Und alle Näh' und alle Ferne
> Befriedigt nicht die tiefbewegte Brust.

Nothing will seem to matter any more and the result will be spiritual apathy.

Medieval theologians, who classified the sins and the progeny of each sin, showed that sloth could lead to Sorrow or Dejection (*tristitia*) and Despair (*desperatio*),[1] both of them destructive of the urge to higher things and conducing to a state in which Mephistopheles' later words 'Staub soll er fressen, und mit Lust' are likely to come true. The final result is apathy. For these reasons Mephistopheles thinks that Faust's feet are already set on a downward path and that he is fair game; in the following scenes we are shown Faust in the grip of *acedia*, and falling a victim to *tristitia* and *desperatio*, to the extent that he even contemplates taking his own life; so there is much to be said for Mephisto's view. The Lord, however, thinks otherwise, but Mephisto is so sure of his diagnosis that he enters into the wager. Like all devils, he is a victim of the sin of pride, that basic sin which caused Lucifer to be cast out of heaven, and which, as Cassian says, is the only sin which is aimed directly at God himself[2] (the others are mere human failings). He thinks he knows better than the Lord. This in fact is his fundamental mistake throughout, and the reason why his undertaking ultimately fails: he always thinks he knows better.

We then find Faust in his study. We are not dealing with a hermit in the desert or with a monk in a monastery, but with a modern parallel, the scholar at his desk. What was originally a religious context is now a secular one and the concept of sloth too has become secularized. What for the monk was an aversion from the pursuit of spiritual things and the performance of spiritual exercises now becomes the scholar's dissatisfaction with intellectual pursuits and traditional intellectual disciplines (a dissatisfaction which in this case has even led him to devote himself to magic). The symptoms are remarkably similar. If we take Cassian's description of them, it is surprising how many recur in Faust's speeches. Let us take them in the order in which Cassian sets them out, though of course not all are equally applicable.

First we have (*a*) 'dislike of the place' and 'disgust with the cell'; this is put explicitly in the section beginning 'Weh! steck' ich in dem Kerker noch? Verfluchtes dumpfes Mauerloch', and is implicit in the whole monologue, especially in the line 'Dafür ist mir alle Freud entrissen', though of course that has general

[1] Wenzel, p. 82; Cassian, *Coll.* v. 16.   [2] Cassian, *Inst.* xii. 7.

application too. Then we have (*b*) 'contempt of the brethren' in the lines 'Zwar bin ich gescheiter als alle die Laffen, Doktoren, Magister, Schreiber und Pfaffen'. Laziness and sluggishness about work and taking no pains about reading (*c*) are sufficiently shown by the circumstance that Faust is talking, not working, but they can be documented in the lines: 'Umsonst, dass trockenes Sinnen hier Die heiligen Zeichen dir erklärt'—intellectual work is 'trockenes Sinnen'—and 'Soll ich vielleicht in tausend Büchern lesen, Dass überall die Menschen sich gequält'—books tell us nothing we did not know before. This is not, of course, what Cassian means; for him 'reading' meant the regular study of the Scriptures, which was a spiritual exercise. Faust is talking about the secularized scholarly equivalent. Cassian's monk groans (*d*) because he can do no good; Faust says 'Es möchte kein Hund so länger leben! Drum hab' ich mich der Magie ergeben'. The monk's feeling that (*e*) he can bear no fruit where he is, with the people he is with, has a rather more distant parallel in Faust's contemptuous attitude towards Wagner, 'der trockene Schleicher'. The monk cut off from spiritual gain (*f*) and benefiting none by his teaching finds a parallel in Faust's lines beginning 'Da steh ich nun, ich armer Tor', though it is not exact. Cassian's monk is complaining that he lacks opportunity to teach; Faust has the opportunity in abundance, but is, he feels, 'edifying none by his teaching'. Faust does not (*g*) 'cry up distant monasteries' or other seats of learning; his rival attractions are pantheistically inspired in a characteristically eighteenth-century way, and take the form of 'Bergeshöhen', 'Wiesen' away from 'Wissensqualm', 'in deinem Tau gesund mich baden', all admirable in themselves, doubtless, but taking him away from the cell. Cassian's monk complains (*h*) that everything about him is rough and even his daily food is difficult to get; Faust, who, unlike him, is not vowed to poverty, complains 'Auch habe ich weder Gut noch Geld Noch Ehr noch Herrlichkeit der Welt'. Cassian's monk feels (*i*) that he will never be well until he leaves his cell; Faust cries 'Flieh! Auf! hinaus ins weite Land'. The monk (*j*) sighs that none of the brethren come to visit him; Faust finds the Devil himself a welcome guest and says to Mephisto, 'Besuche mich nun, wie du magst'. The 'unreasonable confusion of mind' (*k*) of which Cassian speaks is perhaps reflected in Faust's 'Zwei Seelen

Faust and the Sin of Sloth

wohnen, ach, in meiner Brust' speech, but it is sufficiently evident throughout the 'Studierzimmer' scenes. The monk leaves the cloister (*l*) under some pious pretext; Faust takes his Easter walk—'Hier bin ich Mensch, hier darf ichs sein'—and later does not need much persuading by Mephistopheles to leave his cell for good—'Wir gehen eben fort' is all the encouragement he requires. And so, little by little, Faust is (*m*) 'drawn away from his cell and begins to forget the object of his profession', which in his case is not 'meditation and contemplation of divine purity' but intellectual work and striving for higher things. As we saw, as soon as the pact is made we hear no more about his intellectual curiosity, which shows that Mephisto's influence is already making itself felt. But even before that, Faust's case was serious, for he had fallen a victim to a fit of that *taedium vitae* and *desperatio*, self-hatred, despair, and desire for death, which medieval theologians saw as proceeding from, among other things, *acedia*. This is his initial trauma. He had been close to suicide, and was indeed only restrained from it by the memory of earlier religious exercises ('Sonst stürzte sich der Himmelsliebe Kuss Auf mich herab in ernster Sabbatstille [. . .] Erinnerung hält mich nun mit kindlichem Gefühle Vom letzten, ernsten Schritt zurück').

The 'Osterspaziergang' is interesting. For Cassian it is disastrous for the monk to leave his cell; this is his proper sphere and it is here that temptation must be resisted. St. Basil was rather more liberal and even went so far as to allow the monk an occasional emergence from the cell, 'for often the ἀκηδία which besets the soul is dispelled by going out';[1] he was followed by some medieval theologians. The wisdom of this view is exemplified in the case of Faust, for on his return from his Easter walk he settles down to work with renewed zest:

> Entschlafen sind nun wilde Triebe
> Mit jedem ungestümen Tun;
> Es reget sich die Menschenliebe,
> Die Liebe Gottes regt sich nun.

He even uses the word 'cell' in a positive sense:

> Ach, wenn in unsrer engen Zelle
> Die Lampe freundlich wieder brennt,

[1] Wenzel, p. 9; Greek text: *PG* 31, 1368. See also Wenzel, p. 32.

Dann wirds in unserm Busen helle,
Im Herzen, das sich selber kennt,

and he seeks the source of all life, 'des Lebens Quelle', namely God. This search is exemplified by his desire to study scripture —'mich drängt's, den Grundtext aufzuschlagen'; Basil and Cassian would regard this as a spiritual exercise. It would seem that the opening scenes showed only a temporary fit of spiritual sloth, from which Faust is rapidly recovering as a result of the relaxation afforded by his walk. But perhaps Cassian was right after all, for Faust has unwittingly brought the Devil back with him in the form of the poodle. There is nothing incongruous about the poodle in this context, for many hermits and monks are recorded as having made friends with animals and birds: the author of the life of St. Colman in the *Vitae Sanctorum Hiberniae* points out how fitting it is that 'those who have renounced all fellowship and service of men that their spirits may be swifter to serve Him, should themselves receive the good offices of dumb beasts and a kind of human ministering'.[1] It is a neat touch that this should be the means whereby the Devil is enabled to enter Faust's cell, and it is of course the Devil's business to prevent Faust's recovery. It is therefore no accident that Mephistopheles interrupts his Bible study before he has got any further than the first verse of the Gospel according to St. John, and succeeds in distracting him effectively. The next scene, which evidently takes place the following morning, shows Faust beset by a sort of spiritual hangover, irritable—'Wer will mich wieder plagen?' —and again in the grip of *acedia* and despair; this becomes clear from the speech 'In jedem Kleide werd' ich wohl die Pein Des engen Erdelebens fühlen'. He is now ripe for Mephistopheles, because he is still suffering from the restlessness which Mephisto interprets as proceeding from spiritual sloth, and the pact is made.

Sloth is a particularly deadly sin because aversion from spiritual things opens the door to all other vices and lays the subject wide open to temptation, especially when he goes out into the world. As Mephistopheles says:

Ihm hat das Schicksal einen Geist gegeben,
Der *ungebändigt* immer vorwärts dringt, [. . .]

[1] Translated by Helen Waddell, *Beasts and Saints*, London 1934, pp. 146–7.

Faust and the Sin of Sloth

Und hätt' er sich auch nicht dem Teufel übergeben
Er müsste doch zugrunde gehen!

Mephistopheles hopes to reduce Faust to idleness and apathy, but the terms on which Faust enters into the pact show that he himself is thinking of something quite different. He aims not just to hold fast the fleeting moment, but to hold it fast because it is 'so fair'. This excludes apathy (though it does not necessarily exclude idleness). If Mephisto had not been blinded by the sin of pride he would have realized this. But at this decisive point he, as usual, knows better, and so he misses what is *for him* the decisive moment. The Lord knew all along that Faust's restlessness was not really the result of spiritual sloth, closely though his symptoms resembled it, but of a genuine desire for higher, though not strictly spiritual, things:

Der Menschheit Krone zu erringen
Nach der sich alle Sinne dringen.

The title of the scene 'Wald und Höhle' suggests hermits, and in fact we find Faust, having fled from the world and its temptations (in the form of Gretchen), living a hermit's life of communion with God in Nature, from which Mephisto, of course, needs to draw him away, and we witness the last of a series of attempts to achieve this end. Faust's exclamation as he succumbs, 'Schlange! Schlange!' is well chosen, for Mephisto is tempting him away from a paradise of pure contemplation and meditation.[1]

But though he succeeds here, Mephisto's temptations all ultimately fail in Part I, and at the beginning of Part II, when Faust's memory of them and of their disastrous results has been mercifully removed, he is again ready to strive for higher things —'Zum höchsten Dasein immerfort zu streben'. Activity, which Mephisto throughout interprets as restlessness and goallessness arising from sloth, occupies him henceforward, and at the end it is good works undertaken for others. Then comes the last attempt to subdue Faust through sloth—his encounter with Sorge.

The tendency is to think of Sorge in terms of worry, especially about material things, and even Erich Trunz seems to do this

[1] St. Chrysostom thought that the Egyptian desert, because of the life of the hermits who lived there, was better than any Paradise (*In Matthaeum Homil.* viii, iv; *PG* 57, 87): παραδείσου παντὸς βελτίω τὴν ἔρημον ταύτην ὄψει γεγενημένην.

in his commentary on this passage in the *Hamburger Ausgabe*. But it is clear that Sorge means more than that.[1] Her self-characterization is a brilliant, and almost clinical, description of depression or dejection, which numbs the faculties and inhibits all higher striving. Dejection, or *tristitia*, as we saw, has its place in Cassian's list of sins, and he considers it as akin to *acedia*, or sloth. It is characteristic of both that they 'arise without any external provocation' (*Coll.* v. 9), 'stets gefunden, nie gesucht', just as the appearance of Sorge herself is not prepared for in the drama. Dejection, says Cassian (*Inst.* ix. 1), makes the mind 'impatient and rough in all the duties of work and devotion; and as all wholesome counsel is lost and steadfastness of heart destroyed, it makes the feelings almost mad and drunk, and crushes and overwhelms them with penal despair'. The word *Sorge* itself is akin to our word 'sorrow', which is the medieval theologians' rendering of *tristitia* in the sense in which Cassian uses it. Faust, however, rebuffs Sorge; he sees his 'Begehren' as something lofty:

> Wenn Geister spuken, geh' er seinen Gang,
> Im Weiterschreiten find' er Qual und Glück,
> Er, unbefriedigt jeden Augenblick!

This dissatisfaction is a noble one, and quite different from the dissatisfaction arising from mental paralysis with which Sorge threatens him. He succeeds in repulsing her because he does not use magic but resists her with the whole force of his matured personality. All she can do is to strike him blind; she cannot sap his moral fibre.

To sum up: Mephistopheles finds Faust showing all the initial symptoms of *acedia*. He therefore thinks that he can lead him on to the other sins which flow from it. His attempts fail because gluttony (Auerbach's Cellar) disgusts Faust, lust (Gretchen) turns to true love, the temptation of power leads to the discovery of Helen, to the completion of Faust's 'aesthetic education', and finally to the reclamation of land and the renouncing of magic.

[1] Konrad Burdach in 'Faust und die Sorge', *DVJS* 1 (1923), 60, concludes that 'Im Sterben also wird Faust das Kind der Sorge. Aber nicht jenes grauen Dämons, der "atra cura" des Horaz und des Höllendämons der Aeneis, sondern des holderen Genius der Fürsorge'. If you can believe that you can believe anything.

Faust and the Sin of Sloth

Mephisto thinks he can subdue Faust by encouraging him in useless, aimless activity; but Faust *has* an aim—'Zum höchsten Dasein immerfort zu streben'—though he often loses sight of it:

> Ein guter Mensch in seinem dunklen Drange
> Ist sich des rechten Weges wohl bewusst.

This means that his activity is not aimless, and thus negative, but positive, and thus a cure for *acedia*, though a more indirect cure than the hard manual labour prescribed by Cassian (*Inst.* x. 7-25). Mephisto is bound by the contract to assist Faust in his striving, and he believes all along that things are really going his way. The result is that Faust's self-improvement is aided by Mephisto's magic powers, and that Mephisto's scheme is self-defeating. This is because Mephisto is possessed, not by the sin of sloth, but, as we saw, by the even more dangerous and deluding sin of pride. It is precisely because devils are deluded by the sin of pride that they can traditionally be outwitted by human beings, and the 'geprellter Teufel' is a familiar figure in folklore.[1]

There is one fundamental difference between Goethe's conception of these sins and that of Cassian and the medieval theologians who followed him. Their concept of *acedia* is based on original sin and the Fall of man; Goethe considers man as basically good. I would like to make it quite clear that I am not suggesting that *Faust* is a Christian work. Goethe uses Catholic symbolism throughout the drama as a vehicle for his own poetic truth, not as an element of his personal faith; in precisely the same way he used Islamic ideas as a convenient poetic device in the *West-östlicher Divan* without being a Moslem, and like all the poets of his day he used classical mythology throughout his life for the same purpose.

I do not think that the question whether or not Goethe actually read Cassian or the Desert Fathers, interesting though it is, really affects my argument. He must at all events have been familiar with the traditional teaching of the Churches on the seven

---

[1] See Stith Thompson, *Motif-Index of Folk-Literature*, Copenhagen 1955 ff., vol. iii, G303.13. I cannot agree with Eudo Mason, 'Die Gestalt des Teufels in der deutschen Literatur seit 1748' in Werner Kohlschmidt and Herman Meyer eds., *Tradition und Ursprünglichkeit: Akten des Internationalen Germanistenkongresses 1965*, Bern 1966, p. 120, where he says that Goethe's Mephisto has no pride.

deadly sins,[1] whether consciously or not. It is difficult to determine whether his relation to tradition in this respect is conscious, barely conscious, or unconscious. It seems at all events that he did not go back to a discontinued tradition but utilized one which has continued from early times, though in spheres of thought remote from his normal preoccupations. Even if he did not use it consciously, there would be nothing surprising in the circumstance that his own informed diagnosis and analysis of a state with which he, like any intellectual, was familiar should turn out to be so similar to that reached by earlier tradition. What I have tried to show is that certain puzzling aspects of his great and puzzling poem can be better elucidated by taking into account the sin of sloth—whether we call it by that name or by some other name.

[1] On some unsuspected aspects of Goethe's extensive theological knowledge see Elizabeth M. Wilkinson, 'The Theological Aspects of Faust's Credo', *German Life and Letters*, N.S. x (1956–7), 229 ff.

The standard works on the sin of sloth known in the eighteenth century are discussed in Zedler's *Universallexicon*, xliv, col. 1857, s.v. 'Trägheit (geistliche)', especially Johann Daniel Herrenschmidt's *Dissertatio de acedia*, Halle 1713. There is no certain indication that Goethe knew any of them.

T. S. Eliot on Goethe

RONALD PEACOCK

IN Eliot's *The Use of Poetry and the Use of Criticism*, which appeared in 1933, there is a passage on Goethe which to many sounds rather scandalous, and has become notorious. Eliot is speaking about the use of poetry to put across a particular philosophy, and having commented on Wordsworth and Shelley in this connection, he goes on: 'Of Goethe perhaps it is truer to say that he dabbled in both philosophy and poetry and made no great success of either; his true role was that of the man of the world and sage—a La Rochefoucauld, a La Bruyère, a Vauvenargues.[1] The passage is scandalous on the face of it because it offers such an impossibly inadequate judgement of Goethe; very brief, very summary, very rude; and also because it appears in a study in which the author is talking not only about poetry but about the relationship between poetry and criticism, about the critical self-consciousness of a number of great poets: in such a study one would have expected least of all unsubtle critical statements.

I do not know what sort of reception was given to this peculiar statement by Eliot's first audience—the book consists of lectures delivered at Harvard—but in the course of time people have protested against it in England. One has to admit that the protesting voices were mainly those of Germanists, since others lacked the exact knowledge which would have justified them in counter-attacking Eliot, especially since he was at that time at the very height of his prestige as poet and critic and influenced decisively the direction of taste.

Before analysing the passage and commenting on it I want to make clear that I think we have here a remarkable case of a critical blunder only so long as we lift the words out of their context and look upon them as a pungent, epigrammatic sort of statement; a statement perhaps not only, or no longer, deriving from a Mr. Eliot, but having about it the kind of anonymity

[1] *The Use of Poetry and the Use of Criticism*, London 1933, p. 99.

that attaches to a popular saying or quotation. But if one thinks of Eliot as a particular person, a particular poet, and asks the question, 'How did he come to say such a thing?' as he did about Goethe, then the apparently sensational lapse soon changes its appearance; it can be seen as a logical, natural consequence of an aesthetic and philosophical point of view; and it then becomes extremely interesting for the psychology of international literary criticism.

A number of questions arise. What is the basis for such a judgement? What influences affected its formation? Does it depend on national taste, or merely on a personal, possibly an eccentric, taste? Or is it principally determined by fashion, or period taste, or other strong contemporary factors?

All of these things, with different accentuation, can influence judgements of this kind about foreign authors. Since the Renaissance there has been a long tradition which attempted to assert the universality of judgements of taste, although again and again critics and philosophers felt compelled to take into account the undeniable variations in individual taste that exist. David Hume, for instance, believed firmly, as a good rationalist, in a standard of taste which should be able to claim universal validity; such a taste would be founded on those poetic achievements which had survived all the caprices of taste, all errors due to ignorance or envy, and continued through many generations to call for admiration. Hume held the view that variable judgements arise only through deficiency in the critic. The general principles of taste are everywhere the same in human nature; where men differ from one another in their judgement some defect or perversion is always to be observed. But Hume makes a concession which has become more and more important as time has passed. He distinguishes two reasons for difference of taste grounded in nature, namely individual temperament and the manners and customs of a country or age. These give rise to differences which he rather charmingly calls blameless; reason is helpless against them and has no power to reconcile contradictory feelings arising in this way.

Thus it comes about that the judgements of many different men and nations may sometimes be in harmony and sometimes, acceptably, not. There must indeed always be a certain tension between the ideal of an absolute principle or universality and the pressing reality of the conflict of views—and this I think is the case today, even though so many have conveniently committed themselves to relativism in matters of judgement. But certainly there are plenty of examples of blameless misjudgement on the international plane. German critics have always put Keats higher than Wordsworth, whilst the English consensus usually ranks them the other way round. On the other hand people in England have always had a very high estimation of Heine and, at least until a generation ago, been extremely ignorant about Hölderlin or Mörike. Voltaire is known to have had a very low opinion of Shakespeare; on the other hand English taste has radically rejected Corneille and Racine, even though these names represent one of the high peaks of European classicism. Their works are never, literally never, produced in the English theatre; one can only see them played by the Comédie-Française when it makes a special visit to London.

A personally coloured taste is not less important than national taste in respect of the possibilities of confusion it can cause. One can quote from Goethe himself: 'Meine Sachen können nicht populär werden . . . sie sind nicht für die Masse geschrieben, sondern nur für einzelne Menschen, die etwas ähnliches wollen und suchen und die in ähnlichen Richtungen begriffen sind.'[1] No doubt one is meant to understand by this that it is not merely a question of an élite, of being clever enough to understand Goethe, but that one must have got into the same bus and be travelling towards a destination in the same direction on the same assumptions, and in the same frame of mind; only in this way can you understand the man you are travelling with. Goethe, hearing Eliot's remark, might have said that he had got into a different bus, was travelling in a different direction, and had only caught a fleeting, partial, and distorted glimpse of him as he passed.

It is useful to ask what constituted, in the period since Goethe's death in 1832, the history of English taste regarding him prior to Eliot's preoccupation with the problem. How did Goethe, in any case, appear to the English in the nineteenth and early twentieth centuries? One might ask the question, of course, of German literature as a whole. One thing can be said quite briefly: in the development of European literary relations there

[1] Goethe to Eckermann, 11 Oct. 1828.

are now and again periods in which a decisive, radical influence is exercised by one literature on another, or on several others. In the eighteenth century in Germany we observe a long, sustained influence of this kind coming from England: we think of Milton and the Swiss, of Addison and the *Moralische Wochenschriften*, of Lillo and Lessing, of Shakespeare, Ossian, Young and Herder and Goethe, of Richardson and the novel of sensibility. German literature profited not by single, sporadic, accidental, or personal reactions, but from a whole series of literary currents. In the nineteenth century it was the other way round: the idealism of *Humanität*, philosophical idealism in the narrower sense, the concept of culture in personal and social senses, and the different aspects of romanticism radiated a power which left traces throughout our romantic and Victorian literature. It appears in Coleridge, Carlyle, Scott, George Eliot (whose husband Lewes wrote the first Goethe biography); in Matthew Arnold, Browning, and even, towards the end of the century, in Wilde and the young Bernard Shaw, with his creative enthusiasm for Goethe–Faust, Wagner–Siegfried, and Nietzsche–Zarathustra. Then the fruitful centre of Europe shifted again, this time to France, whence a new powerful wave of literary influences swept over Europe; this time England and Germany were both fed from France, and principally, of course, by two very different movements—symbolism in lyric poetry, and naturalism in the novel and the drama.

These things are well known, but I repeat them to emphasize the large and comprehensive sort of movement which determines ideas and taste through a longish period of time, in such a way that one may speak of a predominant intellectual or poetic or artistic climate.

Eliot stood in a movement of this kind in his first years in England. In 1910–11 he had been at the Sorbonne, went on to Germany for a time, after which he came to England, and stayed on when the 1914 war broke out. It was the decade, let us remember, during which in Germany the new expressionist thought and manner displaced and triumphed over the impressionistic and naturalistic styles which had emerged in the later nineteenth century. Many German writers now turned their backs on this century and nearly all its works, from Weimar and romanticism to the literary schools of the nineties. In

England, at the same time, it was the Imagists who played a similar revolutionary role in poetry. T. E. Hulme was their theorist, expounding a form of neo-classicism with which Eliot was in sympathy. Concurrent with this was the spread of symbolist styles. Eliot has reminded us, too, about the new ideal of poetic 'diction' he and Pound conceived, and how the *Morning Post* called them literary bolsheviks. But these developments in the specific field of verse were accompanied in literature and ideas generally by the first great onslaught on 'Victorianism', a term of general reference covering the philosophical, social, and moral attitudes and values that had dominated since the second half of the nineteenth century. Here are the beginnings of a sustained criticism of revolutionary force which changed the intellectual scene, and the style in art and literary forms. Virginia Woolf, D. H. Lawrence, Bernard Shaw, E. M. Forster, James Joyce, Wyndham Lewis, as well as Ezra Pound and Eliot himself, all came to the fore as the protagonists of a 'modern' literature between 1910 and 1925. With the total rejection of the romantic and post-romantic sensibility of the nineteenth century, the rejection of Victorian social and moral values, the final fade-out of German idealistic philosophy which had exercised so strong an influence right down to the pre-1914 years, and the political anti-German hostility associated with the Great War, Goethe's star sank temporarily, quite apart from the particular views of any single person. In 1910 every educated person in England read Goethe; in 1925 very few.

Against this hastily sketched background Eliot's view of Goethe appears already in an altogether different light. It has a context: with even the above few facts about the years 1910 to 1925 in mind, anyone might have *predicted* what Eliot would probably say about Goethe. But the interesting thing is that Eliot's 'distance' from Goethe is shared, as we hinted, by many *German* writers of his own generation, the generation of the *Expressionisten*. A prominent feature there, too, was the displacement of both the Goethean type of *Erlebnislyrik* and the specific rhetoric of romantic feeling. Who was then a favourite poet from the classic–romantic period? Not Goethe, or Schiller, but Kleist, whom Goethe condemned. Even George, who in some ways was traditionalist, once said that much of Goethe was dead wood. In the twenties Max Kommerell wrote a challenging essay called 'Jugend ohne Goethe'. The traditional educational and *Bildungs*-view included still, in a rapidly dying *Bürgertum*, a conventional Goethe image and ingredient; but as a living factor or influence in the creative literary life Goethe was already in Germany itself a remote figure.

Turning to Eliot's book we note that his remarks on Goethe appear in the chapter on Shelley and Keats, and Shelley is a poet for whom he has less sympathy than for almost anyone else. Here we observe that Goethe is not in fact the only poet who comes in for hard words. In this book on the use of poetry and the use of criticism one of the author's principal concerns is to observe how, especially from Dryden onwards, the leading poets do a certain amount of theorizing about their aims. He attempts to relate their criticism to their poetry, and then, in each case, to relate both the poetry and the critical theory supporting it to the main historical development of poetry in England, taking into account social change as well. The book examines the creative relationship between poets' criticism and their work, and also the relationship between poetry at any given moment and the world in and for which it is produced; a prominent assumption is that poets are usually very well aware of the circumstances of their time, and of their audience.

With the romantic poets something very important occurred. Their poetry comes to be associated more deliberately with their individual social or philosophical views, and as a result the relationship between poetry and other things, and how the reader is expected to react, becomes much more complicated. In general, Eliot has very great sympathy for the simple position seen in earlier poets like Dante and Lucretius. They expounded explicit philosophies in their poetry, but they did not create those philosophies: they did not, as poets, use poetry to *evolve* philosophy. Eliot holds firmly to the conviction that the two jobs of poetry and philosophy should be done by different people; neither poet nor philosopher should attempt to do the other's job for him. 'A poet may borrow a philosophy or he may do without one. It is when he philosophises upon his own *poetic* insight that he is apt to go wrong.' This frequently happened, in his view, to the romantic generation, and that is the burden of his charge against them, and against Goethe, who was one of them; nor can one deny that Goethe did a good deal of philosophizing on poetic instinct. In his introductory chapter Eliot observes that Wordsworth and Coleridge begin to make claims for poetry which reach their highest point of exaggeration in Shelley's famous phrase 'poets are the unacknowledged legislators of the world'. He sees here, of course, the beginnings of the development that made poetry first the vehicle of 'religion' and then, with Arnold, a substitute for it. In the present context he reaffirms the argument, particularly against Shelley, who claims too much for the power of poetry, and he makes it clear, too, that he thinks the ideas propagated by Shelley's own poetry poor and muddled. He has more respect for Wordsworth though he believes he made a similar mistake. In Coleridge he sees both a poet and a philosopher inside the same man, but, knowing that Coleridge himself deplored his divided genius, believes that he was only able to exercise the one activity at the expense of the other. All these judgements appear in the space of two pages of argument, and are, so to speak, rounded off with the case of Goethe. Amidst this non-awarding of prizes to some eminent poets the offence to Goethe loses a good deal of its sting. At least, setting the comment in its context both of Eliot's general argument about the use of poetry, and about specifically romantic views of poetry, it is divested of its surface craziness; it is totally inadequate to Goethe as an estimate of the poet, but, deriving logically from Eliot's own creative ideals and his own position in the poetic movement of the second and third decades of this century, it makes sense.

Twenty years later, in 1954, Eliot was awarded a prize carrying the name of Goethe, the Hanseatic Goethe Prize. He may well have felt himself in a cleft stick, but he gave an address at Hamburg University in which he paid a handsome tribute to Goethe.[1]

Let us remark first that this revised attitude is not in any way due to another change in the general attitude to Goethe, even though twenty years have passed. Certainly the literary climate showed a change. I think it can be safely said that some degree of German influence had made itself felt again, as the powerful French pressures from the older generation, above all Valéry, Gide, and Proust, slackened. Rilke and Hölderlin were not only read but assimilated by younger poets; I mean that their work

[1] Printed in *On Poetry and Poets*, London 1957.

came to belong, for younger poets, to the idea of what poetry is. The thirties, too, brought the brilliant translations of Kafka by Edwin and Willa Muir, and Kafka was a powerful presence in the English literary world from then on. Another deep influence —and I am speaking of influences on *writers*, and not just of authors who were read (Thomas Mann, for instance, was read but he was scarcely an influence, either through his themes or his techniques)—in the forties and post-war period was of course Bertolt Brecht. It was a double interest, in his social outlook and subject-matter on the one hand and, on the other, in his innovations in acting and production. Büchner and Kleist were also played or read in this later period. But there were no signs of a revival of interest in Goethe during those years. One or two new translations of *Faust* were conventional tributes in the 1949 bicentenary year. There is, it seems to me, no general context for Eliot's revision of his views on Goethe; it is a personal thing between himself and Goethe: himself as a much older man than he was when he made his earlier criticism, and Goethe as a figure who, as the years had gone by, appeared to him steadily greater and more impossible to ignore.

The basis of Eliot's lecture on *Goethe as the Sage* is, however, in no way a warm, relaxed recognition of either a great poet or a great philosopher, to put in place of the earlier 'he *dabbled* in both philosophy and poetry'. Nor is the lecture a straightforward, detached, balanced piece of criticism of Goethe's works. It flows from a continuing sense that Goethe is a problem to him in a way that Shakespeare and Dante, and some lesser foreign poets, are not. And what one observes as one reads the lecture, what one feels the weight of, is Eliot seeking a relationship with Goethe, and finding it still none too easy, because of the profound clash of philosophy and temperament.

He starts off by admitting to feeling that he 'ought' to make an effort to reconcile himself to Goethe; and his impulse to do this derives from his seeing Goethe as one of what he calls the 'Great Europeans'. Two things seem to be entangled in his mind: first, that everyone *ought* to be able to appreciate a great European, if he is to be called *educated*; and secondly, that if Goethe is a great European, then he, Eliot, *ought* to be able to appreciate him. He speaks of having come to accept him as a great lyric poet. The remarks that ring truest in my opinion are those about Goethe's view of Nature, and his approach to science. Eliot acknowledges in Goethe an experience of Nature of a special kind, and a single origin for the insight expressed in both his poetry and his science. But this does not give him the basis for his particular reconciliation with Goethe. In the end he can only find it, in a slightly roundabout way, in a certain conception of wisdom.

It belongs to this conception that wisdom is expressed and transmitted best in poetry, that it is a feature of the greatest poetry; and thus in his own mind the fusion occurs between wisdom and the notion of the great European poet, the type of poet who clearly transcends locality and national status.

Hence the nice logic in the argument of his lecture. By defining the great European, and Goethe as such, he discovers what it is that Goethe can, and must, mean to him. He presents criteria. Very briefly they include what he calls abundance and amplitude, apparent in variety of interest, and these must be held together by unity in the man's work as a whole. Permanence and universality are important; this kind of poet may not appeal only to a restricted circle. But though transcending his own country and his own age, he must be essentially 'of' both; the great European is not an abstract man. Yet Eliot keeps it all subtle: the great European, though rooted in his own country, Germany or England or Italy, and in one sense 'representative' of it, is never its *average* representative, and may even be in opposition to it; he feels this about Goethe. Beyond all this, however, the test is: what is the quality capable of arousing a direct response of man to man, capable of being recognized by a great diversity of men? He discovers this in wisdom alone, and thus finds the relationship with Goethe for which he has been working so hard.

Having reached this point, Eliot comments on his earlier, grudging remark. Very disarmingly he says he has not read the passage since it was written. He now singles out the word *sage* as right, but he admits error in associating it too closely with *worldly* wisdom, which was too restrictive; what matters is spiritual wisdom. He detects another error in his remark, in that it seems to suggest that wisdom is a sum of maxims, or aphorisms, or wise sayings. This is not so, and indeed Wisdom herself is greater than the actualization of wisdom in any human soul. He then makes a penetrating statement that is a description, almost a definition, of wisdom, and with a simple but far-reaching triad of epithets allows Goethe to appear as a great exemplar of it:

> Wisdom is a native gift of intuition, ripened and given application by experience, for understanding the nature of things, certainly of living things, most certainly of the human heart. In some men it may appear fitfully and occasionally, or once in a lifetime, in the rapture of a single experience beatific or awful: in a man like Goethe it appears to have been constant, steady and serene. But the wise man, in contrast to the merely worldly-wise on the one hand, and the man of some intense vision of the heights or the depths on the other, is one whose wisdom springs from spiritual sources, who has profited by experience to arrive at understanding, and who has acquired the charity that comes from understanding human beings in all their variety of temperament, character, and circumstance. Such men hold the most diverse beliefs; they may even hold some tenets which we find abhorrent; but it is part of our own pursuit of wisdom to try to understand them.[1]

The obligatory attempt to learn wisdom is the reason for frequenting Goethe along with Dante and Shakespeare, and overcoming any aversion or indifference one may have felt. One may hold a philosophy to be right or wrong, but wisdom is λόγος ξυνός, the same for all men everywhere, and Goethe was one of the wisest of men.

Eliot keeps his argument very general, and one misses specific references to Goethe's works. There is one to a part of *Faust*, but otherwise only the general one to 'aphorisms and maxims'. He says, speaking about the unity in a great poet's work, in Dante and Shakespeare especially, that it is not so easy to detect such unity in the work of Goethe: 'For one thing, it is more bewilderingly miscellaneous than that of either of the other men; for another thing, I must confess that there is so much of this vast work that I do not know, or know only superficially, that I am far from being the advocate best qualified to plead the case.'[2] He leaves one wondering how much of Goethe he has in fact covered. Goethe lovers would have liked, perhaps, to hear that Eliot was basing himself partly, at least, on *Torquato Tasso*, and *Die Wahlverwandtschaften*, and the *West-östlicher Divan*, as well as

[1] Op. cit., p. 221.   [2] Op. cit., p. 214.

on *Faust*, all works which to my mind are remarkable for the very quality Eliot is describing. In the two former, one finds all the sense of complexity in character and situation that arises from the experience spoken of in the passage just quoted, and all the charity, the refusal to constrict his seeing or condemn his characters, that comes from understanding human beings in all their variety of temperament and circumstance. An analysis of such works, and of their open, deviating form (as against more conventional, defined, forms) in relation to Goethe's constant tendency to transcend the single aspect or insight in a comprehensive, multi-perspective statement, would, it seems to me, make Eliot's argument still more substantial.

His sincerity about Goethe, however, is beyond doubt. A glance at the range of his own work shows that the search for wisdom was a real preoccupation of his own, and that his references throughout this essay to the desire to learn wisdom and to be able to discern it in poetry are not empty phrases. For many people in England his greatest title to fame may still be his lyric achievement, and his role as poetic innovator. But his writing was comprehensive and his thought touched life at many points. He was a serious student of philosophy and theology; his literary criticism covered problems of *Weltanschauung* as well as poetics; in the twenties and thirties he commented regularly on the political scene in its significance for modern culture; *After Strange Gods* is a book about modern secular beliefs, and *Notes towards the Definition of Culture* one on the problems of modern civilization. Apart from these writings there are the plays, which arouse very different reactions but keep being successfully revived. Their religious themes are, of course, prominent—the problem of sin, of spiritual reality, of true vocation, of humility, of the peace that transcends suffering and mere happiness. But religious though they are, they are not oppressively so; and it has always struck me that part of their attraction for the layman as well as the orthodox believer must lie in their presenting, in a succession that has inner unity, an adequate series of images and situations amidst which the basic problems and mysteries of life are focused and commented on. I think one can say that something like wisdom emanates from these plays, taken as a continuous statement about life, although I do not know that anybody has looked at them in this way. One thinks, to give an example, of some of the speeches of Lord Claverton in *The Elder Statesman*, or of the passage in *The Confidential Clerk* between Colby and Sir Claude about seeking one's vocation, a central theme of the play. If this suggestion is true, it is important for the present argument, because it gives the note of complete legitimacy and sincerity to Eliot's estimate of Goethe as sage. The idea of wisdom being a genuine aspiration for him, his later acknowledgement of Goethe is not a conventional or diplomatic acquiescence but a deeply felt tribute evolved from his deeper judgement.

Die Idee des neuen Lebens: eine Betrachtung über Schillers *Wallenstein*

WALTER MÜLLER-SEIDEL

SCHILLERS *Wallenstein*-Drama hat nach übereinstimmender Auffassung seiner Interpreten in einem berühmten Monolog seine geheime Achse. Man zitiert ihn nicht nur, wenn man die *Wallenstein*-Dichtung interpretiert, sondern führt vorzüglich diesen Monolog an, wenn es darum geht, seine Eigenart zu erläutern. Vom Drama des handelnden Menschen ist in solchen Erläuterungen die Rede, vom Entscheidungsdrama und dem zu ihm gehörenden Monolog, in dem der Handelnde seine Lage überdenkt.[1] Er wird sich der Alternativen bewusst, denen er sich gegenübersieht. Er wird sich des Konfliktes bewusst, der sich in solchen Alternativen zusammendrängt. Der berühmte Monolog — im vierten Auftritt des ersten Aufzugs von *Wallensteins Tod* — wird zum Paradigma der klassischen Dramenform kat' exochen. Es sind jene Verse, die jeder kennt, der das grosse Drama kennt:

> Wärs möglich! Könnt ich nicht mehr, wie ich wollte?
> Nicht mehr zurück, wie mirs beliebt? Ich müsste
> Die Tat *vollbringen*, weil ich sie *gedacht*,
> Nicht die Versuchung von mir wies — das Herz
> Genährt mit diesem Traum, auf ungewisse
> Erfüllung hin die Mittel mir gespart,
> Die Wege bloss mir offen hab gehalten? —
> Beim grossen Gott des Himmels! Es war nicht
> Mein Ernst, beschlossne Sache war es nie.
> In dem Gedanken bloss gefiel ich mir; ...
> (WT. V. 139-48)

Vom Doppelsinn des Lebens wird im Fortgang gesprochen, vom Ernst im Anblick der Notwendigkeit und von tückischen

[1] So etwa bei Paul Böckmann (*Stilprobleme in Schillers Dramen*. Jetzt in: *Formensprache. Studien zur Literarästhetik und Dichtungsinterpretation*, Hamburg 1966, S. 226): 'Seine Dramen sind konzipiert von der Krisis des Geistes aus, von jenem geheimen Einheitspunkt her, wo ein Volk, eine Menschengruppe, ein Einzelner sich in die vieldeutigen Möglichkeiten des Lebens gestellt sieht und wo mit Notwendigkeit eine Entscheidung gefällt werden muss.'

Mächten, 'die keines Menschen Kunst vertraulich macht'. Aber nicht dieser berühmte Teil des Monologs ist der Ausgangspunkt unserer Betrachtung. Wir richten uns auf seine letzten Passagen, die man im allgemeinen seltener zitiert.[1] Zuvor aber vergegenwärtigen wir uns die Situation, in der sich Wallenstein befindet. Als der mit sich selbst Redende ist er sich seiner Stellung unsicher geworden. Er weiss, dass er auf den Kaiser nicht mehr zählen kann. Wallenstein ist sich darüber im Klaren, dass er dessen Vertrauen nicht mehr besitzt. So hat er, seine eigene Politik treibend, im Stillen vorgesorgt. Als die Spielernatur, als die man ihn verstehen kann, hat er auch mit dem Gedanken gespielt, ein zeitweiliges Bündnis mit den Schweden könnte seine Lage verbessern.[2] Hat er mit diesem Gedanken nur gespielt? Der Monolog lässt vermuten, dass es sich in der Tat so verhält: dass es nur ein Gedankenspiel war: 'In dem Gedanken bloss gefiel ich mir . . .', heisst es. Aber gesetzt selbst, dass er mit dem Gedanken zunächst nur gespielt hätte, so bleiben einige Fragen gleichwohl offen. Sollte damit nur die eigene Lage verbessert werden? Geht es in Wallensteins Denken nur um das eigene Ich, wie man seine Äusserungen oft einseitig ausgelegt hat? Oder denkt dieser von der Macht faszinierte Egozentriker doch gelegentlich über die eigene Person hinaus? Der Wallenstein Schillers ist eine eminent politische Persönlichkeit, der es gewohnt ist, zu herrschen und zu gebieten. Seine eigene Position zu festigen, ist er bemüht, wo immer sich die Gelegenheit bietet. Dennoch ist er offenbar nicht einer, der nur Machtpolitik um der Macht willen treibt. Aber sei dem, wie ihm wolle: aus dem Gedankenspiel sind Realitäten entstanden. Die schwedischen Unterhändler warten. Es ist höchste Zeit, dass etwas geschieht, wenn es nicht schon zu spät ist. Seine Freunde — es sind sehr zweifelhafte Freunde — drängen ihn zum Entschluss. Sie drängen ihn zur Entscheidung und zum Verrat, weil sie wissen, dass sie für ihre Person nichts zu erwarten haben, wenn sich ihr Feldherr dem Kaiser unterwirft. Für sie erst recht geht es um alles oder nichts. Aber nicht nur die

---

[1] In seiner *Wallenstein*-Auslegung gibt Benno von Wiese das Zitat in vollem Umfang wieder. Aber eine eingehendere Analyse dieser bedeutungsvollen Aussage verbindet sich damit nicht (*Die deutsche Tragödie von Lessing bis Hebbel*, 5Hamburg 1955, S. 237). Ähnlich in: *Friedrich Schiller*, Stuttgart 1959, S. 660.

[2] Die Spielernatur Wallensteins ist Clemens Heselhaus wichtig: 'Wallensteinisches Welttheater'. In: *Deutschunterricht*, 1960, Heft 2, S. 65.

Eine Betrachtung über Schillers 'Wallenstein'

Freunde locken Wallenstein in den Verrat. Auch der Kaiser selbst und seine Unterhändler tragen durch ihre Intrigenpolitik zum Abfall bei. Sie stossen Wallenstein förmlich in sein Schicksal hinein — ob er es will oder nicht. Die Situation also ist klar: nur rasches Handeln könnte die Dinge wenden. Aber Wallenstein handelt nicht. Er zaudert.[1] Spricht das ein für allemal gegen ihn? Doch wohl nicht! Indem Wallenstein zaudert, ist er nicht ohne weiteres der gewissenlos Handelnde, als den ihn manche Interpreten behandeln. So gibt er denen, die ihn zur Eile drängen, die für ihn bezeichnende Antwort: 'Warte noch ein wenig.' Es ist ihm alles zu schnell gekommen. Er schickt seinen Gesprächspartner — es ist Illo — hinaus und überdenkt die Lage in eben dem Monolog, den wir kennen. In Fragen und Konjunktiven spricht Wallenstein mit sich selbst von der Möglichkeit der Rückkehr, und Rückkehr ist in diesem Drama als eine bedeutungsvolle Metapher gemeint. Jetzt erst wird sich der zum Handeln Gedrängte seiner Lage vollends bewusst. Er soll sich entscheiden. Aber sein Zaudern schränkt die Entscheidung ein; und solche Einschränkungen haben Gewicht:

O! sie zwingen mich, sie stossen
Gewaltsam, wider meinen Willen, mich hinein.
(Picc. V. 701-2)

Die Entscheidungssituation, die man gern als konstituierend für die Schillersche Schaffensweise ansieht, ist gar keine Situation der Entscheidung. Wallensteins Wahl ist eine Wahl des Notwendigen. Aber eine Wahl des Notwendigen ist eigentlich keine Wahl.[2]

Das alles und anderes ist in dem berühmten Monolog enthal-

---

[1] Dass solches Zaudern mit dem Zaudern Hamlets nicht zu verwechseln sei, hat die neuere Forschung wiederholt betont; so Max Kommerell: 'Es ist ein anderes Zaudern als das Zaudern Hamlets, dem alles Handeln schal und willkürlich wird, weil ihn das Sein, das Rätsel des Seins anstarrt. Wallenstein zaudert, weil das Wesen der Tat ihn anrührt . . .' ('Schiller als Gestalter des handelnden Menschen.' Jetzt in: *Geist und Buchstabe der Dichtung*, ³1944, S. 147). Eine geistvolle Deutung dieses Zauderns hat Oskar Seidlin gegeben: 'Wallensteins Zögern ist nicht zu fassen als Charakterzug . . . Sein Zögern entspringt nicht einem inneren Konflikt . . . sondern ist die magistrale Geste eines Menschen, der sich stemmt gegen das unerbittliche und unaufhaltsame Abrollen der Zeit . . .' (*Wallenstein: Sein und Zeit*. Jetzt in: *Von Goethe zu Thomas Mann*, Göttingen 1963, S. 120).
[2] Ähnlich Kurt May: 'Der erste, auch nur halbe Schritt war frei, der zweite ist es nicht mehr. Dann spielt es gar keine Rolle mehr, wie einer gesinnt ist, die Freiheit der Entscheidung ist genommen' (*Friedrich Schiller. Idee und Wirklichkeit im Drama*, Göttingen 1948, S. 110).

ten; uns interessiert sein letzter Teil. Die Bühnenanweisungen schreiben vor: 'Er macht heftige Schritte durchs Zimmer, dann bleibt er wieder sinnend stehen.' Danach heisst es:

> Und was ist dein Beginnen? Hast du dirs
> Auch redlich selbst bekannt? Du willst die Macht,
> Die ruhig, sicher thronende erschüttern,
> Die in verjährt geheiligtem Besitz,
> In der Gewohnheit festgegründet ruht,
> Die an der Völker frommen Kinderglauben
> Mit tausend zähen Wurzeln sich befestigt.
> Das wird kein Kampf der Kraft sein mit der Kraft,
> Den fürcht ich nicht. Mit jedem Gegner wag ichs,
> Den ich kann sehen und ins Auge fassen,
> Der, selbst voll Mut, auch mir den Mut entflammt.
> Ein unsichtbarer Feind ists, den ich fürchte,
> Der in der Menschen Brust mir widersteht,
> Durch feige Furcht allein mir fürchterlich —
> Nicht was lebendig, kraftvoll sich verkündigt,
> Ist das gefährlich Furchtbare. Das ganz
> Gemeine ists, das ewig Gestrige,
> Was immer war und immer wiederkehrt,
> Und morgen gilt, weils heute hat gegolten!
> Denn aus Gemeinem ist der Mensch gemacht,
> Und die Gewohnheit nennt er seine Amme.
> Weh dem, der an den würdig alten Hausrat
> Ihm rührt, das teure Erbstück seiner Ahnen!
> Das Jahr übt eine heiligende Kraft,
> Was grau für Alter ist, das ist ihm göttlich.
> Sei im Besitze und du wohnst im Recht,
> Und heilig wirds die Menge dir bewahren.
> (WT. V. 192–218)

Eine erregende Argumentation![1] Worauf läuft sie hinaus? Wallensteins Denken ist gegen das Überlieferte gerichtet; und das Überlieferte wird von vielen Menschen nur deshalb verehrt, weil es überliefert ist. So auch die Ordnung, die jeweils gilt. Wallenstein wendet sich gegen sie.[2] Er erkennt sie nicht an, nur

---
[1] Die Argumente, die Kurt May beibringt, uns diese Äusserungen Wallensteins als unmoralisch zu verdächtigen, überzeugen nicht (*Friedrich Schiller*, S. 131). Es ist überhaupt auffällig, wie selbstverständlich deutsche Literarhistoriker bereit sind, Wallenstein zu verurteilen, weil er es an Respekt vor der etablierten Ordnung fehlen lässt — einer Ordnung, die es offenbar schon deshalb anzuerkennen gilt, weil sie ist.
[2] Zutreffend spricht Clemens Heselhaus von einer 'Entwertung der Institution, der Legalität, selbst des positiven Gesetzes in Schillers Dichtungen' (ebda., S. 46).

weil sie Ordnung ist. Er wendet sich damit zugleich gegen den Kaiser, der diese Ordnung als die Seine verteidigt. Ein Verteidiger solcher Ordnung ist aber auch Octavio Piccolomini, Wallensteins Gegenspieler. Piccolomini ist ein Vertreter des eigentlich erstarrten Lebens, des Förmlichen, wie es der Brauch an Höfen ist. Wallensteins Gemahlin hat sich vorübergehend dort aufgehalten. Sie ist jetzt zurückgekehrt und berichtet von ihren Erlebnissen am kaiserlichen Hof. Sie beklagt den Wandel, den sie wahrgenommen hat. Aber es ist nicht ein Wandel im Sinne des geschichtlichen Lebens, das sich von Zeit zu Zeit erneuert. Der Wandel, der am Kaiserhof zu beobachten war, ist nicht Fortschritt, sondern Reaktion — eine Veränderung zugunsten des erstarrten Lebens. Die Kategorie der Zeit, zum Verständnis des Wallensteindramas von entscheidender Bedeutung, mischt sich ein. Sie erscheint als das, was war — was immer schon so war und ewig wiederkehrt. Wallenstein bezeichnet diese Wiederkehr des Gleichen als das Gemeine. Er setzt es herab und bezeugt ihm seine uneingeschränkte Verachtung. Und ein Gemeines ist auch das, was sich ewig wiederholt und nur deshalb gilt, weil es immer gegolten hat, weil es die Menge sanktioniert. Man darf den religiösen Wortschatz in der Sprache Wallensteins nicht überhören:

> Das Jahr übt eine heiligende Kraft,
> Was grau für Alter ist, das ist ihm göttlich.
> Sei im Besitze und du wohnst im Recht,
> Und heilig wirds die Menge dir bewahren.
>   (V. 215–18)

Das Heilige und das Göttliche sind aber nicht im wörtlichen Sinne heilig und göttlich. Nur aus Gewohnheit hält man es allenthalben so mit Besitz und Recht. Wallensteins Worte sind voll der Ironie. Denn, was die Menge für heilig und göttlich erklärt, ist nichts als die Sanktionierung des Bestehenden, nur weil es das Bestehende ist. Was die Menge solchermassen sanktioniert, ist also nicht Sein sondern Schein, nicht lebendiges Leben sondern erstarrte Form. Der Wallenstein dieses Monologs, wenn wir seine Worte recht bedenken, gewinnt unsere Sympathien. Denn hat er nicht eigentlich in allem recht? Was ist das für eine Macht — diese Macht der Gewohnheit? Hat man es nicht zumeist nur mit Bequemlichkeit, Egoismus und ungeistigem Verharren zu tun, wenn *diese* Macht im Leben herrscht? Das ewig Gestrige wird von Wallenstein zitiert, und wie sehr ist in der Redewendung schon die Verachtung enthalten, die sich mit ihr verbindet; denn das ewig Gestrige ist in unserer Sprache dubios. Es ist eindeutig Reaktion. Wallensteins Verachtung gegenüber solchen Erscheinungen des Lebens kennt keine Grenzen. Wer will es ihm verdenken! Der Satz, mit dem der Monolog endet, führt den Gedankengang auf den Höhepunkt in den Formen der ironischen Rede, die kaum noch zu überbieten ist:

> Sei im Besitze und du wohnst im Recht
> Und heilig wirds die Menge dir bewahren.[1]

Der Wallenstein dieses Monologs hat andere Vorstellungen vom Recht, als sie die Menge hat. Er denkt in allem nicht an erstarrte Formen, sondern an lebendiges Leben. Er denkt an das lebendig Neue im Bereich der geschichtlichen Welt und will das ewig Alte nicht anerkennen. Dass hier eine Erfahrung der Geschichtlichkeit vorliegt, die nicht bloss Pragmatismus bedeutet, ist unsere Überzeugung.

Von einem, der in allem nur an sich selbst denkt, haben wir uns damit weit entfernt. Wenn es Wallenstein so meint, wie er es hier sagt — und im Monolog hätte die Verstellung wenig Sinn — dann bestimmt nicht nur der Egoismus sondern auch das Soziale sein Denken. Die Bewahrenden als die Besitzenden sind nicht immer die Hüter des geistigen Lebens. Sie hüten nicht selten nur ihren Besitz. Indem sie es tun, glauben sie sich im Recht — nur weil es immer so war und deshalb auch so bleiben soll. Aber wie soll da noch Leben in der Geschichte sein, deren Wesen Wandel ist? Der Wallenstein dieses Monologs in dem Geschichtsdrama Schillers, um das es sich handelt, ist ein Vertreter des geschichtlichen Lebens. Er will etwas Neues. Er treibt nicht nur Politik, die sich in Taktik erschöpft, in Ränken und Intrigen. Dieser Politiker — und das zeichnet den Staatsmann aus — hat eine Vision. Er hat Vorstellungen davon, wie ein zukünftiges Leben aussehen könnte; und er macht sich darüber seine Gedanken. Auch später noch, da sein Stern schon

[1] Dass Wallenstein damit 'in Wahrheit' — aber was heisst hier Wahrheit! — ein Vernichtungsurteil über sich selber spreche, wie Wolfgang Wittkowski behauptet, halte ich wenigstens für 'unbewiesen', von den hier waltenden Interpretationsinteressen ganz zu schweigen ('Octavio Piccolomini'. In: *Jahrbuch der Deutschen Schillergesellschaft*, 5 (1961), S. 32).

Eine Betrachtung über Schillers 'Wallenstein' 85

sinkt, ist das der Fall, wenn er in der Vision vom Ende der spanischen Herrschaft einen Sieg des neuen Glaubens erkennt:

> Die Erfüllung
> Der Zeiten ist gekommen, Bürgermeister,
> Die Hohen werden fallen und die Niedrigen
> Erheben sich, ...[1] (WT. V. 2604–7)

Wallenstein hat bestimmte Vorstellungen von einer Zeit, die anders als die Gegenwart ist. Als künftige Zeit ist es zugleich die erfüllte Zeit, die Oskar Seidlin als eschatologische Vision des Endes und der Aufhebung alles Zeitlichen interpretiert: 'Echo chiliastischer Prophezeiung aus Vergils Viertem Hirtengedicht'.[2] Eine Vision idyllischen Lebens zeichnet sich ab. Der ihr das Wort redet, ist einer, dem Kampf und Krieg über alles zu gehen scheint. Doch deutet vieles darauf hin, dass Wallenstein den Krieg nicht um seiner selbst willen schätzt. Das Ziel seiner Pläne ist bestimmt von einer Idee des Friedens, von der Vorstellung eines neuen Reiches, das er sich — wie zu den Zeiten Vergils — als ein Friedensreich erträumt. Es liegt nahe, an die Abhandlung *Über naive und sentimentalische Dichtung* zu erinnern. Die Ausführungen über die Idylle sind auf ein solches Friedensreich der Zukunft bezogen. Zwar ist diese Dichtungsart zumeist den Anfängen der Kultur zugewandt. Aber die Idylle ist nicht minder zukunftsbezogen: Die poetische Darstellung unschuldiger und glücklicher Menschheit sei der allgemeine Begriff dieser Dichtungsart. Weil aber solche Unschuld mit den künstlichen Verhältnissen der Gesellschaft nicht vereinbar sei, habe der Dichter den Schauplatz der Idylle in den einfachen Hirtenstand verlegt. Schiller fährt fort: 'Aber ein solcher Zustand findet nicht bloss vor dem Anfange der Kultur statt, sondern er ist es auch, den die Kultur, wenn sie überall nur eine bestimmte Tendenz haben soll, als ihr letztes Ziel beabsichtet.'[3] Wie sehr Wallenstein in allem an sich selber denkt, an seine Macht und an seinen Besitz — einen solchen Zustand des Friedens herbeizuführen, fühlt er sich gleichwohl berufen. Möglicherweise ist er der einzige unter seinen Zeitgenossen, der dazu in der Lage wäre. Es wäre ungerecht, das alles nur als Vorwand und

---
[1] Vgl. K. May, ebda., S. 130; O. Seidlin, S. 122.
[2] O. Seidlin, ebda., S. 123.
[3] *Über naive und sentimentalische Dichtung. Schillers Werke. Nationalausgabe*, Bd. 20, hg. von Benno von Wiese, Weimar 1962, S. 467.

Heuchelei zu verdächtigen. Schiller hat seinen Helden auch mit solchen Zügen ausgestattet — anders als in der *Geschichte des Dreissigjährigen Krieges*. Der Wallenstein seines Dramas ist kein Tugenheld. Aber er ist noch weniger der Verbrecher, der es verdient, dass wir ihn mit Schulbegriffen wie Schuld und Sühne messen. Schillers Wallenstein ist zumal von diesem bedeutenden Monolog her gesehen ein revolutionärer Idealist, und dass man einen 'Visionär mit solchen Gesichten' mehr als ein Jahrhundert lang einseitig mit dem Etikett des Realisten versehen hat, ist in der Tat erstaunlich.[1] Mit Max Piccolomini, dem von aller Weltkenntnis entfernten Idealisten, dürfen wir ihn darum nicht verwechseln. Wallenstein unterscheidet sich von diesem durch die Kenntnis, die er von der Welt und von der Politik in dieser Welt hat. Er unterscheidet sich auch in der Kenntnis der Mittel, und er weiss sie zu gebrauchen. Wallenstein ist diesem Monolog zufolge ein revolutionärer Idealist. Von seinem revolutionären Willen zum lebendig Kraftvollen hat man gesprochen.[2] Aber er ist zugleich der Realist des politischen Lebens, der die Intrige kennt und sich ihrer auch, wenn es sein muss, zu bedienen weiss. An verdecktes Planen und Handeln ist er gewöhnt. Er belehrt die Seinen, wenn sie ihn allzu einfach und unkompliziert sehen:

> Und woher weisst du, dass ich ihn nicht wirklich
> Zum besten habe? Dass ich nicht euch alle
> Zum besten habe? Kennst du mich so gut?
> Ich wüsste nicht, dass ich mein Innerstes
> Dir aufgetan...
>
> (Picc. V. 861-5)

Das sagt er zu Terzky und bezeichnet damit das aus Prinzip Hintergründige seines Charakters. Zumal in solchen Zügen — wir denken an den Marquis Posa des *Don Carlos* — ist Wallenstein der Handelnde, den man aus Schillers Dramen kennt. Im Intrigengeflecht des politischen Lebens kennt er sich wie wenige aus. Da haben die Idyllen des einfachen Lebens nichts mehr zu suchen. Da werden die Mittel gewählt, die zu wählen sind. Aus den unbedenklich Handelnden werden die grossen Verschwörer, die wie Fiesco, Marquis Posa, Mortimer oder Demetrius ihr gewagtes Spiel treiben. Wallenstein ist ein Idealist, wenn er

---

[1] Im Sinne Oskar Seidlins (*Wallenstein: Sein und Zeit*, S. 123).
[2] Benno von Wiese, *Die deutsche Tragödie*, S. 238.

Eine Betrachtung über Schillers 'Wallenstein'

sich in Gedanken an die Vision einer besseren Zeit verliert, die er heraufzuführen hofft. Er ist Realist durch und durch, wenn er die Mittel bedenkt, die er dafür einsetzen muss. Er ist Idealist und Realist zugleich. Ein mit solchen Zügen ausgestatteter Staatsmann ist so rasch nicht schuldig zu sprechen, wie es oft geschieht. Es geht in allem nicht nur um seine Person und um die Macht, die er für sich erstrebt. Etwas Allgemeines steht in Frage: der Friede der Zukunft und mit ihr eine neue Zeit, ein neues Leben. Von solchen Überlegungen her ist Wallensteins Verrat nicht mehr ausschliesslich als der Verrat eines Abenteurers und Opportunisten zu interpretieren. Seine Untreue ist nicht einseitig gegen die Treue auszuspielen, die Octavio Piccolomini dem Kaiser hält; denn was diesen an den Kaiser bindet, ist in hohem Masse die Treue zum Gewohnten, wenigstens in Wallensteins Sicht. Schiller hat in Wallensteins Gegenspieler keinen kleinlichen Intriganten gezeichnet, und er hat ihn ausdrücklich gegenüber jenen in Schutz genommen, die ihn im Verständnis des Dramas zum Bösewicht degradiert sehen wollen. Es habe nicht in seiner Absicht gelegen, schreibt Schiller 1799, 'dass sich Octavio Piccolomini als einen gar so schlimmen Mann, als einen Buben darstellen sollte'.[1] Auch Piccolomini ist auf seine Weise im Recht, wenn er sich auf seine Treue zum Kaiser beruft. Auch er hat in gewissen Grenzen Grösse. Dennoch: wenn sie alle so denken, wie Octavio denkt, dann würde sich alles Leben in ein Dasein verwandeln, das kein Leben mehr ist, sondern Gewohnheit, Förmlichkeit und Zeremoniell. Die Partei des Rechts und der Ordnung, die Octavio Piccolomini vertritt, ist mit einer Formulierung Kurt Mays die Ordnung 'einer erstarrten Konvention des staatlich-gesellschaftlich-kirchlichen Zusammenlebens und seiner aus ehrwürdiger Tradition vererbter Gesetze.'[2]

Genau hier, da wir es mit dem Lebendigen gegenüber dem Gewohnten und Veralteten zu tun haben, sind Max und Thekla einzubeziehen: der Sohn des kaisertreuen Politikers und die Tochter des Feldherrn, der sich gegen den Kaiser stellt. Das Verhältnis der jungen Menschen ist kein Verhältnis übers Kreuz. Der Sohn Piccolominis hält zu Wallenstein, den er

---

[1] An Böttiger vom 1. März 1799. — Zur Interpretation des Briefes vgl. auch C. Heselhaus, ebda., S. 44.
[2] Kurt May: *Friedrich Schiller*, S. 124.

verehrt. Aber Wallensteins Tochter hält nicht zu Octavio Piccolomini. Sie halten als Liebende vereint zu Wallenstein und sind aus dessen engerem Lebenskreis nicht wegzudenken. Auf Wallenstein, nicht auf Octavio Piccolomini, sind die jungen Menschen, die Vertreter blühenden Lebens, bezogen. Weil Octavio vorwiegend ein Repräsentant des Alten ist, mit allen Rechten des Alten und Gewohnten, haben die Jüngeren nicht seine Nähe, sondern die Nähe Wallensteins gewählt, auch wenn vieles sie von dessen Verhalten trennt. Max wie Thekla sind Gestalten des Schönen, des Ideals und eines jugendlichen Lebens. Sie sind als jugendliche Idealgestalten Symbole des lebendigen Geistes, wie die Vision einer schöneren Zeit der Ausdruck des lebendigen Geistes ist. Von solch zukünftigem Leben spricht Max, indem er das vieldeutige Bild der Heimkehr verwendet:

> O schöner Tag! wenn endlich der Soldat
> Ins Leben heimkehrt, in die Menschlichkeit,
> Zum frohen Zug die Fahnen sich entfalten,
> Und heimwärts schlägt der sanfte Friedensmarsch.
> (Picc. V. 534–7)

Heimkehr in die Menschlichkeit! Es ist ein tiefsinniges Wort, das Schiller den jungen Piccolomini sagen lässt; und Max spricht davon in Bildern, die auch die Bilder Theklas sind. Die häufigste Zeitform in ihrer beider Sprache ist das Futur, und dass der panegyrische Hymnus des jungen Piccolomini auf den Frieden in vieler Hinsicht der Ankündigung einer neuen Ordnung der Dinge durch Wallenstein entspricht, bleibt in der Tat zu bedenken.[1] Beide, Max und Thekla, sind vorzüglich auf eine Zukunft gerichtet, in der jedes schöne Glück und jede schöne Hoffnung blühen soll. Von der goldenen Zeit ist die Rede, wo jede neue Sonne die Menschen vereint. Max sieht sie als die schon gewesene gegenüber der Wirklichkeit des Lebens entschwinden. Er ahnt die Schwierigkeit, die darin beruht, unschuldiges Leben zu bewahren. Auch Thekla ist von solchen Bildern erfüllt. Ihre Liebe zu Max ist der Ausdruck ihrer Sympathie mit dem neuen Leben. Doch weiss sie auch zugleich, dass es sich um eine Idee handelt, die man nicht auf die Dauer bewahren kann. Alles Hohe und Schöne, alles Hoffnungsfreu-

---

[1] In Übereinstimmung mit O. Seidlin, S. 127.

Eine Betrachtung über Schillers 'Wallenstein' 89

dige und blühende Leben wird in diesen Menschen Gestalt. Aber sie sind gleichsam zum Tode verurteilt in einer Welt, die sich nicht mehr im Zustand der Unschuld befindet. Was Max und Thekla wollen, bleibt Idee, und im Grunde sind sie nur Verkörperungen dieser Idee — eines Ideals noch vor aller Wirklichkeit. Max verweigert dieser Wirklichkeit in seinem Denken jedes Daseinsrecht. Die Belehrung, die Octavio seinem Sohn hierüber erteilt, ist geboten: die Ideale, wenn man sie ohne Wirklichkeit haben will, werden zur Illusion:

> Mein bester Sohn! Es ist nicht immer möglich,
> Im Leben sich so kinderrein zu halten,
> Wie's uns die Stimme lehrt im Innersten... (Picc. V. 2447-9)

Was aber haben solche Bilder eines neuen zukünftigen Lebens mit Wallenstein zu tun? Sie haben mit ihm sehr viel zu tun; denn er ist in einem durchaus nicht oberflächlichen Sinne empfänglich für sie. Auf ergreifende Art spiegelt es sich wieder in der Erinnerung an Max, den er vor anderen geliebt hat, auch wenn er ihm in der ihm eigenen Überheblichkeit die Hand der Tochter verweigern wollte. Von ihm, dem Dahingegangenen, spricht Wallenstein mit bewegten Worten:

> Doch fühl ichs wohl, was ich in ihm verlor.
> Die Blume ist hinweg aus meinem Leben.
> Und kalt und farblos seh ichs vor mir liegen.
> Denn er stand neben mir, wie meine Jugend,
> Er machte mir das Wirkliche zum Traum,
> Um die gemeine Deutlichkeit der Dinge
> Den goldnen Duft der Morgenröte webend —
> Im Feuer seines lieblichen Gefühls. (WT. V. 3442-9)

Wer so spricht, kann derjenige nicht sein, für den man ihn oft gehalten hat: 'ein Mensch ohne Liebe'.[1]

Wallenstein kennt also noch anderes als Politik und politisches Intrigenspiel, wie notwendig diese auch im politischen Leben sein mögen. Er kennt noch anderes als nur Berechnung, Kalkül und Rationalität. Dieser Feldherr, dem sich die jungen Menschen, die Symbole des neuen Lebens, so innig verbunden

---
[1] K. May (*Friedrich Schiller*, S. 125): 'Wallenstein ist ein Mensch ohne Liebe.' In der Kommentierung der in Frage stehenden Szene selbst wird das schroffe Urteil beträchtlich modifiziert: 'Auch das Machtmenschentum dieses Mannes ist aus einer breiteren Menschlichkeit zu beherrschender Grösse entwickelt...' (S. 144).

fühlen, ist empfänglich für Neues in der Welt. Er denkt über das gewohnte Leben hinaus. Er lebt und denkt und glaubt mit den Sternen. Es ist kein Zweifel, dass der Sternenglaube Wallensteins nicht nur etwas Suspektes darstellt, wie Goethe zutreffend erkannte.[1] Die Motive sind ambivalent. Sie bedeuten Vermessenheit im Berechnen und Verfügenwollen über die Zukunft. Der Sternenglaube Wallensteins beleuchtet eine Seite des Irrationalen in dieser sonst auf Rationalität und Berechnung gerichteten Person. Berechnung ist unerlässlich für jeden, der im politischen Leben bestehen will. Wer aber nichts kennt als Berechnung, muss sich misstrauisch zu anderen verhalten. Weil Wallenstein auch Irrationales kennt, hat er zugleich Vertrauen bewahrt. Er vertraut Octavio Piccolomini. Hermann August Korff hat gemeint, es sei dies der schwächste Punkt in Schillers Tragödie.[2] Wir wollen es bestreiten. Auch das Vertrauen Wallensteins ist ein Teil derjenigen Welt, die Max verkörpert. Nicht zufällig ist dieses Vertrauen mit dem Sternenglauben verknüpft. Wenn Wallenstein seinem Gegenspieler Piccolomini so unverständlich lange vertraut, so hängt das zugleich mit seiner Astrologie zusammen. Es hängt zusammen mit der Lebensrettung, die er Octavio verdankt, einer unbestimmten Dankbarkeit im Menschlichen, einem Moment des Irrationalen in seiner Existenz. Dass es solche Dankbarkeit als Vertrauen gegenüber anderen gibt, zeichnet ihn aus; dass es dabei um das eigene Leben geht, bringt zugleich einen Zug dämonischer Selbstliebe hinein. Wallensteins Vertrauen ist verhängnisvolle Unkenntnis der Welt und der Menschen. Aber es ist daneben auch eine Erscheinungsform der Menschlichkeit, in die Max heimkehren möchte und später, wenngleich um den Preis des Todes, heimkehrt. Wie immer diese Idealwelt der beiden jugendlichen Gestalten gedeutet werden mag: sie trägt Züge des Staates, wie ihn Schiller in den Briefen über die ästhetische Erziehung des Menschen beschreibt. Das Lebendigste ist in den Formen des Zukünftigen da. Auf solche Formen des Zukünftigen sind Max wie Thekla bezogen. Aber auch Wallenstein ist es auf seine Weise, wie wir gesehen haben. Oskar Seidlin hat das zutreffend

---

[1] Vgl. Goethes Brief vom 8. Dezember 1798: 'Der astrologische Aberglaube ruht auf dem dunkeln Gefühl eines ungeheuren Weltganzen ... Diesen und ähnlichen Wahn möchte ich nicht einmal Aberglaube nennen.'
[2] Herm. Aug. Korff: *Geist der Goethezeit*, Bd. 2, S. 258.

Eine Betrachtung über Schillers 'Wallenstein'

erkannt. Er hat erkannt, dass Wallenstein auf ein solches Reich als auf ein Reich des Schönen blickt. Zugleich wird zwischen der geschichtlichen Existenz, in der Wallenstein steht, und der ästhetischen, auf die er gerichtet ist, unterschieden. Wallenstein versuche, sagt Seidlin, aus der geschichtlichen Lage in die ästhetische Existenz überzutreten. Darin läge die Hybris, deren er sich schuldig macht: 'dass er Geschichte leben und gestalten will, als unterstünde sie den Wesensgesetzen des Schönen.'[1] Dass es Vermessenheit in Wallensteins Tun und Denken gibt, bestreiten wir nicht. Seine Absicht, dem jungen Piccolomini die Hand der Tochter zu verweigern, ist als eine solche zu bezeichnen. Aber auch sie hängt mit seiner politischen Wirksamkeit zusammen, mit Berechnungen, die ihn von der Menschlichkeit des Menschen entfernen. Gleichwohl ist er auf Berechnungen angewiesen, und zumal der Staatsmann kommt ohne sie nicht aus. Die Grenzen zwischen dem noch Erlaubten und dem nicht mehr Erlaubten bezeichnen unmerklich die Verfallenheit an das tragische Leben. Aus diesem Grunde erscheint uns der Begriff der Hybris bedenklich, weil er dem Doppelsinn des Lebens nicht gerecht wird, in dem sich der Handelnde verstrickt. Der Begriff der Hybris bleibt ähnlich problematisch wie der in der neueren Forschung so bevorzugte Terminus der Nemesis.[2] Durch beide Begriffe dringt das voreilig moralische Urteil in die Wallensteindeutung ein, das es zu vermeiden gilt, wenn man auf die Tragik der Tragödie sieht; denn die ist niemals identisch mit eindeutiger Schuld, über die eindeutig moralische Urteile möglich sind. Wir wollen daher nicht voreilig von Hybris sprechen hinsichtlich dessen, was Wallenstein versucht. Dass er Unmögliches begehrt, mag sein. Aber erst damit beginnt die Tragik seines Tuns, die im Versuch des Unmöglichen angelegt ist. Was denn eigentlich will er?

Wallenstein will Unmögliches in vielerlei Gestalt, und dass er es will, zeichnet ihn vor anderen aus — trotz der Irrtümer, die

[1] *Wallenstein: Sein und Zeit*, S. 124.
[2] Vgl. zur Nemesis-Problematik vor allem: Clemens Heselhaus ('Die Nemesis-Tragödie'. In: *Der Deutschunterricht*, 1952, Heft 5). Emil Staiger: 'Schillers Agrippina'. Jetzt in: *Die Kunst der Interpretation*[2], Zürich 1957, S. 132–60.—Wolfgang Wittkowski: 'Octavio Piccolomini'. In: *Jahrbuch der Deutschen Schillergesellschaft*, 5 (1961), S. 10–11. Auch Kurt May (*Friedrich Schiller*, S. 129) spricht von einem 'nemesisartigen Vorgang'. Zu kanonischem Ansehen des problematischen Begriffes hat Benno von Wiese in seinen neueren Arbeiten über Schiller das meiste beigetragen.

sich damit verbinden. Er will unter anderem Irrationales mit den Mitteln der ratio berechnen. Mit dem Irrationalen in seiner Vorstellungswelt ist Verschiedenes gemeint: das Zukünftige, das Schöne, das Menschliche und das Neue nicht zuletzt. Wallenstein will derart Irrationales, weil er sich mit dem Weltganzen verbunden weiss, während seine Gegenspieler vorzüglich an ihre Besitztümer denken. Das Irrationale — also das Schöne, das Menschliche, das Neue und Lebendige im weitesten Sinn — berechnen zu wollen, mag vermessen sein. Wallenstein mag im Versuch solcher Berechnungen das Menschliche verfehlen. Aber derjenige verfehlt es nicht minder, der sich des Irrationalen als des Schönen, Neuen und Lebendigen nicht versichern will, der nur auf den Tag sieht — ein Taktiker des letztlich sinnlosen, weil nur in sich kreisenden Erfolgs. Um der tragische Held zu sein, der er von Schiller her werden sollte, muss Wallenstein die über das Irdische hinausliegenden Dinge wollen. Zugleich muss er das Irdische wollen: das Planen und Berechnen und was sonst zur rauhen Wirklichkeit gehört, wenn sie sich nicht zu Traum und Illusion verflüchtigen soll. Wallenstein muss beides wollen: die Realität und die Idealität, das Irdische und das Überirdische, das Rationale und die Irrationalität.[1] Das eben ist sein Schicksal. Es ist nicht das Schicksal eines Charakters, der so veranlagt ist. Von jedem Charakterdrama sind wir weit entfernt.[2] Es ist vielmehr der Charakter der Idee, die ihm zum Schicksal wird. Wallenstein ist lebendig in menschlicher Grösse, durch die sein Heer erst das ist, was es ist. Aber er hat darum die Regungen für die Grösse des Menschlichen nicht völlig erstickt, wie man an seinem Umgang mit Max und Thekla erkennt. Er will auch hier beides: die menschliche Grösse und die Grösse des Menschlichen, den Realismus der Macht und die Idealität

[1] Hinsichtlich der Begriffe Idealism(us) und Realism(us) in *Wallenstein* ist die aufschlussreiche Äusserung gegenüber Humboldt vom 21. März 1796 zu vergleichen; hierzu auch Wolfgang Binder: 'Die Begriffe "Naiv" und "Sentimentalisch" in Schillers Drama.' In: *Jahrbuch der Deutschen Schillergesellschaft*, 4 (1960), S. 155. — Das Ineinander von Idealismus und Realismus hat man in der neueren Schillerforschung mit wechselnder Zielsetzung öfters betont, so Friedrich Sengle (*Das deutsche Geschichtsdrama*, Stuttgart 1957, S. 42): 'Ist sonst das Stück ein stark realistisches Geschichtsdrama, so springt es in der Lösung um so deutlicher ins idealistische Drama über.' Ähnlich Kurt May: 'Im Wallenstein-Drama sind demnach ... zwei Tragödien ineinandergelagert ... in deren Mitte je ein Repräsentant des dämonischen Realismus und des ethischen Idealismus steht' (S. 168).

[2] In Übereinstimmung mit O. Seidlin: 'aber es geht eben nicht um Charakterologisches' (S. 123).

Eine Betrachtung über Schillers 'Wallenstein'

eines künftigen Reiches. Wallenstein muss, um tragisch zu sein, beides wollen, und muss sich damit in das Geflecht verstricken, das ihm zum Verhängnis wird. Er ist nicht in der Lage, sich für eine Seite zu entscheiden, weil er der anderen das gleiche Recht zugesteht. Wallenstein wird letztlich tragisch, weil er nicht einsinnig denkt. Er wird verklagt vom Doppelsinn des Lebens. Die Einsinnigkeit der anderen ist das, was ihn von diesen trennt: von den einsinnigen Realisten ebenso wie von den einsinnigen Idealisten. Zu den ersteren gehört Octavio, der nur das Altgewordene kennt, die bestehende Ordnung und die Treue zum Kaiser; ähnlich kennt die Gräfin Terzky nur die baren und öden Realitäten, die Berechnung und die Kalkulation. Nirgends denken sie darüber hinaus. Aber auch Max Piccolomini ist festgelegt. Auch er gehört zu den Einsinnigen des Dramas, dessen Tod uns ergreift, ohne dass er das volle Gewicht des Tragischen erhielte. Sie alle können sich leichter entscheiden, weil sie sich für eine Seite im Geflecht der Gegensätze entscheiden. Wallenstein kann das nicht:

> Schnell fertig ist die Jugend mit dem Wort,
> Das schwer sich handhabt wie des Messers Schneide;
> Aus ihrem heissen Kopfe nimmt sie keck
> Der Dinge Mass, die nur sich selber richten.
> Gleich heisst ihr alles schändlich oder würdig,
> Bös oder gut ... (WT. V. 779–84)

Hier nun vollends wird sichtbar, was es mit dem sogenannten Entscheidungsdrama auf sich hat. Nicht nur ist der Wallenstein Schillers der Held eines Dramas, über den schon entschieden ist, wenn er sich entscheidet. Auch die klare Entscheidung derer wird problematisch, die nur einer Seite folgen. Wallenstein, weil er vieles will, ist dieser Einseitige nicht. Er hat an beiden Reichen teil. Das Scheitern der Vereinigung, die er versucht, ist die Folge. Wer darin in erster Linie Hybris sieht, macht das Ende des Dramas zur moralischen Belehrung. Aber das Ende des *Wallenstein*-Drama wollen wir gerade als eine moralische Belehrung nicht verstehen. Was ist der Sinn der letzten Szenen? Gewiss sind sie vom Walten der tragischen Ironie geprägt, und tragische Ironie bedeutet stets, dass derjenige etwas noch nicht weiss, von dem sie bereits Besitz ergriffen hat. Gleichwohl ist es wichtig, aus der Tragödie Schillers den Moralismus zu entfernen, der sich eindrängen muss, wenn man entscheidende Dinge im Vorgang des Dramas mit Begriffen wie Hybris oder Nemesis umschreibt. Welchen Sinn also hat Wallensteins Tod? Der Wallenstein dieser letzten Szenen weiss nicht, was ihn erwartet. Dennoch befindet er sich in einer Todesstimmung, die zur Sphäre des Erhabenen gehört, wie sie Schiller versteht. Wallenstein hat sich in das Unabänderliche geschickt, ohne seine Sache aufgegeben zu haben, und Aufgeben würde die Verleugnung jenes neuen Lebens bedeuten, zu dem er sich in unserem Monolog bekannt hat. Doch ist er anders einsichtig als zuvor. Er hat dem Sternenglauben entsagt und den Tod Max Piccolominis als eigene Schuld angenommen. Er scheint in den Bereich jener Menschlichkeit heimgekehrt zu sein, die Max als Traum durch sein irdisches Dasein begleitet hat. Jetzt völlig sind wir in die Zone des Tragischen eingetreten, die Scheitern, Untergang und Katastrophe bedeutet und uns dennoch versöhnend stimmt infolge der Nähe solcher Menschlichkeit, die Goethe zutreffend erfasste, wenn er im Brief vom 18. März 1799 den grossen Vorzug des letzten Stückes betonte, 'dass alles aufhört politisch zu sein und bloss menschlich wird . . .'[1] Ihrer werden wir inne, wenn wir den Todgeweihten sprechen hören, als würde alles schon in einem Zwischenreich gesprochen, in dem sich Sinn und Widersinn, Wissen und Nichtwissen seltsam vermischen:

      Leuchte, Kämmerling.
Du auch noch? Doch ich weiss es ja, warum
Du meinen Frieden wünschest mit dem Kaiser.
Der arme Mensch! Er hat im Kärntnerland
Ein kleines Gut und sorgt, sie nehmens ihm,
Weil er bei mir ist. Bin ich denn so arm,
Dass ich den Dienern nicht ersetzen kann?
Nun, ich will niemand zwingen. Wenn du meinst,
Dass mich das Glück geflohen, so verlass mich.
Heut magst du mich zum letztenmal entkleiden,
Und dann zu deinem Kaiser übergehn —
Gut Nacht, Gordon!
Ich denke einen langen Schlaf zu tun,
Denn dieser letzten Tage Qual war gross,
Sorgt, dass sie nicht zu zeitig mich erwecken!
      (WT. V. 3665–79)

[1] Zum Dualismus zum Menschlichen im Denken Goethes vgl. Wolfgang Paulsen: 'Goethes Kritik am Wallenstein'. In: *DVJS* 28 (1954), 79.

Eine Betrachtung über Schillers 'Wallenstein' 95

Zunehmend nähert sich Wallenstein einer Menschlichkeit von der Art, die uns an Max und Thekla ergriff. Die an den Realitäten Gescheiterten sind ihm im Tod vorangegangen. Die einen wie die anderen sind dem Tod geweiht, und nur die Subalternen überleben; die Vertreter der alten Ordnung, die dafür sorgen, dass alles genau so bleibt, wie es immer war. 'Mit diesen allen kann kein neues Zeitalter beginnen, noch nicht einmal eine anständige Restauration'; so kommentiert Kurt May die letzten Szenen des grossen Dramas.[1] Aber nur Wallenstein hat die tragische Einsicht des Wissenden, auch wenn er Entscheidendes — seine Ermordung — nicht wissen kann. Seine Überlegenheit wird offenkundig, was Octavio und dessen Ordnung betrifft.[2] Die ihrerseits bleibt im Recht, aber um welchen Preis! Doch nicht um die Tragik einer Person, sondern um die Tragik der Idee ist es Schiller zu tun; und es ist die Tragik der Idee, an dem Realisten zu scheitern, den sie braucht, wie es die Tragik des Realisten ist, dass er sich für die Ideen und Ideale interessiert und also noch anderes kennt als die blosse Wirklichkeit. Der eine Teil im Geflecht der Dinge benötigt den anderen. Aber derselbe Teil schliesst den anderen aus. Es sind immer wieder solche Antinomien, deren Tragik Schiller in seinen Personen gestaltet, indem er das Scheitern der Idee gestaltet.[3] Auch im vorklassischen Drama, in *Kabale und Liebe* oder im *Don Carlos*, ist das der Fall. Aber erst im *Wallenstein*-Drama steht die Idee des neuen Lebens im Zentrum des dramatischen Geschehens. Da wir es mit einer Idee zu tun haben, ist sie, wie jede Idee, zum Scheitern verurteilt. Indem sie Schiller als Thema seiner Dramen verwendet, verwendet er keine beliebige Idee. Es ist im Gegenteil die bestimmende der Epoche, die wir Klassik nennen. Die Idee des Neuen ist die Idee der Geschichtlichkeit und des Wandels der Geschichte. Ihre Entfaltung ist seit 1790 auch im Denken Goethes deutlich zu verfolgen, ehe sie Schiller auf seine Weise umschreibt.

Die Idee des neuen Lebens ist eine Grunderfahrung des europäischen Denkens seit der Renaissance. Die Erneuerung der antiken Geisteswelt ist damit aufs engste verknüpft. Das

---
[1] Ebda., S. 164.
[2] Hierzu Herbert Singer: 'Dem Fürsten Piccolomini'. In: *Euph.* 53 (1959), S. 301.
[3] Clemens Heselhaus: 'Wallensteinisches Welttheater', S. 46.

Erlebnis einer solchen Welt in einer sich wandelnden Welt des geschichtlichen Lebens wird Goethe erstmals in Rom zuteil. Er gibt unter dem Datum vom 3. Dezember 1786 dafür die Begründung: 'denn an diesen Ort knüpft sich die ganze Geschichte der Welt an, und ich zähle einen zweiten Geburtstag, eine wahre Wiedergeburt, von dem Tage, da ich Rom betrat.'[1] Die Idee des sich erneuernden Lebens begleitet ihn fortan auf dieser Reise. Als sich der Tag jährt, an dem er sich unbemerkt von Karlsbad wegstahl, denkt er zurück und notiert sich: 'Welch ein Jahr! und welch eine sonderbare Epoche für mich dieser Tag, des Herzogs Geburtstag, und ein Geburtstag für mich zu einem neuen Leben';[2] ähnlich lesen wir es in der Niederschrift aus Rom vom 2. Dezember 1786: 'Überhaupt ist mit dem neuen Leben, das einem nachdenkenden Menschen die Betrachtung eines neuen Landes gewährt, nichts zu vergleichen...'[3] Jede Idee des Klassischen als einer Wiedergeburt vergangenen Lebens ist auf irgendeine Weise mit dieser Idee verknüpft und muss es sein: denn die blosse Nachahmung, die nicht mit eigenem Sinn erfüllte Wiederholung wäre der Tod. Das alte Wahre soll in einer Klassik wie der deutschen gelten. Aber die Idee des lebendigen Neuen nicht minder. Mit Goethes italienischer Reise beginnt die Epoche der deutschen Klassik in dem Sinn, dass im Alten ein lebendig Neues entdeckt wird. Das besagt, dass weder das Alte der antiken Geisteswelt einseitig herrscht noch das Neue als das bloss Revolutionäre der eigenen Zeit. Ein neuer Stil geht daraus hervor, der den Stil des Sturm und Drang als etwas Veraltetes zurücklässt, das der Zeit nicht mehr genügt. In seiner Rezension der Gedichte Bürgers redet Schiller einer Erneuerung der Lyrik das Wort — keiner zeitlos klassischen, sondern einer solchen, die mit der Zeit fortschreitet, die, wie es wörtlich heisst, 'in ihrem verjüngendem Licht der Erstarrung eines frühzeitigen Alters' entginge. Das *Wallenstein*drama ist das erste Drama nach zehnjähriger Pause. Wie in keinem Drama zuvor werden Handeln und Entscheidung eingeschränkt. Die Determiniertheit in der Herrschaft des Notwendigen ist umfassend. 'Man sieht in dieser ungeheuren Empirie nichts als Natur und nichts von dem, was wir Philosophen so gern Freiheit nennen möchten', schreibt Goethe im

---

[1] *Italienische Reise. Gedenkausgabe*, 1949, Bd. 11, S. 160.
[2] Ebda., S. 433. [3] Ebda., S. 150.

Eine Betrachtung über Schillers 'Wallenstein' 97

Jahre 1802 an Schiller, und man dürfte den Satz gut und gern auf den *Wallenstein* beziehen. Der Dichter der Freiheit, als den man Schiller so oft feiert, ist ein Dichter des Notwendigen in hohem Mass. Er ist es zumal in der beginnenden Klassik, indem er sich an der antiken Tragödie und an ihren Determiniertheiten orientiert.[1] Aber natürlich ist er weit entfernt von einer Nachahmung dieser Tragödie. Schiller ist sich darüber im klaren, als Deutscher geboren zu sein und bezüglich des griechischen Geistes durch Imagination zu ersetzen, was die Wirklichkeit vorenthält, um so 'gleichsam von innen heraus und auf einem rationalen Wege ein Griechenland zu gebähren'.[2] Schiller verbindet mit dem überlieferten Alten das Neue des antiken Dramas in vielerlei Gestalt. In *Wallenstein* entfaltet es sich als eine das ganze Drama umgreifende Idee des geschichtlichen Lebens. In dem Masse, in dem sich der Held des Dramas als Anwalt des Neuen gegen die Macht der Gewohnheit und gegen das Recht der Besitzenden wendet, nur weil es ein Gewohnheitsrecht ist, spürt man die Nähe zur Ideenwelt der Französischen Revolution. Die Idee des Neuen im Denken Wallensteins gewinnt Gestalt in einem neuen Reich, das er schaffen will, um das veraltete des Kaisers abzulösen. Aber genau besehen, ist dieses Reich selbst eine Idee, wie Schillers ästhetischer Staat auch. Sein Drama gestaltet die Antinomie dieses irrational Neuen als einer Idee, die notwendigerweise an der rationalen Wirklichkeit scheitert. Geschichte umfasst jetzt nicht mehr nur das Herrschaftsgebiet des politischen Handelns, der Berechnung und des Kalküls. Im Motiv des Neuen als einer Kategorie der Zeit, die das Drama so entscheidend konstituiert, geht es zugleich um ein Irrationales, das sich der Berechnung entzieht. Es geht letztlich um das Geschichtliche selbst als einer Erscheinung des lebendigen Geistes. Der Machtstaat als der wirkliche und der ästhetische Staat als ein solcher der Zukunft sind dialektisch aufeinander bezogen in dem Geschichtsdrama Schillers, das wir als Drama der deutschen Klassik bezeichnen — aber einer Klassik, die nichts Zeitloses ist, sondern

---

[1] Vgl. Benno von Wiese (*Die deutsche Tragödie von Lessing bis Hebbel*, ³Hamburg 1955, S. 222): 'aber gerade seine Tragödie entwickelt sich seit dem 'Wallenstein' immer stärker in Aneignung einer von den Griechen, von Sophokles und Euripides gelernten tragischen Analysis, die den poetischen Stoff in eine tragische Fabel verwandelt . . .'
[2] An Goethe vom 23. Aug. 1794, Jonas, iii, S. 473.

die zeitbedingte Antwort auf die weltgeschichtliche Lage in dichterischer Form. Auf das Ereignis von 1789 antworten Goethe wie Schiller nicht einfach mit dem Rückzug in eine ferne Vergangenheit, in diejenige der antiken Geisteswelt. Sie denken nicht daran, ihrer Gegenwar den Rücken zu kehren. Beide sind sie keine Vertreter der Reaktion so wenig wie sie Anwälte der Revolution sein wollen. Was sie beide wollen, ist ein Drittes, wie es Goethe in Italien aufgegangen war. An den Sitten der Völker hatte er gelernt, 'wie aus dem Zusammentreffen von Notwendigkeit und Willkür, von Antrieb und Wollen, von Bewegung und Widerstand ein drittes hervorgeht, was weder Kunst noch Natur, sondern beides zugleich ist . . .'[1] Was wir deutsche Klassik nennen ist ein derart Drittes: eine 'Vermittlung' zwischen Vergangenheit und unmittelbarer Gegenwart, zwischen den bestehenden Verhältnissen hier und den neuen Verhältnissen dort.

[1] *Italienische Reise*, S. Bd. 17, S. 84/5.

Three Scenes from *Wilhelm Tell*

G. W. McKAY

THE ambiguities and difficulties of *Wilhelm Tell* continue to exercise the minds of critics and producers alike. Perhaps no play of Schiller's is at one and the same time so theatrically effective and so dramatically puzzling. Perhaps no other work of his has suffered so much critically from its popularity; the *Volksstück* seemed to lend itself all too readily to nationalistic, even Nazi, interpretation, and even its dire quotability has made it to such a degree a part of popular culture that it is now difficult to see it, or indeed its author, with unprejudiced eyes. This point is strongly made by Muschg in his article 'Schiller — die Tragödie der Freiheit'.[1] Muschg rightly insists that 'Schiller ist interessanter und aktueller als die Legende, die das neunzehnte Jahrhundert um ihn gewoben hat', and seeking to sketch the new image of Schiller which has been appearing in recent years, he finds it necessary to define this image 'gleichsam einen Schiller ohne Wilhelm Tell'. It is probable that *Tell* has contributed more to the picture of Schiller as the German national poet than any other work; and even for that reason it is necessary to examine the play free from the accrued historical bias that so long bedevilled German criticism of it.

Two English scholars have attempted such a radical revision of the critical view of *Tell*, W. G. Moore in a stimulating short article, 'A New Reading of *Wilhelm Tell*',[2] and Professor W. F. Mainland in the very interesting introductory essay to his recent edition of the play.[3] Moore sees Tell as a tragic figure, an idealist forced to commit murder, and is able to make sense of the notoriously debatable Parricida scene as 'the only scene in which Tell is faced with the inevitable consequences of his act';[4] and so this is the tragedy of the ruin of an idealist. In my view this does rather beg the question why Schiller called his

---

[1] In the volume of essays *Schiller. Reden im Gedenkjahr 1959*, ed. B. Zeller.
[2] *German Studies presented to H. G. Fiedler*, Oxford 1938, pp. 278 f.
[3] Schiller, *Wilhelm Tell*, ed. W. F. Mainland, London 1968.
[4] Op. cit., p. 288.

play 'ein Schauspiel', after he had earlier described it in his letters as a tragedy.[1] It is nevertheless entirely possible to see the Parricida scene as a dawning, towards the end of the play, of tragic comprehension on the part of a hero hitherto an unlikely candidate for tragic stature in the Schillerian canon; only I think that Tell is faced with something other than simply the moral implications of his deed, which he has already pondered to the maximum of his not very profound capacity in the Hohle Gasse scene. And it should be remembered that the play ends with a kind of apotheosis of Tell, even if he himself remains—uncharacteristically but possibly revealingly—dumb, in the final scene.

Mainland's much more radical and full discussion takes a refreshingly un-pious view of Tell himself and sees the play much more as a drama about the movement of history. He does not consider it to be a nationalistic play, and utters in this connection a warning, which all critics of Schiller's dramas should constantly bear in mind, against being 'tempted to attribute to Schiller himself sentiments expressed by characters in his play'.[2] 'The dramatic theme of the play', he states, 'is the building up of a legend and the revelation of its ultimate weakness.'[3] This seems to me a wise insight which allows the popular, nationalistic *Volksstück* element its proper place, while still allowing us a deeper view into history than the participants in history can ever themselves attain. Mainland talks of Schiller's irony and pity towards his characters; yet beyond irony and pity one feels in *Wilhelm Tell* the poet's respect for individual people caught in the toils of history and attempting to act with dignity and humanity within it. The fact that they cannot control it and finally misinterpret it does not make them its dupes, but rather shows their determination to assert their humanity where the facts of history would implicitly attack it.

It is arguable that traditionally too much attention has been paid by critics of Schiller to the relevance of his dramaturgical and aesthetic writings to his plays.[4] Martini, for example, implies that Schiller sets out deliberately to illustrate his theories

[1] e.g. letter to Wolzogen, 21 Sept. 1803.
[2] Mainland, p. xxv. Indeed, Mainland points out the positive sarcasm with which Schiller speaks of the *Volksstück*; for example, in his letter to Wolzogen of 27 Oct. 1803.
[3] Op. cit., p. xxxvii. [4] Cf. Muschg, op. cit.

Three Scenes from 'Wilhelm Tell'

in his play, when he states that 'Der Tell in der Parricida-Szene ist aus dem Kampf und Leidensfeld der geschichtlichen Welt in die Idylle heimgekehrt'.[1] One finds Benno von Wiese likewise talking of 'der zum Erhabenen entschlossene Mensch'[2] as if, one is tempted to say, the hero or heroine in Schiller's later plays were aware of a duty to attain a state of *Erhabenheit* which he or she can know of only from a perusal of *Über das Erhabene*. While there is indubitably much mutual fructification between the aesthetic and dramaturgical writings and the plays, such insistence on a straight applicability of the data of the former to the creation of the latter seems to do a disservice to our view of Schiller as a man of the theatre. Clearly he was a writer with an inborn theatrical instinct and a profound respect for the potentialities of the stage. He remarked in the essay *Über den Gebrauch des Chors in der Tragödie* with which he prefaced *Die Braut von Messina* (a play whose theatrical qualities deserve attention): 'Aber das tragische Dichterwerk wird erst durch die theatralische Vorstellung zu einem Ganzen: nur die Worte gibt der Dichter . . .' *Wilhelm Tell* is a highly theatrical play, full of carefully managed stage effects, memorable encounters, unforgettable sayings, brilliantly managed crowd scenes, precise stage directions, and cunningly used musical effects. Its continuing popularity in performance is well attested and well merited. It might be that by careful attention being paid to its theatrical qualities something can be learned of its dramatic purposes. I propose to examine in some detail three scenes whose theatrical implications seem to me crucial and which in their different ways reveal important aspects of the hero Tell, and of Schiller's view of the history in which Tell has posthumously become the great mythical hero. They are the first 35 lines of the opening scene, Act I, scene 1; the Rütli scene, Act II, scene 2; and the Parricida scene, Act V, scene 2. Ironically, the first and last scenes have in common that they are not infrequently entirely omitted (e.g. they were omitted in a major production in the Staatstheater in Stuttgart in 1966; the Parricida scene both in the production and in the published text of the production in the open air at Interlaken in 1950). The Parricida scene has proved

---

[1] Cf. 'Der aesthetische Staat und der aesthetische Mensch', *Deutschunterricht*, 12 (1960), 2, 117.
[2] B. v. Wiese, *Schiller, eine Einführung in Leben und Werk*, Reclam, p. 71.

a stumbling-block from the very start, for Schiller had to work hard to persuade Iffland to retain it in the Berlin production.[1] The opening scene of *Wilhelm Tell* is clearly in the style of the opening scenes in many contemporary *Singspiele*, in which the populace is depicted at work or at play and the social and/or historical setting is established. Operatically conceived scenes are not uncommon in Schiller's later plays; for example, Johanna's farewell to her home, scene 4 of the prologue to *Die Jungfrau von Orleans*, and Beatrice's scena in the garden ('Garten, der die Aussicht auf das Meer eröffnet') in *Die Braut von Messina*.[2] The setting at the opening of *Wilhelm Tell* is idyllic—the rocky shore of Lake Lucerne opposite Schwyz, with a view over the lake to the meadows, farms, and villages on the other side. On the left are the peaks of the Haggen range, on the right in the distance snow-capped mountains. Three representative members of the Swiss community are seen: a fisher-lad in a boat, a shepherd on a mountain, and an Alpine hunter on the top of a cliff. They each in turn sing a verse of a song to the accompaniment of the *ranz des vaches*, each of them standing on a different level on the stage; and the content of each verse corresponds schematically to the landscape level of the singer on stage and to the natural landscape level of his normal working life. The song is in the nature of work songs, in which the populace expresses its feelings about its daily round, its common task, much as, say, miner's ballads or sea-shanties. In their clearly intended representative function the characters can be felt to be only a step away from the mythical.

The first verse, sung by the *Fischerknabe*, at the lowest level of the theatrical (and natural) landscape, recalls Goethe's poem *Der Fischer*. The fisher-lad sings of how a boy falls asleep beside a peaceful lake, and in his dream hears

ein Klingen
Wie Flöten so süss,

[1] Cf. letter of 14 Apr. 1804, where he insists, and says that Goethe agrees with him, on the necessity of its inclusion; yet Goethe in conversation with Eckermann, 16 Mar. 1831, agreeing that the scene throws an unfortunate light on Tell, says 'allein Schiller war dem Einfluss von Frauen unterworfen, wie andere auch, und wenn er in diesem Fall fehlen konnte, so geschah es mehr aus solchen Einwirkungen als aus seiner eigenen guten Natur'!

[2] Cf. R. Longyear, *Schiller and Music*, Chapel Hill, University of California Press, 1965.

Three Scenes from 'Wilhelm Tell'

> Wie Stimmen der Engel
> Im Paradies.

But waking out of his blissful dream he finds the water lapping round his chest, and a voice from the depths of the lake calls to him:

> Lieb Knabe, bist *mein*!
> Ich locke den Schläfer,
> Ich zieh' ihn herein.

This is a remarkable way to open an apparently idyllic scene; the *Singspiel* convention is used here for purposes very different from such harmlessly jolly choral openings as No. 2 in the Goethe/Schubert *Claudine von Villa Bella* or No. 1 in the Körner/Schubert *Der Vierjährige Posten*. The fisher-boy's landscape is ambivalent and frightening. Now the lake is frequently the setting in the rest of the play, and in its most striking appearances it is a place of danger which only the bravest can master: firstly in the scene immediately following this ambivalently idyllic opening, in which, when even the ferryman has declared that no man in his senses would risk his life by putting out on the raging lake, Tell himself resolutely takes the boat and masterfully ferries Baumgarten to safety; and secondly in Tell's description (ll. 2218–2270) of how, during the crossing after Gessler has declared his freedom forfeit, Gessler asks him to save the ship and its company when a sudden storm threatens their lives. In both these scenes the proverbial near-miraculous prowess of Tell is underlined:

> *Ruodi*. Wohl bessre Männer tuns dem Tell nicht nach,
> Es gibt nicht zwei, wie der ist, im Gebirge.
> (ll. 163–4)

and

> *Fischer*. Tell, Tell, ein sichtbar Wunder hat der Herr
> An Euch getan, kaum glaub ichs meinen Sinnen.
> (ll. 2271–2)

The second verse is sung by the shepherd on the mountain. His job makes him an archetype of what the Swiss feel themselves to be: 'ein Volk der Hirten'. His song contains nothing of the threat of the verse sung by the *Fischerknabe*. Rather it reflects the quiet continuity of pastoral life. He sings a shepherd's autumn song as he drives his flocks from the rich summer pastures of the Alps down for wintering in the plains:

> Wir fahren zu Berg, wir kommen wieder,
> Wenn der Kuckuck ruft, wenn erwachen die Lieder.

But we quickly discover that the pastoral life is indeed threatened, and by a human agency, when in the continuation of the scene the Vogt's henchmen punish the shepherd for his complicity in the rescue of Baumgarten by slaughtering his flock.

The first two singers were on stage when the curtain opened. The third makes a dramatic appearance on the top of the rock to sing his verse; he is the *Alpenjäger*. The very element of his song is constant danger, as the first line already shows:

> Es donnern die Höhen, es zittert der Steg.

The inhabitant of the upper heights where such danger is his constant element is the *Schütze*, who, the singer says, knows no fear; he strides boldly over glaciers, with a sea of mist beneath his feet; his life is far from society and the landscape level where most men live and work; he sees the world far beneath him through a break in the cloud; indeed such is his height above the normal level that its elements seem to change their place and he sees

> Tief unter den Wassern
> Das grünende Feld.

The hunter's sphere, then, is danger, height, and distance from normal humanity. Now there is only one notable hunter in the play: Tell himself. Danger is indeed his element; and his isolation, his separation from normal life, even from his family, is constantly reiterated. Indeed, so far is Tell from normal affairs that he seems to lack a proper practical judgement of men and cannot see, as his wife does, that his previous encounter with Gessler has made the latter his enemy for life.[1]

It is my contention that this pastoral, *Singspiel*-like opening has, theatrically, four important functions. Firstly, it establishes three areas of landscape that are of great importance in the

---

[1] Cf. Mainland's discussion of Tell's isolation, pp. lii–liii. It is even arguable that his superhuman quality is in danger of turning into inhumanity, so far does he disregard the natural fears of both his wife and the confederates—cf. Johanna speaking from the height of her vocation to the Archbishop and the Dauphin in *Die Jungfrau von Orleans*, Act III, scene 4.

Three Scenes from 'Wilhelm Tell'

theatrical and emotional imagery of the play, and establishes them in a hierarchy at the top of which stands the Hunter. Secondly, it expresses something of the Swiss view of themselves, taking three archetypal figures as representative of the populace and in the words of each figure either expressing or ironically prefiguring an element of danger which stands in contrast with the overtly idyllic nature of its setting and action. Thirdly, and perhaps more importantly, it initiates a process of myth-making, conscious on Schiller's part, though of course generally unconscious in the Swiss, which can be felt to be one of the most important elements in the play. The feeling of the inhabitants of a landscape for its qualities, and their qualities within it, readily takes on a mythical quality, as we see in the feelings of the French in *Die Jungfrau von Orleans* and of the chorus of Sicilians in *Die Braut von Messina*. In both plays, the feeling of ownership in the 'rightful' inhabitants of the landscape goes far beyond the merely geopolitical. The mythical affabulation of Joan with the Virgin Mary, against the background of a rural Catholic populace, and of the turbulent Sicilians with ever-threatening Mount Etna is in each case a strong, partly unconscious binding element among the native inhabitants themselves and creates a powerful solidarity in them *vis-à-vis* their rulers, the foreign English or Norman dynasty. This mythical solidarity is even stronger among the Swiss in *Wilhelm Tell*: their feeling for the land (the word *Land* in the play has a spectrum of meaning which stretches from 'soil' to 'fatherland'), their unquestioning belief that God is on the Swiss side, the mythicizing imagery, all point to a mythical bond of unity amongst the Swiss, in which their individual concerns and ambitions, in themselves egoistic and not necessarily converging, become submerged. Fourthly, the opening functions as a prefiguration of Tell as a mythical hero. Both the danger in the deep and the danger in the heights prove to be elements that he alone can deal with, and his prowess in these elements is already proverbial. His mythical function is already known to the Swiss, as it clearly is to Gessler, for in both of Gessler's encounters with Tell on stage the one quality he picks on, and in which he may be said to recognize the mythical importance of Tell's prowess, is his famed ability with the bow. The scene, then, is prefigurative at a profound level; the prefiguration is most specific, though, in the figure and song of the *Jäger*: his sudden appearance, his physical dominance of the stage from the height of the rock, and import of his song, all point to the great bowman Tell.

I have said that a process of mythicization is initiated in this scene. It is continued throughout the play, particularly in the landscape imagery; but its political activation is strikingly contrived in the Rütli scene, and the character who operates it is Stauffacher.

The theatrical effect of the Rütli scene is powerful and very carefully engineered by Schiller. Mainland, while admitting the theatrical excellence of the scene, stresses rather its satirical content both in the light of the subsequent development of the *Bund* and in its actual disorderliness when viewed as a parliamentary meeting. Clearly, the elected Chairman, Reding, quickly has the control of the meeting taken from him by Stauffacher, and only exercises his Chairman's power to confirm a unanimous vote (l. 1309), call the meeting to order (ll. 1396-8), and put the proposal to delay action to the vote (l. 1417). Theatrically speaking, the man in charge of the scene is Stauffacher, who even technically usurps the Chairman's powers when he invites Konrad Huhn to report on his visit to the Emperor (l. 1322). Mainland describes him as the 'prototype of the chroniclers who wrote the story of the days when the Confederation was founded . . . the means by which he promotes the cause of the cantons repay the most careful scrutiny.' In fact, Stauffacher can be seen as a clever and by no means disinterested politician manipulating and interpreting history, even history in the making, in the interest of his own views on its desirable development. Tell can be seen as one of the pawns in this game, and Stauffacher certainly encourages the *post hoc* self-justifying interpretation of events in the spirit of nationalism with which, in my view ironically, the play ends (cf. ll. 3016 ff. and 3082-6). It is as a nationalistic politician that he operates in the Rütli scene, and he does it by making a maximal appeal to the mythical solidarity of the Confederates. This is his long speech (ll. 1165-1201) which purports, according to him, to be a story that old shepherds—archetypes of the *Hirtenvolk!*—tell. He retells it, apparently, to an audience not particularly familiar with it, in response to Winkelried's question and request:

So ist es wahr, was in den Liedern lautet,
Dass wir von fernher in das Land gewallt?
O, teilts uns mit, was Euch davon bekannt,
Dass sich der neue Bund am alten stärke. (ll. 1161-4)

One might remark that this is a heaven-sent opportunity for a clever politician and gifted orator to influence a willing audience. The scene and the participants' mood are solemn: they are agreeably aware of their own importance and behave with ceremonial rectitude, as upright citizens and men of peace; and furthermore, as men with possessions, traditions, and families to defend, they are ready game for an orator who can appeal to their mythical sense of national identity. This is a fine theatrical moment, carefully prepared by stage effects, well-chosen props, and creation of mood, and Stauffacher rises magnificently to the occasion, telling a mythical tale well calculated to arouse the profoundest feelings of mutual loyalty and adherence to ancient rights. The three landscape elements distinguished in the opening scene play their part in the myth—the raging lake where a ferryman sat waiting (a figure unexpected in this area, since 'nicht Menschenspuren waren hier zu sehen'!), the land with its woods and springs, and the *Weissland*, the mountains beyond which 'ein andres Volk in andren Zungen spricht'. At the end of his tale he plays out his last trump, consanguinity:[1]

Aus all den fremden Stämmen, die seitdem
In Mitte ihres Lands sich angesiedelt,
Finden die Schwyzer Männer sich heraus,
Es gibt das Herz, das Blut sich zu erkennen.

This myth concerns, not the foundation of Switzerland as a political entity, but that of Canton Schwyz, so that it is not strictly an answer to the question put by Winkelried, who is a man of Uri. But what is happening here is something parallel to the widening of reference of the word *Land* as mentioned above. Schwyz, even if it is immediately contrasted with the other cantons in its greater freedom, is felt by the men of all three cantons to mean something more than Canton Schwyz: they all shake hands, saying:

Wir sind *ein* Volk, und einig wollen wir handeln.

[1] Cf. the remark, albeit ironical, of R. Leroux in his article 'L'idéologie politique dans "Guillaume Tell"', *Études germaniques*, 10 (1955), 131: 'Schiller serait-il donc un précurseur des théoriciens de la race?'

This sense of mythical solidarity seems to coexist with what the modern Swiss call the *Kantönligeist*. Stauffacher in his next speech perhaps somewhat insensitively harps on the special excellence of the men of Schwyz, till Rösselmann retorts that they too of Uri opted voluntarily for the protection of the Empire. Even after the solemn affirmation of unity, a petty squabble at cantonal level breaks out (ll. 1387–95), whose result is that the men who have solemnly proclaimed their unity and their intention of undertaking unified action find it necessary to postpone their attack on the Austrian forts. And even their postponed plan does not have to be fully activated, since it will be overtaken by two events entirely outside the control and without the approval of the Confederates: the murder of Gessler by Tell and, politically more important, the murder of the Emperor by his nephew John, Duke of Swabia.

Why, in view of the fact that extraneous events render the proposed action of the newly founded Confederacy largely irrelevant, does Schiller take such pains with this scene? Clearly, it is not because the liberation of the forest cantons stems directly from the foundation of the Confederacy. The actions which in the play constitute the workings of history are emphatically not teleologically linked; if we seek such a teleological explanation, we are forced, I think, either to accuse Schiller of technical incompetence or to suspect him, as I do, of a darker, more ironical view of history.

Though the Rütli scene stands at the heart of the play and is theatrically one of its greatest moments, then, neither does it unite all the Swiss activists (Tell is absent) nor is it the source of the most important actions to follow. Rather, it seems to me, its function is to establish the mythical solidarity of the Swiss which the actions in themselves do not illustrate.[1] The nation united here in its representatives accepts myth as historical truth ('so ist es wahr', etc.) when it considers its past history; and it will do the same at the end of the play when it hails the apolitical individualist, Tell, as the saviour of the country. The workings of history are haphazard and unteleological; it is in

[1] All the main characters have individual, and not necessarily converging, interests to defend; and ironically the Rütli scene itself produces evidence of divergent loyalties between members of the different cantons (ll. 1388–95), social distinction between free men and serfs (ll. 1140–1), and basic disagreement about the timing of their proposed action (ll. 1386–1419).

the interest of those who have benefited by it to see it as teleological, indeed as divinely ordered; and it is in this sense that Tell can indeed be properly greeted as the hero whose mythical qualities, rather than his historical importance, make him a suitable and flattering national symbol. Thus, at the end of the play the mythical quality of Tell, already prefigured in the opening scene, and the mythical unity of the Swiss established in the Rütli scene can find common cause. History then is a kind of mythical (which does not imply dishonest!) and unselfconscious *post hoc* reinterpretation of events in the interests of national feeling. The rugged theatrical grandeur of the Rütli scene, the solemnity and highmindedness of the participants in it, its powerfully emotional association of them with the landscape which is theirs—all these elements forbid us to see these same men later as wilfully self-deluding in their interpretation of the events: rather we can see that the truth of myth is perhaps greater than the facts of history.

Men engaged in the making of history, unless they be great statesmen, are not aware, cannot be aware, of the part they are playing in it. Tell is a man engaged in history; and this is a notion entirely foreign to his outlook. His actions are never the result of consideration of the requirements of the wider historical situation; he acts rather in immediate response to the demands of the moment, except when, against his nature, he is forced to ponder on the social and familial implications of his decision to murder Gessler in the Hohle Gasse scene. It seems to me that one scene alone forces Tell to see himself in the context of history: the Parricida scene.

The fifth Act has found many detractors and few to praise it. As early as January 1805 Fritz von Stein, in a letter to Schiller's wife, wonders 'ob bei einer Vorstellung auf dem *Theater* der fünfte Akt nicht wegzulassen sei'.[1] On the Parricida scene we find Edwin Rödder, after a century of Schiller criticism, remarking: 'Die Parricida-scene hat, soviel ich weiss, bis jetzt erst einen Verteidiger gefunden. Trotz grosser Schönheiten im einzelnen soll ihr auch hier das Wort nicht geredet werden', and proceeding to suggest judicious excisions to temper 'das Unangenehme

---

[1] Quoted by A. Schmidtgen, *Die bühnengerechten Einrichtungen der Schillerschen Dramen für das Königliche National-Theater zu Berlin, erster Teil: Wilhelm Tell*, n.p. (Berlin?), 1906, p. 45 n.

der Szene'.[1] But clearly all is not over bar the shouting by the end of Act IV. The tumultuous shout of the Swiss in Act IV, scene 3, line 2821, 'Das Land ist frei', is not a statement of a political fact. The fifth Act has still a few surprises in store.

Admittedly, little overt political activity is shown. The liberation of the cantons is, perhaps prematurely, and, in spite of the caution of Walther Fürst (ll. 2852–5), triumphantly proclaimed in a series of announcements, and the demolition of the fort Zwing Uri enthusiastically begun. Melchthal describes how he and Rudenz rescued Berta from the castle of Sarnen where she was held prisoner; the fateful hat of Gessler is produced. But Walter Fürst again warns the confederates that 'Das Werk ist angefangen, nicht vollendet' (l. 2926). At this point Rösselmann enters to announce, and Stauffacher to describe graphically, the murder of the Emperor, and immediately after this the widowed Queen Elsbet's request for extradition of the murderers, read by an imperial messenger, is refused by the populace.

By this time the stage is filled with a milling throng of people, so that their displeasure at the Queen's request seems tantamount to rebellion, particularly after the speeches of Stauffacher and Walter Fürst, which in effect dissociate the Swiss from their loyalty to the Empire. Never have the leaders risked so much plain-speaking to a representative of the imperial authority. It is ironical, therefore, that they do not thank Heaven for the liberation, which has been made possible chiefly by the death of the Emperor, but instead set off at the end of scene 1, encouraged by Stauffacher, to seek out and thank the absent Tell, now described by Stauffacher as 'unsrer Freiheit Stifter' (l. 3083). It must surely be clear that the most important political fact in this situation is not Tell's deed but Parricida's; but already myth (and especially the mythagogue Stauffacher) is at work on the facts to turn them into 'history'.

From the excited bustle of the crowd scene, then, we move to Tell's home, where his wife and children await him. They too are in no doubt that Tell has saved the country. The outcast Parricida appears, dressed as a monk; he is clearly disorientated and his strange behaviour arouses fear in Tell's wife. What is

---

[1] E. Rödder, 'Kritische Nachlese zu Schillers Wilhelm Tell', *Zeitschrift für den deutschen Unterricht*, 19 (1905), 495.

beginning to be a tense situation is then interrupted by the entry of Tell, and after the reunion of the family the Parricida scene begins. Now it is interesting to notice a parallel in Hedwig's behaviour towards the as yet unrecognized Parricida and towards her husband Tell: she forbids Parricida to touch her or her children; she hesitates to take her husband's hand, for it is the hand of a murderer. Thus already a parallel is implied, at a still partly unconscious, instinctive level, between the two murderers.

The main reason which Schiller himself gave for insisting on the inclusion of this scene, in his letter to Iffland, 14 April 1804, namely the completion of the defence of Tell's murder of Gessler by contrasting it with Parricida's murder of the Emperor, must, if we stick to it, lead us to accuse Schiller of dramatic and theatrical incompetence. Logically, if he is anxious to justify Tell, he must make him sympathetic; but this he does not do; indeed in no scene in the play is such an unsympathetic light cast on the hero as in this one, at the moment before his apotheosis. It is not as if Tell were dealing with an unrepentant, hardened murderer, for Parricida is a broken man who feels himself an outcast from human society; at this moment Tell's self-righteous abuse of him can only serve to awaken pity for Parricida and dislike for Tell. It might be thought, indeed, that Goethe's explanation mentioned earlier (p. 102 n. 1) may have some substance, but in a different sense from that which Goethe gives it: Schiller may have recognized that in appearing to satisfy last scruples about Tell's act of murder he could ironically bring home to Tell and to a discerning audience the real relevance of the comparison of his deed with Parricida's.

If we bear this idea in mind, the confrontation becomes dramatically and possibly theatrically much more arresting. Tell's desperate insistence on seeing the confrontation as a moral issue can be seen as an attempt on his part to avoid other, perhaps deeper, issues which he, as a simple man, is incapable of dealing with. If, heeding Mainland's warning, we see Tell, not Schiller, as conducting his moral defence, we can also see the other side of the coin: that whatever the differences in *intention* may be, the two murders are comparable in their *effect*. They have both played their part in the destruction of recognized authority, and in doing so their perpetrators have become involved in the movement of history. Admittedly Tell's deed lacks the immediate political importance of Parricida's: nevertheless it has implications beyond the family sphere within which he would like to confine it. The cheerfully unmeditative Tell, then, is offered an insight into the wide historical implications of his action, and to a man who prefers the paradoxical safety of loneliness (adumbrated already in the *Jäger*'s song!) such an insight could be not merely disturbing but destructive. This, perhaps, explains Tell's helpless and very touching cry, 'Kann ich Euch helfen? Kanns ein Mensch der Sünde?' (l. 3222), even if, immediately after, he is enabled to rescue himself back into his old role of helper and adviser. Parricida *does* (I think with symbolical significance) seize Tell's hand, and Tell's withdrawal with the words 'Lasst meine Hand los' (l. 3228) could be played in such a way as to make it clear that he is shudderingly rejecting the fearful insight offered him. Yet, however enthusiastically he reassumes his old role, ordering his wife to refresh Parricida and load him with gifts, Tell, when faced with the rejoicing Swiss, utters not a word. He is faced now with the apotheosis of his mythical role, a role that could only successfully be sustained as long as (like Joan in *Die Jungfrau von Orleans*) he was not forced into a destructive and potentially tragic self-awareness. Historically he has not saved his people, and has been forced against his nature into a pitiless murder; but mythically he is properly the hero of his people. Perhaps the disparity between these two truths has in some degree entered his consciousness. His silence at the end, as he stands amid his rejoicing compatriots, is eloquent.

Blume und Stein
Zur Deutung von Ludwig Tiecks Erzählung *Der Runenberg*

WOLFDIETRICH RASCH

DIE hohe Bedeutung des 'Lebendigen', die Bewunderung des 'Organismus' bei Goethe ist so offensichtlich und so allgemein bekannt, dass es eines Beleges dafür nicht bedarf. Man weiss ebenso, dass Herder dieses Organische überaus hoche einschätzte und es mit starkem Wertakzent gegen das 'Mechanische' ausspielte; das Kunstwerk, Erzeugnis einer schöpferischen Kraft im Menschen, in der die Natur selbst wirkt, wird bei Herder wie bei Goethe als 'Organismus' verstanden, und gerade diese Struktur des Kunstgebildes bezeichnet seinen Wert.

Gewiss hat Goethe, der gesamten Natur betrachtend und forschend zugewandt, auch die anorganische Welt der Mineralien als Hervorbringung der natura naturans verehrt und sie untersucht, um das Walten der ewigen Kräfte auch in ihnen aufzuspüren und anzuschauen. Aber diese Kräfte sind in den Lebewesen, im vegetabilischen und tierischen Leben intensiver anschaubar und bilden hier die höchsten Erscheinungsformen jener Ganzheit, in der alle Teile unlösbar und unverrückbar miteinander verbunden und aufeinander bezogen sind. Eben diese organische Ganzheit, die das Lebendige gesetzmässig ausbildet, macht es dem Anorganischen überlegen; denn diese Ganzheit ist ein höchster Wert für Goethe. Er schreibt z. B. im Vorwort des ersten Heftes zur Morphologie: 'Das Lebendige ist zwar in Elemente zerlegt, aber man kann es aus diesen nicht wieder zusammenstellen und beleben. Dieses gilt schon von vielen anorganischen, geschweige von organischen Körpern.'[1]

Goethes Naturanschauung, für die diese Wertung des Organischen entscheidend ist, hat weithin gewirkt, wurde auch

[1] *Goethes Werke*, Hamburger Ausgabe in 14 Bdn., Hamburg 1948 f., Bd. 13, S. 55.

von den Romantikern aufgenommen und entwickelt und hat eine Tradition gebildet, die im neunzehnten Jahrhundert weiterlebt. Auch das ist bekannt genug. Aber es ist bemerkenswert, dass diese Goethische Anschauung doch in ihrer Geltung schon in der Zeit ihrer Ausbildung, schon um 1800 nicht unangefochten ist, dass diese Tradition bereits bei den Romantikern, die sie als nachfolgende Generation zuerst übernehmen, eine Brechung erfährt. Das gilt freilich nicht nur für spezifische Momente der Goethischen Naturanschauung sondern für das Verhältnis zur klassischen Dichtung und Weltdeutung Goethes überhaupt, das eigentümlich aus Bewunderung und Kritik, aus Rezeption und Abkehr gemischt ist. Novalis' Ofterdingen-Roman ist ebenso Goethisch wie antigoethisch. Die traditionsbildende Kraft des Goethischen Werkes wird von den Romantikern zugleich erfahren und verleugnet.

Die folgende Untersuchung gilt einem Einzelphänomen. Darum wird der Zusammenhang mit dem Gesamtverhältnis der Romantik zu Goethe nur leise angedeutet, und das Interesse wird darauf gelenkt, dass in einer Erzählung von Ludwig Tieck die genaue Umkehrung der Goethischen Wertungsweise der Naturbereiche erscheint. Das anorganische Mineralische hat hier den Vorrang, die stärkere Anziehungskraft gegenüber dem organischen Leben. Da man die Grundzüge der romantischen Naturauffassung in der Nachfolge Goethes zu sehen pflegt, scheint diese Umwertung unerwartet. Man rechnet offenbar so wenig mit ihr, dass man Tiecks 1802 geschriebene Erzählung *Der Runenberg*[1] bisher überhaupt nicht genau verstanden hat. Auf die Radikalität der Abwertung des Organischen war man, so scheint es, nicht gefasst. Auch die allerdings sehr knappen Deutungsansätze in der jüngsten Ausgabe der Erzählung, die von Marianne Thalmann stammen, zeigen ein auffälliges Unverständnis für ihre entscheidenden Motive.[2]

'Ein junger Jäger sass im innersten Gebirge nachdenkend bei einem Vogelherde, indem das Rauschen der Gewässer und des Waldes in der Einsamkeit tönte. Er bedachte sein Schicksal...'

---
[1] Die Erzählung wird hier zitiert nach der von Marianne Thalmann besorgten Ausgabe der *Werke* L. Tiecks, Bd. 2: *Die Märchen aus dem Phantasus. Dramen*, München 1964. Die in Klammern den Zitaten beigegebene Seitenzahl bezeichnet die entsprechende Seite dieser Ausgabe.
[2] Vgl. Nachwort und Anmerkungsteil von Bd. 2 der von M. Thalmann besorgten Tieck-Ausgabe.

(S. 61). So beginnt der Erzähler, und indem er dann das Nachdenken Christians mitteilt, erfährt der Leser, dass dieser seine Heimat und Familie verlassen hat, 'um sich aus dem Kreise der wiederkehrenden Gewöhnlichkeit zu entfernen' (S. 61). Er war ins Gebirge gezogen und Jäger geworden. Das fröhliche Jägerlied, das er singt, vertreibt jedoch seine Trübseligkeit nicht, er denkt an seine Kindheit und Jugend in der Heimat, 'und er sehnte sich in alle diese Umgebungen zurück, die er freiwillig verlassen hatte, um sein Glück in unbekannten Gegenden, in Bergen, unter fremden Menschen, in einer neuen Beschäftigung zu finden' (S. 62). Es war also nicht, wie es zunächst scheinen konnte, blosse romantische Wanderlust und Abenteuerfreude, was ihn aus der Heimat vertrieb, sondern das Bedürfnis nach anderer 'Beschäftigung' und nach einem Leben 'in den Bergen'. Beide Motive werden deutlicher in dem Lebensbericht, den Christian etwas später — die Interpretation greift hier vor — einem Fremden erzählt, der plötzlich an seinem Rastplatz am Rande eines Baches auftaucht und mit ihm weitergeht. Diesem Fremden berichtet er, dass er das Dasein in der heimischen Umwelt nicht aushielt; 'wie mit fremder Gewalt' wurde er weggetrieben, verstrickt 'in seltsamen Vorstellungen und Wünschen' (S. 63). Die berglose Ebene seiner Heimat hat 'Wiesen, fruchtbare Kornfelder und Gärten (S. 63), sein Vater ist Gärtner im Schloss, liebt leidenschaftlich die Pflanzen. Er wollte den Sohn zur Gartenarbeit überreden oder zwingen, aber dem war sie zuwider. Auch am Beruf eines Fischers, eines Kaufmanns fand er keinen Gefallen. Als aber der Vater 'von Gebirgen' erzählt, 'von den unterirdischen Bergwerken und ihren Arbeitern, von Jägern und ihrer Beschäftigung', da erwachte in ihm 'der bestimmteste Trieb', im Gebirge als Jäger zu leben (S. 64). Was ihn daran anzieht, ist nicht etwa der ästhetische Reiz der Berglandschaft, sondern — das wird später noch deutlicher — die Gesteinsmassen, die unterirdischen Schätze und das wilde Treiben der Jagd. Vom Gestein, das in der Gebirgswelt überall sichtbar ist, geht eine merkwürdige Faszination für Christian aus ('Meine Einbildung erschuf sich ungeheure Felsen', S. 64). Christian bevorzugt die vegetationsarme Natur im Gebirge statt der fruchtbaren Ebene und statt der friedlich-pfleglichen Gartenarbeit lockt ihn die beutegierige Jagd, 'das Geschrei der Hunde und des Wildes' (S. 64). Doch es geht nicht allein um einen Gegensatz zweier Lebensformen und Lebensräume. Dieser ist vielmehr nur die erste Erscheinungsform der Grundspannung, die die ganze Erzählung bestimmt. Christians Verlangen nach der Gebirgswelt ist nicht nur in einer Vorliebe für sie motiviert, sondern er wird 'wie mit fremder Gewalt' (S. 63) hingetrieben. Andererseits ist ihm die heimische Welt nicht bloss langweilig und uninteressant, sondern er hasst und verabscheut sie. 'Die Ebene, das Schloss, der kleine beschränkte Garten meines Vaters mit den geordneten Blumenbeeten, die enge Wohnung, der weite Himmel, der sich ringsum so traurig ausdehnte, und keine Höhe, keinen erhabenen Berg umarmte, alles ward mir noch betrübter und verhasster' (S. 64). Das ausgeglichene, friedlich geregelte Dasein in der fruchtbaren, von einem grossen Fluss durchströmten Ebene und das liebevolle Hegen der Gewächse im Garten erscheint Christian als völliger Leerlauf, als öde und verfehlt. Die Zufriedenheit der Menschen in diesem Lebensbereich hält er für unbegründet, sie scheint ihm nur dank ihres mangelnden Bewusstseins von ihrer wahren Lage möglich. 'Es schien mir, als wenn alle Menschen um mich her in der bejammernswürdigsten Unwissenheit lebten, und dass alle ebenso denken und empfinden würden, wie ich, wenn ihnen dieses Gefühl ihres Elendes nur ein einziges Mal in ihrer Seele aufginge' (S. 64). Es ist sehr auffällig, dass Christians Kennzeichnung der heimischen Lebenssituation durchaus nicht jene Merkmale des Leidens, der Not, etwa durch Krankheit, Enttäuschungen, Konflikte, Beschränkungen enthält, die gemeinhin die negative Beurteilung, die Klage über das 'Elend' der Menschen rechtfertigt. Vielmehr ist es gerade das friedliche, wohlgeordnete Dasein, das Gedeihen des Lebens in dieser ländlichen Welt, das von Christian abgewertet wird und seinen Abscheu hervorruft. Woran eigentlich leidet er? Da er das nicht direkt ausspricht, muss man es erschliessen. Offensichtlich ist es die Domestizierung des Daseins in seinem Lebenskreis, die es für Christian auch ohne Nöte und Sorgen unerträglich machte. Das geordnete, im Einverständnis mit den Naturgegebenheiten geregelte und angepasste Leben wird von Christian verabscheut aus einer Regung jenes 'Unbehagens in der Kultur', dessen Quelle Sigmund Freud in dem unbewussten Fortleben ursprünglicher Triebwünsche entdeckt hat. Unbewusst wird die Tatsache registriert, dass die Ordnung und Sta-

Zur Deutung von Ludwig Tiecks 'Der Runenberg'

bilität des Kulturzustandes mit schmerzlichem Verzicht auf nur verdrängte, nicht aufgehobene Triebwünsche erkauft ist. Freuds Erkenntnisse, mehr als ein Jahrhundert nach der Entstehung von Tiecks Erzählung entwickelt, lassen sich ohne weiteres auf diese anwenden, weil Tieck intuitiv, ohne methodische psychologische Beobachtung Vorgänge darstellt, die den Einsichten Freuds erstaunlich genau entsprechen. Diese Einsichten sind zur exakten Interpretation der Erzählung überaus hilfreich, ja unentbehrlich.

Die Richtung von Christians Wünschen gibt Aufschluss über sein Leiden. In Auflehnung gegen die domestizierte Lebensform ersehnt er statt der gehegten Gärten und der Agrikultur die unbearbeitete Gebirgsnatur, das rauhe und unfruchtbare Gestein. Christian leidet nicht (oder nur mittelbar) unter dem von der 'Kultur' auferlegten sexuellen Triebverzicht. Weder in seinem heimatlichen Leben noch in der Zeit seines Jägerdaseins ist irgendeine Liebesbeziehung oder ein Liebesbedürfnis angedeutet. Er leidet jedoch, mit einseitiger Akzentuierung, an der Unterdrückung dessen, was Freud als 'Aggressionstrieb' bezeichnet. 'Wenn die Kultur nicht allein der Sexualität, sondern auch der Aggressionsneigung des Menschen so grosse Opfer auferlegt, so verstehen wir es besser, dass es dem Menschen schwer wird, sich in ihr beglückt zu finden.'[1] Freud legt erkennend frei, was den Menschen unbewusst die Kultur verleidet. Unter Kultur versteht er 'die ganze Summe der Leistungen [...], in denen sich unser Leben von dem unserer tierischen Ahnen entfernt und die zwei Zwecken dienen: dem Schutz des Menschen gegen die Natur und der Regelung der Beziehungen der Menschen untereinander'.[2] Auch Christian, der die Anpassung an die heimatliche Lebensform verweigert, tut das nicht in klarer, die Gründe des Protestes reflektierender Bewusstheit. Doch sein Verhalten entspricht der Feststellung Freuds: 'Es wird den Menschen offenbar nicht leicht, auf die Befriedigung dieser ihrer Aggressionsneigung zu verzichten; sie fühlen sich nicht wohl dabei.'[3]

[1] Sigmund Freud, *Das Unbehagen in der Kultur*. In: *Gesammelte Werke*, chronologisch geordnet, unter Mitwirkung von Marie Bonaparte, Prinzessin Georg von Griechenland, hrsg. von Anna Freud, E. Bibring, W. Hoffer, E. Kris, O. Isakower, Bd. 14 (Frankfurt a. M. 1968⁴), S. 474.
[2] Ebd., S. 448 f.
[3] Ebd., S. 473.

Nun würde die steinige Gebirgswelt als solche für Christian keine Möglichkeit für eine Ersatzbefriedigung seines Aggressionstriebes bieten. Aber es zeigt sich eine solche Möglichkeit, dem unbewussten Aggressionstrieb in den Grenzen der gegebenen Ordnung eine Befriedigung zu verschaffen, in der Tätigkeit des Jägers, der das Wild tötet. Der Vater erzählt nicht nur von Gebirgen und Bergwerken, sondern auch 'von Jägern und ihrer Beschäftigung', und dabei erwacht in Christian der 'bestimmteste Trieb' zu diesem Dasein ('das Gefühl, dass ich nun die für mich bestimmte Lebensweise gefunden habe') (S. 64). Er berichtet: 'Meine Einbildung erschuf sich ungeheure Felsen, ich hörte in Gedanken das Getöse der Jagd, die Hörner, und das Geschrei der Hunde und des Wildes; alle meine Träume waren damit angefüllt...' (S. 64). In der Tat ist er dann später, als er wirklich Jäger im Gebirge geworden ist,'überaus glücklich', wie er dem Fremden mitteilt (S. 65) — wenigstens für drei Monate.

Christians Verhalten ist fast ein Musterbeispiel dafür, was eine Bemerkung Freuds als Ausweg aus der Unterdrückung des Aggressionstriebes beschreibt, die Sublimierung der Triebziele in der Berufsarbeit. 'Besondere Befriedigung vermittelt die Berufstätigkeit, wenn sie eine frei gewählte ist, also bestehende Neigungen, fortgeführte oder konstitutionell verstärkte Triebregungen durch Sublimierung nutzbar zu machen gestattet.'[1] Christian setzt die Wahl des Jägerberufes gegen den Willen seines Vaters durch, der den Sohn zum Gärtner machen möchte und ihn, obwohl er ein sanftmütiger Blumenfreund ist, dennoch 'mit Drohungen' zu dieser Tätigkeit 'zu zwingen versuchte' (S. 64) — ein Moment der Unterdrückung wird hier wahrnehmbar.

Jedoch, das Leben als Jäger im heimatfernen Gebirge macht Christian nur vorübergehend glücklich, nach drei Monaten kommt er sich 'so verloren, so ganz unglückselig vor' (S. 65). In dieser Lage trifft er den Fremden, der ihm bald wie 'ein alter Bekannter' (S. 63) erscheint. Darin deutet sich die innere Verwandtschaft mit diesem Manne an, der zur unterirdischen Gesteinswelt gehört, auch wenn er nicht als Bergmann bezeichnet wird. Er wohnt bei einem 'alten Schacht' (S. 65), und er sagt von sich: 'Die Erze sind meine Nachbarn' (S. 65). Er er-

[1] Ebenda, S. 438.

Zur Deutung von Ludwig Tiecks 'Der Runenberg'

muntert Christian, auf den Runenberg zu gehen. Der junge Jäger wandert dann bei Nacht zu diesem düsteren Berg, getrieben von unwiderstehlichem Verlangen, in das sich Schauder mischt, bis er mit Angst und Entzücken in einem verfallenen Gemäuer das riesige dämonische Bergweib in einem mit 'Gesteinen und Kristallen' (S. 67) verzierten Saal erblickt und von ihr eine magische Tafel mit eingelegten Edelsteinen erhält. Die Steine bilden eine geheimnisvolle Figur, 'die unsichtbar sogleich in sein Inneres überging' (S. 68). Nach dem Abstieg vom Runenberg schläft er unten ein und hält beim Erwachen am Morgen — die Tafel ist verschwunden — alles für Traum oder Wahn.

Diese Deutung bleibt auch für den Leser zunächst möglich und wird erst in Frage gestellt, wenn Christian später die magische Tafel wiederfindet und sie dem Vater zeigt (S. 78). Damit scheint bestätigt, dass Tieck die Begegnung mit dem Bergweib als nicht nur geträumt, sondern als transzendente Erfahrung Christians darstellen will, dass er also die Erzählung ins Märchenhafte hinüberführt. Aber der Unterschied ist nicht so gross, wie es zunächst scheinen mag. Die Funktion der Annäherung an das Bergweib ist die gleiche wie die eines Traumes, d. h. eine imaginäre Erfüllung eines Triebwunsches, der in der Wirklichkeit nicht befriedigt werden kann.

Aber welcher Triebwunsch wird mit diesem Vordringen in den anorganischen Naturbezirk erfüllt? Der Vorgang scheint nicht mehr aus dem Aggressionstrieb erklärbar, als dessen sublimierte Erfüllung das Jägerdasein sich deuten liess. Freilich war schon Christians Aufbruch aus der Heimat nicht allein vom Wunsch nach dem Jägerdasein bestimmt, sondern zugleich vom Verlangen, in die steinige Bergwelt zu gelangen. Diese Begierde erfüllt sich jetzt höchst intensiv — aber wie gehört sie mit dem Jägerdasein zusammen, was hat diese Wendung mit dem Aggressionstrieb zu tun?

Für die Beantwortung dieser Frage, die den Kern der Erzählung betrifft, ist Freuds Analyse der Triebnatur unentbehrlich. Sie bestimmt den Aggressionstrieb als 'Abkömmling und Hauptvertreter des Todestriebes'.[1] In der Schrift *Jenseits des Lustprinzips* von 1920 hat Freud dargelegt, 'es müsse ausser dem Trieb, die lebende Substanz zu erhalten und zu immer grösseren

[1] Ebenda, S. 481.

Einheiten zusammenzufassen, einen anderen, ihm gegensätzlichen geben, der diese Einheiten aufzulösen und in den uranfänglichen, anorganischen Zustand zurückzuführen strebe. Also ausser dem Eros einen Todestrieb . . .'[1] Er ist 'dazu bestimmt, den eigenen Todesweg des Organismus zu sichern und andere Möglichkeiten der Rückkehr zum Anorganischen als die immanenten fernzuhalten . . .'[2] Ihm ist die Aufgabe gestellt, 'das organische Lebende in den leblosen Zustand zurückzuführen . . .'[3] Dieser Trieb aber, sagt Freud, sei schwer fassbar, weil er 'stumm im Inneren des Lebewesens an dessen Auflösung arbeite'.[4] Freud hebt jedoch hervor, 'dass sich ein Anteil des Triebes gegen die Aussenwelt wende und dann als Trieb zur Aggression und Destruktion zum Vorschein komme'.[5] Die Aggressionsneigung ist also eine Komponente, eine Äusserungsweise des Todestriebes, der in ihr erfassbar wird. Christian ist entscheidend bestimmt von diesem Todestrieb, der sich bei seinem Aufbruch aus der Heimat in beiden Komponenten wirksam zeigt. Als Aggressionsneigung sucht er eine sublimierte Erfüllung im Jägerberuf, als ichbezogener Todestrieb äussert er sich in Christians Verlangen nach der Nähe der Gesteinswelt. Tieck findet als Ausdruck des Todestriebes, den er als solchen nicht wahrnimmt, aber offensichtlich dunkel spürt, das Bedürfnis nach engem Kontakt mit dem Mineralischen, dem Anorganischen. Es genügt nicht, für 'das primäre Interesse Tiecks am Anorganischen und seine zeichenhafte Verwendung' auf die 'Begegnung mit dem europäischen Volksmärchen' hinzuweisen, weil es die Verwandlung des Vegetabilischen ins Anorganische kennt und in Metallen und Erzen das 'Geheimnis des Erdinnern' und Momente des Wunderbaren sieht.[6] Gewiss vermittelt das Märchen literarisch verwendbare Motive, die Tieck zur Darstellung der seltsamen Erfahrungen Christians benützt. Aber das triebhafte, ihm selbst nicht verständliche Verlangen nach dem Mineralischen, das nicht identisch ist mit der

---

[1] Ebenda, S. 477 f.
[2] S. Freud, *Jenseits des Lustprinzips*. In: *Gesammelte Werke*, Bd. 13 (Frankfurt a. M. 1967⁵), S. 41.
[3] S. Freud, *Das Ich und das Es*, ebd., Bd. 13, S. 269.
[4] Ders., *Das Unbehagen in der Kultur*, ebd., Bd. 14, S. 478.
[5] Ebenda, S. 478.
[6] Siehe P. G. Klussmann, *Die Zweideutigkeit des Wirklichen in Ludwig Tiecks Märchennovellen*, ZfdPh 83 (1964) 445.

Begierde nach Schätzen (die Tieck allerdings zuweilen mitwirken lässt), und die radikale, hasserfüllte Abwertung des Organischen, die im Märchen kein Vorbild hat und aufs engste mit der Bevorzugung des Mineralischen zusammenhängt, lassen sich nicht aus der Märchentradition verstehen.

Deutlich ist die starke Anregung, die von Novalis ausgeht. Im *Ofterdingen* berichtet der böhmische Bergmann von der tiefen Faszination durch die unterirdischen Erze und Mineralien, auch durch einen Steinhaufen, 'den man Halde nennt'.[1] Er spricht von dem tiefen Glück beim ersten Begehen des Bergwerks. Er fühlt dort 'diese wundersame Freude an Dingen, die ein näheres Verhältnis zu unserm geheimen Dasein haben mögen . . .'[2] Aber bei Novalis muss der Bergbau 'von Gott gesegnet werden', er erhält 'die Unschuld und Kindlichkeit des Herzens reiner' als andere Künste.[3] Im Runenberg dagegen ist die Gesteinswelt dämonisch, gefährlich und gottfern. Auch ist sie hier nicht ein Symbolbereich für die schöpferische Existenz des Dichters, was sie nach der Deutung Werner Vordtriedes bei Novalis und in der Entfaltung des 'Unterreich'-Motivs im 19. Jahrhundert ist.[4]

Tiecks Erzählung gibt der Gesteinswelt in ihrer scharf akzentuierten Gegensätzlichkeit zur vergänglichen organischen Welt einen besonderen Sinn. Der Todestrieb ist nicht auf absolute Vernichtung gerichtet, sondern auf Auflösung des organisch Lebendigen, nämlich darauf, 'das Lebende in den anorganischen Zustand zu überführen'.[5] Das Lebende ist aus diesem Anorganischen entstanden und löst sich beim Tod wieder in dieses auf. Freud erkennt 'im Mit- und Gegeneinanderwirken der beiden Grundtriebe'[6] die Totalität des Lebens. Tieck konnte selbstverständlich ohne das Instrumentarium der Psychoanalyse die menschliche Triebstruktur nicht erklären, aber er erfasste intuitiv und beobachtend die Wirksamkeit eines lebensfeindlichen Prinzips im Menschen, und er schildert im Schicksal

[1] Novalis, *Schriften*, hrsg. von Paul Kluckhohn und Richard Samuel. Zweite, nach den Handschriften ergänzte, erweiterte und verbesserte Auflage in 4 Bdn., Stuttgart 1960 ff., Bd. 1, S. 240.
[2] Ebenda, S. 242.   [3] Ebenda, S. 244.
[4] Werner Vordtriede, *Novalis und die französischen Symbolisten*, Stuttgart 1963, S. 49, 53 u. ö. Tiecks *Runenberg* wird in diesem Buch nicht erwähnt.
[5] S. Freud, *Abriss der Psychoanalyse*. In: *Gesammelte Werke*, Bd. 17 (Frankfurt a. M. 1966⁴), S. 71.
[6] Ebenda, S. 71.

Christians mit äusserster Konssequenz, wie dieses Prinzip dominant wird und im Verlangen nach dem Anorganischen sich manifestiert. Dieses unwiderstehliche Verlangen bleibt auch dem Erzähler zuletzt unerklärlich. Er sagt z. B. bei der Schilderung von Christians gefährlichem Gang zum Runenberg: 'Er achtete nicht auf die Tiefe, die unter ihm gähnte und ihn zu verschlingen drohte, so sehr spornten ihn irre Vorstellungen und unverständliche Wünsche' (S. 66).

Die Interpretation muss noch einmal zu jener Stelle der Erzählung zurückkehren, an der Christians Aufbruch aus der Heimat dargestellt wird. Es ist jetzt deutlich, dass sein Leiden an der heimischen Welt eine doppelte Wurzel hat. Zunächst ist es, wie ich zeigte, verursacht durch die von der 'Kultur' geforderte Triebunterdrückung. Weiterhin aber lässt sich erschliessen, dass Christian weiss: diese durch grosse Opfer erkaufte Daseinsordnung erreicht keinen wahren Gewinn, kein dauerhaftes Gut, sondern sie dient nur der Erhaltung eines wachstümlichen Lebens, das ohnehin und trotz aller Mühen und Opfer hinfällig, vergänglich, wesenlos, ein ständiges Sterben ist. Nicht nur die Triebunterdrückung, sondern auch diese Einsicht in die Nichtigkeit des wachstümlichen Lebens bleibt den Menschen unbewusst, und deshalb kann Christian sagen, dass sie 'in der bejammernswürdigsten Unwissenheit lebten', und dass alle wie er selbst denken würden, 'wenn ihnen dieses Gefühl ihres Elendes nur ein einziges Mal in ihrer Seele aufginge' (S. 64).[1] Dass Christians Feststellung aus seiner Lebensfeindlichkeit verstanden werden muss, bestätigt eine bisher bei der Interpretation ausgesparte Stelle des vorangehenden Erzählungsteils: Christians Reaktion beim Klagelaut der Alraunwurzel, die er unbeabsichtigt ausreisst (S. 62). Tieck benützt hier das Sagenmotiv vom Wurzelmännchen, das, wenn man es ausreisst, einen durchdringenden Schrei ausstösst, der den Ausgräber tötet. Christian gibt jedoch dem Vorfall eine eigentümliche Deutung. 'Der Ton durchdrang sein innerstes Herz, er ergriff ihn, als wenn er unvermutet die Wunde berührt habe, an der der sterbende Leichnam der Natur in Schmerzen verscheiden wolle' (S. 63). Die wachstümliche Natur sieht Christian als 'sterbenden Leichnam' (S. 63), d. h. er sieht sie

[1] Die Menschen erkennen nach Christians Meinung ihr Elend so wenig, wie es z. B. die Kunstreiterin in Kafkas Erzählung *Auf der Galerie* erkennt.

unter dem lebensfeindlichen Aspekt des Todestriebes. Seine Worte weisen voraus auf eine spätere Stelle der Erzählung, an der sich Christian an die Alraunwurzel erinnert, die ihm 'das Unglück der ganzen Erde bekannt gemacht hat' (S. 77). Christian bekennt hier ausführlich seine Lebensfeindlichkeit. Es ist die Schlüsselstelle der ganzen Erzählung, von der noch zu sprechen sein wird. Dieses 'Unglück der ganzen Erde' macht also jenes 'Elend' der Menschen aus, dessen sie sich nicht bewusst werden. Es ist bedeutsam, dass in dem Augenblick, als Christian erschrocken den Klagelaut der Alraunwurzel vernommen hat, unvermittelt 'der Fremde' auftaucht: der Repräsentant der anorganischen Welt, der Erze und Metalle, die frei sind von der 'Wunde' der organischen Natur und nicht an der Vergänglichkeit, der Krankheit zum Tode leiden.

Dieser Fremde weist Christian auf den Runenberg, er erklärt suggestiv, 'wie schön und anlockend das alte Gestein zu uns hinblickt' (S. 66). Das dämonische Bergweib, das Christian später erblickt, ist eine Inkarnation der mineralischen Welt: übermenschlich gross (wie die Riesengestalt der Felsen), mit schwarzem Haar und weissen Gliedern 'wie Marmor' (S. 68), ohne Lebensfarben, mit goldenem Schleier ums Haupt, das Gesicht 'streng' (S. 67). Es ist kein erotischer Dämon, und wenn Christian die Erscheinung trotz Übergrösse und Strenge unvergleichlich 'schön' findet, so bezeichnet das die Anziehungskraft, die die anorganische, lebensferne Natur für ihn besitzt. Sie wirkt auch im funkelnden Glanz der Juwelen auf der magischen Tafel, deren geheimnisvolle Figur, unentzifferbar, wohl als Todeszeichen verstanden werden muss. Wenn sie 'sogleich in sein Inneres überging' (S. 68), so ist damit ausgedrückt, dass er als Lebender das anorganische Tote in sich aufnimmt und eine symbolische, man darf vielleicht sagen: sublimierte Erfüllung seines Todestriebes findet. Sein Vater, dem er später die wiedergefundene Tafel zeigt, deutet die Lineamente als Zeichen einer grausamen Macht: 'sieh her, wie kalt sie funkeln, welche grausame Blicke sie von sich geben, blutdürstig, wie das rote Auge des Tigers. Wirf diese Schrift weg, die dich kalt und grausam macht, die dein Herz versteinern muss' (S. 78).

Es ist völlig einleuchtend, dass in Christian, in dem der Todestrieb so einseitig dominiert, nach dessen Befriedigung der Lebenstrieb neue Geltung gewinnt. Beide Triebe sind im

Menschen nach der Lehre Freuds stets wirksam, in wechselndem Mischungsverhältnis. Der Umschlag erfolgt bei der tiefen Verwirrung Christians nach dem nächtlichen Abenteuer. Er geht ins Flachland, Gärten und Felder scheinen ihm jetzt anziehend. 'Seine Empfindungen und Wünsche der Nacht erschienen ihm ruchlos und frevelhaft', als 'gottlose Gefühle' (S. 69). Christian hat nichts Böses getan, erkennt aber jetzt seine Begegnung mit der Bergwelt als Schuld, weil sie eine lebensfeindliche Welt ist, die das von Gott geschenkte Leben und seine Erhaltung abwertet, die Christian den Priester in seiner Predigt feiern hört.

Christian wird Gärtner bei einem wohlhabenden Pächter, heiratet dessen Tochter, zeugt ein Kind, fühlt sich 'ganz einheimisch und befriedigt' (S. 71). Ebenso einseitig wie vorher der Todestrieb regiert ihn jetzt der lebensfreundliche Eros, er fügt sich ein, beugt sich der Kulturforderung nach Triebunterdrückung. Er hat sich also völlig den Ansprüchen des Vaters unterworfen, wandert nun folgerichtig zu diesem, um die Aussöhnung zu besiegeln. Der Vater ist seinerseits auf dem Wege zu ihm, Christian trifft ihn auf seiner Wanderung. Der Konflikt Vater-Sohn ist behoben. Christian trifft den Vater — eine überdeutliche Symbolik — beim liebevollen Betrachten einer seltenen Blume. Diese ist nicht, wie Marianne Thalmann meint, 'Hieroglyphe der Enge', sondern Symbol des Lebendigen, des Wachstümlichen-Organischen, so wie Stein und Metall nicht 'Symbol der Weite' sind, sondern Zeichen für das Leblose, die anorganische Materie.[1]

Der Vater zieht — er ist inzwischen Witwer — in das Haus des Sohnes, in 'das gute, fromme, ebene Land' (S. 73). Christian lebt viele Jahre völlig angepasst, aber der verdrängte Todestrieb bleibt in seinem Unbewussten wirksam und regt sich schliesslich wieder, das Pendel schwingt zurück. Er deutet hellsichtig seine eigene seelische Konstitution, wenn er später dem Vater sagt: 'ich kann auf lange Zeit, auf Jahre, die wahre Gestalt meines Innern vergessen, und gleichsam ein fremdes Leben mit Leichtigkeit führen: dann geht aber plötzlich wie ein neuer Mond das regierende Gestirn, welches ich selber bin, in meinem Herzen auf, und besiegt die fremde Macht' (S. 76). Sein eigentliches

---

[1] Vgl. Anmerkung 63, S. 894 in Bd. 2 der von M. Thalmann herausgegebenen Tieck-Ausgabe.

Zur Deutung von Ludwig Tiecks 'Der Runenberg'

Ich ist lebensfeindlich, von der Leidenschaft für das Anorganische erfüllt. Es gewinnt die Oberhand, als 'ein Fremder' ins Haus kommt und nach langer Besuchszeit beim Abschied eine grosse Geldsumme in Goldmünzen hinterlässt. Christian hat die frühere Begegnung mit 'dem Fremden' so entschieden verdrängt, dass er den Besucher nicht genau erkennt; doch 'es kam ihm vor, als kenne er den Reisenden schon von ehemals' (S. 74). Das zurückgelassene Geld fasziniert ihn, und zwar als Metall, nicht als Geld mit Kaufkraft, wenn er auch dem Vater gegenüber sein übermässiges Interesse an dem Gold durch seinen Vermögenswert für die Familie motiviert und später wirklich seinen Landbesitz damit vermehrt. Aber diese Umwandlung des dauerhaften, unveränderlichen Goldes in Dinge, die dem von Vergänglichkeit bestimmten Lebensprozess dienen, ist im Grunde nicht nach seinem Sinn. (Tatsächlich geht nach Christians Weggang später der durch das Gold erworbene Landbesitz schnell durch Seuchen, Misswachs usw. verloren, Christians Frau und ihr neuer Mann verarmen.) Christian zählt nachts die Goldstücke und sagt zu seinem Vater: 'seht, wie es mich jetzt wieder anblickt, dass mir der rote Glanz tief in mein Herz hineingeht! Horcht, wie es klingt, dies güldene Blut! das ruft mich, wenn ich schlafe . . .' (S. 74 f.). Der vergrösserte Landbesitz hält Christians zunehmende Verstörung nicht auf, sein Lachen ist 'wild und frech, sein Blick irre und fremd' (S. 75). Er will nicht mehr in Feld und Garten arbeiten, so berichtet die besorgte Frau dem Vater, er 'scheint sich vor allen Pflanzen und Kräutern wie vor Gespenstern zu entsetzen' (S. 75 f.). Der Vater beklagt den 'verwüstenden Hunger nach dem Metall', den Christian in der 'Gesellschaft der verwilderten Steine' erworben habe (S. 76).

'Nein', sagte der Sohn, 'ich erinnere mich ganz deutlich, dass mir eine Pflanze zuerst das Unglück der ganzen Erde bekannt gemacht hat, seitdem verstehe ich erst die Seufzer und Klagen, die allenthalben in der ganzen Natur vernehmbar sind, wenn man nur darauf hören wolle; in den Pflanzen, Kräutern, Blumen und Bäumen regt und bewegt sich schmerzhaft nur eine grosse Wunde, sie sind der Leichnam vormaliger herrlicher Steinwelten, sie bieten unserm Auge die schrecklichste Verwesung dar. Jetzt verstehe ich es wohl, dass es dies war, was mir jene Wurzel mit ihrem tiefgeholten Ächzen sagen wollte, sie vergass sich in ihrem Schmerze und verriet mir alles. Darum sind alle grünen Gewächse so erzürnt auf mich, und stehn mir nach dem Leben; sie wollen jene geliebte Figur in meinem Herzen auslöschen, und in jedem Frühling mit ihrer verzerrten Leichenmiene meine Seele gewinnen' (S. 77).

Hier ist gedanklich ausformuliert, was in der Erzählung vor sich geht: die Umkehrung, die Vertauschung der Werte, bei der das Anorganische als das Höhere erkannt, dass Organisch-Lebendige abgewertet wird. Die Gewächse, das vegetabilische Leben 'sind der Leichnam vormaliger herrlicher Steinwelten, sie bieten unserm Auge die schrecklichste Verwesung dar'. Der Organismus ist nicht eine Höherentwicklung der anorganischen Materie, sondern Verfallsform, das minderwertige Abfallprodukt der 'Steinwelten', die mittels der Verwandlung in pflanzliches Leben in Verwesung übergehen. Die Mineralien und Metalle sind nicht vergänglich und verweslich, sondern von dauerhaftem Bestand, und daher überlegen.

In einem Fragment von Novalis heisst es: 'Krankheiten der Pflanzen sind Animalisationen, Krankheiten der Tiere Rationalisationen, Krankheiten der Steine Vegetationen [...] Pflanzen sind gestorbene Steine, Tiere gestorbene Pflanzen.'[1] Diese Formulierungen sind nicht abwertend, sondern sie bezeichnen eher den Versuch, das Anorganische in die Gesamtheit eines allumfassenden Lebens einzubeziehen.

Der Todestrieb ersehnt statt des dem Sterben verfallenen Lebens das dauerhafte Dasein der anorganischen Substanz des Steins. Die Wirklichkeit unter dem Aspekt des Todestriebes zu sehen, bedeutet bei Tieck: das organische Leben nicht als blühendes Wachstum, sondern von seiner Gegenseite aus, als ständigen Prozess des Vergehens, des Absterbens zu begreifen.

Wenn Christian dem Vater diese lebensfeindliche Sehweise mitteilt, so spürt der alte Gärtner entsetzt, dass er damit sein eigenes Menschsein, das zur Lebenswelt gehört, verleumdet und sich ihm entfremdet, 'als wenn ein andres Wesen aus ihm, wie aus einer Maschine, unbeholfen und ungeschickt herausspiele' (S. 77). Tieck, in seiner Darstellung sehr konsequent bis in die Metaphern, bezeichnet mit dem Maschinenvergleich das Nichtorganische, das Mechanische in dem sich selbst entfremdeten Christian.

[1] *Novalis, Werke, Briefe, Dokumente*, hrsg. von Ewald Wasmuth, Heidelberg 1953-7, 3. Bd., Fragmente II, S. 151.

Es ist sehr bezeichnend, was in Christian, der noch eine Weile in seinem Landleben verharrt, den Entschluss zu seinem zweiten Aufbruch ins Gebirge auslöst. Es ist eine neue Wahrnehmung des Vergehens alles Lebendigen, nämlich im Altern seiner Frau, die 'nicht mehr ein blühendes kindliches Mädchen' ist (S. 77). Er sagt sich: 'so habe ich mutwillig ein hohes ewiges Glück aus der Acht gelassen, um ein vergängliches und zeitliches zu gewinnen' (S. 78). Er verlässt sein Haus, geht in den Wald, meint dort von fern den Fremden zu sehen, aber die sich nähernde Gestalt ist ein altes hässliches Waldweib, das ihn anredet. Als sie weggeht, erscheint sie Christian wie das Bergweib mit dem goldenen Schleier. Er findet dann die magische Tafel wieder, die ihn nun endgültig in den Bann der mineralischen Welt zieht. Er geht in den verfallenen Schacht, bleibt verschwunden, gilt im Dorf als umgekommen.

Wenn er nach Jahren zum letzten Mal, alt und verkommen, in dem Dorf auftaucht und seine inzwischen wiederverheiratete Frau und seine Kinder trifft, so ist sein seltsames Gebaren bei dieser Wiederkehr nur auf Grund seiner vorausgehenden Geschichte richtig deutbar. Tieck lässt ihn nicht etwa Bergmann werden, was nahezuliegen scheint, aber dem Sinn der Erzählung zuwiderlaufen würde. Denn die sinnvolle Arbeit des Bergmanns dient jenem Leben, von dem sich Christian abwendet. Sie wäre, mit Freuds Begriffen interpretiert, Verlagerung libidinöser Energien in notwendig-nützliche Tätigkeit. Christian sucht Schätze im 'rauhesten Gebirge auf Erden' (S. 81), aber er hat nur wertlose Kiesel in seinem Sack. Er hält sie für Edelsteine. Kostbare Edelsteine lassen sich nicht am Wege finden, sondern nur in harter Arbeit unter Tage gewinnen. Dazu ist Christian nicht bereit, er folgt nur seinem Triebe, der ihn leblose Steine zu suchen zwingt, und er findet und sammelt sie in ihrer armseligsten Form. Aber Christian bleibt trotz seiner Verstörung und Selbstentfremdung doch noch an die Bedingungen des menschlichen Lebewesens gebunden, und so möchte er, dass die Steine 'Auge und Blick' (S. 81) hätten, dass sie farbig leuchteten und damit, trotz der Kälte dieses Glanzes, an die Farben des Lebendigen erinnerten. So versucht er, die Kiesel zur Hergabe ihres Glanzes zu zwingen. Das Feuer ist in ihnen verborgen, 'aber man muss es nur herausschlagen, dass sie sich fürchten, dass keine Verstellung ihnen mehr nützt . . .' (S. 81).

Er schlägt die Steine heftig gegeneinander, so dass Funken sprühen. Marianne Thalmann deutet diese abschliessende Szene als 'Triumph des Vorstellungsvermögens über die wahrgenommene Welt'.[1] Schon die gewaltsame Behandlung der Kiesel widerlegt diese unhaltbare Deutung. Christian ist am Schluss verstört, vom Wahn umfangen. Das ist die Folge seiner Selbstzerstörung durch den übermächtigen Todestrieb. Im Grunde sind die Steine als solche, auch in ihrer alltäglichsten Form, für ihn schon das Wertvolle; sie sind der Schatz, den er unbewusst im Banne des Todestriebes sucht. Dass er sich dabei in dem Wahn verfängt, deutet Tiecks Distanzierung von dieser extremen Figur an. Tieck geht es hier nicht um Romantisierung der Wirklichkeit, sondern eher darum, die Begrenzung menschlicher Existenz, ihr Angewiesensein auf das 'Realitätsprinzip', die Gefahr einer Abwendung vom Lebensvollzug zur Geltung zu bringen. Das weist voraus auf Tiecks Spätwerk, in dem der conditio humana ihr Recht widerfährt.

[1] Vgl. Anm. 81, S. 895 in Bd. 2 der von M. Thalmann herausgegebenen Tieck-Ausgabe.

Keller's *Der Grüne Heinrich* the Pattern of the Labyrinth

FREDERICK STOPP

ALL literary history, like political history, is an attempt to infer a sequent order in the living raw material, rooted as it is in an order of reality which is in the last analysis refractory to the discursive mind. The historian announces 'the rise of the merchant classes', and seeks thereby to impose a pattern; the literary historian proclaims the 'Bildungsroman', and seeks to infer a tradition. Against the daily evidence of discontinuity and inconsequentiality in human affairs, he posits continuity between A and B, in this case between Goethe's *Meister* and Keller's *Grüner Heinrich*. Such terms are maieutic: they direct attention, invite examination, stimulate discussion. They are also power surrogates, take-over bids—the latest case is 'emblematic'—and last only as long as the old stag is not challenged by a younger one.

The 'Bildungsroman' is said to be a narrative of 'eine gesetzmässige Entwicklung... im Leben des Individuums angeschaut' (W. Dilthey).[1] In this strict sense it is anchored in the culture of the eighteenth century; indeed, the concept is mainly and originally inferred from the leading example, *Wilhelm Meisters Lehrjahre*. This novel, as described by nineteenth-century scholars, is the type-fossil. But the field geologists then get to work, and find further examples far and wide. It is 'die Grossform des deutschen Romans im klassisch-romantischen Zeitalter'. Or it is 'die deutsche Grossform des Romans überhaupt'. *Simplicissimus* and *Der Zauberberg* are now linked up. *Parzival* too must not be forgotten; *Stopfkuchen* is brought in; *Heinrich von Ofterdingen* is a kind of 'Bildungsroman' upside down. Anything which is not a 'Bildungsroman' becomes a 'Gegenströmung'; novels of our century represent the 'decline' or 'decay 'of the 'Bildungsroman'. The terms 'deutsch' and 'Grossform' bring in the big battalions; any further critical discussion must skate

[1] This and other formulations in these two paragraphs are from H. H. Borcherdt, 'Bildungsroman', in *Reallexikon*, 2nd edn., pp. 175-7.

on the thin ice of 'comparative literature' and national psychology, where many noble minds have come to grief.

Keller has a word for this. 'Es wird Revalenta arabica gemacht in der Kunst und Wissenschaft' (*GH* IV. 4, see below);[1] as a creative artist he had every right to this view. But if we, as critics, do not wish to skate on thin ice, we should take our position on firmer ground, and emphasize discontinuity where we can. *Der grüne Heinrich* provides such firm ground. Admittedly, Heinrich Lee does work his way through spheres of human experience in the classical manner: family, love, religion, society, politics, art; what educated man can avoid such confrontations? His aim is, if not 'Bildung', at least some kind of self-clarification; again, who does otherwise? But the 'einheitliche Grundlinie: vom Irrtum zur Wahrheit, von Verworrenheit zur Klarheit, vom Unbewussten zum Bewussten' is at least not very evident, and the patent tragedy of the first version, the muted harmonies of the second, and indeed the very length of the book enjoin caution. Further, the work is strongly autobiographical; must we then assume that, even if Heinrich Lee did not progress from confusion to clarity, his creator at least did? The interminable gestation of the work alone would throw doubt on this.

In the space available we cannot deal with the problem of Lee versus Keller, nor with intellectual currents of the time, and especially the influence of Feuerbach—though it will be quite clear where he might be brought in; nor with the other works of Keller. But there is one image in the work which takes us near the heart of the matter, that of the labyrinth, with its related cluster of associations. There are few things more basic to the human mind than the image of the labyrinth, and few images closer to the very nature of the poetic imagination. It is archetypal and it arouses in the poet's mind such consistent poetic ideas as 'Gewebe' (Goethe) and 'Textur und Faser der Wirklichkeit' (Keller); so that, with its aid, we may read something of his instinctive processes in a field which is as little affected by 'cultural overlay'—I mean the effect of a writer being consciously influenced by a revered poetic model, in this

[1] References are to the thin-paper Hanser edition by Clemens Heselhaus, which prints in one book (*Sämtliche Werke*, Band I) both first and second versions, the first to IV. 15 (book and chapter will be cited thus), and the second from III. 9 (break at p. 773). Page references are given after direct quotations, also to this edition.

the Pattern of the Labyrinth 131

case *Wilhelm Meister*—as are the basic traits of a man's handwriting. We may for instance note, with its aid, the extent to which Keller was preoccupied with the destructive effect in a man's relations with his fellows of the uncontrolled and unbridled exercise of the poetic imagination in its disordered form (what W. Preisendanz calls 'die Unverantwortlichkeit der Einbildungskraft'). Lastly, because of its archetypal content, the image of the labyrinth is capable of being charged with a great variety of tones, from positive to negative, and of degrees of significance, from concretion to abstraction, so that we can follow it in numerous disguises through all the spheres of Heinrich Lee's progression. It is like a trace element as used in physiological experiments. In this manner we shall be in a good position to observe by inference the real discontinuity of the work from others with which it may seem, at first sight, to be linked in a historical tradition.

There is a well-known passage in a letter (dated 31 August 1794) from Schiller to Goethe: 'denn gewöhnlich übereilte mich der Poet, wo ich philosophieren sollte, und der philosophische Geist, wo ich dichten wollte.' It is much less well known that Keller has an almost identical statement in *GH* IV. 1, where he is describing the effect on him of the lectures on human anatomy and physiology which he attended in Munich:

> Indem die Lehre von unserer Menschennatur sich zusehends abrundete, bemerkte ich nicht ohne Verwunderung, wie die Dinge neben ihrer sachlichen Form in meiner Einbildung zugleich eine phantastisch typische Gestalt annahmen, welche zwar die Kraft des Vorstellens in den Hauptzügen erhöhte, hingegen das genauere Erkennen des Einzelkleinen gefährdete. Das rührte von der Gewöhnung des malerischen Bildwesens her, die sich jetzt einmischte, wo das Gedankenwesen herrschen sollte, während dieses sich wiederum an die Stelle drängte, die jenem gebührte. (p. 918.)

The extent to which this was in fact true of either writer is not for discussion at this point; my purpose here is rather to point out that the next sentence gives an example of this imaginative intuition of a scientific truth, namely the circulation of the blood, which is of the greatest significance for the poetic structure of the novel:

> So sah ich den Kreislauf des Blutes gleich in Gestalt eines prächtigen Purpurstromes, an welchem wie ein bleiches Schemen das

weissgraue Nervenwesen sass, eine gespenstische Gestalt, die, in den Mantel ihrer Gewebe gehüllt, begierig trank und schlürfte und die Kraft gewann, sich proteusartig in alle Sinne zu verwandeln.

To isolate in summary form the items of this description: a lifegiving, all-pervasive system supports a principle which is capable of unlimited, protean transformation. I next refer briefly to two occasions where the image is used in quite different contexts, as a kind of type and anti-type of the same basic pattern.

Firstly the type, generalized and applied in a social context. Quite late in the novel, when Heinrich has failed in his primary artistic ambitions, and is feeling a deep lack of the sustaining strength which comes through contact with the home soil of Switzerland, one of his dreams features the constant procession of people across a bridge, and their intermingling with a series of Swiss classes, occupations, and types, shown on numerous wall-paintings depicted in a 'Brückenhalle' (p. 659, cf. also p. 663). The life of a community, with its changing composition in time, the interaction of past and present in the national memory, and their joint promise for the future, is seen under the splendid image of the 'wunderbar belebten Brücke', and is finally summed up by Keller thus: 'und der ganze Verkehr war wie ein Blutumlauf in durchsichtigen Adern.'

Again, in a quite different sphere, the reverse or anti-image is brought in to describe the deluded convictions of the unfortunate artist called Römer, that the whole round of European government and politics is only kept going by a draining of his creative genius and intellectual energies: 'Doch bald darauf deutete er mir an, dass alle Fäden der europäischen Politik in seiner Hand zusammenliefen' (p. 423): so that a moment's relaxation of mental concentration on his part would result in general confusion in public affairs. At the same time, of course, he is the victim of a wicked plot to deprive him of the fruits and rewards of this universal utilization, so that he is at one and the same time 'der verborgene Mittelpunkt aller Weltregierung' and 'das Opfer unerhörter Tyranneien und Misshandlungen', in that 'sie ihm täglich gerade soviel von seinem Genius abzapften, als sie zu ihrer kleinlichen Weltbesorgung gebrauchten'. The image is a deranged inversion of that of the organic circulation of blood in a human or social body: a man preyed upon,

the Pattern of the Labyrinth

tortured by the world-wide power-net of which he is the secret centre and vivifying principle, forced to supply his life-blood or mental energy as required through a system of inhuman conduits, 'das Räderwerk meines Geistes' (p. 424).

The image of blood-circulation is, however, a much more highly developed and sophisticated form of one which in Keller occurs more commonly in the less differentiated mode of 'Gewebe' (fabric or texture), 'Gewirre' or 'Wirrnis', 'Wirrsal', and 'Netz', and, finally, 'Labyrinth'. In the earlier chapters of the work, in Books I and II, where, under the heading of 'Zurück zur Natur', Heinrich describes the young Heinrich's sojourn with his relatives in the country after the frustrations of town life, Nature, that rich, burgeoning, colourful, ever-fertile mother of us all, is referred to constantly under the term 'Wildnis', 'Wirrnis', 'Gewebe', 'Gewirre'. At random one may pick out 'eine reizende Wirrnis', 'eine grüne Wirrnis', 'die holde Wildnis', 'stille grüne Wildnisse'. The reason for this, of course, is that Keller is here emphasizing, in the locality which preserves the roots of his own family, the never-ending sequence of generations which make up the life-history of a community, and the constant renewal of life out of death. So the graves in the ancient village cemetery are covered by wild flowers and bushes, 'und nur der Totengräber kennt genau die Grenze in diesem Wirrsal, wo das frisch umzugrabende Gebiet anfängt'; the bushes, flowers, and insects, with their eternal buzzing, which cover the graves are a 'zartes Gewebe' over past centuries of communal history. Here first love can declare itself without embarrassment: when Heinrich and Anna exchange their first kisses over the fresh grave of Heinrich's grandmother, we read of 'die verworrenen Schatten der üppigen Grabgesträuche' (p. 248).

As before, there is the counter-image, commonly using the term 'Netz': against this positive criterion of 'Natur', all forms of 'Un-Natur' in *Der grüne Heinrich*, and especially in the early part, are measured and found wanting. For Heinrich, the one jarring note in the village is the unattractive, eighteenth-century church, pointing the contrast between the bloodless formalism of established religion and the divine spark in the soul of man, not to be imprisoned in 'das hanfene, dürrgeflochtene Netz eines Katechismus' (p. 27). Other examples of negative, compulsive, life-denying activities in the work are: the invasion of life by fiction, family degeneracy brought about by cheap reading, in two episodes in I. 12 (version 2) called 'Die Leserfamilie, Lügenzeit', 'so dass wir uns in ein ungeheures Lügennetz verwoben und verstrickt sahen' (p. 133); the boy to whom Heinrich boasted of a non-existent 'Geliebte', and who 'umwickelte mich mit einem moralischen Zwangsnetze' (p. 136); and the other tempter of Heinrich's younger years, the pestiferous Meierlein, who possessed in a high degree the gift of 'mit verständiger Besprechung alles zu überspinnen, Verhältnisse auszuklügeln und mit vielsagender Miene Aufschlüsse und Vermutungen aufzustellen, welche über unser Alter hinausgingen' (p. 152). Finally, on the burlesque level, the first long day spent by Heinrich in the village, full to the brim with new and confusing impressions, new contacts, and the unmerciful teasing of his flirtatious female cousins, ended with his tumbling into— an apple-pie bed: 'Mit sehr gemischten Empfindungen machte ich vorsichtig das Fenster zu und suchte in meinem boshaften Leinwandlabyrinth Mädchen, Liebe, Mainacht und Verdruss zu vergessen' (p. 284).

The image is indeed ambivalent, both morally and in its subservience or otherwise to the human will: 'ein zartes Gewebe' can in a moment change its nature and become 'ein Zwangsnetz'; so especially in the sphere of love, as when associated with the beautiful and sensual Judith, she being—like many of Keller's female figures—half Pomona, half Circe. His first meeting with his charming distant cousin is bathed in the innocence of nature, when she comes into the house with an apronful of new apples and fresh-cut flowers: 'Dies schüttete sie alles auf den Tisch, wie eine reizende Pomona, dass ein Gewirre von Form, Farbe und Duft sich auf der blanken Tafel verbreitete' (p. 192). But after Heinrich's relations with Judith *and* Anna have become more conscious, his visits to Judith in the village at night, 'als sie mich bei der Hand nahm und zwischen Hecken und Mauern durch ein dunkles Wirrsal führte' (p. 380), and again, his seeking her out in the mist—'Ich sah mich bald in ein Netz von schmalen Garten- und Wiesenpfaden versetzt'— show how guilt can arise out of innocence. Before the episode where, rising from the water of the stream, she shows herself naked to Heinrich, the two 'gingen gerade dem Waldbache entlang, über welchem der Mond ein geheimnisvolles Netz von *the Pattern of the Labyrinth*

Dunkel und Licht zittern liess' (p. 444). Here and in other passages, the painterly note of chiaroscuro is used by Keller to show the close association between innocence of intention and guilt of conscious realization which is the very stuff of life as it is lived. When Heinrich saunters along the same stream with Anna, '[sie] schritt anmutig neben mir her durch das Helldunkel, durch welches die heimlich leuchtenden Wellen über rosenrote, weisse und blaue Steine rieselten' (p. 239).

In the same way as the profusion of human experience can hold guilt and innocence in suspension, so the profusion of natural abundance is a great unifier of differences: where divisions are not sharpened dialectically into direct opposites, as with the 'Un-Natur' of established religious practice, the resulting mood is irenical. So in the description of the house and village of Heinrich's uncle and his family, and of their mode of life, unifying notes are to be found on every page (see especially pp. 193–5). The house, once the seat of an aristocrat, had had wedged into it all the peasant activities of the present incumbent of the parish, 'dass sich beide Elemente, das junkerhafte und das bäuerliche, verschmolzen und durch wunderliche Türen und Durchgänge verbanden' (p. 193). Round the parsonage there was a 'reizende Wildnis', with kitchen and flower garden, juniper bushes, fountains, a small bridge over water leading to a mill, so that 'Das Ganze war eine Verschmelzung von Pfarrei, Bauerhof, Villa und Jägerhaus' (p. 195). The happy Heinrich, released from the inhibitions and restrictions of town life, found his early 'Spieltrieb' converted into a serious desire to work and create, to write, draw, or paint, 'was weiss ich was alles!'; his creative urge focuses, for the moment, on landscape-painting. To return to our opening image, the deep red healing stream circulates through him and releases the life-energy, with its protean capacity to express itself, potentially, in any of the spheres of the senses.

In counterpoint with the house of Heinrich's uncle is the timber-merchant's yard which is described much later: productive confusion in an industrial rather than a peasant and rustic setting. It occurs when Heinrich receives his first lesson in public affairs and the interrelation of private interest and public advantage at the hand of the 'Stadthalter'. The question is, whether a new road projected by the community shall run along the hill, where the innkeeper who has taken the part of Tell in a 'Volksspiel' has his family property, or along the line of the river where the timber-merchant has established his yard. His commercial activities are the epitome of fertile chaos and productive confusion; the master-plan is to have no masterplan, in the sense of one who

> es vorzieht, unscheinbare räucherige Gebäude, Werkstatt an Werkstatt, Schuppen an Schuppen zu reihen, wie es Bedürfnis und Gewinn erlauben, bald provisorisch, bald solid, nach und nach, aber immer rascher mit der Zeit, dass es raucht und dampft, pocht und hämmert an allen Ecken, während jeder Beschäftigte in dem lustigen Wirrsal seinen Griff und Tritt kennt. (p. 353.)

> Brenn- und Bauholz, Kohlen, Eisen und Stein bildeten in ungeheuren Vorräten ein grosses Labyrinth. (p. 354.)

> Es lag ein grosser Reichtum darin, aber dieser änderte täglich seine äussere Gestalt. (p. 355.)

'Aber dieser änderte täglich seine äussere Gestalt'; we are reminded again of the hypostatized figure of the 'weissgraues Nervenwesen' in Keller's description of the blood-circulation, 'eine gespenstische Gestalt, die . . . die Kraft gewann, sich proteusartig in alle Sinne zu verwandeln'.

After these youthful episodes in a Swiss setting, there follows the account of Heinrich's inner odyssey in the artistic capital of Munich: his increasing despair on failing to become an artist, his love for Hulda, the humble seamstress, and the apparent solution of his problems offered by Dortchen Schönfund. This inner odyssey is accompanied by labyrinth images indicative of his progressive loss of constructive inspiration in his art, and a failed sense of colour, motivated by long absence from the soil of his homeland and the link with his mother.

At some stage in these hundreds of pages we may and do ask: what kind of pictures *does* he paint? The answer is clear and very depressing. We hear of 'Seine ungeheuerlichen Kartons mit den abenteuerlichen Kompositionen, die grossen blassen Bilder auf Leinwand bildeten zusammen ein Labyrinth von verschiedenen helldunklen Gelassen und Winkeln . . .' (p. 559). Then again, there are historical compositions from the Germanic past, an Auerochs hunt, a medieval township. One striking masterpiece of futility and spiritual anaemia, and telling evidence of his progressive melancholia, is an enormous cartoon of framed grey paper, showing on its lower edge a summary foreground of pine-trees, while the rest of the expanse is covered with an apparently senseless network of strokes: 'Über den ganzen übrigen leeren Raum schien ein ungeheures graues Spinnennetz zu hangen.... An eine gedankenlose Kritzelei, welche Heinrich in einer Ecke angebracht, um die Feder zu probieren, hatte sich nach und nach ein unendliches Gewebe von Federstrichen angesetzt, welches er jeden Tag und fast jede Stunde in zerstreutem Hinbrüten weiterspann, so dass es nun den grössten Teil des Rahmens bedeckte' (p. 560). Closer examination, however, showed that there was an incipient method in this madness: this is a genuine labyrinth, presenting a theoretical, but as yet undiscovered, way of escape. This 'Wirrsal' of lines was 'ein Labyrinth, das vom Ausgangspunkte bis zum Ende zu verfolgen war'; while the presence of numerous minor decorative patterns and convoluted, knotted areas showed that the artist was at least seeking a way out of these 'Irrgänge'—'dass das träumende Bewusstsein Heinrichs aus irgendeiner Patsche hinauszukommen suchte' (p. 561). Kerényi has shown with a wealth of illustration from ancient motifs, both mythical and artistic, that the labyrinth as an archetypal image stands for the underworld, but does offer a way of escape by its very regularity, since there *is* a centre and a way out. But the way out is normally via the centre, by accepting the rules of the labyrinth, rather than by trying to break down the hedges.

It is doubtful whether Heinrich is ever liberated finally from this net of indecision, since both offers of release come from without, through the assertion of the will of some stronger and less complicated personality: Erikson and Dortchen Schönfund. First, Erikson, who simply walks behind the monstrous cartoon and thrusts his fist through the middle: 'Was soll das Gekritzel? Frisch, halte dich oben, mache dich heraus aus dem verfluchten Garne! Da ist wenigstens ein Loch!' (p. 910). But Erikson's solution to Heinrich's lack of real inspiration, husbanding his artistic resources and marrying the rich widow Rosalie, is not that of Heinrich himself.

Secondly, Dortchen Schönfund. Heinrich's despairing project of returning to the revivifying maternal soil on foot is positively delayed by his stay with Dortchen and her adoptive father; and he does not, in the end, offer marriage at the right moment. So he both loses a wife and contributes further to his mother's death. Significantly, instead of proceeding by the direct highway to Switzerland, Heinrich is led astray at night by successive confusing road-forks (the labyrinth again, cf. Reinhart's arrival at Lucie's house in *Das Sinngedicht*), and ultimately seeks refuge from the rain in the most inviting corner of the chapel on the estate—which turns out, appropriately, to be a confessional (pp. 673 and 684). Here, at the estate, there awaits him welcome financial assistance: the Count produces fragments of one of his larger 'Kartenkompositionen' (which Heinrich had sold piecemeal to make a few coppers a sheet), pays him handsomely for the sheets, and commissions him to reassemble them, after which, he is assured, 'es wird ein Netz von feinen Fugen sichtbar bleiben, das nichts schadet' (p. 1030). But this reassembly of the associated Germanic fantasies of his Munich years, leaving only the faint scars of suffering in the mind ('ein Netz von feinen Fugen'), is not a final solution, since sorrow and guilt cannot be banished from Heinrich's life while his mother remains alive—and only just.

The death of the mother and Heinrich's own death were to form the 'zypressendunklen Schluss, wo alles begraben wurde', as Keller wrote, of the first version. But, even before he leaves Munich, Heinrich is brought a truly heart-rending account of her life, again in the form of a net image: 'Sie sitzt den ganzen Tag am Fenster und spinnt, sie spinnt jahraus und ein, als ob sie zwölf Töchter auszusteuern hätte, und zwar, wie sie sagt, damit ... wenigstens ihr Sohn für sein Leben lang und für sein ganzes Haus genug Leinwand finde. Wie es scheint, glaubt sie durch diesen Vorrat weissen Tuches ... Ihr Glück herbeizulocken, gleichsam wie ein aufgespanntes Netz ...' (646–7). The image strikes home in Heinrich's mind, and recurs in his dreams: 'Am Bächlein aber stand ihr Spinnrad, das mit Schaufeln versehen und eigentlich ein kleines Mühlrad war und sich blitzschnell drehte; sie spann nur mit der einen Hand den leuchtenden Faden, der sich nicht auf die Spule wickelte, sondern kreuz und quer dem Abhang herumzog und sich da sogleich zu grossen Flächen blendender Leinwand bildete' (p. 656). The endless spinning and weaving of a fabric is a mirror-image of Heinrich's lone 'Kritzelei'. The mother, who *the Pattern of the Labyrinth*

appears 'uralt und gebeugt' in his dream, has received a transfusion from the mythical figure of the Norn of Fate spinning the thread of life; both are engaged in an archetypal activity of which the only term is death or a return to the maternal soil and reuniting of mother and son. No amount of philosophical and ethical reorientation in Dortchen Schönfund's country house can alter this.

We may, I think, at this point draw a brief comparison with *Seldwyla*. Here the labyrinth image plays the role of illuminating satirically the personalities of his more memorable eccentrics: Pankraz, Züs Bünzlin, Jon Kabys, Strapinsky. One example: the story of *Der Schmied seines Glückes* is based on the folk-situation of the schemer hoist with his own petard. John Kabys carried round with him 'das komplizierteste und zierlichste aller Geldtäschchen mit unendlich geheimnisvollen Abteilungen', a summary in a nutshell of his own tortuous plans and character. When, finally, with his own effective assistance, the wife of his benefactor bears a child and heir, 'er zappelte in einem unzerreisslichen Netze'. Type and anti-type are used at important points: the labyrinth is exciting and engrossing till bearings are lost; eine reizende Wirrnis' then becomes 'ein Netz', from which there is no escape. But the tone is mainly one of farce and burlesque.

The problem really becomes serious when the image of the labyrinth acquires moral implications, and this happens in *Der grüne Heinrich*. Keller shows a keen intuition here of the manner in which human moral responsibility is interwoven contrapuntally of apparent opposites, when human sufferings are 'durcheinander gemischt und mit Schuld und Unschuld so durchwebt . . . dass ein eigener Linné nötig wäre, sie einzureihen' (p. 31). And again, when discovering that the objectionable person called Gilgus has at least the merit of having had a devoted mother, Heinrich reflects: 'So ist unser Leben aus Wirrsal gewebt, dass wir dem Nächsten kaum einen Tadel zuwenden, den wir nicht, noch eh er ihn vernommen, auf uns selbst beziehen können' (p. 1062). And always, the disordered imagination is deeply implicated. Very early in the book, when describing the deep imaginative impact made on Heinrich's mind by the exciting and esoteric treasures of Frau Margot's 'Trödlerladen', Keller uses the image of the warp and the woof:

'Mit all diesen Eindrücken beladen, zog ich über die Gasse wieder nach Hause und spann in der Stille unserer Stube den Stoff zu grossen träumerischen Geweben aus, wozu die erregte Phantasie den Einschlag gab' (p. 104), and he follows up this statement by a disquisition on the strength of his luxuriant and inventive imagination as a child, and then immediately there is the account of an episode at school where Heinrich, through his innocent inability to distinguish between moral truth and imaginative lies, involves some other boys in serious trouble (pp. 105–8).

Goethe used the identical image of the warp and the woof in his famous description of 'das Dämonische' in *Dichtung und Wahrheit*, Book 20: 'so steht es [das Dämonische] vorzüglich mit dem Menschen im wunderbarsten Zusammenhange und bildet eine der moralischen Ordnung, wo nicht entgegengesetzte, doch sie durchkreuzende Macht, so dass man die eine für den Zettel, die andere für den Einschlag könnte gelten lassen.' But the difference is wide and instructive. Goethe is concerned with a cosmic view: the relations between actions within the moral order and the logic of events as they seem determined from without. Keller is concerned with a view of the mind: how imagination can inform reality, deflecting the mind from moral truth, or can part company with reality and the nourishing material basis of experience, and develop a false and debilitating form of fantasy. In both cases a problem is set and a dilemma involved. Goethe's cosmic view requires Ottilie to escape from the conflict between the moral and the daemonic order by transcending it and rising to the metaphysical, and vistas are opened to problems dealt with by Hebbel. Keller, before concluding his exploration of the life problem of Heinrich, engages in a broad conservative criticism of society for permitting and fostering a growing alienation from basic materials and from a concern with useful, though humble, goods and activities. These views form a canvas against which Heinrich's final solution for life can be seen, and are contained largely in the latter and artistically inferior parts of *Der grüne Heinrich*. But they are closely linked with the problems of the artistic imagination on the personal plane; and, in so far as Keller is speaking here *in propria persona*, they tell us much about his own kind of poetic imagination.

Keller reveals here two preoccupations, obsessions almost, both turning on a form of alienation from reality, as he sees it: the one, the contrast between reality and abstraction in the mind; the other, that between true and false values in society, summed up in his references to a patent food which burst upon Europe in mid century, called 'Revalenta arabica'.

In the course of his reflections on the lessons of German history and law, to which Heinrich turns after his disappointment with his artistic career in Munich, the crux comes in the statement: 'So gewann nun Heinrich durch die unmittelbare Anschauung solcher Dinge, erst eine lebendige Liebe zu der Geschichte, wie überhaupt die unmittelbare Kenntnis der Faser und der Textur der Wirklichkeit tiefere, nachhaltigere und fruchtbarere Begeisterung erweckt in allen Übungen als alles abstrakte Phantasieren' (p. 590). The following passages contrast again, in violent terms, the 'organisch-notwendige Gewebe' and 'Textur der Dinge' with 'alles gewaltsame Räsonnieren' which causes people to 'eine ungleichmütige Verwirrung bald feiger, bald übermütiger Stimmungen und Forderungen über die Dinge auszugiessen, die sie nicht begreifen'. Similarly, artists and writers, especially those inferior 'Schriftmenschen' who are engaged in something they are pleased to call 'cultural life', are so isolated from the natural foundations of normal food, goods, and materials that they cannot be said to receive these material foundations of life from the primary producers, directly, but only through other middlemen, and are thus doubly removed from 'nature': 'und eine künstliche abstrakte Existenz führen, so dass der ganze Verkehr ein Gefecht in der Luft, eine ungeheuere Abstraktion ist, hoch über dem festen Boden der Mutter Natur' (p. 601). This view can be seen as a generalization of Heinrich's own personal situation: on his way south towards home—in fact towards Dortchen Schönfund—he is able to rescue from a bullying forester an old woman gathering firewood, and he feels the warmth of a good deed percolating through his cold and hungry frame: 'und es wollte ihn bedünken, als ob eine solche fortgesetzte und fleissige Tätigkeit in lebendigem Menschenstoffe doch etwas ganz anderes wäre als das abgeschlossene Phantasieren auf Papier und Leinwand . . .' (p. 677).

I turn to 'Revalenta arabica' and what it teaches us concerning true and false values in society. There is a curious story behind this reference to a food product whose name is now totally forgotten.[1] It was launched on a gullible public about 1851 and acquired considerable fame and notoriety as an alleged invalid food. It was, quite simply, a mixture of ground common or red lentils and barley flour. First called '*Er*valenta' (from *Ervum lens*, or lentil, on the analogy, no doubt, of Polenta), the name was changed to '*Re*valenta', so that, under this new title, 'the article was better concealed and some mystification gained', as a correspondent wrote in 1864. Our own Sir Richard Burton wrote, in his 'Pilgrimage to El Medina and Meccah' (1855), speaking of an Arabian dish of lentils: 'This grain is cheaper than rice on the banks of the Nile—a fact which enlightened England, now paying a hundred times its value for "Revalenta Arabica", apparently ignores.' The product was therefore an early form of commercial exploitation and of food adulteration. Keller was scathing about certain material inventions, which are often based on pure speculation, such as 'Revalenta arabica', and of such preparations says: 'das Ganze [ist] ein skandalöser Schwindel und sein Kern eine hohle Nuss . . . eine ungeheuere Blase der Zeit . . .' (p. 603). But such speculative developments, he continues, are also not uncommon in intellectual life, where the total result may be of no greater value, and indeed amounts to a dangerous deceit: 'Es wird Revalenta arabica gemacht in der Kunst und Wissenschaft, in Theologie und Politik, in Philosophie und bürgerlicher Ehre aller Art' (p. 103).

What has all this to do with the image of the labyrinth? Simply this: in our opening quotation, under the impact of a scientist's lectures on physiology, Heinrich, and surely Keller speaking through his fictional creation, noted 'nicht ohne Verwunderung, wie die Dinge neben ihrer sachlichen Form in meiner Einbildung zugleich eine phantastisch typische Gestalt annahmen, welche zwar die Kraft des Vorstellens in den Hauptzügen erhöhte, hingegen das genauere Erkennen des Einzelkleinen gefährdete' so that the 'Gewöhnung des malerischen Bildwesens . . . sich einmischte, wo das Gedankenwesen herrschen sollte . . .'. One fundamental pictorial image which runs throughout the work is that of the labyrinth and its associated

[1] My information is derived from old issues of *Notes and Queries*.

the Pattern of the Labyrinth 143

sub-images: a perfect instrument in a poetical context, since by the very reason of its protean convertibility it can be soaked in concrete intuitions and yet can also emerge at the level of life-denying abstraction. When the fictional canvas is enlarged beyond the personal problems of love, art, and the factors in a man's environment which operate directly on the life of his imagination and his art—regional roots, family ties, and a mother's love—the image is retained, but transformed, and an attitude of emotional negation drains the broad prospect of significance. Established habits of imaginative reaction endanger 'das genauere Erkennen des Einzelkleinen', and the multifarious activities of a sophisticated, civilized community are seen in terms of nearness or remoteness from primary production, or in terms of the adulteration of food. To draw on the analogy of Heinrich's 'Kartenkompositionen', such a society is a meaningless network of etiolated human relations.

We might, of course, offer a social explanation of this situation, and say that Keller is a writer whose instinctive loyalties are to a small, settled, and stable community, such as his ancestral village home with which the work begins, and note the two prefaces to the *Seldwyla* books, in which useful, small-town, and petty bourgeois occupations are contrasted with a paper-dominated speculative society. This would entail a negative attitude to the large national community, such as the active and self-confident German national state after 1870, and even to the loss in values pervading its cultural life ('es wird Revalenta arabica gemacht in der Kunst und Wissenschaft'). But how deep is this obsession stemming from the poetic imagination is shown when, after developing the view at length, he suddenly thinks of Schiller, whose work he admires highly, and yet in praise of whose art he can find no more suitable terms than the number of people to whom the works of Schiller give legitimate employment and material prosperity: paper-makers and printers, book-sellers, commentators, and the like are all engaged in an industry concerned with the exploitation of a national product based, in the last analysis, on genuine values: 'Dies ist, im Gegensatz zu der Revalenta arabica manches Treibens, auch eine umfangreiche Bewegung, aber mit einem süssen und gehaltreichen Kern, und nur die äussere derbe Schale eines noch grösseren und wichtigeren geistigen Glückes der reinsten nationalen Freude' (pp. 604-5). The superlative excellence of Schiller's dramatic work can seldom have been lauded in such a curious manner.

Whatever construction we put on such passages of social criticism, it seems clear that Keller's immersion in the poetic texture of life as it is lived prevents him from postulating any ulterior principle of idealism working through the warp and woof of poetic reality as he sees it, still less any cosmic principle working from without. Just as Keller has no social theory to offer which covers the life of a large community, so there is little philosophical or theological superstructure in this work. He is concerned, first and last, with the 'Faser und Textur der Wirklichkeit', as is his fictional *alter ego*, Heinrich, when he turns to the colourful reality of German history and law. So Heinrich's recollection of the guilt and innocence, the sufferings and joys of his youthful experience, implies no lasting regret but also no genuine liberation, and, particularly, no possibility of emergence on a higher plane to find a permanent solution to his problem of self-isolation from the fertilizing ground of home and the mother, except by simple return to his roots, sharing his memories with another person, and acceptance. Return: but he has directly caused the death of his mother, so that there is nothing left but the filling of a minor post of service to his fellow men. Sharing: his confession to Judith, 'Du hast mich erlöst, Judith!' (p. 1122). Acceptance: after Judith's death and in accordance with her will, the autobiographical account of his early life which he had entrusted to her came back to him: 'Ihrem Willen gemäss habe ich es aus dem Nachlass wieder erhalten und den andern Teil dazu gefügt, um noch einmal die alten grünen Pfade der Erinnerung zu wandeln' (p. 1125—last sentence in the work). But 'die alten grünen Pfade' are no less crooked in retrospect than they were when first trodden, though now they are overgrown with elapsed time and by the aid of Nature, for which in this work Judith is the hieroglyph. Retrospection does not imply insight, and Heinrich's humble dedication to the service of his fellow men does not carry the willed intent which is the note of Wilhelm Meister's final self-commitment to the profession of surgeon. Keller's ultimate solution of the problem of the form of the work is the sign of this: incapsulation of the *Jugendgeschichte* is resolved and the simple tem-

the Pattern of the Labyrinth

poral sequence restored; for when all is retrospective, no part can be more so than the rest.[1]

Keller's immersion in a form of realism with few idealistic overtones, as it emerges from this examination of his use of the labyrinth and associated images, explains in some degree why he could never accept established Christian doctrine. In the passage on human physiology quoted at the outset of this inquiry Keller remarks how an apparent teleology in the structure of the animal organism, 'die wunderbar scheinende Zweckmässigkeit der Einzelheiten des tierischen Organismus', might by some be seen to postulate the existence of a transcendental planner, but not for the lecturer—nor, we may add, for Keller: 'Aber nachdem der Lehrer die Trefflichkeit und Unentbehrlichkeit der Dinge auf das schönste geschildert, liess er sie unvermerkt in sich selbst ruhen und so ineinander übergehen, dass die ausschweifenden Schöpfergedanken ebenso unvermerkt zurückkehrten und in den geschlossenen Kreis der Tatsachen gebannt wurden' (p. 917). In the final analysis, for Keller, the labyrinth of human experience and the texture of reality as it is lived crystallize into the 'geschlossenen Kreis der Tatsachen', and no metaphysical dimension is either perceived or sought for. On the plane of world affairs, no greater discontinuity with the eschatological tendencies of Schiller or of Kleist could be imagined, and, on the personal plane, no greater discontinuity with Goethe's quest for 'Steigerung', whether in the apotheosis of Ottilie, the metaphysical justification of Faust, or that broadening of the range of experience granted to the Wilhelm Meister of the *Wanderjahre*.

[1] See Wolfdietrich Rasch's demonstration of how, in *Wilhelm Meisters Lehrjahre*, retrospective narration within the main story in the classical epic style operates against the sense of time passing, in 'Die klassische Erzählkunst Goethes' (*Formkräfte der deutschen Dichtung vom Barock bis zur Gegenwart*, Kleine Vandenhoeck-Reihe, Sonderband 1, Göttingen 1963).

Nietzsche and Klinger

MALCOLM PASLEY

LITERARY and cultural tradition appeared generally discontinuous to Nietzsche, since he was concerned less with humdrum traffic than with messages and examples passed from mountain-top to mountain-top across the centuries. He located the classic artistic achievements of mankind primarily in pre-Socratic Greece, and after his disenchantment with Wagnerian art he attached great value to the literature of post-Renaissance France from Montaigne to Voltaire ('die französische Form', he says, i. 578,[1] is 'die einzige moderne Kunstform'). Here alone he was prepared to recognize the existence of a relatively continuous literary tradition, which was, however, shattered by the restless and disruptive spirit of the latter eighteenth century: 'Man hat die "unvernünftigen" Fesseln der französisch-griechischen Kunst abgeworfen, aber unvermerkt sich daran gewöhnt, alle Fesseln, alle Beschränkung unvernünftig zu finden; — und so bewegt sich die Kunst ihrer *Auflösung* entgegen . . .' (i. 580).

The entire course of modern German literature must therefore, so it seems, be viewed in a negative light: as a process of disintegration, a plunge into a new dark age of barbaric disorder. This is certainly the impression we first gain from reading *Menschliches, Allzumenschliches*. Yet even at this stage Nietzsche's verdict on modern German art and culture was not a simple negative. Since every great or classic human achievement was understood by him, always, as a powerful response to a powerful challenge, 'Sturm und Drang' could be seen as providing such a challenge, because it injected into 'Aufklärung' culture those very energies which were indispensable for the display of the highest classical control. The 'moderne Geist' with its 'Hass gegen Mass und Schranke' (i. 579) could in theory provide a

---

[1] Nietzsche is quoted where possible from the handiest available edition, by Karl Schlechta, Munich 1954–6, 3 vols., by volume and page number only, thus: i. 578. Quotations from the Musarionausgabe are marked M and appear thus: M V 253. Quotations from the Kritische Gesamtausgabe by Colli and Montinari, Berlin 1967 ff., are marked CM and appear thus: CM IVi 361.

positive stimulus for that '*Bändigung* der darstellenden Kraft', that 'organisierende Bewältigung aller Kunstmittel' (ibid.) which he found exemplary. He admired Goethe's later work so much precisely because Goethe had found the strength to weather the German storm unleashed by Rousseau and Shakespeare: 'Gerade weil seine Natur ihn lange Zeit in der Bahn der poetischen Revolution festhielt, gerade weil er am gründlichsten auskostete, was alles indirekt durch jenen Abbruch der Tradition an neuen Funden, Aussichten, Hilfsmitteln entdeckt und gleichsam unter den Ruinen der Kunst ausgegraben worden war, so wiegt seine spätere Umwandlung und Bekehrung so viel . . .' (i. 580).

His lasting admiration for the work of the late Goethe is quite consistent with the argument he advances in the first part of *Die Geburt der Tragödie*, where he holds that the greatest artistic achievements depend on rigorous formal control being imposed on man's strongest energies and most vivid awareness of life. These energies and this awareness he calls 'Dionysian', the ordering and controlling power 'Apolline'. Of what he calls the 'Apolline Greek' ('der apollinische Grieche') he writes: 'sein ganzes Dasein, mit aller Schönheit und Mässigung, ruhte auf einem verhüllten Untergrunde des Leidens und der Erkenntnis, der ihm wieder durch jenes Dionysische aufgedeckt wurde. Und siehe! Apollo konnte nicht ohne Dionysus leben! Das "Titanische" und das "Barbarische" war zuletzt eine eben solche Notwendigkeit wie das Apollinische!' (i. 34). It was a cardinal tenet of his general cultural theory that the Titanic excess of Dionysian awareness and feeling must first emerge and assert itself before it can be mastered by the power of Apollo, in man's highest achievements. In other words that wild and abundant energy, which it is man's supreme achievement to tame, must first break out. Goethe's *Novelle*, for example, impressed him so deeply[1] because it expressed this truth as well thematically as by its artistic form and style. The image of the child surpassing the lion in *Also sprach Zarathustra* ('Von den drei Verwandlungen', ii. 293f.) certainly recalls Goethe's story, in which we are told: 'und wirklich sah das Kind in seiner Verklärung aus wie ein mächtiger, siegreicher Überwinder, jener [sc. the lion] zwar

---

[1] See his letter to Peter Gast of 19 Apr. 1887; cf. also E. Förster-Nietzsche, *Der junge Nietzsche*, Leipzig 1912, p. 38.

nicht wie der Überwundene, denn seine Kraft blieb in ihm verborgen, aber doch wie der Gezähmte, wie der dem eigenen friedlichen Willen Anheimgegebene.'

As with Goethe's late work, so with the great art of ancient Greece ('das Klassisch-Hellenische', iii. 209): its clarity and simplicity, its apparent lightness and ease, must be understood—so Nietzsche never tires of telling us—as a constant triumph over outbreaks or threatened outbreaks of energetic barbarity: 'die Gefahr eines Rückfalls ins Asiatische schwebte immer über den Griechen, und wirklich kam es von Zeit zu Zeit über sie wie ein dunkler überschwemmender Strom mystischer Regungen, elementarer Wildheit und Finsternis. Wir sehen sie untertauchen, wir sehen Europa gleichsam weggespült, überflutet... aber immer kommen sie auch wieder ans Licht, gute Schwimmer und Taucher wie sie sind, das Volk des Odysseus' (i. 820). Classical achievements are never easy, as he asserts against Schiller in *Die Geburt der Tragödie* (i. 31) and against Lichtenberg in *Menschliches, Allzumenschliches* (i. 819): they are hard-won victories which have been made to look easy. In the truly classical work energy and pain must still be sensed beneath the unruffled surface, and there is no contradiction from this point of view between his early praise of Attic tragedy and his later praise of Stifter's *Nachsommer*—one of the few German books he was willing to admire after 1876.

Now we may take Nietzsche's word for it that he had been deeply intoxicated by Schopenhauer and Wagner during the decade 1865–75. In simple terms, there were two drugs to which he had been exposed and whose effect he wished to counteract: that of a pessimistic–idealistic *Weltanschauung*, and that of high-flown poetic modes of expression. Schopenhauer had dispensed only the first, while Wagner—correspondingly more potent—had dispensed both. The 'anti-romantische Selbstbehandlung' which ensued (i. 739) involved the almost total denigration of German thought, art, and culture. The standards of judgement which he adopts in the immediate post-Wagnerian phase seem to derive primarily from his study of ancient Greek prose writing, and from his reading of Montaigne, Pascal, and La Rochefoucauld. The 'heldenhaftes Hindurchringen zur leichten reinen Composition' which he traces in the history of Greek prose (M V 253; cf. i. 819) becomes a guiding principle for all great literary (and not just literary) achievements. In Section 195 of the first volume of *Menschliches, Allzumenschliches* (i. 565) he writes: 'Die höhere Stufe der Kultur . . . hat eine grosse Ernüchterung des Gefühls und eine starke Konzentration aller Worte vonnöten, worin uns die Griechen im Zeitalter des Demosthenes vorangegangen sind. Das Überspannte bezeichnet alle modernen Schriften . . . Strenge Überlegung, Gedrängtheit, Kälte, Schlichtheit, überhaupt An-sich-Halten des Gefühls und Schweigsamkeit — das kann allein helfen.'

Now it is plain that in *Menschliches, Allzumenschliches* and subsequent works Nietzsche was not merely offering prescriptions for the kind of literary product that he associated with the 'höhere Stufe der Kultur': he was also attempting to provide examples. 'Ruhe Einfachheit und Grösse!' he notes in the summer of 1876 (CM IVii 397), 'Auch im Styl ein Abbild dieses Strebens, als Resultat der concentrirtesten Kraft meiner Natur.' The change in form and style of his discursive prose must be taken seriously, not dismissed as just a side-effect of the changed conditions of his working life. The facts of ill health, eye-strain, and frequent removals, which have often been adduced in explanation, cannot tell us much about his decision not to proceed further with the *Unzeitgemässe Betrachtungen* along the original lines. They can tell us even less about the dramatic shift in style which occurs in 1876, that is to say, the abandonment of that 'Stil des unreinen Denkens' (CM IVi 361; cf. i. 548) which he was still employing when he completed the fourth *Unzeitgemässe Betrachtung* in the spring of that year. The following may serve as an example of the rejected manner: '. . . das alles schaut der Gott, dem der waltende Speer im Kampfe mit dem Freiesten zerbrochen ist und der seine Macht an ihn verloren hat, voller Wonne am eignen Unterliegen, voller Mitfreude und Mitleiden mit seinem Überwinder: sein Auge liegt mit dem Leuchten einer schmerzlichen Seligkeit auf den letzten Vorgängen, er ist freigeworden in Liebe, frei von sich selbst' (i. 433).

It is generally accepted that, when Nietzsche turned from the elevated pathos of such writing to his so-called 'aphoristic' manner, he drew special encouragement from the example of the French moralists. Certainly it was part of his strategy at the time to suggest that there was hardly any German prose worthy of emulation. Even those few Germans whom he exempts from his general ban are paid distinctly back-handed compliments: thus the prose style of Goethe and Schopenhauer is declared only comparatively free from the German faults of 'das Dunkle, Übertriebene und gelegentlich wieder Klapperdürre' (i. 961) and does not approach the 'Helligkeit und zierliche Bestimmtheit' of Montaigne, La Rochefoucauld, etc. However, it is permissible to discount some of this anti-Germanism and to suppose that, in developing his aphoristic manner, he owed rather more to German predecessors than he was ready to admit: not merely to the aphorisms of Lichtenberg (which he does indeed openly praise, i. 921), Goethe's *Maximen und Reflexionen*, and Schopenhauer's *Aphorismen zur Lebensweisheit*, but also, as I want to suggest here, to the *Betrachtungen und Gedanken* of Friedrich Maximilian Klinger.

Klinger's *Betrachtungen und Gedanken über verschiedene Gegenstände der Welt und der Literatur* appeared in its final form in 1809.[1] According to a recent critic this book 'macht Klinger zu einem jener Moralisten und aphoristischen Schriftsteller, die in unserer Literatur die Ausnahme sind und oft gegenüber den ästhetischen Künstlern vernachlässigt werden'.[2] He goes on: 'Eine Tradition zeichnet sich hier ab, in der sich der Autor als Gewissen seiner Nation empfindet und zugleich im Auftrage der Wahrheit über die Grenzen des Vaterlandes hinauswirkt.' The notorious discontinuity of this tradition of aphoristic German prose is underlined by the fact that Klinger pays no attention to Lichtenberg, while Nietzsche in his turn apparently pays no attention to Klinger. Both Klinger and Nietzsche declare themselves chiefly indebted to Greek, Roman, and French models, but in Nietzsche's case we should remember that he had his own special reasons for playing down his debts to his German predecessors. The fact that he makes no reference to Klinger in his published works is rather misleading: we now have definite evidence that he knew the *Betrachtungen und Gedanken*, and this in turn suggests that the parallels between this work and *Menschliches, Allzumenschliches* may be more than coincidental.

[1] Fr. M. Klinger, *Werke*, Bd. 12 (1809). Quotations are from this edition.
[2] Christoph Hering, *Fr. M. Klinger*, Berlin 1966, p. 372.

In a recently published passage (CM IVi 89) Nietzsche noted: '*Klinger* sagt "die Kultur ist eine Frucht freierer furchtloserer Gefühle".' He was quoting from No. 581 of Klinger's *Betrachtungen*, where the remark stands in the following context:

Man vergleiche nur die Erziehung und den Unterricht der jetzigen Zeit mit der Erziehung und dem Unterrichte der vergangenen Jahrhunderte. Sagt man, dieses sei eine Folge der Kultur, so antworte ich: Die Kultur selbst ist eine Frucht freierer, furchtloserer Gefühle. Klagt man in einem Staate über schlechte Erziehung und zweckwidrigen Unterricht, so ist das ein Beweis, dass sich die Menschenkräfte auf einen höhern Punkt richten, als die Regierung ihnen vorgezeichnet hat . . .

Nietzsche made his excerpt from this in March 1875, at a time when his immediate intention was to write the two *Unzeitgemässe Betrachtungen* on Wagner and on the educational value of classical studies ('Wir Philologen'). This was the critical point in Nietzsche's career, when he was already finding it necessary to defend the cult of genius against himself, already struggling to maintain his Wagnerian position, and it was presumably for this reason that he seized on Klinger's proposition that 'die Kultur ist eine Frucht freierer furchtloserer Gefühle'. It was probably not by chance that he used the same alliterative formulation when he finished the *Unzeitgemässe* on Wagner early in 1876: 'es bedarf des freien furchtlosen Menschen, welcher . . . von sich aus die dem Gotte versagte Tat vollbringt'; 'der freie furchtlose Mensch erscheint, er ist im Widerspruche gegen alles Herkommen entstanden'; 'Und die Freien, Furchtlosen, in unschuldiger Selbstigkeit aus sich Wachsenden, die Siegfriede unter euch?' (i. 433 f.).

The point at issue is this: in the years 1875–6 Nietzsche made the decisive shift from his glorification of creative genius to his advocacy of free intellectual inquiry. While Schopenhauer could provide a negotiable bridge from 'genius' to 'free spirit', Wagner could not, and was thus the occasion of a traumatic rupture. In Klinger Nietzsche found a German author particularly fitted to support the transition from 'Geniekult' to cool inquiry and classical control. For by the stage of the *Betrachtungen und Gedanken* Klinger had profoundly modified, or overcome, the 'Sturm und Drang' enthusiasms which he had originally proclaimed. He certainly still insisted that the release of strong emotional energy was necessary for great literary and other cultural achievements, but he emphasized at least equally the need for the rational and artistic discipline of such energy. The stress on vigour marches in step with the stress on order, and the work breathes a reinvigorated 'Aufklärung' spirit which has much in common with *Menschliches, Allzumenschliches*.

Menschliches, Allzumenschliches was in due course dedicated to Voltaire, to whom Nietzsche nominally switched his allegiance after the break with Wagner. One of his earliest quotations from Voltaire is an indirect one, via Klinger,[1] and this strengthens the case for supposing that he made a careful reading of the *Betrachtungen und Gedanken* in 1875. At that time he was certainly on the point of reaching Klinger's conclusions on a number of points, for example that the 'aufblühende Mystik' of those 'poetische Poeten'[2]—the Romantics—was to be deplored, and that any enfeebling resignation to the idea of a Higher Fate should be strongly resisted. The following quotations from the *Betrachtungen und Gedanken* may indicate that Nietzsche had indeed lighted on a kindred spirit:

> Wenn ich auch die höchste und dünnste Stufe der skeptischen Leiter bestiegen habe, so führt mich immer die Poesie (im hohen Sinne des Wortes) einige Stufen abwärts . . . (No. 3.)
>
> Dass die Menschen einen ruhm- und herrschsüchtigen, zur Zerstörung geneigten, nach Übermacht und Gewalt über ihresgleichen dürstenden Geist mit auf die Welt bringen, das beweisen der Enthusiasmus, mit welchem wir in der Jugend die Taten solcher Männer in der Geschichte lesen, und die Langeweile, womit wir gähnend das durchblättern, was stille Weise und Gesetzgeber zum Besten der Menschen getan haben. . . . Ohne diesen Geist wären wir nun zwar ein sehr gutmütiges, sanftes, aber auch ein sehr langweiliges Geschlecht und wahrscheinlich gar moralisch totgeboren. Also Kräfte her; aber nur auch Licht dazu! (No. 255.)
>
> Ich hasse die kränkliche sogenannte moralische Empfindsamkeit und Empfindlichkeit . . . (No. 375.)
>
> Die orientalischen Metaphern, Hyperbeln und Bilder, die wir in

---

[1] Klinger (No. 94): 'Voltaire sagt irgendwo: "Wenn die Bewunderer Homers aufrichtig wären, so würden sie die Langeweile eingestehen, die ihnen ihr Liebling so oft verursacht."' Nietzsche (CM IVi 103): '*Voltaire* hat gesagt: "wenn die Bewunderer Homers aufrichtig wären, so würden sie die Langeweile eingestehen, die ihnen ihr Liebling so oft verursacht."'

[2] See No. 570 and No. 722 of the *Betrachtungen*.

Nietzsche and Klinger 153

der frühsten Jugend, als ersten Unterricht, in den Grundbüchern der Religion lesen, sind es, die die Köpfe der meisten so verwirren, exaltieren und verzerren, dass sie späterhin der nordische, kältere Sinn selbst nicht mehr heilen kann. . . . Fragt nur einen darüber, in dessen Kopf die klassische Literatur nicht etwas aufgeräumt hat. (No. 453.)

Mit einer neuen Moral, einer neuen Götterlehre müssen dann doch die Deutschen endlich Männer wie die Griechen werden . . . (No. 680.)

More striking perhaps are those passages, less obviously in the stream of eighteenth-century thought, where Klinger reflects on the potential cultural value of sickness:

Ein Mann, der immer gesund gewesen ist, kennt sich und den innern Menschen nur vom Hörensagen. Krankheiten entwickeln Kenntnisse von Dingen in ihm, die er vorher gar nicht geahndet hat; es ist, als wenn Abspannung, Schwäche, zu gespannte Kraft, Nervenreiz, Fieberhitze und ihr ganzes hässliches Gefolge die innere Seele so ängstigten, dass sie nun im Drang ihrem eignen Besitzer die längst verborgenen Geheimnisse offenbaren müsste. (No. 123.)

Das Geistige im Menschen scheint beinahe nicht ganz, nicht recht ausgebildet werden zu können, ohne dass das Physische etwas erkranke. Das, was wir höhere, feinere Kultur nennen, muss unsre rohe Muskelkraft erst schwächen, unsre starken Nerven für die Eindrücke empfindlicher, reizbarer, das heisst kränklicher, krampfhafter machen. (No. 283.)

This is a line of thought which leads from Klinger via Nietzsche to Thomas Mann. It is worth noticing that the famous passage in *Menschliches, Allzumenschliches* entitled 'Veredlung durch Entartung' (i. 583f.) was first sketched in the summer of 1875 (CM IVi 335), against Darwinism as a 'Philosophie für Fleischerburschen'.

To draw another parallel we may set the first of Nietzsche's reflections in *Menschliches, Allzumenschliches* (entitled 'Chemie der Begriffe und Empfindungen') beside Klinger's reflection No. 540 in the *Betrachtungen und Gedanken*. Nietzsche declares that we require 'eine *Chemie* der moralischen, religiösen, ästhetischen Vorstellungen und Empfindungen, ebenso aller jener Regungen, welche wir im Gross- und Kleinverkehr der Kultur und Gesellschaft, ja in der Einsamkeit an uns erleben', and he suggests that a 'chemical' science of this nature is likely to lead to the conclusion 'dass auch auf diesem Gebiete die herrlichsten Farben aus niedrigen, ja verachteten Stoffen gewonnen sind' (i. 447). His general argument in the passage is that it is an 'Irrtum der Vernunft' for us to apply the logical category of simple opposition to moral phenomena, since they arise from a complex process of interaction among natural drives. Klinger, for his part, speaks of the need to construct a scale ('eine Tonleiter') 'wodurch alle hohe, mittlere, niedere Triebe, Begierden, Neigungen, Eigenschaften, Fähigkeiten, physische und geistige, durch welche die Gesellschaft sich bildet, verbildet, verunreinigt, verwirrt, erfreut, plagt, glücklich, unglücklich macht und doch besteht, genau bestimmt, angegeben und nach ihren Wirkungen gegeneinanderüber gestellt werden'. He goes on:

> Wäre diese Leiter nun mit der gehörigen scharfen Bestimmtheit und dem kalten Abwägen, ohne alle Vorliebe, entworfen, so würde man erkennen, dass oft aus dem Erhabenen, Grossen und Guten Elendes, Kleines, Niedriges, Böses, aus dem Weisen Törichtes, aus dem Klugen Unsinn, aus dem Besten das Schlechteste und so umgekehrt entsteht oder sich doch so untereinander vermischt und durcheinanderläuft, dass man es gar nicht begreift, wie Gift zur wohltätigen Arznei und wohltätige Arznei zu Gift wird.... Wer da glaubt, dass ich damit auf gut leibnizisch-theologisch dem Optimismus das Wort rede, der irrt sich. Ich sehe nur ein Stück Notwendigkeit, an dem wir alle weben, ohne zu wissen, wo der Einschlag des Gewebes hängt....

Klinger seems to anticipate Nietzschean thoughts and formulations of the latter 1870s in a variety of ways, for example in what he has to say about dreams and about music. In his reflection No. 531 he writes: 'Vielleicht ist gar die Musik die Hauptquelle aller der Gefühle und hoher Ahndungen, welche späterhin die Philosophen zu Begriffen zu machen strebten, vielleicht haben sie gar ihre Metaphysik daraus aufgeführt.' He goes on to suggest that 'dieses wunderbare Ahnen und Träumen' was given to man 'als Würze zum Leben, als Gegengift gegen alle Übel, die ihre Fähigkeiten zur höheren Kultur nach und nach hervortreiben mussten', adding finally that whoever actively pursues these valuable dreams 'bezahlt gewöhnlich die Reisekosten nach jenem Feen- und Dichterlande mit seinem eigenen Verstande'. This is surely the language of *Menschliches, Allzumenschliches*. We may note especially Klinger's use of that toxico-

Nietzsche and Klinger

logical imagery to which Nietzsche became increasingly addicted after 1875.

Klinger's reflections, like Nietzsche's but unlike La Rochefoucauld's, are rarely cast in the short, pithy, and pointed form of the maxim proper: their average length is about a third of a page and they may run to short essays of two or three pages. All the same the book is, for want of a better word, 'aphoristic' like Nietzsche's: a compendium of thought-explorations which covers a wide range of moral, philosophical, social, and literary topics and which deliberately resists systematization. In reflecting at large on human behaviour and human affairs Klinger gives us a necessarily groping account of the personality of man in general and of his own personality in particular. But he asserts that despite the book's apparent confusion 'es läuft doch ... ein einziger Geist und Sinn hindurch' (No. 416). Nietzsche on his side exclaims rhetorically: 'Meint ihr denn, es müsse Stückwerk sein, weil man es euch in Stücken gibt (und geben muss)?' (i. 787).

Klinger was a good deal less rude than Nietzsche about other German prose writers, but his complaints ran on similar lines. He was one of the first to be really sharp about 'das deutsche, schwerfällige, mit Terminologie beladne, auf Stelzen gehende, philosophisch-ästhetische Gewäsche' (No. 68), and he inquires 'Wann werden die Grazien die Sohlen unserer Prosaisten beflügeln, wie sie den französischen Prosaisten so gefällig tun?' (No. 23). He was indeed not wholly successful in emulating the clarity and elegant brevity which he admired. But he made it quite plain what his prescriptions were, and they fell in with the prescriptions which Nietzsche was formulating when he read Klinger's book.

Nietzsche read the *Betrachtungen und Gedanken* in 1875, at the time of his most critical inspection of German prose writing. Two years earlier, in the first *Unzeitgemässe Betrachtung*, he had expended his anger on the style of D. F. Strauss. What annoyed Nietzsche was not so much the obvious fact that Strauss wrote bad prose as the current opinion that he was 'eine Art von klassischem Prosaschreiber' (i. 188). By attacking Strauss, whose style lacked all personal vigour and certainty, he was making his dispositions in advance. He wanted to make it quite clear that the classical prescriptions towards which he was moving should never be confused with the pseudo-classical prescriptions of the 'Bildungsphilister'. 'Darum hassen sie', he writes of his contemporary Germans, 'mit instinktiver Einmütigkeit alle *firmitas*, weil sie von einer ganz anderen Gesundheit Zeugnis ablegt, als die ihrige ist, und suchen die *firmitas*, die straffe Gedrungenheit, die feurige Kraft der Bewegung, die Fülle und Zartheit des Muskelspiels zu verdächtigen' (i. 195). A prose style embodying such qualities, and exhibiting above all the required 'Einfachheit und Straffheit im Denken' (ibid.), was to be found in Schopenhauer, who was the model held up here against Strauss.

Prose style is only one of many cultural indicators, but for Nietzsche it was perhaps the most important of all during the decisive years of the mid 1870s. The ability to write clear and disciplined prose was for him a *sine qua non* of 'higher' culture in his immediate post-Wagnerian phase, and all 'poetic' writing was viewed as self-indulgence or worse. His final efforts, in 1875–6, to defend Wagner's writing appear particularly strained: he declares that it is merely petty to decry the 'häufigere Dunkelheiten des Ausdrucks und Umschleierungen des Gedankens' in Wagner's work, 'wo eine solche allerseltenste Macht sich äussert' (i. 415). But such attempts to maintain the priority of expressive energy over rational and formal control carry no conviction, for what he really wanted to assert was the opposite. In 1878 he expresses horror at the fact that he had ever approved Wagner's manner of writing (CM IViii 396), and already in the spring of 1876 he says: 'Es ist die *rechte* Zeit, mit der deutschen Sprache sich endlich artistisch zu befassen. Denn ihre Leiblichkeit ist ganz entwickelt: lässt man sie gehen, so entartet sie jählings. Man muss ihr mit Wissen und Fleiss zu Hülfe kommen und die Mühe an sie wenden, die die griechischen Rhetoren an die ihre wendeten... Es muss ein Handwerk entstehen, damit daraus einmal eine Kunst werde' (CM IVi 355).

In 1876 Nietzsche set about this task on his own account, presenting himself as a follower of Greek and French models and progressively playing down the classical efforts of all mere German forerunners. Even Goethe, whose success in controlling the expressive power of his youth—and hence the German literary language itself—could scarcely be denied, was not allowed to belong properly to Germany: he was some kind of displaced Greek, 'in der Geschichte der Deutschen ein Zwischenfall ohne Folgen' (i. 928). What he now admired and recommended was 'möglichste Bestimmtheit der Bezeichnung' and 'vorsichtigste Mässigung im Gebrauch aller pathetischen und ironischen Kunstmittel' (CM IViii 392). Hence, for instance, his hostile remarks about Heine (CM IVi 397), whom he was obviously not yet ready to admire.

The aim of this essay has been to argue that Nietzsche owed something to Klinger, and at the same time to stir up the larger question of his relation to his German predecessors. Our difficulty in assessing his shifting attitude to these predecessors (and indeed to literary and cultural tradition generally) arises from a central uncertainty in his own mind. Does he wish to judge them historically? Or does he wish to judge them by the immediate contribution they can make to the culture of his day? Or does he finally wish to judge them by what they can offer him personally at a particular stage of his development? We go least wrong if we regard this last criterion as the important one, and assume that he praises, for example, Gottfried Keller because he thinks Keller is good for him after Wagner. Historically speaking, Nietzsche finds himself in a post-classical period in which a Baroque style is permitted (see i. 791 f.), but as far as his personal development is concerned the vigorous varieties of the Baroque remain forbidden fruit until he has submitted himself to the firmest course of classical restraint. When he writes in 1876: 'Es muss ein Handwerk entstehen, damit daraus einmal eine Kunst werde', he is thinking of his own development first of all. The 'Handwerk' of the years 1876–81 paves the way for the 'Kunst' of *Also sprach Zarathustra* and the late lyrics, in which the major German tradition of evangelical pathos reasserts itself—at a supposedly higher level—after prolonged and painful repression. It was only at this late stage that the renewed expression of high fervour was permissible. Similarly, at the earlier stage which we have been considering, the cult of moderation and formal control was only proper to one who had—like himself and like Klinger—experienced to the full the excitements of the 'Geniekult'.

Thomas Mann and Tradition
Some Clarifications

T. J. REED

I

'You have taken it wiselier than I meant you should.'
The Tempest

'THOMAS MANN treffe ich höchstens zufällig und dann schauen 3000 jahre auf mich herab.' Brecht, who was somewhat sensitive about his height, was not an admirer of Thomas Mann. But coolness may further insight. The sardonic comment in a letter of the forties[1] registers a prominent feature of Mann's public image. Increasingly since *Der Zauberberg* (a *Bildungsroman* in two senses) Mann had come to be thought of as an elevated exponent of culture. After 1933, the circumstances of his exile, his opposition to Nazism as a cultural degradation as well as a political evil, thrust him into the role of an embodiment—for many people, *the* embodiment—of German culture. Even if he never spoke the words 'Wo ich bin ist die deutsche Kultur',[2] they sum up a posture which the times justified. In the same period, the Joseph-tetralogy and the Goethe novel caused new stress, in criticism and appreciation, on Mann's learning—history of religion, literary scholarship—and on his philosophy. In large measure he was accepted in America (so he complained) as a 'ponderous philosopher' (Br iii. 55).[3] In a country which he found painfully lacking in tradition, his 'heritage of culture' (xi. 218) was revered at least as much as his narrative art was enjoyed.

All this might seem only a consistent development in a writer who had always made use of philosophical and literary allusion.

---

[1] Quoted by Wolfdietrich Rasch, 'Bertolt Brechts marxistischer Lehrer', in Rasch, *Zur deutschen Literatur seit der Jahrhundertwende*, Stuttgart 1967, p. 250.
[2] Heinrich Mann, *Ein Zeitalter wird besichtigt*, Stockholm [1946], p. 231.
[3] References in the text are to Thomas Mann, *Gesammelte Werke*, in 12 vols., Frankfurt 1960; and to *Briefe*, 3 vols., Frankfurt 1961–5.

Some Clarifications 159

Still, the sceptical implications of Brecht's remark are worth following out. Its irony is concrete and direct. By compressing the time-span of Western culture into Thomas Mann's glance at a casual meeting, Brecht hints at the incongruity of identifying an individual with the totality of culture. Perhaps he implies disapproval of Mann the public figure for allowing the identification, when Mann the writer certainly knows what precarious arrangements lie behind the façade of the cultural edifice. Brecht speaks as one member of a guild who finds another member's relations with the outside world part irritating, part contemptible. We need not take his judgement as final, but it will do no harm to take it as a warning. For if truth, in Brecht's favourite phrase, is concrete, then the statements literary historians make will need to be so too if they are to command belief. They must correspond, that is, to a conceivable reality and be plausible descriptions of literature as an individual's activity—especially when they try to relate this to the complex abstractions of 'period' or 'literary tradition'.

In this, Thomas Mann scholarship has sometimes been incautious, even naïve. It is easy to find statements like Brecht's '3000 Jahre' offered in good earnest. Mann is 'a latecomer and heir to the whole of Man's cultural past';[1] the 'full rich score of his work resounds with our living past and can be adequately explained only by what would come close to a history of our intellectual world';[2] his works have an 'um Jahrhunderte, ja Jahrtausende zurückreichendes Gedächtnis';[3] and, coming to particulars, we may read of a 'Traditionslinie, die von Paulus über Luther zur Romantik und von da zu Thomas Mann führt'.[4] Now there may be senses in which statements like these are true, but they need more careful definition than they have yet had. All too often, critics have worked with the tacit assumption that any feature or phase of standard culture, especially German literary and philosophic culture, is axiomatically relevant to

---

[1] R. A. Nicholls, *Nietzsche in the Early Works of Thomas Mann*, Berkeley 1955, p. 6.
[2] Fritz Kaufmann, *Thomas Mann. The World as Will and Representation*, Boston 1957, p. xii.
[3] Reinhard Baumgart, 'Beim Wiederlesen Thomas Manns', in *Sinn und Form*, Sonderheft Thomas Mann, Berlin 1965, p. 178.
[4] Herbert Lehnert, *Thomas Mann. Fiktion, Mythos, Religion*, Stuttgart 1965, p. 190.

Thomas Mann's works of any period and may be taken to lie behind them. The opinions just quoted only make this assumption explicit.

Various kinds of confusion are at work here, and a deal of interplay with the attitudes and dicta of Thomas Mann himself. It is perhaps time to clarify the principles involved, and to mark out some essentials of Thomas Mann's real relations with tradition.

A good point from which to start is Kaufmann's erudite study, which sets out to locate in Western philosophical history those 'problems not deliberately invoked, various types of solution, reminiscences from time immemorial' which (we are told) used to 'rise around' Thomas Mann as he wrote (p. 17). This might mean simply that a historian of philosophy can identify old philosophical themes in Mann's fiction (as no doubt in many other places). Such echoes and connections are then in the mind of the historian, and claim no real reference—except on a Hegelian view of the Absolute Spirit's imperturbable progress through history. This is how one would read, for instance, the suggestion that 'Thomas Mann challenges the Aristotelian–Scholastic tradition of God's immutability' (p. 19), or that Mann 'has to be seen in the wake of the romantic tradition, i.e. the intellectual movement from Böhme through Baader and Schelling to Scheler' (p. 25). But on occasion Kaufmann seems to mean that an actual event has taken place in time: 'In Mann it is a very personal *appropriation* of the wisdom of Angelus Silesius' (p. 18); or 'Mann's typology *developed originally from* Schiller's classical antithesis between naive and sentimental' (p. 27); after which 'Mann *accepts* Schelling's and Nietzsche's dialectical amendments of Schiller' (p. 29, all italics mine). This phrasing colours our view of what is implied elsewhere, and we feel moved to object that the links Kaufmann establishes are either so general that they are relevant 'essentially' to many modern writers, or so specific that they can be disproved in the case of Thomas Mann.[1] Mann himself disclaimed some of the

[1] For example, Mann seems to have made his first contact with Schiller's typology in his sources for *Schwere Stunde* (1905). The foundations of a typological outlook had been laid well before this under the influence of Nietzsche and of Merezhkovsky, whose *Tolstoi und Dostojewskij* Mann read about 1903. (His copy with annotations and date 1903 in Thomas-Mann-Archiv, Zürich, referred to henceforth as TMA.) As for Angelus Silesius, there is, for example, a quotation from

Some Clarifications

fruits of Kaufmann's labours, with a touch of unconscious comedy: 'Einfluss Leibnizens sehr indirekt. Ebenso Schellings' (Br ii. 296). But his reproof was gentle, his comment on Kaufmann's method of the friendliest. It bore clearly enough, he said, the mark of the 'deutsche geisteswissenschaftliche Tradition'—but why should that not be as welcome in America as the object of Kaufmann's study had proved? One obvious reason is the traps that attend such a method. In Kaufmann's book, the fallacy *post hoc ergo propter hoc* has had a field-day. And the confusions of this approach are compounded when a scholar ignores such simple facts as are known. A study of Mann and Romanticism under the banner of *Problemgeschichte* will naturally incline away from the concretely historical to the 'essential' patterns of detectable problems. Even so, to say that 'es ist kein Zufall, dass um jene Zeit *Schiller* zur Gestalt einer Dichtung Thomas Manns wurde'[1] is (to say the least) unobservant. Precisely the historical chance of the centenary of Schiller's death in 1905 led to Mann's commission to write a Schiller story for *Simplicissimus*—just as the 1932 Goethe centenary was to intensify his interest in Goethe. Even the Hegelian Spirit sometimes likes Its elbow jogged.

At least with the Romantics, unlike so many of the names pressed into Kaufmann's book, we are among writers with whom Mann did at some stage make contact. Yet problems still remain. What kind of contact? When did it occur? What was its demonstrable effect? The later Mann devoted two essays to Kleist, but is Kleist's essay on the *Marionettentheater* to be assumed relevant to the early *Tonio Kröger* and its dance-motif?[2] Internal evidence (rarely a conclusive argument) is all there is to go on, and that (*pace* its proponent) weak. If one must at all costs have a literary source, surely Nietzsche—Mann's most fully documented early influence and repeated source—is the first to be considered?[3] But why not allow a place to simple

him at a key point in the essay on Schopenhauer (ix. 556), but it is one taken from the pages of Schopenhauer Mann worked on for the essay (*Welt als Wille und Vorstellung*, 4. Buch, § 68, with annotations in Mann's copy).

[1] Käte Hamburger, *Thomas Mann und die Romantik*, Berlin 1932, p. 82.
[2] Paul Weigand, 'Thomas Mann's *Tonio Kröger* and Kleist's *Über das Marionettentheater*', *Symposium*, 12 (1958).
[3] e.g. *Also sprach Zarathustra*, erster Teil, 'Vom Lesen und Schreiben'; vierter Teil, 'Vom höheren Menschen' 19.

experience as Mann himself did when he recalled the 'braunbezöpfte Tanzstundenpartnerin, der weitere Liebeslyrik galt' (xi. 100)? It would of course be wrong to speak of an 'intraliterary fallacy', since so much of Mann's work is demonstrably of intra-literary provenance. Even so, a sense of proportion is needed. Had Thomas Mann at twenty-six read Kleist's essay? A banal question. Yet it is a banal truth that all of us—even writers destined themselves to become classics—read the classics one after the other, in the course of time, and are not born ready-equipped with them. (Mann, for instance, read nothing of Stifter till he was forty, and thought he was Swiss.[1]) We must not turn Thomas Mann into a mere pawn in the *Geistesgeschichte* game, a timeless cultural entity operating at all stages with the full range of materials which the literary past potentially constitutes, or with the full range of techniques which he later developed. Any method which does this—assumes, for example, that Mann's first story must necessarily have used Wilhelm Meister's 'Marianne-Erlebnis' as a source[2] because both concern a young man's love for an actress—can only be called naïve. And certainly, some naïvety is needed to suggest that when Tony Buddenbrook greets her brother Thomas on his return from an Italian honeymoon with the words 'Habt ihr das Haus gesehen: auf Säulen ruht sein Dach?' we are being 'an Mignons Italienlied . . . *und damit auch* an die Lehrjahre verwiesen'[3] (italics mine). Goethe's novel is in no real sense drawn into this quotation from a poem which is accessible and familiar to many moderately educated Germans who might not dream of reading the *Lehrjahre*.

This last would be a trifling quibble if it did not once more point to a recurrent fallacy—to which scholars are particularly prone—which we may call the fallacy of misplaced completeness. This consists in assuming that, rather as the tip of an iceberg implies the presence of vastly more ice under the surface, any detectable literary allusion implies the hidden presence and functional relevance of the larger whole to which it belongs—

[1] Ernst Bertram to Ernst Glöckner in *Thomas Mann an Ernst Bertram*, Pfullingen 1960, p. 214.
[2] Jürgen Scharfschwerdt, *Thomas Mann und der deutsche Bildungsroman*, Stuttgart 1967, p. 30. The section is headed 'Die erste Erzählung und ihr Traditionsbewusstsein'—surely almost a contradiction in terms.
[3] Scharfschwerdt, op. cit., p. 15.

Some Clarifications

and of that whole as known and understood by scholars. The virtuoso application of this fallacy is Erich Heller's discussion of *Buddenbrooks* and Schopenhauer.[1] This is worth examining in some detail.

As early as 1913, Wilhelm Alberts[2] pointed out the congruence of Schopenhauer's main argument and the line of development of *Buddenbrooks*. His cue was the prima-facie evidence of that episode in which Thomas Buddenbrook reads some Schopenhauer. Alberts also, like Heller, pointed to the place where Thomas misunderstands his philosopher and draws a life-affirming—Nietzschean—message from an essentially negating work. Later on, Mann provided accounts of the impact which reading Schopenhauer had had on him personally. But he also made it quite clear that *Buddenbrooks* was far advanced in composition when this occurred. Thus Mann was immediately able to give thanks for his experience by weaving it into his novel, which had reached the point 'dass es galt, Thomas Buddenbrook zu Tode zu bringen' (xii. 72). Accepting Mann's confirmation of the impact, but ignoring the unequivocal statement about the chronology, Heller was able to assert that *Buddenbrooks* 'derived its intellectual plot from Schopenhauer' and that 'the imagination which conceived it bears the imprint of Schopenhauer's thought' (pp. 30, 27). Yet even the choice of words in Mann's second account of the matter makes this impossible: 'mein überbürgerliches Erlebnis einzuflechten' (xi. 111) must mean the adding of a strand to an existing design and cannot be twisted to mean the first forming of that design, even were we to have recourse to some elaborate hypothesis of a late total recasting of the novel.[3]

But for Heller's oversight,[4] we should lack an eloquent reading of *Buddenbrooks*; because of it, we have a highly misleading account of the novel's genesis. Once more, the lapse is important

[1] In *The Ironic German*, London 1957.
[2] *Thomas Mann und sein Beruf*, Leipzig 1913, ch. 3.
[3] It is evident from Mann's earliest notebook sketches for the novel that the pattern of decline through four generations was his immediate reaction to the problem of how to expand his original idea for a 'Knabennovelle' about Hanno. See Paul Scherrer, 'Bruchstücke der Buddenbrooks-Handschrift und Zeugnisse zu ihrer Entstehung 1897–1901', *Neue Rundschau*, 69 (1958).
[4] It has been pointed out before, by Eberhard Lämmert in *Der deutsche Roman*, ed. B. von Wiese, Düsseldorf 1965, ii. 438, but without any probing of the assumptions which may have led to it.

as a symptom, namely of the iceberg assumption. Given the use of a piece of Schopenhauer as material, the idea that the whole of him was a determinant of form had irresistible appeal. So much so that it not only overbore clear contrary evidence: it also suggested to the critic that the Schopenhauer episode in *Buddenbrooks* functions in a way which simply is not plausible. For Heller, it is 'an inevitable consummation demanded by the syntax of ideas' in the narrative (p. 57). Yet if we look with attention at the Schopenhauer materials Mann used, they are precisely *not* in harmony with the underlying thesis of *Buddenbrooks*. If we will but leave on one side whatever else we may know about Schopenhauer's ideas, Thomas Buddenbrook's misreading becomes at once comprehensible. His almost ecstatic tone may well echo Nietzsche, in a similar way to other passages in Mann's early works.[1] But given that Thomas Buddenbrook did not read all of *Die Welt als Wille und Vorstellung*, but skipped a good deal to get to what Mann calls 'das eigentlich Wichtige' (i. 655), no effort was required to extract a consoling mysticism. For the chapter 'Über den Tod und sein Verhältnis zur Unzerstörbarkeit unseres Wesens an sich' *is* consoling, taken in isolation. It states the continuity of life despite the decay of individual phenomena. Now in the total argument of the work this is not meant to be consoling. Individual decay is illusory only because individuality as such is illusory. Nirvana will ultimately be shown preferable to individual existence. But all this is far from evident to the reader of the single chapter. Links with the main argument are perceptible only to the reader who has been following that argument. Thomas Buddenbrook, who has not, is weary of his individuality because it is 'ein Hindernis, etwas Anderes und Besseres zu sein' (i. 657); he is disappointed in his weakling son Hanno. Understandably he welcomes what Schopenhauer at this point seems to be evoking: mystical communion with more successful incarnations of the Will, whom he envies and would have wished to be like. When Schopenhauer writes: 'Demnach können wir jeden Augenblick wohlgemuth ausrufen: "Trotz Zeit, Tod und Verwesung sind wir noch alle beisammen"',[2] he could not be easier to misconstrue.

[1] Cf. the passage in *Der Bajazzo* (viii. 125) beginning: 'Es gibt eine Art von Menschen, Lieblingskinder Gottes ...'
[2] *Sämtliche Werke*, ed. Arthur Hübscher, Wiesbaden 1961, iii. 548.

Thus, far from epitomizing the theme of Mann's novel, the content of this episode is at cross-purposes with it—and not even primarily because of any 'Nietzschean' reading of Schopenhauer. It must go back to being a finely conceived and executed passage, and none the worse for that. It is there because it corresponds to a vivid experience of Mann's own: the basis of his work, even in this most apparently objective novel, is autobiographical. The episode was taken to be something more than this when a part was wrongly thought to entail the whole; and this in turn depended, surely, on a false mental model of the artist's procedures. Unlike the scholar, he is not out to understand exhaustively, but to make piecemeal use of what attracts him. Moral: in the critic, a lot of knowledge is a dangerous thing.

A postscript will show how, nevertheless, the artist is edged into the position of a cultural pundit by the mere fact of having used 'cultural' materials. It is of no significance for a novel if one of the characters in it (or even the author himself) misunderstands a philosopher. But Thomas Mann may have felt a little awkward about his presentation of the 'essentials' of Schopenhauer. In the *Lebensabriss* he says: 'Nicht . . . um die Heilslehre der Willensumkehr, dies buddhistisch-asketische Anhängsel . . . war es mir zu tun: was es mir antat auf eine sinnlich-übersinnliche Weise, war das erotisch-einheitsmystische Element dieser Philosophie' (xi. 111). Of Schopenhauer as the great negator he is now aware. He suggests that he knew this aspect, but rejected it in favour of another. Yet to relegate the negation of the Will in Schopenhauer to a mere appendage is idiosyncratic to the point of the absurd, barely possible but for the need to defend an earlier misreading. Subsequently, when Mann comes to write his essay on Schopenhauer (1938), at least he feels able to refer to the 'naive Missbrauch einer Philosophie' of which artists like Wagner and himself are capable. But still he sticks to his contradictory idea of Schopenhauer's 'erotische Süssigkeit'.[1] And an earlier draft of the passage 'So gehen

---

[1] Aside from the possible perverting influence of Wagner's *Tristan*, the whole idea may stem from two remarks of Nietzsche's on Schopenhauer and the importance of the age at which a philosophy is conceived (*Menschliches, Allzumenschliches*, ii. 271 and *Genealogie der Moral*, iii. 6). Mann refers to them in his later essay on Nietzsche (ix. 560). But conceiving a philosophy at an age when the erotic dominates is not at all the same as conceiving an erotic philosophy.

Künstler mit einer Philosophie um, — sie "verstehen" sie auf ihre Art, eine emotionelle Art' (ix. 562) was less conciliatory, and read '... und "verstehen" sie dabei im Grunde besser als die Moralisten'.[1]

When we come to Mann's major claimed affinity, that with Goethe, the confusions already located recur, now worse confounded by a typological-mythical-mystical supposition to which Mann's talk of a 'unio mystica' (Br ii. 72) gave rise. We read of how, despite a 'natural shyness', a 'long and painful process of self-examination qualified Mann at last to identify himself with Goethe. They became truly one.'[2] In so far as such a statement has any meaning at all, it is hardly a critic's statement. It takes what was subjectively true for the writer and repeats it parrot-fashion. Not that critics have an absolute duty to debunk what an author says. But they must look beyond its immediate meaning to its significance.[3] Whatever effects Mann's sense of 'unio mystica' had on him, the effects of his hint on criticism have been wholly unfortunate. Goethe becomes the first line of inquiry for source and influence at any stage. Hence the sledgehammer of *Wilhelm Meister* to crack the nut of *Gefallen*. Later proves earlier, part entails whole, the critic has a *carte blanche*.

Der Zauberberg furnishes an example of what may result. The work certainly uses some (in themselves hardly recondite) Goethe materials—the parallel of Joachim Ziemssen and Valentin, the Walpurgisnacht re-enactment. Why not conjecture a Goethean source for the chapter 'Schnee'? That Castorp's vision is mildly reminiscent of classical landscapes might not itself justify the conclusion that the *Italienische Reise*[4] was a source; but the Goethean *carte blanche* will bridge any gaps of doubt. Moreover, birds are singing in Castorp's vision—not named birds, but the description of their song suggests they could be nightingales—and did not Goethe hear nightingales in Sicily? 'Beweisen lässt sich ein Zusammenhang zwischen den Nachti-

---

[1] TMA Mp ix. 190, sheet 4. I wish to express my thanks to Frau Katja Mann for permission to publish passages from Thomas Mann's papers.

[2] B. Biermann, 'Thomas Mann and Goethe', in *The Stature of Thomas Mann*, New York 1947, pp. 249, 251.

[3] One cannot accept—for any writer, and certainly not for Thomas Mann— the equation 'der beste Interpret, der Dichter selbst' proposed by E. Wirtz, 'Zitat und Leitmotiv bei Thomas Mann', *GLL* 7 (1953), p. 128.

[4] Herbert Lehnert, 'Hans Castorps Vision', *Rice Institute Pamphlet* 47 (1960). Henceforth RIP.

Some Clarifications

gallen, die Goethe hörte, und denen in Hans Castorps Traum natürlich nicht' (p. 14). But never mind. Some recent alternative suggestions are less 'traditional' but somewhat more convincing. Derivative the vision certainly is, but not from so canonical a source. The text of the section 'Von der Schönheit' in Mahler's *Lied von der Erde*[1] and, especially, some *Jugendstil* paintings by Ludwig von Hofmann,[2] one of which Mann possessed, yielded exact details of the scenery and the disposition of figures in 'Schnee'.

Again a moral is pointed. The scholarly interpreter, perhaps even without Mann's seductive hints, is likely to engage in a rather high-level selection, a precipitate flight to the peaks of the literary landscape, grown timeless through scholarship and syllabus. But were these peaks the sole abode of the writer? To suppose so is to ignore what actually went on in the obscurer unmapped valleys, among cultural undergrowth now long since faded, but which was very alive to contemporaries. (*Jugendstil* provides the perfect example of a rich period source of literary style and motif which is now just in process of being rediscovered.[3]) If we jump too readily to 'Goethean' conclusions, we block off all view of the more characteristic period influences. Our account gains in neatness and unity, but is false. The modern writer is assimilated into a view of literature as a self-perpetuating classicity. He is canonized, but unhistoried.

Here yet another confusion is at work, this time between literary history and criticism. The evaluating critic feels impelled to link in some way those writers he esteems: since they show the art at its highest, it is in comparing them that its technical and moral possibilities can best be appreciated. He may even speak of his favourites as a 'tradition'. Yet this word really denotes a historical process, not just a sequence.[4] The comparative evaluation may thus slide into suggestions of historical connectedness, but without offering evidence. The *locus classicus* of

[1] Michael Mann, 'Eine unbekannte "Quelle" zu Thomas Manns *Zauberberg*', *GRM* 46 (1965).
[2] Heinz Saueressig, *Die Bildwelt von Hans Castorps Frosttraum*, Biberach an der Riss 1967.
[3] See especially Wolfdietrich Rasch, 'Thomas Manns Erzählung "Tristan"', in Rasch, op. cit., with references (p. 306) to related work.
[4] i.e. it is not enough to see (as Northrop Frye puts it) 'the miscellaneous pile strung out along a chronological line' in such a way that 'some coherence is given it by sheer sequence' (*Anatomy of Criticism*, Princeton 1957, p. 16).

this is F. R. Leavis's *The Great Tradition* (which, it has been suggested, could well have been called 'Novels I've Liked').[1] Leavis's opening chapter teems with statements which straddle the border between history and criticism. What stands in for the missing proof of contacts and fruitful study is the always obliging but always question-begging 'internal evidence'. (Henry James's admiration for Jane Austen is called 'that obvious aspect of influence which can be brought out by quotation'.[2]) Perhaps it is too late for us to rescue the term 'tradition' for the role its etymology claims, but at least we do well to recognize the multitudinous sins looser usage covers.

Yet surely, it will be objected, Thomas Mann's hints justify some attention to Goethe for that phase when his influence is documented? Indeed. But even here we must distinguish between some generalized, neutral, scholars' Goethe and the specific, angled, limited Goethe Mann knew and used. It is these uses we must look at; we may not extrapolate from them in any direction we please. As Hume wrote, on a subject similarly conducive to unfounded assumption: 'When we infer any particular cause from an effect, we must proportion the one to the other and can never be allowed to ascribe to the cause any qualities but what are exactly sufficient to produce the effect.'[3] In our case, from observed effects (Mann's use of particular Goethe materials) we may not infer causes (a global knowledge of and interest in Goethe) which are then taken as sufficient to produce further effects (Goethe at every turn).

Yet surely, our objector will persist, there are signs that Mann *did* have just such a global knowledge of Goethe. If two motifs from *Faust I* do not add up to a sovereign manipulation of the Goethe corpus, and if the Goethe essays are admittedly made up largely of biographical anecdote and a small range of often repeated quotations, what of *Lotte in Weimar*, a rich weave of fact, quotation, and allusion? Did that not demand (as Ernst Cassirer felt[4]) a constant retention of Goethe's works, conversations, and letters in Thomas Mann's memory?

[1] Harry Levin, 'The Tradition of Tradition', in *Contexts of Criticism*, Harvard University Press 1957, p. 63.
[2] *The Great Tradition*, London 1948, repr. 1962, p. 19.
[3] 'Of a Providence and Future State', in *Essays Moral, Political, and Literary*, ed. Grose and Green, London 1882, ii. 112.
[4] 'Thomas Manns Goethe-Bild', *GR* 20 (1945), p. 181.

Some Clarifications 169

Such certainly is the immediate impression. Yet such was the impression left by other works which rested on a highly economical montage technique about which we now know a good deal:[1] a purposeful reading of limited sources and a reverbalization of derived verbal materials. We know how superficial the appropriation of substance could be while still giving a sense of depth and solidity—a *Schein* at two or three removes from reality and quite unlike that of Weimar aesthetic theory.[2] The early *Schwere Stunde* was a similar weave of specifically literary allusion: the idea occurred to nobody that it might rest on anything other than total command of the primary sources. The short cuts possible in an Alexandrian age were left out of account— the preselection of materials in secondary works and the stimulus value of the coherent, ready-made picture a critical account can provide.[3]

True, Mann reconstructing Goethe in 1936 is (on our own principle) not necessarily the same as Mann reconstructing Schiller in 1905. To some extent he has certainly experienced what Sartre put in the words: 'La Comédie de la culture, à la longue, me cultivait.'[4] But in fact Mann's technique of montage —present in *Schwere Stunde*, confessed in the transparent allegory of *Königliche Hoheit* (chapter 'Der hohe Beruf') and confirmed in a passage of the *Betrachtungen* (xii. 301 f.)—proves to have been the same in *Lotte in Weimar*. The central incident once chosen, intense concentration ensued: on the relevant parts of Bielschowsky's biography, on the areas of Goethe's works and his *Annalen* leading up to 1816, on works which give access to the characters to be evoked—Riemer's *Mitteilungen* (an old source for the more

---

[1] From Gunilla Bergsten, *Thomas Manns Doktor Faustus. Untersuchungen zu den Quellen und zur Struktur des Romans*, Uppsala 1963; Hans-Joachim Sandberg, *Thomas Manns Schiller-Studien*, Oslo 1965; and Hans Wysling, *Quellenkritische Studien zum Werk Thomas Manns* (Thomas-Mann-Studien, Band 1), Berne 1967, esp. pp. 258–325.

[2] A connection suggested by E. M. Wilkinson, 'Aesthetic Excursus on Thomas Mann's *Akribie*', *GR* 31 (1956).

[3] Mann told Stefan Zweig in 1920 that great criticism—he had Merezhkovsky in mind—could be more stimulating to him than primary literature. Criticism generally seems to have had this effect, even making direct inspection of the object superfluous, like the hearsay which could stimulate medieval courtships. The extreme case is James Joyce, who fascinated Mann as a phenomenon in the forties although he never read a word of his works. See Lilian R. Furst, 'Thomas Mann's Interest in James Joyce', *MLR* 64 (1969).

[4] *Les Mots*, Paris 1964, p. 57.

jaundiced parts of the essays) and Wilhelm Bode's book on Goethe's son, August. Also used were other works Mann chanced to have to hand, not necessarily authoritative, but suggestive: a book on Schiller's role in the composition of *Faust*[1] becomes the sole interpretative basis for a view of Goethe's and Schiller's relationship, which Mann's rendering will make authoritative and popular. Chance also turns up useful newspaper articles—on Goethe's use of spas, on a public lecture devoted to Goethe's vocabulary.[2] The material accumulates—*Lotte* is a longer work than *Schwere Stunde*. It is copied and re-copied, notes are followed by abbreviated notes on the notes, until finally dovetailing begins, and details of Goethe's spa visits are at last built into speech:

'Vater war doch früher immer sommers in Böhmen zur Kur, in Karlsbad, Franzensdorf, Töplitz, schon seit 1784, aber auch nach Italien (1794). Dann wieder 1806 in Franzensbad (Egerwasser) und 1808, 10, 11, 12. Anno 12 wird er irre an Karlsbad, weil er dort einen schweren Anfall von Nierenstein-Koliken hat. Er ging dann 1813 noch nach Töplitz, verbrachte den ganzen Sommer da und badete 158 mal. Aber dann k̶a̶m̶ die letzten 3 Jahre Berka, Wiesbaden, Tennstädt. — *Vor zwei Jahren, Sommer 14*, fuhr er in die Rhein- und Maingegenden: Erfurt, Hünfeld, *Frankfurt* (seit 17 Jahren zum erstenmal). Dann *Wiesbaden* mit Zelter und Oberbergrat Cramer, Mineraloge. Rochuskapelle (Altarbild). *September 14 bei Brentanos in*
Einwurf:
Winkel am Rhein. Wiesbaden. Wieder *Frankfurt* (Oberpostamtszeitung).
September
Wohnt bei Fritz Schlosser. O̶k̶t̶o̶b̶e̶r̶ ̶1̶4̶ ̶B̶e̶k̶a̶n̶n̶t̶s̶c̶h̶a̶f̶t̶ mit Willemer, alter Bekannter. Marianne (*16 jährig*) *Landsitz am Obermain*, '*Gerbermühle*'. (*Einwurf*) — *Heidelberg*. *Oktober 14 findet er sie verheiratet. 18 Oktober Höhenfeuer.*'[3]

Urzidil's article and Bielschowsky, chapters 13 and 14[4] of volume 2, between them account for these details. The passage is a specimen—rare in Thomas Mann's preserved papers—of a

[1] K. A. Meissinger, *Helena. Schillers Anteil am Faust*, Frankfurt 1935. TMA, with annotations.
[2] Johannes Urzidil, 'Patient und Kurgast Goethe', *Basler National-Zeitung*, 24. Mai 1936; unidentified cutting 'Goethe als Wortschöpfer', reporting a public lecture by Professor Otto Pniower. The examples quoted in the report go into Mann's notes. Both items in TMA Mat. 5 (Materialien zu 'Lotte in Weimar'), nos. 5 and 33.
[3] TMA Mp xi. 14, sheet 38.
[4] Mann's copy, with a dedication dated 1905 and annotations, in TMA.

Some Clarifications 171

transition from 'sources' to 'text'. It begins resolutely conversational (August is the speaker), but gets burdened increasingly with references to acquired facts. It reverts to the historical present tense or the verblessness of the preparatory notes. Factual corrections are still being made, archaizing touches are in progress—'Teplitz' is already 'Töplitz', though 'Kur' is not yet 'Cur'. Already the points where Lotte must interpose something to break the flow of factual matter are indicated by 'Einwurf'. Much thinning out and rearranging is still to do, as the final text shows (ii. 578 ff.). But the procedures are clear.

We should note in passing that the novel's structure is also affected by them. The way it creates anticipation through the successive portraits Goethe's intimates paint of him, before we eavesdrop on his reflections in the seventh chapter, has often been admired, and it is admirable in effect. But the quasi-monologues also allowed a not too complicated block-use of each area of source-material: the *Mitteilungen* for Riemer, Bode's book on August for August. *Lotte in Weimar* is more complex than *Schwere Stunde* as well as longer; but complexity has been kept manageable by making a structural virtue out of a genetic necessity. (Imagine the problems of making the various speakers interact plausibly for the whole novel.)

Not the erudition of the scholar, then, but the economy of the constructivist accounts for the *basis* (to be carefully distinguished from the meaning expressed through it) of Mann's novel. There may be some reluctance to give up the image of Thomas Mann as a repository of learning. But why keep an inaccurate picture of his methods? Indeed—and this is the crucial question—why are knowledge and learning thought important in themselves? Are they any enhancement, let alone criteria, of artistic value? As Lessing pointed out in the thirty-fourth part of the *Hamburgische Dramaturgie*, the creative writer is allowed not to know a thousand things that any schoolboy knows. It is not for what his memory holds that we appreciate him. And if we overrate the importance of 'tradition' in the sense of mere quantities of learning, we risk a corresponding and equally irrelevant deflation of the writer's reputation if his learning is queried. T. S. Eliot, whose situation was analogous in some ways, wrote: 'In my earlier years I obtained, partly by subtlety, partly by effrontery, and partly by accident, a reputation among the credulous for learning and scholarship, of which (having no further use for it) I have since tried to disembarrass myself. Better to confess one's weaknesses, when they are certain to be revealed sooner or later, than to leave them to be exposed to posterity: though it is, I have discovered, easier in our times to acquire an undeserved reputation for learning than to get rid of it.'[1]

Knowledge as such—what his correspondent Karl Kerényi well called 'statische Kultur'[2]—is indeed, on an objective view, less important in Mann's relations with the culture of the past than its *use*;[3] and both are preceded and guided by *need*—the demands of the writer's impulse to analyse or express himself, or the exigencies of the times, the 'Forderung des Tages'. Since our rejection of such earnestly held views of Thomas Mann obliges us to make some positive suggestions, to these needs and uses we now turn.

II

Und irrend schweift mein Geist in alle Runde,
Und schwankend fass' ich jede starke Hand.
THOMAS MANN, 'Monolog' (1899)

Space allows us only to sketch an approach, but Mann's relationship to Nietzsche and to Goethe will yield essentials and provide a contrast: the one a formative influence, the other a chosen 'affinity'.

Nietzsche was virtually the only begetter of Mann's fundamental ideas—on art, disease, genius, vitality, human typology; and of his basic attitudes—critical, analytic, ironical, self-querying. Acknowledgement is not lacking, and Mann's reservation in the 1930 *Lebensabriss*—'ich nahm nichts wörtlich bei ihm, ich *glaubte* ihm fast nichts' (xi. 110)—is inaccurate, a product of its time, when repudiation of Nietzsche's more hysterical

[1] Opening paragraph of 'The Classics and the Man of Letters'.
[2] Thomas Mann — Karl Kerényi, *Gespräch in Briefen*, Zurich 1960, p. 200. Kerényi's comments are relevant to our further discussion: 'Der alte statische Begriff der stofflichen "Bildung" ist längst antiquiert, er hat sich auch moralisch unmöglich gemacht, indem er nicht die mindeste Widerstandsfähigkeit gegen totalitäre Angriffe der Unbildung oder Scheinbildung aufgebracht hat oder heute noch aufbringt.'
[3] Although Herman Meyer's chapter on Mann in *Das Zitat in der Erzählkunst*[2], Stuttgart 1967, studies use, it still makes rather much of the *poeta doctus*—despite reservations implicit in earlier chapters (e.g. on Rabelais, p. 52 and note).

doctrines was a necessary political act. In fact, Mann read and re-read Nietzsche,[1] he experienced through the categories of his thought and re-enacted its conflicts. Thus, having long taken Nietzsche as the patron of a critical intellectualism (even while for most contemporaries he was the inspiration of an anti-rational vitalist current of thought), Mann achieved a volte-face in 1914, abjured the ideals the intellectual Nietzsche had inspired—psychology, critical distance, 'literature', and other superficialities—to support the vital interests of Germany's organic, allegedly non-political culture. This is debased Nietzsche, paralleling the contradiction which runs through all his thought, and Mann realized it. Reading his friend Ernst Bertram's book on Nietzsche,[2] which had grown up side by side with his own *Betrachtungen eines Unpolitischen*, he saw the affinity and asked whether Bertram could ever have understood Nietzsche and his 'ganze antithetische Lebensintensität' so well 'wenn Sie den grossen Gegenstand nicht, gewissermassen, in gewissem Umfange, im Kleinen noch einmal erlebt hätten'. The book gave Mann 'Übersicht des eigenen Lebens, Einsicht in seine Notwendigkeit, ein Verständnis meiner selbst . . . neue Lust, mich zu Ende zu führen'.[3]

To take self-comprehension to the lengths of identifying with another's life may seem strange, but had in this case some justification. What Mann had absorbed of Nietzsche helped to make him what he was, his uncertain allegiances repeated Nietzsche's, and Nietzsche was thus a proper medium through which to understand himself. Moreover, his actual knowledge of Nietzsche made a judicious comparison possible in retrospect. Yet neither of these things was essential before identification could take place. The prime factor was emotional, the product of Mann's early self-doubt and sense of isolation. He needed support, confirmation, community—so acutely that he could go more than half-way to meet any potential provider of them.

Thus the impassioned entering into Schiller's situation in

---

[1] Abundant internal evidence is supported by Mann's many discussions of Nietzsche's role and by his preserved Nietzsche collection, which shows a lifelong preoccupation with Nietzsche's thought. Especially the Naumann Grossoktavausgabe, which Mann acquired as it came out from 1895 on, shows intensive use in almost all volumes, with layers of annotation in the handwriting of different periods.
[2] *Nietzsche, Versuch einer Mythologie*, Berlin 1918.
[3] Ed. cit., p. 76.

Schwere Stunde grew from the discovery in a centenary article that Schiller's difficulties, aims, limitations were akin to his own. The material sources of the story are slender.[1] But broad knowledge was not at issue, only an intensely felt sense of familiarity inspired by certain common experiences. In Joseph's words: 'War er dir also bekannt oder nicht? Er war dir vertraut. Das ist mehr als bekannt' (v. 1429).

But it is also undeniably less, when so produced. Identification—quite unlike that with Nietzsche—becomes a narrowly focused self-recognition, an inspired jumping to conclusions. And this is essentially what it remains. 'Vom Individuellen loszukommen ist immer Wohltat', Mann wrote in 1929, at the height of his interest in myth (xi. 409). But we must ask how far he ever did get outside himself and the pattern of his own preoccupations. Was his Goethe-image ever composed of elements other than those which self-concern (albeit sometimes a critical self-concern) made sympathetically accessible? If it was not, then identification was identification with himself, self-reaffirmation through the selected fragments of another's existence, as is hinted in Mann's observation 'dass Jeder in Büchern nur sich selbst findet'.[2] As a generalization this is overstated, as a confession it is significant. The tautology it implies became the basis for Mann's essay-writing method. In 1932, asked to write a book on Goethe, he wrote to Bertram 'dass ich mich auf dies Leben so gut oder besser verstehe, als Emil Ludwig und dass meine Art, es auszusprechen, vielleicht ihr Rechtmässiges, ihre Legitimität hätte'. Not because of knowledge, which Mann disclaims (he has not actually read Emil Ludwig's book, and is requesting Bertram's suggestions of what to read), but because he can 'aus *Erfahrung* reden — über Goethe aus Erfahrung: eine mythische Hochstapelei, mit der vielleicht die Brücke vom "Joseph" zum "Goethe" geschlagen wäre'.[3]

The problem is obvious: how does one know that one's experience is relevant? The claim to empathy is the perfect circular argument. It is inspired (or justified) by a favourite quotation from Nietzsche. In 1915 Mann wrote apropos *Der Tod in Venedig*:

[1] See Sandberg, op. cit., ch. 3.
[2] Note 3 for 'Geist und Kunst', in Wysling, op. cit., p. 151.
[3] Ed. cit., p. 172.

Some Clarifications

Wie einfältig die meisten Leute über das Bekenntnis denken! Wenn ich vom Künstler handle, oder gar vom Meister, so meine ich nicht 'mich', so behaupte ich nicht, ein Meister oder auch nur ein Künstler zu sein, sondern nur, dass ich von Künstler- und Meistertum etwas *weiss*. Nietzsche sagt irgendwo: 'Um von Kunst etwas zu verstehen, mache man einige Kunstwerke.' Und er nennt die lebenden Künstler wärmeleitende Medien, deren Thun dazu diene, 'das Bewusstsein der grossen Meister zu gewinnen'. Wenn ich mich genau prüfe, so war dies und nichts anderes immer der Zweck meines 'Schaffens': das Bewusstsein der Meister zu gewinnen. . . . Indem ich künstlerisch arbeitete, gewann ich Wissenszugänge zur Existenz des Künstlers, ja des grossen Künstlers, und kann davon etwas sagen.[1]

This only restates the difficulty: will not the 'grosse Meister' be given Thomas Mann's 'Bewusstsein' instead of the reverse? The passage does not refer to Mann's essays, but it is demonstrably relevant to his method in them, for it recurs in the manuscript notes for the Goethe essays of 1932: 'Nietzsche: "Will man von Kunst etwas verstehen, so mache man einige Kunstwerke." Wir sind wärmeleitende Medien zwischen dem Grossen und der heutigen Welt. Anders als die Gelehrten, haben wir Erfahrung mit ihm, weil wir seine Erfahrungen wiederholen. "Freundschaft" mit den Grossen ist so gemeint.'[2] The only hint that Mann sensed the dubious nature of the assumption, its possible arbitrary results, comes in the words from Degas which are at the head of his notes: 'Ein Bild muss mit demselben Gefühl gemacht werden, wie ein Verbrecher seine Tat ausführt.'[3]

Besides the logical limitation on Mann's approach, there is a material one—his concentration on the biographical. In the letters just quoted, he claimed understanding of 'dies *Leben*' and of the '*Existenz* des grossen Künstlers'. Mann's main quarry for the materials of his essays on Goethe was Biedermann's great collection[4] of Goethe's conversations and the accounts left by

---

[1] *Briefe an Paul Amann*, Lübeck 1959, p. 32.
[2] TMA Mp. ix. 173, sheet 24. Mann's earliest use of the quotation also related to Goethe, though not yet to himself. In note 22 for 'Geist und Kunst' (Wysling, op. cit., p. 165) he wrote: 'Hofmannsthal betrachtet sich ohne Weiteres als eine Art Goethe. Wir haben das "*Bewusstsein der grossen Meister gewonnen*" (Nietzsche). Sympathisches daran. Grössere Verpflichtung. Höheres, strengeres, ernsteres Leben.'   [3] TMA Mp ix. 173, sheet 1.
[4] Annotated copy in TMA. The pagination does not correspond to the page references in the MS. notes of 1932. It is clear Mann worked through these materials

contemporaries of meetings with Goethe. As in Mann's essays on other writers, what most differentiates them—their works—are relatively neglected here. The *Sprüche* are what he most often quotes—a type of work nearest to the writer's everyday life and his immediate human reactions. Without Mann's Princeton duties, it seems unlikely there would ever have been essays on *Werther* and *Faust*.

Such a predominantly biographical interest is common in writers, but does not normally lead to assertions of identity. In Mann, it bypasses essentials and blurs distinctions. Identification is facilitated—made easier, made more facile. The important differences between Mann and Goethe—in their relationship to nature, the status of their language as a response to experience, the originality of their thought—are either excluded, or minimized by drawing a Goethean phenomenon into the sphere of Mann's outlook. For example, the *Westöstlicher Divan* is regarded as parody; Goethe's connection with the learning of his time is turned into nothing but an exploitation of others' expertise akin to Mann's; Goethe's insight into recurrent experience is assimilated to Mann's ideas on myth.

How should we view Mann's accounts of Goethe, if not as objective illumination? Not as inadequate essays, nor as acts of presumption—querying the 'identity' myth need not mean arguing Mann's inferiority to a shibboleth Goethe. A more positive view is possible. If, by the logic of empathy, it would take a great artist to know fully what the mind of a great artist is like, it is equally true that a great artist is the last person likely to achieve unclouded insight into the mind of his predecessors. His own themes and commitments will come between him and the object: he will use this for his own ends. Hence Mann's approach to Goethe via the concepts 'Bürgerlichkeit' and 'Schriftstellertum' in 1932—what better clues to the Mann-centredness of those essays! Hence too the 'socialist' Nietzsche and the 'democratic' Goethe of the thirties and forties.

I propose we take Mann's use of the past as a perfect case of what Nietzsche called 'monumentale Historie'. It is often overlooked that Nietzsche saw uses as well as drawbacks in the historical consciousness. He set use against mere accumulation of

exhaustively over again in a replacement copy after the loss of most of his library in 1933.

knowledge, against the teams of fact-collectors ('les historiens de M. Thiers'), against the ideal of impersonal objectivity. The past could serve as an ally: 'Die Geschichte gehört vor allem dem Tätigen und Mächtigen, dem, der einen grossen Kampf kämpft, der Vorbilder, Lehrer, Tröster braucht und sie . . . in der Gegenwart nicht zu finden vermag.'[1] But Nietzsche is clear that such use demands simplifications: 'Wieviel des Verschiedenen muss, wenn sie jene kräftigende Wirkung tun soll, dabei übersehen, wie gewaltsam muss die Individualität des Vergangnen in eine allgemeine Form hineingezwängt und an allen scharfen Ecken und Linien zugunsten der Übereinstimmung zerbrochen werden!' For nothing repeats itself exactly in history (short of a theory of eternal recurrence, which at this stage Nietzsche does no more than glance at). So the seeker for allies must dispense with 'volle ikonische Wahrhaftigkeit', and may even come close to 'freie Erdichtung'. There are periods, in fact, 'die zwischen einer monumentalischen Vergangenheit und einer mythischen Fiktion gar nicht zu unterscheiden vermögen'. At such times, the sources of history flow 'wie eine graue, ununterbrochene Flut, und nur einzelne geschmückte Fakta heben sich als Inseln heraus'. The epitome of Nietzsche's argument is: 'Die monumentale Historie täuscht durch Analogien.' This is also an epitome of Mann's method.

This surely brings us nearer the truth about the nature of tradition than (for example) T. S. Eliot's insistence on the impersonality of writers' relations with the past.[2] For what we repeatedly observe as historians of literature is the way new personal imperatives wrench tradition from its course, impose new meanings on its components, and use these—reinterpreted, misinterpreted, turned into a symbol, an idol, an Aunt Sally— for present purposes.

It thus becomes pointless to test Mann's texts for their accuracy, on the 'hier irrt' principle. We must simply understand them as uses of the past for self-expression, self-assertion, self-defence. On this principle what—aside from Mann's delight in intimate personal parallels—do we discover? In *Goethes Laufbahn als Schriftsteller* we find a riposte to current anti-intellectualism,

[1] This and following quotations from section 2 of *Vom Nutzen und Nachteil der Historie für das Leben.*
[2] In the essay 'Tradition and the Individual Talent'.

now become decidedly political, in the form of a claim that the most sacrosanct 'Dichter' was one of the accursed race of 'Schriftsteller'. (The distinction, long resented and long combated by Thomas Mann, had long been a blunt instrument used against him in place of more subtle modes of criticism.) Mann's original title was even more provocative: 'Goethe der Schriftsteller.'[1] The essay *Goethe als Repräsentant des bürgerlichen Zeitalters* was similarly political in over-all import, warning bourgeois society, from a Marxian historical viewpoint, that now was perhaps its last chance. How deeply this piece is rooted in political concern is clear from the way consecutive passages from the early drafts (which make up a single argument, obviously written *currente calamo*) went into the Goethe essay and the *Rede vor Arbeitern* held in Vienna in the same year.[2] It is here that the socialist Nietzsche joins hands with the 'future-oriented' Goethe as Mann's political allies. ('Zukunft/Vergangenheit' is the notation in this period for rational clarity and socialism on the one hand, reactionary irrationalism, fascism, obscurantism on the other.)

'Nietzsche the socialist' ideally illustrates Nietzsche's concept of monumental history. A great struggle was indeed in progress, with Nietzsche himself, the vitalist and critic of 'devitalizing' intellect, as an authority claimed by Mann's antagonists. Why not turn the enemy's guns round on him (as Mann said of his use of myth in *Joseph*) and answer the jibes against socialist materialism with Nietzsche's 'Ich beschwöre euch, meine Brüder, bleibt der Erde treu' (xi. 898)? History was not an anodyne seminar where rights and wrongs of interpretation could be analysed at leisure: allies were needed whose sheer authority would count. Myth had to be opposed by myth, one historical hero by another (or by the same one viewed another way). Hindenburg had been put out as a latter-day 'getreuer Eckehart' (xii. 749); Stefan Zweig veiled his feelings behind the presentation of his *Erasmus*, which Mann regretted, because it implied the equation of Hitler with Luther (xii. 746). It is the 'deutsche Wille zur Legende' (xii. 748) that both sides try to exploit, with historical analogizing sunk to an all-time low: against Nietzsche's words 'wer allen am nötigsten tut? Der Grosses befiehlt' Mann notes bitterly 'Wie sehr müssen Schwach-

[1] TMA Mp ix. 180, sheet 1.   [2] TMA Mp ix. 173, sheets 47 ff.

Some Clarifications

köpfe versucht sein, im Hitler-Wahn dies alles "wiederzuerkennen"'.[1]

This makes it quite clear that Mann understood the workings of 'monumentale Historie'. But did he also grasp the fact that his own essay technique and beloved identifications were not different in kind? The word 'wiedererkennen' might suggest he did. Yet in the post-war essay on Nietzsche (where incidentally he is still in places arguing with the pro-Nazi Nietzsche of Alfred Bäumler)[2] he calls the title of *Vom Nutzen und Nachteil der Historie für das Leben* 'insofern inkorrekt, als von dem Nutzen der Historie kaum—und desto mehr von ihrem Nachteil . . . die Rede ist' (ix. 688). True, it is the negative part of Nietzsche's account of history that gives Mann's essay its central theme; still, history's use is strangely ignored by one who had so effectively used it. A key to self-understanding is missed. Missed or suppressed? Mann's papers for the essay include some skeleton notes on *Vom Nutzen und Nachteil,* and among the sparse quotations one stands out: 'Monumentalische Vergangenheit und mythische Fiktion garnicht zu unterscheiden.'[3]

III

Wer nicht von dreitausend Jahren
Sich weiss Rechenschaft zu geben,
Bleib im Dunkeln unerfahren,
Mag von Tag zu Tage leben.
GOETHE, *Westöstlicher Divan.*

But can a writer ever fully understand himself? Perhaps not while there is an ounce of literary life left in him, since 'understanding' automatically becomes a new creative act of some kind, and demands a new appraisal. Nevertheless, from early on Thomas Mann strove for the form of understanding usually

[1] In his copy of Josef Sommer, *Dionysos. Friedrich Nietzsches Vermächtnis*, Leipzig n.d., p. 71.
[2] Much of Mann's preparatory work for the essay was done on vol. 4 of a 1931 Reclam edition. It contains Bäumler's selection from Nietzsche's works and introductory essays headed 'Der Philosoph' and 'Der Politiker'. The pro-Nazi bias evident in these, especially the second, also affected the selection. Hence Mann was meeting the opposition on its own ground, and a comparison of his essay with Bäumler's text (e.g. ix. 695 and p. 57) shows how far Mann was arguing simultaneously with Nietzsche and with his intellectual progeny.
[3] TMA Mp ix. 199, sheet 1.

left to critics and historians—trying to 'place' himself, musing not so much about particular influences and traceable historical processes as about patterns of similarity which he had been unaware of while writing. 'Man weiss nicht, was man tut,' he wrote in 1954 to Max Rychner,[1] 'erfährt es aber gern, besonders wenn man soviel Wert darauf legt, wie ich, sich in einer festen, möglichst weit zurückreichenden Tradition stehend zu wissen.' 'Tradition' here means the perspective in which *Zauberberg* is seen to be 'really' a quester-novel;[2] in which Mann can see the great medieval poets—parodists in an age which cared little for originality—as his essential predecessors;[3] in which it is significant that his works reproduce (deepest of satisfactions) the authentic patterns of myth.[4]

But Mann's pleasure in these things, and in the mirror of *Geistesgeschichte* which Fritz Kaufmann held up to his Narcissus-gaze (the term is Mann's own[5]) must not be confused with assertions about his creative process or the cultural range of his works as a part of their conscious communication. Of course, with sufficient goodwill connections and parallels and echoes can be found with almost anything; but perhaps for clarity's sake, as Hans Eichner suggested, 'eine Portion böser Wille'[6] is what we need. This may help us to watch Mann the artist at work—with a large enough volume of materials and a subtle enough range of means, in all conscience—but delighting in the effects rather than gaping at the erudition, drawing no undue inferences about the 'cultural representative', whose role was dictated by factors outside his work.

[1] *Blätter der Thomas-Mann-Gesellschaft*, 7 (1967), p. 24.

[2] Taking up a suggestion made in a university dissertation. See 'Einführung in den "Zauberberg"', xi. 615.

[3] In the source-material for *Der Erwählte*. See Wysling, op. cit., p. 290.

[4] As Karl Kerényi several times assured him. See Mann–Kerényi, op. cit., e.g. p. 202.

[5] See Br ii. 295: '. . . das Vergnügen, mit dem ich hineingeblickt habe, war zu nachdenklich, als dass ich es eitel nennen möchte, — obgleich ja ein gewisser Narzissmus von einem bewusst geführten und kultivierten Leben wohl unzertrennlich ist.'

[6] 'Thomas Mann und die Romantik', in *Das Nachleben der Romantik in der modernen deutschen Literatur*, Heidelberg 1969, p. 156. Eichner shows very precisely how much Thomas Mann's thought, attitudes, and work differ from those of the Romantics; how much his use of Novalis in the essays of the twenties bends or even contradicts Novalis's meaning (monumental history again); and that what Mann understood by Romanticism had more to do with Wagner and Nietzsche than with any earlier phase of literary history.

Some Clarifications

We shall then be able also to allow him his 'geistesgeschichtliche Interessiertheit'[1] (the word bears two meanings) without necessarily taking over his conclusions: mindful of Robert Faesi's comment on *Die Entstehung des Doktor Faustus*, that Thomas Mann 'ist sein eigner Literarhistoriker und nimmt uns die Mühe ab, — oder verdoppelt sie'.[2]

[1] The phrase occurs in a letter thanking Käte Hamburger for her book *Thomas Mann und die Romantik* (Br i. 323): at this point there also occurs the first semi-public (because to a critic) suggestion of Mann's 'Gefühl ähnlicher Prägung' with Goethe.

[2] Thomas Mann–Robert Faesi, *Briefwechsel*, Zürich 1962, p. 89.

The Rise of Primitivism and its Relevance to the Poetry of Expressionism and Dada

J. C. MIDDLETON

IT would be bookish to affirm that the European cultural tradition has been continuously rational. The works of reason have, no doubt, assured a degree of continuity. Yet the socio-economic conditions have been such that what emerged was a complex of shifting tensions evolving through time and enjoying precious few moments of equilibrium. At such moments, reason and unreason entered a relationship which was fruitful. When split apart, each became the other's evil. The massive splitting in wars and revolutions during this century may even have destroyed Europe as a cultural continuum. The German literary tradition is certainly not one in which reason has always been sovereign. Yet it has been one in which Europe's peculiar tensions appear in sharp outline. There has been a rational decorum of sorts, with periodic bursts of unreason nourishing a literature that plies between manners and manias, folk modes and sublime ones, logic and music. Rationality even triumphed during the bourgeois epoch. Yet that epoch's most incandescent writers—Lessing, Büchner, Nietzsche—were men in whom reason fought some of its fiercest palace revolutions, ousting all sorts of deceptions and ossifacts. During the period of Expressionism and Dada, as the revolt against reason took new forms, Primitivism was one of the factors bedevilling aesthetic rationales. The tension was such that reason seems to have been hungering, or sickening, for primitive unreason in the first place: a tired Tithonus, praying to his Aurora. This primitivism has been both a vital and a deadly force in social and cultural life ever since its epiphany around 1900. Possibly its rise can be linked, though not causally, with the decline of humanitarian values. For Serenus Zeitblom, at least, in Thomas Mann's *Doktor Faustus*, there is a relation between primitivism in modern art and atavism in totalitarian politics, between 'Ästhetizismus' and 'Barbarei' as forces coalescing in a general brutalization of

The Rise of Primitivism

culture. Early in this century some of the sweetest reasoners among the artists were looking back, or inwards, to primitive modes in feeling or in art, as correctives to rationales which they believed to be unsound or unfit in an age of such internal uncertainty and external complexity. On the one hand, amazing advances in the physical sciences were seeming to assure at least secular progress; on the other, the primitive in art came to be seen as an index to the formative powers of the unconscious, or as a prism refracting the light which dawns at the birth of culture. But this immense new intellectual horizon had terrors in store. The rage for simple essence in the arts differed from Rousseauism, to be sure; but its public sequel was no less subversive, because it became cruelly distorted. And never before had the sublimations of culture been so tellingly questioned, so eroded by doubt. No Greek or Latin poet (except perhaps Theocritus) aimed to purify his rhetoric, as poets early in this century did, by dosing it with supposedly primitive elements. Yet even primitivism, in its quest for the preconditions of culture, lost innocence amid crushing conflicts between dogma and spontaneity, in which mass killing became programmatic in the name of order, and global destruction itself could be got up to look rational.

Before outlining some of the stages by which the value 'primitive' became positive and desirable, I should declare a few preliminaries. The gist is epitomized in Harold Rosenberg's sentence: 'Before any poetic event can happen, the cultural clatter must be stopped.'[1] In general, primitivism was an active force in experiments which challenged the venerable view of art as a perspectival simulation of nature with a theory of art as visionary fact. The new theory was first formulated by Kandinsky in his *Über das Geistige in der Kunst* (published 1912). In particular, primitivism has many facets, ten of which I list at once:

1. 'Prelogical' or 'savage' art, without support from later ethnological findings.
2. 'Naïve' European art (excluding folk art), e.g. Henri Rousseau.

[1] Harold Rosenberg, *The Tradition of the New*, London 1962, p. 89. Cf. Herwarth Walden (in *Der Sturm*, 1915): 'Der gebildete Mensch muss das Gebildete vergessen oder verlieren, um Künstler, das heisst bildender Mensch sein zu können' (quoted from P. Pörtner, *Literatur-Revolution*, Bd. 1, Neuwied 1960, p. 398).

3. Alogism in poetry: Russian Futurists, Hugo Ball, Hans Arp.
4. Infantilism, positive and negative. In Russia, Kruchenykh, as in his *Duck's Nest of Bad Words* (1913). Gregor Samsa's infantile eating in *Die Verwandlung* belongs here; so does the revaluation of children's art and the child's imagination, from *Zarathustra* to Morgenstern, *Der blaue Reiter*, and Paul Klee (1912).
5. Resuscitation of folk forms: again the Russian Futurists, pre-eminently Khlebnikov in his epics; also folk woodcuts, Bavarian glass-paintings, and votive paintings, in *Der blaue Reiter*.
6. 'Anti-aestheticism' including the 'Ästhetik der Hässlichkeit' first mapped by Kandinsky in a footnote to *Über das Geistige in der Kunst* (2nd edn., 1912, p. 71). Various versions of this in, for example, Rilke, Benn, and Brecht.
7. Feigned illiteracy (chiefly in some Russian Futurist poems).
8. Exoticism in some cases: Gauguin, for example, whose colours inspired the *fauves* and *Die Brücke*, or Klee's experience of colour in Tunisia in 1914. Descriptions of Africa and South America in popular journals (e.g. *Die Gartenlaube*, during the 1890s) might have nourished fantasies of primeval landscapes and primitive paradises as Europe took stock of its dominions.
9. 'Das Elementare', a crucial concept in Expressionism and Dada. Thus Hugo Ball: 'Das Elementare, Dämonische, springt dann zunächst hervor; die alten Namen und Worte fallen' (8 April 1916, in *Die Flucht aus der Zeit*). Later: Antonin Artaud's idea of a primordial theatre.
10. Atavism: Jarry's *Ubu* (1896), Brecht's *Baal*, Jahnn's *Perrudja* (1929). Also Kokoschka's plays of the period 1907–18.

This list gives some notion of the word's semantic range. It also indicates how widespread and how magnetic the phenomenon was. Even the most Socratic writers of the period were in some way touched by primitivism, if only in respect to subject-matter. Mann's dreaming Aschenbach regresses, to experience his primitive Dionysiac vision. Kafka's Gregor regresses: often in Kafka, too, there are scenes with the angular flat stillness of 'naïve' paintings. Hermann Broch noted this 'primitive' side in Kafka. Musil's Törless experiences the regressive unreason of sado-masochism; later, the Moosbrugger episodes in *Der Mann ohne Eigenschaften* are dialectical versions of the idea of the primitive. By then the idea had been demagnetized by a generation's thought. The turning-point towards irony in fiction might have come in 1924, with Thomas Mann's analytic treatment of atavism in the 'Schnee' chapter of *Der Zauberberg*. To mention the later Rilke's quiet priapism is not to blur the field. Here he meets, if only half-way, with D. H. Lawrence. One should certainly not equate primitivism with regression (infantile or archaizing) as an outcome of anxiety; but in some cases there are connections, within the psychology of post-Romantic nihilism. Less obvious connections exist between primitivism and poetic structure. German primitivism in poetry was not as conspicuous as it was at the same time in Russia. But the phenomenon is there, and the term is one which profiles several in-between areas that are not satisfactorily defined by the host of terms clustering around the concepts *Abstraktion* and *Ausdruck*.

Maurice Vlaminck has said that he took to Picasso in 1905 a negro sculpture which he had found in a Paris *bistro*. Max Jacob has said that Picasso first saw a negro sculpture in Matisse's studio. At all events, Vlaminck, Matisse, and Derain are usually thought to have been the first modern European artists to admire African works of art.[1] Picasso's *Les Demoiselles d'Avignon* and *La Danseuse* (1907) are two paintings which show the first 'influence' of primitive art: Negro masks from the French Congo, and Bakota statuettes, respectively.[2] The conventional

[1] There had been much interest in Japanese woodcuts among artists during the 1880s and 1890s. Pierre Loti's writings also were widely read (Henri Rousseau painted his portrait, *c*. 1890). Late nineteenth-century ethnology tended to regard primitive artefacts as implements, not as works of art; the important revaluations, and their sequel in official aesthetics (Hein, Stolpe), also the growth of museums, are discussed by Robert J. Goldwater in his *Primitivism in Modern Painting*, New York and London 1938 [Vintage Books, rev. edn., 1967]. Artists preceded scholars in encouraging the decisive revaluations early in the twentieth century.

[2] Cf. W. G. Archer and R. Melville, *40,000 Years of Modern Art*, London n.d., p. 24, where the differing views of Henri Kahnweiler and Christian Zervos are quoted. Let it be said that supposedly primitive works from Africa came from cultures once deeply sophisticated, like the Western Sudanese Timbuktu culture of the sixteenth century. These cultures had been eroded by over four centuries of slavery

1905–7 dateline can be shifted ten years back if one listens for the first real stirrings. For Germany the ground was being prepared during the 1890s, as it had been prepared in France by exotic art (notably Japanese). In Berlin during the 1890s the first connections were being made between primitivism and 'soul' art. In February 1894 Stanislaw Przybyszewski, who was closely associated with Edvard Munch and Strindberg, wrote of Munch's paintings that they were visions of an inner world, direct expressions of psychic energy, without cerebral mediation.[1] Then towards the end of 1894 Strindberg met Gauguin in Paris.[2] On 31 January 1895 Strindberg visited Gauguin's studio yet again, in order to refresh his mind for his 'letter' which introduced the catalogue of Gauguin's 1895 exhibition. Here he concluded: 'Now I too begin to feel an irresistible drive to become a primitive and to create a new world.'[3] Within two years Strindberg had written his *Inferno*, an anti-Tahiti, to be sure but a fiction which created a new psychological world by exploring forbidden psychic depths (Gauguin appears in it as 'one man who possessed genius, an untamed spirit').[4] The narrator in *Inferno*, moreover, is impressed by a charcoal draw-

(between 1444 and 1850, 20,000,000 Africans were sold into slavery in the New World, another 20,000,000 died in captivity before getting there). Europe grew fat on slavery during the eighteenth and nineteenth centuries: in some ways the term 'primitive' is still tainted by European cultural pride, ignorance, and guilt. See Lerone Bennett, *Before the Mayflower*, Baltimore 1966, pp. 18–30.

[1] In *Das Werk Edvard Munchs*, Berlin 1894. My source: Evert Sprinchorn's introduction to A. Strindberg, *Inferno, Alone, and Other Writings*, New York 1968, p. 44.

[2] They met in the salon of William and Ida Molnard in the Rue Vercingétorix. Henri Rousseau lived near by and was sometimes a visitor. See Strindberg, p. 58, also Roger Shattuck, *The Banquet Years*, New York 1958, p. 56. Sex was a powerful force in the proto-primitivism of Munch, Strindberg, and Przybyszewski in Berlin and Paris. In Berlin there had been Dagny; in Paris there was Mme Lecain, the English sculptress ('a demon, a man-eater' (Gauguin)). For Przybyszewski, whose experiments were extreme and disastrous, the 'loved one . . . is merely a projection of the hero's Unconscious' (Strindberg, p. 74).

[3] Strindberg, p. 64.

[4] Strindberg, p. 132. Gauguin introduced Strindberg to Balzac's mystical fiction *Séraphita*, a work which influenced him decisively. The link between primitivism, as a psychological *descensus ad inferos*, and mysticism is not unusual among German heirs of the 1890s symbiosis. Hugo Ball passed via political journalism from Dada to the study of mystical doctrines in the Eastern Church (*Byzantinisches Christentum*, 1923). The madman in Georg Heym's story 'Der Irre' becomes a murderous animal ('like a hyena') and then a visionary. Kafka's Gregor Samsa trembles on this threshold: 'War er ein Tier, da ihn Musik so ergriff? Ihm war, als zeige sich ihm der Weg zu der ersehnten unbekannten Nahrung' (*Erzählungen und kleine Prosa*, Berlin 1935, pp. 119–20).

to the Poetry of Expressionism and Dada 187

ing by his sculptor friend, 'sketched from the floating weeds in the Lac des Suisses' at Versailles; and he exclaims: 'Here was a new art revealed, an art taken from Nature herself! Nature's clairvoyance... may the harmony of matter and spirit be born again.'[1] This constellation of new values was followed and developed by primitivism a decade later by the artists of *Die Brücke* and *Der blaue Reiter*. The equation was: primitive = psyche = pure energy = *natura naturans* (rather than *natura naturata*) as spontaneous creation of spirit. Twenty years later, Hans Arp is found studying, on the shores of an actual Swiss lake, the primal shapes of pebbles, lumps of wood, and other organic flotsam.[2]

The date of Ernst Ludwig Kirchner's first visit to the Dresden Ethnographic Museum is usually given as 1904.[3] The *Die Brücke* painters were inspired by precedents as various as Grünewald, El Greco, and masks and sculpture from Africa and Oceania: works whose expressive distortion and defined energy served them as landmarks, just as much as the moderns Gauguin and Van Gogh did. Gauguin had upgraded primitive art in terms which appealed strongly to artists, like those of *Die Brücke*, who believed that a new art pertained to a complete reform of Western culture, to a rebuilding of its spiritual basis. Gauguin wrote: ' "Refined art" springs from sensuality and subserves nature. Primitive art springs from the spirit and uses nature.'[4] Kandinsky, in his *Über das Geistige in der Kunst*, also wrote with such radical reform in mind: 'Ebenso wie wir, suchten diese reinen Künstler [meaning primitive artists] nur

[1] Strindberg, p. 167.
[2] Hans Arp, *Unsern täglichen Traum*..., Zürich 1955, p. 12: 'In Ascona zeichnete ich mit Pinsel und Tusche abgebrochene Äste, Wurzeln, Gräser, Steine, die der See an den Strand gespült hatte. Diese Formen vereinfachte ich und vereinigte ihr Wesen in bewegten Ovalen, Sinnbildern der ewigen Verwandlung und des Werdens der Körper.' See also Hugo Ball, *Die Flucht aus der Zeit*, Lucerne 1947, p. 74 (Mar. 1916): 'Wenn er [Arp] für das Primitive eintritt, meint er den ersten abstrakten Umriss, der die Komplikationen zwar kennt, aber sich nicht mit ihnen einlässt.'
[3] The date 1904, from Kirchner's *Chronik der Brücke* (1916), is upheld by Goldwater (1938 and 1967), whereas H. K. Röthel gives 1905 ('Die Brücke', in *Der deutsche Expressionismus: Formen und Gestalten*, ed. Hans Steffen, Göttingen 1965, p. 192).
[4] Archer and Melville, p. 9. Gauguin, in *Avant et après* (1903), also seems to have sparked the interest in children's art: 'Sometimes I went very far back, further than the horses of the Parthenon... to the wooden rocking-horse of my childhood' (quoted from Oto Behalji-Merin, *Modern Primitives*, London 1961, p. 17).

das Innerlich-Wesentliche in ihren Werken zu bringen, wobei der Verzicht auf äusserliche Zufälligkeit von selbst entstand.'[1] Here also, for the first time, Kandinsky related primitive and abstract art: 'Je freier das Abstrakte der Form liegt, desto reiner und dabei primitiver klingt es.'[2] Yet Kandinsky firmly stressed the limitations of this sympathy between the finest modern artistic sensibility and the primitive. The moderns, he wrote, are plagued by doubt and by the 'nightmare of materialist ideas' (a hangover from the nineteenth century). Accordingly, there can be no more than a passing passion for the art of primitives. The primitive is like an ancient vase which has been dug up, but which has a crack in it.[3] Towards the end of his book, all the same, Kandinsky returned to the question: the new dance (Isadora Duncan) has also looked back to earlier times for a model, namely, to the Greeks, 'aus demselben Grunde ... aus welchem die Maler bei den Primitiven Hilfe suchten'.[4] The primitive here is still *one* sacred fount in which 'das Innerlich-Wesentliche' dwells, and across whose surface 'feinere seelische Vibrationen' have played. It is, moreover, an object-lesson for artists who are exploring 'das Objektive der Form', who are working towards a systematic non-figurative 'Konstruktion zum Zweck der Composition'.[5]

The most dramatic result of sympathy with the primitive was *Der blaue Reiter* (1912). Here the spectrum included, besides Cézanne, Matisse, Gauguin, Van Gogh, Delaunay, and other new painters, European 'naïve' painting (Henri Rousseau),

---

[1] *Über das Geistige in der Kunst*, Munich 1912 (2nd edn.), p. 4. Kandinsky had certainly read Nietzsche, cf. p. 116: 'Dieses Prinzip [unbeschränkte Freiheit ... auf dem Grunde der inneren Notwendigkeit] ist nicht nur das der Kunst, sondern das des Lebens. Dieses Prinzip ist das grösste Schwert des wirklichen Übermenschen gegen das Philistertum.' Nietzsche's *Der Wille zur Macht* (1901, 1904) contained numerous statements on such lines as: 'Der "wilde" Mensch (oder, moralisch ausgedrückt: der *böse* Mensch) ist eine Rückkehr zur Natur — und, in gewissem Sinne, seine Wiederherstellung, seine Heilung von der "Kultur"'; or the famous phrases, 'der Mut zur psychologischen *Nacktheit* ... Um sich aus jenem Chaos zu dieser Gestaltung emporzukämpfen — dazu bedarf es einer Nötigung ... Problem: wo sind die *Barbaren* des zwanzigsten Jahrhunderts?' (*Werke in drei Bänden*, ed. K. Schlechta, Bd. 3, Munich 1956, pp. 742, 690).
[2] Op. cit., p. 60. R. N. Maier's analysis of abstraction in poetry, *Paradies der Weltlosigkeit*, Stuttgart 1964, includes much detail about theories of painting, but nothing is said about primitivism or contacts between primitivism and abstraction.
[3] Op. cit., p. 5. Cf. Franz Marc's aphorisms 39 and 78, of early 1915.
[4] Op. cit., p. 107. [5] Op. cit., p. 112.

Russian and German folk art (woodcuts, carvings, votive paintings), children's drawings, and primitive works (masks, wood carvings, statuettes) from twelve different cultures. By now Wilhelm Uhde's monograph on Henri Rousseau had appeared (1911). Rousseau was being recognized as having been, since he first exhibited in Paris in 1885, a 'native who turned up on the shore when the exploratory voyages of modern art arrived in the new world'.[1] Most striking was the range of the primitive *exotica*: South Borneo (Dayak), South America (Yuri-Taboca), Easter Islands, Cameroons, Mexico (Aztec), New Caledonia, Alaska, Marquesas, Bali, Benin, Ceylon, Guatemala (the last not in the original edition).[2] Here, too, the word 'primitiv' occurs in some new contexts. Franz Marc, whose 'Animalisierung der Kunst' has mystical features in any case, wrote of the new German 'Wilde': 'Die Mystik erwachte in den Seelen und mit ihr uralte Elemente der Kunst.'[3] David Burliuk, writing of Russian developments, advocated a militant barbarization of art.[4] August Macke stressed the strength of form in primitive masks: 'Schaffen von Formen heisst: leben. Sind nicht Kinder Schaffende, die direkt aus dem Geheimnis ihrer Empfindung schöpften, mehr als Nachahmer griechischer Form? Sind nicht die Wilden Künstler, die ihre eigene Form haben, stark wie die Form des Donners?'[5] No sign here of the later ethnological view that primitive works are 'expressions of deeply rooted art traditions which dictated to a large extent the basic designs that the professionally trained primitive artists

[1] Shattuck, p. 112. J. de Rotonchamp's book on Gauguin had appeared in Paris in 1906.
[2] *Der blaue Reiter: dokumentarische Neuausgabe*, ed. Klaus Lankheit, Munich 1965. There were also Japanese pen drawings and woodcuts, Egyptian silhouette figures, and a Gabon mask wrongly identified as Chinese. Old German woodcuts and children's drawings had also been an influence on the painters of *Die Brücke*.
[3] Op. cit., p. 30.
[4] Op. cit., p. 48: 'das neuentdeckte Gesetz aller der obengenannten Künstler ist aber nur eine aufrechtgestellte Tradition, deren Ursprung wir in den Werken der "barbarischen" Kunst sehen: der Ägypter, Assyrier, Skythen usw.' Burliuk's anti-academicism predates Italian Futurism by three or four years. See V. Markov, *Russian Futurism: a History*, Berkeley and Los Angeles 1968, ch. 2 ('Hylaea'). Burliuk's terms in *Der blaue Reiter* anticipated those of the (undated) *Vital English Art* manifesto of Marinetti and C. R. W. Nevinson (*c.* 1914); but that manifesto attacked all 'Neo-Primitives'.
[5] Op. cit., p. 55. The statement is flanked by reproductions of a stooping carved figure from the Easter Islands, and a carved wooden block from the Cameroons.

were required to follow'.[1] On the other hand, the absence of 'pictorial exactness', starkness of form, form as the pulse of mind recording contact with the elemental—these were primitive features which appealed to Marc, Macke, and Kandinsky, and which later inquiry endorsed. The accent on untutored spontaneity was an intrusion from the new myth about the primitive; hence the tendency at this time to merge primitive art, children's art, and even mad art, which prevailed for some time to come and was still troubling André Malraux in the 1920s.

It is not hard to see how Kandinsky's concepts of 'innere Einheitlichkeit' and 'Seelenvibration' codified his responses to the primitive works that he knew. A model for his theory of abstract art (in *Über das Geistige in der Kunst*) had been music. His theory was anchored in concepts of psychic tone, immateriality, and dissonance. In *Der blaue Reiter*, too, music is a context in which primitivism appears. N. Kulbin, writing on 'Free Music', advocated the use of quarter-tones and eighth-tones, as tones existing in nature (musical instruments might have to be redesigned). At the time Delius, Mahler, and Scriabin were among the composers to whom this vitalistic notion of music as the polyphony of nature had its appeal. It was perhaps the strongest source of inspiration for early twentieth-century music. But Kulbin's dream of plugging music in to nature did not match the more radical realities which were already on the scene: eruptive syncopated rhythms animating tonal structures of ravishingly intricate ambiguity. Bartok's *Allegro barbaro* is dated 1910. Stravinsky was writing his *Sacre du printemps* in 1911 and 1912; the ballet was first performed on 29 May 1913.[2] In his *Ragtime* (1919) primitive and jazz metres are combined

[1] Paul S. Wingert, *Primitive Art: its Traditions and Styles*, Cleveland and New York 1965, p. 9.
[2] Details in William W. Austin, *Music in the Twentieth Century*, New York 1966, e.g. p. 258: 'his beats are often marked by a thud in the accompaniment while the main melody has a gasp of silence, and then the motions of the melody occur as syncopated accents of the second or third unit with the beat' (the 'Glorification' and 'Victim's Dance' sections of *Sacre du printemps*). The main features here are violent contrast, eruptiveness, unpredictability, syncopation, staccato accents. See also the analysis of 'violently syncopated accents' and of the 'innumerable changes of time signature' in Eric Walter White, *Stravinsky: the Composer and his Works*, Berkeley and Los Angeles 1966, pp. 172–6. White describes the instrumentation as a 'highly sophisticated means . . . employed to get a deliberately primitive effect' (p. 175).

in a highly sophisticated montage. Stravinsky's instrumental finesse dominates one end of the scale. At the other came the cardboard-box drumming to a simultaneous poem, first performed on 29 March 1916, by the Zürich Dadas (their version of 'musique bruitiste', invented in 1913 by the Italian Futurist Luigi Russolo). That same programme of 29 March included 'Chant nègre I et II', accompanied by small exotic drums to a quasi-African melody provided by Jan Ephraim, owner of the Cabaret Voltaire.

Kandinsky's essay 'Über die Formfrage' scanned the various themes in *Der blaue Reiter*: children's art, the coexistence, in a single image, of real and abstract elements, Cubism, the compositional genius of medieval and folk art, and the 'neue grosse Realistik' of Henri Rousseau, master of the mental image. 'Das rein Kompositionelle' was the common denominator which Kandinsky inferred for the new art of a new cultural epoch.[1] The transition was thus made from the emotional or 'romantic–symbolic' attitude to the primitive, which had still marked *Die Brücke*, to an analytic concern with structure.[2] By the time *Der blaue Reiter* appeared, with its momentous conception of structure as a graph of unspoiled psychic activity, primitivism was capturing many of the outstanding minds of the time. In his *Formprobleme der Gotik* (1912) Wilhelm Worringer struck the main nerve of modern interest with his theory of relations between primitive dread of a hostile incomprehensible world and the creation of 'absolute' abstract forms on plane surfaces (suppression of the 'tridimensionality of the actual world').[3]

[1] *Der blaue Reiter*, p. 172.

[2] Goldwater, p. 92, stressed the emotional side of primitivism in *Die Brücke*, notably in Max Pechstein's and Emil Nolde's paintings of 1911–15: 'the romantic–symbolic attitude toward nature and toward the primitive in its union with nature that we have seen in Gauguin and the *fauves*.' At the same time, Goldwater distinguished the primitivism of 1904–5 from its romantic precedents: 'Where the nineteenth century thought of the primitive... as calm and reasonable, the twentieth sees it as violent and overwhelming' (p. 95). This (Nietzschean) revaluation even occurs in Rilke's poem 'Geburt der Venus' (early 1904): the dolphin as bloody uterus from which the goddess is born. Rilke's predilection at that time for supposedly archaic (pre-fourth-century) Greek sculpture is realized in the phonics of the poem: see my 'Rilke's "Birth of Venus"', *Arion*, 7 (1968), 372–91.

[3] Worringer had probably not read Lévy-Bruhl's *Les Fonctions mentales dans les sociétés inférieures* (Paris 1910). His concept of abstraction excludes the careful distinction made by Lévy-Bruhl between 'abstraction mystique' and 'abstraction logique' in ch. 3. There is also Lévy-Bruhl's argument that the primitive mind, as revealed in drawings, has no conception of homogeneous space: the meaning of

192   *The Rise of Primitivism and its Relevance*

1912–13 was the year of Freud's *Totem and Taboo*; read or not, his *Traumdeutung* and *Psychopathologie* were being discussed by writers from about 1909 onward. Jung's *Die Psychologie des Unbewussten* (1912) suggested another perspective on archaic patterns active in the modern psyche.[1] Morgenstern had already nominated the child as the 'deathless creator in man'.[2] Paul Klee discovered children's art in 1912.[3] In April 1914, 'possessed' by colour in Tunisia, he added a fresh nuance to the bond between the primitive and the exotic: 'Very fine belly dances. One doesn't see such things at home.'[4] Long before the First World War George Grosz discovered his form of primitive art: graffiti on public lavatory walls, also the crude paintings and panoramas of images without perspective which he had seen at circuses, all of which influenced his drawings during the period 1916–20.[5] The first analysis of African sculpture was Carl Einstein's *Negerplastik* (1915).[6] Einstein was already known as

an image may vary according to where it is placed (pp. 124–31, 2nd edn., 1912). Worringer's idea about 'plane surfaces' was good for Munich or Paris, but not for Central Australia. In fact, his 'primitive man' was a bold figment in Ur-Gothic costume, e.g.: 'He must therefore endeavour to recast the incomprehensible relativity of the phenomenal world into constant absolute values' (*Form in Gothic*, New York 1964, p. 16).

[1] Notably (in Jung) the theory that each individual psyche contains an epitome of the psychic history of mankind. Georg Heym uses a Freudian term ('Sexualverdrängung') in his journal for 20 Dec. 1910 (Hamburg 1960, p. 154). The morning after writing *Das Urteil*, in Sept. 1912, Kafka noted in his *Tagebücher*: 'Gedanken an Freud natürlich' (New York and Frankfurt 1954, p. 294).

[2] From his fragmentary foreword to *Galgenlieder*: M. Bauer, *Christian Morgensterns Leben und Werk*, Munich n.d., p. 152: 'dieses "Kind im Menschen" ist der unsterbliche Schöpfer in ihm.'

[3] *The Diaries of Paul Klee 1898–1918*, Berkeley and Los Angeles 1968, p. 266: (on *Der blaue Reiter*) 'These are primitive beginnings in art ... Children also have artistic ability, and there is wisdom in their having it! The more helpless they are, the more instructive are the examples they furnish us ... Parallel phenomena are provided by the works of the mentally diseased; neither childish behaviour nor madness are insulting words here ... All this is to be taken very seriously.' Siegfried Levinstein's *Kinderzeichnungen bis zum 14. Lebensjahr* had appeared in 1905 (Leipzig). Goldwater (p. 187) mentions a German translation (1906) of the first book on children's art, published in Italian in 1887, but does not name author or title.

[4] *The Diaries*, p. 288.

[5] George Grosz, *A Little Yes and a Big No*, New York, pp. 26–9. Cf. Jean Dubuffet's engraving, 'Venus of the Sidewalks' (1946), reproduced in René Huyghe, *Art and the Spirit of Man*, New York 1962, fig. 278.

[6] Reprinted in Carl Einstein, *Gesammelte Werke*, ed. by Ernst Nef, Wiesbaden 1962, pp. 80–103. Primitivism in Herwarth Walden's momentous exhibition of 1913 ('Erster deutscher Herbstsalon') had drawn from some Berlin critics vituperations like 'Hottentotten im Oberhemd' and 'Säuglinge im Frack' (Robert Breuer).

to the Poetry of Expressionism and Dada 193

the author of the canonical early Expressionist fiction, *Bebuquin* (1909), in which the hero had found reason rocked by something like Worringer's 'metaphysical dread' and man doomed unless his consciousness could be transformed: 'Die Logik hat nicht eine Grundlage', 'die materielle Welt und unsere Vorstellungen decken sich nie', 'Herr . . . Ich bin geschaffen zu erkennen und zu schauen, aber Deine Welt ist hierzu nicht gemacht; sie entzieht sich uns; wir sind weltverlassen.'[1] In 1916 and 1917 Einstein also published in *Die Aktion* his seven translations of African negro poems, which have some stylistic kinship with the compressed 'abstract' lyrics of August Stramm.[2] The purity of the paradisal vision was volatile. Even some of Stramm's poems show how, in poetry, a straining after the primordial could result in teutonic grunting, rather than in the spirited crystalline transparency envisaged by Kandinsky and Klee. By 1914 there are already signs of primitivism becoming a cliché. Yet one phrase by Klee, in his Tunisian diary, epitomizes the pre-1914 mood: 'When is the spirit at its purest? In the beginning.'[3] And at the end of 1915 Hugo Ball takes up the question in terms which anticipate a whole new extension of the idea into the constructive iconoclasm of early Dada:

In einer Zeit wie der unsern, in der die Menschen täglich von den ungeheuerlichsten Dingen bestürmt werden, ohne sich über die Eindrücke Rechenschaft geben zu können, in solcher Zeit wird das ästhetische Produzieren zur Diät. Alle lebendige Kunst aber wird irrational, primitiv und komplexhaft sein, eine Geheimsprache führen und Dokumente nicht der Erbauung, sondern der Paradoxie hinterlassen.[4]

The question was even discussed, on 12 Apr. 1913, in parliament, where 443 delegates agreed that paintings akin to savage art and child art were 'krankhaft' and unfit for museums. See Nell Walden and Lothar Schreyer, *Der Sturm: ein Erinnerungsbuch*, Baden-Baden 1954, pp. 121–2 (quoting also Fritz Stahl's racist defamation of negroid features).
  [1] *Gesammelte Werke*, pp. 227, 230, 234.
  [2] Einstein's own poems were influenced by Stramm, who is said to have composed 'Negersagen' as a young man ('Ihn lockte das Urtümliche', his daughter said). See August Stramm, *Das Werk*, Wiesbaden 1963, p. 403.
  [3] *The Diaries*, p. 312. The period is also one of large-scale pioneering research into African languages (Meinhof) and cultural systems (Frobenius). Einstein's book on negro sculpture was written largely in Brussels, where there was by now a large ethnological collection.
  [4] *Die Flucht aus der Zeit*, p. 70. Cf. Richard Huelsenbeck's later statement about the search for 'a new beauty' in Zürich Dada: 'Wir hatten mit Nietzsche die

The alliance of primitivism and abstraction is one of the most copiously documented facts of the period under question. Both were ways of training imagination to pounce intuitively on the unsuspecting essence. Both were ways of baring the nerve of 'primary sensations' and of seeing universal forms as 'impressions of rhythm' (Malevich). As such, both were central to the deep changes in sensibility pervading all the arts by about 1913.[1] Many writers have studied these changes in the visual arts. The motives and forms of abstraction in German poetry have also received much attention recently, R. N. Maier's treatment being the most detailed and most acid (*Paradies der Weltlosigkeit*, 1964). Applied to poetry, the new value 'primitive' was clean contrary to the languishing idioms of the time, from the ornate sublime to the declamatory diffuse. It suggested a poetry of stark pre-logical metaphor, word dislocation, and new patternings of sound. This meant not merely a sporadic walloping of entrenched norms. The primitive was not just an anti-world, it was a world in itself. It promised a mode of imagining with its own rhythms and with an immediacy of vision which might break the spell of reason by reading it backwards. Here one might suspect that abstraction and primitivism colluded only up to a certain point. Abstraction was not always an end in itself, but was one means of preparing language for primitive effects (as in Stramm, and most notably in Carl Einstein's extra-

Relativität der Dinge und den Wert der Skrupellosigkeit gelernt ... ausgeklügelte Mittel, Intellektualität jeder Art mussten aufgegeben werden, wir verstanden von fern den Sinn der Primitivität — Dada, das Kinderlallen, das Hottentottische — die Primitivität, die das Zeitalter durch seine Vorliebe für Negerplastik, Negerliteratur und Negermusik anzudeuten schien' (*Dada siegt*, Berlin 1920, pp. 12–13). In retrospect on early Dada, Ball himself wrote in a letter to August Hoffmann, 7 Oct. 1916: 'meine Idee vom Dadaismus ... die Idee der absoluten Vereinfachung, der absoluten Negerei, angemessen den primitiven Abenteuern unserer Zeit' (*Briefe 1911–27*, Einsiedeln–Zürich–Cologne 1957, p. 66).

[1] Goldwater (pp. 130–40) discusses primitivistic traits in Suprematism (Malevich), Purism (Ozenfant), and Neo-Plasticism (Van Doesburg): 'plastic and associative elements heretofore used by painters are to be simplified, purified, or eliminated altogether, and the admittedly desirable synthesis of these analytic parts is to be obtained only from a combination of the barren remnants ... and in so far as the combination of such elements is deliberately limited in its richness and complication, we may correctly speak of the "primitivising" tendency of such theories' (p. 133). Cf. C. Malevich, *Die gegenstandslose Welt*, Munich 1927, p. 74, where the use of geometrical elements is compared to primitive marks of primitive men 'which in their ensemble do not portray an ornament but the impression of rhythm'. Malevich's early work is contemporaneous with primitivism in Russian poetry.

to the Poetry of Expressionism and Dada 195

ordinary poem 'Der tödlicher Baum'). It is not, I think, anachronistic to refer here to Hermann Broch's later evaluation of the primitive; it does apply to features in the imagery of Heym and Trakl which the fine terminology of abstraction seems to abuse:

> Die Welt wird wieder zum ersten Male gesehen, und zwar in einer Unmittelbarkeit wie sie sonst bloss dem Kinde und dem Primitiven . . . zu eigen ist, und so wird auch der Weltausdruck zu dem des Kindes, des Primitiven, des Träumenden: er vollzieht sich in einem Akt neuer Sprachschöpfung. . . . So ist daraus nun . . . etwas völlig Neues emporgeschossen, die Ur-Symbolik irrationalunmittelbarer Weltsicht.[1]

Primitivism was, at all events, an active force in the 'Umwortung aller Worte', the disarming of bourgeois language, which Morgenstern had begun with his 'humour' (as a species of psychic eruption) and his 'childlike' genius for breaking the sleep of words.[2] The poem as a magical exposure of psychic happenings, a meta-language, only lightly misted over by existing linguistic rationales: this was the mermaid left singing on the shore as nineteenth-century rationalism ebbed away. An ambiguous mermaid—deprived of her element, the ordering insulations of art, she could become a bloated demon bewitching all with new toxic illusions. Freud's *Gedanken über Krieg und*

[1] From 'Hofmannsthal und seine Zeit', *Dichten und Erkennen*, Bd. i, Zürich 1955, p. 58. In the 'Zerfall der Werte' sections of *Huguenau oder die Sachlichkeit* (1932) Broch had traced abstraction in Western thought back to the break-up of a supposedly unified value-system, that of the Christian Middle Ages. He implicated abstraction in the secular malaise of modern times, with God 'versunken in die unendliche Neutralität des Absoluten', and society, emptied of actual unifying value-content, splitting into countless isolated and purely functional sub-systems, or 'Wertgebiete'. Does the *dialectical* relation of primitivism and abstraction before 1914 imply that the former was a counter-agent to abstraction so construed? There are signs (Picasso, Klee, Hugo Ball) that the momentum of abstraction had by 1912–14 reached a point at which it became polarized into abstraction and primitivism, with primitivism as an attempt to resuscitate, or reify, the sense of the numinous—that 'God' which abstraction had turned into a neutral absolute, exiled from a polluted world. Three of Broch's examples of 'Sprachschöpfer' in the later essay are Van Gogh, Cézanne, and Henri Rousseau.

[2] For Morgenstern, Palmström meant freedom from 'jenem Zustande des ganz "Drinnenseins" in der Welt der Erscheinung, der den Menschen von heute in so hohem Masse gefangen und geknebelt hält'. The play of language might shake off 'die erdrückende Schwere und Schwerfälligkeit des sogenannten physischen Plans, der heute mit dem ganzen Ernst einer gott- und geistlos gewordenen Epoche als die alleinige und alleinseligmachende Wirklichkeit dekretiert wird' (Morgenstern's words, quoted in M. Bauer, *Christian Morgenstern*, pp. 177, 186).

Tod (1915) showed, at least, how he inferred from the war that the savage agitating under a skin-deep civilization has traits which are not paradisal at all, but plain brutish.

Ten facets of primitivism were listed at the start of this essay, and that list is not by any means complete. It is also a historical fact that primitivism in the twentieth century is as much a question of individual stylistic nuance as realism was in the previous century. There is, moreover, a 'false primitivism', which arises when the primitive or the archaic exerts a spell that paralyses critical and moral judgement (the Kridwiss circle in *Doktor Faustus*). Apart from motifs in poems, there are modulations in poetic structure which are an almost unexplored field among the cultural changes inspired by primitivism.[1] I propose now to plant some tentative markers in that field.

First, there is the matter of perspective. My suggestion is that primitivism has to do with plane surfaces, in painting and in poetry. It has often been noticed that naïve paintings and early abstract paintings suppress central perspective. Depth is reduced, and forms come to occupy a frontal plane. Kandinsky was concerned with this change in balance between plane surface (the canvas itself) and perspectivic modelling (depth of image): between 'flache Fläche' and 'ideelle Fläche'. The loss of 'possibilities' by flattening, he proposed, might be repaired by two methods: thinner or thicker lines with forms intersecting, and variable intensities of colour. Both methods could make the image psychically resonant, 'zu einem in der Luft schwebenden Wesen, was der malerischen Ausdehnung des Raumes gleichbedeutend ist'. Neither need relapse into illusionistic three-dimensional perspective, or into Cubism's 'impoverished plasticity'.[2] Worringer's view of primitive drawings also took up

[1] Examples of motifs: Jakob van Hoddis, 'Carthago'; Georg Heym, 'Das infernalische Abendmahl' (section II); possibly Heym's 'Die Gorillas'; Benn, 'Hier ist kein Trost', and 'Gesänge' (II). I would exclude Else Lasker-Schüler's child-persona poems, but not Kurt Schwitters's 'Grünes Kind' and his prose collage 'Aufruf! ein Epos' (in *Anna Blume und ich*, Zürich 1965, pp. 201–4). Schwitters's version of primitivism is one of the liveliest spectacles of the period; his use of 'base' material in collage is one aspect of it.

[2] *Über das Geistige in der Kunst*, pp. 94–5. Heinrich Hoerle (later a Constructivist) published in *Die Aktion* in 1917 (20 Jan.) a note in praise of plane surface in Picasso: 'Picasso wandte sich ab von der bildhaften Darstellung und kehrte — der wirkliche Primitive — zum Ursächlichen zurück = Bildebene' (*Ich schneide die Zeit aus*, ed. Paul Raabe, Munich 1964, p. 269).

to the Poetry of Expressionism and Dada

the problem: the savage artist is seen as a creator of absolute abstract forms on plane surfaces, who ignored the 'tridimensionality of the actual world'.[1] There is also a third factor: Nietzsche's critique of cognition and morals since the Renaissance, which culminates in *Der Wille zur Macht*. The 'world' is not identical with the world of our perspectives. These perspectives shape only its 'Scheinbarkeit'. But Nietzsche reverses idealism: he exclaims, 'Als ob eine Welt noch übrig bliebe, wenn man das Perspektivische abrechnet!' And he adds: 'Der Gegensatz der scheinbaren Welt und der wahren Welt reduziert sich auf den Gegensatz "Welt" und "Nichts".'[2] The existing 'perspektivische Welt' is a fiction fitted to the values of good and evil which men with eroded instincts have mistakenly set on things. The subversion of these values and of the opaque semeiotic system which enshrines them is the task of independent and creative minds, who dare to face the 'Nichts' without self-deception, and to project new and future values into it. Now can one correlate these four fields: Nietzsche's critique of mental perspectivism, the plane-surface theory of primitive art, Kandinsky's advance into abstraction from the zero point of the canvas as plane surface, and the converging of forms in flat frontal planes in Henri Rousseau? I would speculate, firstly, that this is a family of phenomena, though I cannot state how closely knit the family is; and, secondly, that the family does have a none-too-distant relation in a plane-surface factor to be found in the poetic imagery of Trakl, Jakob van Hoddis, and Lichtenstein. Trakl's patterning of tenses in his poems of 1912–14 creates a semblance of flat time, or simultaneity. Quasi-mythic events occur in the present tense of the poem, which is not the 'eternal present' of older lyric poems.[3] Trakl's present

[1] Source as in n. 4, p. 191.
[2] *Werke in drei Bänden*, Bd. 3, pp. 705–6. Cf. Paul Hatvani (in *Die Aktion*, 17 Mar. 1917), linking relativity theory with Expressionist dynamism in terms of perspective: 'die "psychozentrische Orientierung" des Denkens und Fühlens verbietet es, Standpunkte zu haben. So fliesst alles dorthin zurück, woher es einmal gekommen ist: ins Bewusstsein . . . Bewegung: darauf kommt es an' (*Ich schneide die Zeit aus*, pp. 276–7).
[3] Correspondences between the last section of 'Helian' and Paul Klee's painting *Scheidung abends* are discussed in a perceptive article by Jürgen Walter, 'Orientierung auf der formalen Ebene', in *DVS* 42, Nov. 1968. At points Walter's argument about Trakl's open texture verges on the plane-surface problem: 'Trakls Gedicht gibt weder nur den Eindruck eines "Äusseren" wieder, noch ist es rezeptiver Ausdruck eines "Inneren", es ist weder ganz im Emotionalen verwurzeltes visionäres

tenses are often bracketed by preterites which profile the mythic present without shifting it, or their own contexts, into a background. Present and past contexts occupy luminously the same imaginative time-plane. Time as succession is almost blotted out by time as visionary momentum, a kind of open-textured omnipresent, in which moments constellate in a planimetric time. This is the case in 'Helian' and in 'Elis' (I and II). In 'De Profundis' the time-plane also bends, without achieving anything like volume: the 'sanfte Waise' is gleaning (still), while, in the next stanza, shepherds *found* her corpse in the thorn-bush. In Jakob van Hoddis's poem 'Weltende' and Alfred Lichtenstein's 'Die Dämmerung' (to cite two well-known models of early Expressionist poetry), simultaneity again results in a flattening of time-perspective. In 'Die Dämmerung', additionally, the optics of the imagery become flat through the reduction of emphasis on any words denoting a presumptive or preformulated awareness. Thus Lichtenstein tucks the adjective 'fetter' away behind the emphatic verb 'klebt' in the line 'An einem Fenster klebt ein fetter Mann'. The montage here is of a kind which suppresses both optic depth and temporal sequence. This is the case in many poems of the time, in which simultaneity was the object, with plasticity held to a minimum, in favour of graphic abruptness and rapid visionary sweep. These poets need not have thought this new way of seeing to be primitivistic; but their imagery manifests features which were thought to be primitivistic by men who were pioneering the new visual aesthetics of the time.

Secondly, a more conspicuous (and perhaps antithetic) fruit of primitivism: Hugo Ball's sound poems of June 1916. Abstraction here eliminated lexicality almost entirely. Only soundpatterns are there, and in four of the poems the sounds are from African languages, notably Bantu and Swahili. Ball put an African mask on the European lyric, as Picasso in 1907 had put African mask-faces on two of his ladies of Avignon. Ball's endeavour was to rescue the 'innerste Alchimie des Wortes' from journalism's ravages;[1] later he dissociated this endeavour

Schauen, das "notwendig" zu einer bestimmten Gestaltungsform drängt, noch will es einen irgendwie gearteten Entwurf, eine Stimmung, eine Erinnerung "einholen", als Inhalt formal erfassen, als Gedicht realisieren' (p. 647).

[1] *Die Flucht aus der Zeit*, p. 100.

to the Poetry of Expressionism and Dada 199

from the rude onomatopoeic explosions of Marinetti, which he thought were all too naturalistic.[1] The African elements constitute a kind of transcultural pidgin: numerous Bantu and Swahili words do occur, but Ball could not have gone much further in rupturing their semantic relations, even if he had known (which seems unlikely) that they meant something.[2] The effect of such magical incantation, for a non-Bantu or non-Swahili speaker, is to extinguish all the lexical tensions which make and integrate 'meaning' symbolically.[3] On the other hand, as Goethe observed of the ballad, it all depends on the quality of the performance. Tonally and rhythmically, these poems oscillate between solemnity and fun, between incantation and irony. Their first performance was, for Ball, traumatic, in so far as a stratum of repressed childhood feeling was released in a discharge of mental images amid religious overtones.[4] But his catharsis included the moment of liberation which the ironic oscillation enshrines. This irony is, paradoxically, the mark of the 'truly primitive' in modern art. Without it, the critical distance

[1] *Briefe 1911–27*, Einsiedeln–Zürich–Cologne 1957, pp. 278–9: 'Die Wort-Analyse der Futuristen waren naturalistisch, Ihre eigenen Versuche dagegen, lieber Arp, und die meinen sind magisch' (22 Nov. 1926). Ball's later study of mystical ceremonies did not shake his idea that primitivizing could be a form of ritual regression to psychic origins: 'Ein unerschöpflicher Sinn wohnt den Riten und Zeremonien inne. Ihrem göttlichen Einfluss vermag sich niemand zu entziehen. Laternen und Lichter in leuchtender Symmetrie; ein primitives Gemisch von Tier- und Kinderlauten; eine Musik, die in längst verschollenen Kadenzen schwingt; all dies erschüttert die Seele und erinnert sie an ihre Urheimat' (*Byzantinisches Christentum*, Munich–Leipzig 1923, p. 132). In *Doktor Faustus*, such magic is in the terms of Leverkühn's contract with the devil ('das Archaische, das Urfrühe, das längst nicht mehr Erprobte'). In Leverkühn's *Apocalypsis cum figuris*, there is choral music with elements akin to Ball's idea: 'Chöre also, die durch alle Schattierungen des abgestuften Flüsterns, geteilten Redens, Halbsingens bis zum polyphonsten Gesang gehen, — begleitet von Klängen, die als blosses Geräusch, als magisch-fanatisch-negerhaftes Trommeln und Gong-Dröhnen beginnen und bis zur höchsten Musik reichen' (Moderne Klassiker edn., Frankfurt a. M. 1967, p. 373; the 'das Archaische' phrase, p. 237).
[2] There might have been sources for 'Katzen und Pfauen', 'Totenklage', 'Gadji beri bimba', and 'Karawane' (*Gesammelte Gedichte*, Zürich 1963). Three possibilities: Carl Meinhof's linguistic writings, Jan Ephraim (much-travelled proprietor of the Holländische Meierei), and 'die dicke Negerin Miss Ranovalla de Singapore', whom Ball met in a Basel *Wirtsstube* in Nov. 1915 (*Die Flucht aus der Zeit*, p. 58). I am grateful to Dr. Marcel van Spaandonck of the Merelbeke Institute for information about African words in these poems, and plan to publish the details separately.
[3] See R. Brinkmann, ' "Abstrakte" Lyrik im Expressionismus und die Möglichkeit symbolischer Aussage', in *Der deutsche Expressionismus*, esp. pp. 105–9.
[4] *Die Flucht aus der Zeit*, pp. 98–100.

shrinks and false primitivism, spell-binding and stupefying, raises its Medusa head. Irony controlled the inter-animation of meaning and unmeaning, or meaning and counter-meaning.

Thirdly, Hans Arp's word-fracturings. Arp's treatment of words exemplifies his own distinction between *Unsinn* and *Gegensinn* in *Unsern täglichen Traum* . . . There is much talk of the 'destruction of meaning' in Dada. Dada did mean the subversion of cliché, a form of violence implicit in poetry at most times, which now reached an intensity unthinkable before Rimbaud. But Dada also showed both that the unmaking of false meaning admits new life into art, and that meaning is not so easily unmade. Creative shocks may shatter certain norms, vernacular or poetic, but they also induce fresh integrations. Or ghostly coherences survive, in which the 'human substance' may not be so attenuated as conservative critics (like R. N. Maier) suppose. Arp makes not *Unsinn* but *Gegensinn*, in so far as strong traces of speech-norm survive as the frame in which a 'destruction' has been made. What determines the impact of the *Gegensinn* is often precisely the quality of the trace. 'Variante als Nr. 2', from *Behaarte Herzen*, contains the mild paronomasia,

> das schiff ist unglücklich
> schon seit kindesbeinen und -armen
> fühlt es die kerne in seinem innern (. . .)

Another version of the middle line, in *Die gestiefelten Sterne*, reads:

> schon seit kindesarmen (. . .)[1]

The semantic shift affects the phrase 'seit kindesbeinen'. In 'Variante als Nr. 2', the juxtaposition of norm and shift sharpens the point. In the other version, the pun is much flatter. Michael Polanyi's terms 'focal awareness' and 'subsidiary awareness' shed light on this and similar shifts.[2] The norm 'von kindesbeinen' is one on which we bear with focal awareness ordinarily, and in which we would notice nothing of intrinsic interest. But our subsidiary awareness realizes the tacit meaning in the *parts* of such a norm. Arp invents (usually from nouns) by structuring

[1] *Gesammelte Gedichte*, Bd. i, Zürich 1963, pp. 163, 161.
[2] *Personal Knowledge*, Chicago and London 1958; also 'Sense-Giving and Sense-Reading', *Philosophy*, 42 (1967), no. 162.

to the Poetry of Expressionism and Dada 201

his highly active subsidiary awareness and by feeling out the discrete properties of such parts. In 'von kindesbeinen und -armen' he is raising his subsidiary awareness to parity with the focal awareness. In 'von kindesarmen' he has allowed the subsidiary awareness almost, but not quite, to replace the focal awareness. The word 'heufische' in 'kaspar ist tot' is a more striking case of the shift. The norms *heu, haifisch, häufig, heuschrecke* become parts that are integrated in a neologism which has 'counter-meaning' and which then spins out its own web of phonic and semantic surprises. As subsidiary intrudes on focal awareness, so do parts and wholes change their relationships: *beileibe/beiseele, wagehalsig/wagenasig, katafalken/kataspatzen, spazierstockdunkle frauenzimmer, zum beinspiel*. This redisposal of levels of linguistic awareness was a key to many secret chambers of the mind. Yet with dead-pan cadences, absence of punctuation marks and of capitals, and with many nuances of under-emphasis, it sounds 'on the level', as indeed it is. For everything is done to make the 'denaturing' of speech-norms introduce a new 'nature' on the level of the planimetric word-configuration which raises to focal positions the elements of *Gegensinn* submerged or tacit in ordinary language. This is a German version of 'Zaum', or 'transrational language', as conceived at the time by Khlebnikov and Kruchenykh. Benedict Livshits's account of his first response to Khlebnikov's manuscripts is relevant: 'I saw before me language come alive. The breath of the original word seared my face . . . The baring of roots . . . was a real myth-making, an awakening of meanings dormant in the word, as well as the birth of new ones.'[1] In Arp the word reveals itself as a sparkling field of perception the moment when silent supports of meaning rush, dance, hop, or creep out of hiding and become its positive structure. His method added to the plane-surface element of primitivism two further elements: childishness is regained on a highly structured level of ironic intelligence, and we witness the actual unfolding of processes which initiate language and so shape our sense of a world. Primitivism had become a way to realize meaning precisely where language

[1] V. Markov, *Russian Futurism: a History*, p. 14. See also p. 141, on Victor Boris Chlovski's early views on 'making it strange' and the startling renewal of the poetic image by word-distortion (*Voskresenie slova*, 1914). On 'Zaum' see Markov, pp. 345–50, where Kruchenykh's 'Declaration of Transrational Language' (1921) is translated.

seemed to be doing nothing; or, to quote Klee: 'Die Genesis als formale Bewegung ist das Wesentliche am Werk.'[1]

The structural features on which I have touched indicated new modes of perception, a new creative sensibility. Public primitivism during the first half of this century faced the other way: it meant the recrudescence of archaic instincts in deadly modern guise and with hideous instruments—aggressiveness, violence, even supine collaboration with terror as 'fate', as 'the historical dialectic', 'the white man's burden', and so forth. But there have also been joyous effects, like the primitivism of 'negritude' in body-based dance and song, which since 1963, at least in the U.S.A., has been bending, if not breaching, the labyrinthine racial barriers, unfreezing the 'soul' amid the ferment of 'America's attempt to unite its Mind with its Body, to save its Soul'.[2] Certainly in art and anti-art, primitivism now seems to have sounded a positive note among the cacophonic desublimations and the ecstasies of destruction. It sought to achieve the ingression of new salutary life-instincts into civilized man. It helped to shatter 'illusionistic art' and those ideologies which such art shields. It challenged, with its reversals of 'meaning', the pseudo-nature imposed on people's senses by the repressive rationality of unfree social systems. It was an early signal of the present 'Great Refusal': it promised liberation from those compulsions which make men stupid, brutal, and automatic. Yet now these early primitivisms have mainly been absorbed. They are accepted as art, safe in museums and books, overshadowed or neutered by what Herbert Marcuse has called 'the technical reaches of powers whose terrible imagination organizes the world in their own image and perpetuates, ever bigger and better, the mutilated experience'.[3] Heavy, indeed, are the odds against any eventual realization, in societal terms, of the three forms of new sensibility outlined here. Specifically:

[1] Paul Klee, *Das bildnerische Denken. Schriften zur Form und Gestaltungslehre*, Basle 1964, p. 457.
[2] See Eldridge Cleaver, *Soul on Ice*, New York 1968, pp. 202–4.
[3] Herbert Marcuse, *An Essay on Liberation*, Boston 1969, p. 45. Erich Kahler (in *The Disintegration of Form*, New York 1968) views with profound suspicion the desublimations in which Marcuse detects cathartic changes in 'the historical *topos* of the aesthetic' leading towards a 'transformation of the *Lebenswelt*' (op. cit., p. 45). It seems to me that Marcuse does disregard a real difference between sensibility which creates and that which can only destroy.

(1) in plane-surface poetic imagery, a model for a balanced visionary optics of time, with psychological and historical tensions mastered without violence, without their doing violence to one another; (2) in the sound-poem, signs that even down among the translexical nerve-roots of language rhythm and song are facts of life (here, in my view, the irony in the structure is a token of intellectual joy in invention, liberation from the spell of regression); (3) in Arp's word-fracturings, a lucidity which denies that word and world can be stereotyped, which understands the silences embedded in language, and which announces that imagination's linguistic universe has an ordering as well as an analytic function in the transformation of the senses, and of their world.

DADA DANCES
Hugo Ball's *Tenderenda der Phantast*

SIEGBERT PRAWER

> Seine Verse sind ein Versuch, die Totalität dieser unnennbaren Zeit mit all ihren Rissen und Sprüngen, mit all ihren bösartigen und irrsinnigen Gemütlichkeiten, mit all ihrem Lärm und dumpfen Getöse in eine erhellte Melodie aufzufangen. Aus den phantastischen Untergängen lächelt das Gorgohaupt eines masslosen Schreckens.
>
> HUGO BALL on Richard Huelsenbeck, 11 March 1916

> We had fed the heart on fantasies,
> The heart's grown brutal from the fare;
> More substance in our enmities
> Than in our love; o honey-bees,
> Come build in the empty house of the stare.
>
> W. B. YEATS, *Meditations in Time of Civil War*, 1922

JUST a year after the outbreak of the First World War, in neutral Zürich, Hugo Ball noted in his diary:

Wie mag einem Menschen zumute sein, wie muss einer leben, der sich zugehörig empfindet und in verhängnisvoller Weise geneigt erschiene, alle Art Abenteuer, alle Verwirrung der Probleme und der Delikte auf seine eigene, alleinige Konstitution zu beziehen? Wie möchte sich ein Wesen behaupten, dessen phantastisches Ich nur dazu geschaffen scheint, das Unerhörte, den Widerspruch, die Empörung all dieser losgelassenen Kräfte in sich zu empfangen und auszuleiden? Wenn uns die Sprache wahrhaft zu Königen unserer Nation macht, dann sind ohne Zweifel wir es, die Dichter und Denker, die dieses Blutbad verschuldet und die es zu sühnen haben. (FadZ 40.)[1]

When he set down these words, Ball had already begun the

---

[1] In quoting from Hugo Ball's works, the following abbreviations have been used: B = *Briefe 1911–27*, ed. A. Schütt-Hennings, Benziger Verlag, Einsiedeln 1957; FadZ = *Die Flucht aus der Zeit*, Verlag Josef Stocker, Lucerne 1946 (all quotations from Ball's diaries are taken from this work. The original, unexpurgated, and unedited versions have not been published); TdP = *Tenderenda der Phantast*, Verlag der Arche, Zürich 1967.

Hugo Ball's 'Tenderenda der Phantast' 205

novel that was to depict a number of such 'fantastic selves' destined to feel upon their pulses the chaos, the disorder, the cruelty of the time—the novel which obsessed him for six years and to which he finally gave the title *Tenderenda der Phantast*. Completed in 1920, it was not published until 1967, exactly forty years after its author's death. This belated publication has made available, at last, a book of which admirers of Ball had had tantalizing, all too brief glimpses in *Die Flucht aus der Zeit*, and one which confirms all the hopes such glimpses could have aroused. It combines what Ball called his *Sprachzucht* (disciplined cultivation of strange linguistic blooms) with gaiety and irony, and all three with a deep and pervading sense of horror, outrage, and the necessity of expiation. It allows us to experience for ourselves something of that fascination attested by contemporaries who heard Ball read extracts from his novel at the Cabaret Voltaire and the Galerie Dada—a fascination Ball himself analysed when he compared his own work with that of Richard Huelsenbeck:

Die Verwendung von 'Sigeln', von magisch erfüllten fliegenden Worten und Klangfiguren kennzeichnet unsere gemeinsame Art zu dichten. Solcherlei Wortbilder, wenn sie gelungen sind, graben sich unwiderstehlich und mit hypnotischer Macht dem Gedächtnis ein, und ebenso unwiderstehlich und reibungslos tauchen sie aus dem Gedächtnisse wieder auf. Ich erlebe es häufig, dass Leute, die unvorbereitet unsere Abende besuchten, von einem einzelnen Worte oder Satzglied derart beeindruckt wurden, dass es sie wochenlang nicht mehr verliess. (FadZ 94.)[1]

From the first vision of Donnerkopf, conveyed in solemn, Biblical locutions and rhythms: 'Siehe, er sass vor Atlanten und Zirkeln und kündete Weisheit der oberen Sphären. Lange Papyrusrollen liess er, mit Zeichen und Tieren bemalt, vom Turme herab und warnte damit das Volk, das unter den Nestern stand, vor den kreischenden Scharen der Engel, die wütend den Turm umflogen' (TdP 13), and the sound of ancestral voices prophesying war in the chapter entitled 'Das Karussellpferd Johann: 'Ein Kopf war gefunden worden, der

[1] How closely Ball and Huelsenbeck collaborated can be deduced from Ball's diary entry dated 15 June 1916: 'Huelsenbeck kommt, um auf der Maschine seine neuesten Werke abzuschreiben. Bei jeder zweiten Vokabel wendet er den Kopf und sagt: "Oder ist das etwa von Dir?"' (FadZ 93).

schrie 'Blut! Blut!' unstillbar, und Petersilien wuchsen ihm über die Backenknochen. Die Thermometer standen voll Blut, und die Muskelstrecker funktionierten nicht mehr. In den Bankhäusern diskontierte man die Wacht am Rhein' (TdP 22), the reader finds himself borne along on waves of horror and laughter to the final sections of the novel, with their unforgettable images, rhythms, and vowel-harmonies: 'Wir Fratzenschneider, im Feuermantel tanzend ums Wasserfass' (TdP), their sonorous invocations and questions: 'Oh dieses Jahrhundert aus Glühlicht und Stacheldraht, Urkraft und Abgrund! Was sollten hier Dokumente der Qual? (TdP 111), and their parodies of epigrams and commonplaces, concealing sense in nonsense: 'Auf einer Höllenmaschine kann man nicht Kaffee kochen' (TdP 124). To savour *Tenderenda* to the full, one must read it aloud, or at least cultivate the inner ear sufficiently to imagine Ball's public readings of 'Das Karussellpferd Johann', 'Der Untergang des Machetanz', and 'Grand Hotel Metaphysik'. Ball himself attached the greatest importance to such readings:

> Nirgends so sehr als beim öffentlichen Vortrag ergeben sich die Schwächen einer Dichtung. Das eine ist sicher, dass die Kunst nur solange heiter ist, als sie der Fülle und der Lebendigkeit nicht entbehrt. Das laute Rezitieren ist mir zum Prüfstein der Güte eines Gedichtes geworden, und ich habe mich (vom Podium) belehren lassen, in welchem Ausmasse die heutige Literatur problematisch, das heisst am Schreibtische erklügelt und für die Brille des Sammlers, statt für die Ohren lebendiger Menschen gefertigt ist. (FadZ 75–6.)

If nothing else, *Tenderenda der Phantast* demonstrates incontrovertibly Ball's unfailing ear for the rhythms of German speech and the potential musicality of the German language.

Nothing, however, could have been further from Ball's mind than to think of his novel as appealing solely to the ear. The creator of the finest sound-poems (*Klanggedichte*) ever written was no advocate of art for art's sake, of a 'pure' poetry that sought no public and made no comment on its own time. 'Man kann wohl sagen', he wrote of himself and his fellow Dadaists, 'dass uns die Kunst nicht Selbstzweck ist — dazu bedürfte es einer mehr ungebrochenen Naivität —, aber sie ist uns eine Gelegenheit zur Zeitkritik und zum wahrhaften Zeitempfinden' (FadZ 81). And he continues, in words that clearly state the problem he set himself to solve with *Tenderenda der Phantast*:

Hugo Ball's 'Tenderenda der Phantast'

'Was besagt ein Roman, der von Bildungs wegen zwar gelesen wird, der aber weit davon entfernt ist, die Bildung auch zu bewegen?' (ibid.). *Tenderenda*, therefore, plays with the fragments of a culture that revealed its bankruptcy in the First World War in order to bring home to its readers one poet's horror at the world he was forced to inhabit, along with glimpses of its end. Its grave buffoonery sorts well with Ball's famous definition of the spirit of Dada as he and the other founders envisaged it in their Zürich days: 'ein Narrenspiel aus dem Nichts, in das alle höheren Fragen verwickelt sind; eine Gladiatorengeste; ein Spiel mit den schäbigen Überbleibseln; eine Hinrichtung der posierten Moralität und Fülle' (FadZ 91). It is *the* novel of Dada, as Marinetti's *Mafarka le Futuriste* is *the* novel of Futurism and Breton's *Nadja* the novel of Surrealism[1]—but Ball's decision not to publish it during his lifetime showed that he had put Dada behind him, that he had, in fact, worked Dada out of his system in the act of writing this very book:

Ich kann das Büchlein nur mit jenem wohlgefügten magischen Schrein vergleichen, worin die alten Juden den Asmodai eingesperrt glaubten. Immer wieder in all den sieben Jahren habe ich mich zwischen Qualen und Zweifeln mit diesen Worten und Sätzen verspielt. Nun ist das Büchlein fertig geworden und ist mir eine liebe Befreiung. Alle jene Anfälle der Bosheit mögen darin begraben sein, von denen der hl. Ambrosius sagt:

> Procul recedant somnia
> Et noctium phantasmata,
> Hostemque nostrum conprime.
>
> (TdP 135.)

The title he then gave to his book, *Tenderenda der Phantast*, suggests in its rhythm, sound-pattern, and grammatical structure that Ball may have had *Mafarka le Futuriste* in mind; but whether this is true or not, the novel may certainly be seen as a counterblast to Futurist glorifications of violence, worship of machinery, irreligiosity, and rejection of the human along with the humane.

The figure of Tenderenda does not turn up until relatively late in the evolution of the novel, as far as this can be traced in

---

[1] Cf. Christa Baumgarth, *Geschichte des Futurismus*, Reinbek 1966, pp. 62–4 and 247–9; Roger Shattuck, 'The Nadja File', *Cahiers de l'Association internationale pour l'étude de DADA et du surréalisme*, i, Paris 1966, pp. 49–56; and Armin Arnold, *Die Literatur des Expressionismus*, Stuttgart 1966.

Ball's diaries and in various handbills and posters announcing public readings from his work. From the first, however, the title was to have proclaimed the pre-eminence, in the book, of fantasy and those who live by fantasy; we find it variously referred to as 'Die Phantasten', 'Phantastischer Roman', 'Phantastenroman', and 'phantastisch = pamphletisch = mystische[r] Roman' (FadZ 56, 117, 135, 141, 264; B 57). It is therefore relevant to inquire what *das Phantastische* meant to Ball.

The diaries show clearly that Ball saw in what was generally called *phantastisch* a more fitting representation of modern 'reality' than any produced by naturalistic means. The scientists, he believed, had shown how mistaken it was to believe in the 'solidity' of the objects that confronted us in our everyday lives —a conclusion anticipated and confirmed by philosophical epistemologists; while the behaviour of nations made a mockery of everything which might be considered fundamental moral principle. The world *was* fantastic, and nothing but fantasy could hope to catch its essence: 'Bei genauerem Hinsehen lösen die Dinge sich im [*sic*] Phantasmata auf... Was man gemeinhin Wirklichkeit nennt, ist, exakt gesprochen, ein aufgebauschtes Nichts... Wer an die Wirklichkeit dessen glauben wollte, was ringsum geschieht, der müsste schon sehr kurzsichtig und schwerhörig sein, dass ihn kein Grauen und Schwindel ergriffe über die Nichtigkeit dessen, was frühere Generationen Humanität genannt haben' (FadZ 66). Fantasy might reach the essence of reality more surely than any self-styled 'realism'; Ball, therefore, clearly distances himself from the poets he introduces into the final section of his novel, poets who have escaped Armageddon only to busy themselves with cataloguing putrefaction and toning down the fantastic aspects of everything that surrounds them: 'eifrig damit beschäftigt, die Verwesung zu registrieren und die phantastische Wirklichkeit zweckmässig abzuschwächen' (TdP 89). Fantasy, however, was more to Ball than a registration of modern reality—it could also be a criticism of that reality. By jumbling and distorting the elements of our daily perception, a writer could show disrespect for the world and its lack of principle: 'Die Gegenwart ist nicht in Prinzipien sie ist nur noch assoziativ vorhanden. Also leben wir in einer phantastischen Zeit, die ihre Entschlüsse mehr aus der Angliederung als aus unerschütterten Grundsätzen bezieht.

Der gestaltende Geist kann mit dieser Zeit beginnen, was ihm beliebt. Sie ist in ihrer ganzen Ausdehnung Freigut, "Materie"' (FadZ 102). Ball does not think of fantasy as a means of escaping from an unpleasant reality—on the contrary, he thinks that a 'phantastisches Ich' is menaced by destruction precisely because it feels the chaos of the world more strongly than the sober Philistine. Such a consciousness is peculiarly apt, in Ball's own words, 'das Unerhörte, den Widerspruch, die Empörung all dieser losgelassenen Kräfte in sich zu empfangen und auszuleiden' (FadZ 40). At the same time, however, Ball allows himself to speculate—as did so many of his contemporaries—on the regenerative effect fantastic art might have on modern life. Did it not oppose the world of the child to a world grown senile? Was it not good to play out 'alles kindlich Phantastische, alles kindlich Direkte, kindlich Figürliche gegen die Senilitäten, gegen die Welt der Erwachsenen' (FadZ 101)? Well, perhaps; the diary entry of 5 August 1915 is an apology for the deliberate childishness of Dada, its 'Sich überbieten in Einfalt und Kindsköpfigkeit' (FadZ 102); but this same diary entry shows Ball's awareness that the imagination of children is terrifyingly prone to corruption, 'aller Verderbnis und aller Verkehrtheit ausgesetzt'. What follows in the diary is therefore a series of notes for an Essay Against Fantasy, 'Ein hübscher anti-phantastischer Aufsatz' (FadZ 102), whose chief thesis would have been that if it is wrong to confuse logic with *logos*, it is no less wrong to confuse *logos* with the human imagination.

There was another argument, however, which Ball himself had used in defence of the possible regenerative power of fantasy. Might it not lead men into a world of *Urbilder* (FadZ 68), that world of the mothers to which Goethe had made his Faust descend? Might not the creation of fantastic art have a liberating, cathartic effect on those who have to endure the rush of modern life? Here Hugo Ball clearly anticipates arguments that were later to be used by the French Surrealists:

Das Betreiben irgendeiner Kunst wird ihnen guttun, vorausgesetzt, dass sie in ihren Sujets keine [*sic*] Absicht, sondern der freien und fessellosen Imagination folgen. Der selbständige Phantasieprozess fördert unfehlbar diejenigen Dinge wieder zutage, die die Bewusstseinsgrenze unzergliedert überschritten haben. In einer Zeit wie der unsern, in der die Menschen täglich von den ungeheuerlichsten

Dingen bestürmt werden, ohne sich über die Eindrücke Rechenschaft geben zu können, in solcher Zeit wird das ästhetische Produzieren zur Diät. (FadZ 70.)

The result of such a descent into the unconscious will be—so Ball believed in 1915—a living art: 'Alle lebende Kunst aber wird irrational, primitiv und komplexhaft sein, eine Geheimsprache führen und Dokumente nicht der Erbauung, sondern der Paradoxie hinterlassen' (ibid.). In the following year he introduced a group of such 'poets of fantasy' (what we have since learnt to call 'surrealist' poets) into his novel, and made its spokesman pride himself on his irreverent irrationality: 'Sehr geehrter Herr Feuerschein! Ihr konföderiertes Naturburschentum, Ihre Latwergfarbe, das imponiert uns nicht. Noch Ihre entliehene Kinodramatik! Aber ein Wort zur Aufklärung: Wir sind Phantasten. Wir glauben nicht mehr an die Intelligenz. Wir haben uns auf den Weg gemacht, um dieses Tier [='Das Karussellpferd Johann', which gives the chapter its title], dem unsere ganze Verehrung gilt, vor dem Mob zu retten' (TdP 26). But as Ball was the first to note (in *Die Flucht aus der Zeit*), the character who speaks these words is himself treated with irony—his very name, Stiselhäher, makes it difficult to take him seriously. *Tenderenda der Phantast* is anything but a document of confident irrationalism. Was irrationality, after all, not a hallmark of the very world that Ball hated? Did not that world regress to the primitive, only making its primitiveness more loathsome and barbarous with its technological inventions? Might not therefore the suspension of intellect in the service of individual fantasy mean playing the world's game? As the diary proceeds, such questions move more and more into the foreground:

> Die Kunst unserer Zeit hat es in ihrer Phantastik, die von der vollendeten Skepsis herrührt, zunächst nicht mit Gott, sondern mit dem Dämon zu tun; sie selber ist dämonisch. Alle Skepsis aber und alle skeptische Philosophie, die dieses Resultat vorbereiteten, sind es ebenso. (FadZ 83–4.)

> Die Kunst in ihrer Phantastik . . . verdankt sich der vollendeten Skepsis. Folglich münden die Künstler, soweit sie Skeptiker sind, in den Strom der phantastischen Zeit; sie gehören dem Untergang,

Hugo Ball's 'Tenderenda der Phantast'

sind seine Emmissäre und Blutsverwandte, wie sehr sie sich gegensätzlich gebärden mögen. Ihre Antithese ist eine Täuschung. (FadZ 102.)

Fantasy could lead—as so many Surrealist works were later to demonstrate—to visions of cruelty and bestiality that paralleled only too exactly what went on in the world whose regeneration Ball devoutly wished. He therefore found himself less and less willing to follow Dada along the path later trodden, with little resistance, by Tristan Tzara: the path that led to Surrealism. He left Zürich, and in his diary he solemnly abjured the *spiritus phantasticus*: 'Die Metapher, die Imagination, und die Magie selbst, wo sie nicht auf Offenbarung und Tradition gegründet sind, verkürzen und garantieren nur die Wege zum Nichts; sie sind Blendwerk und Diabolik. Vielleicht ist die ganze assoziative Kunst, mit der wir die Zeit zu fangen und zu fesseln glauben, ein Selbstbetrug' (FadZ 158). This is dated May 1917; yet in 1919 we find him working on his novel again, the novel whose very title paid tribute to his *spiritus phantasticus*, the dearest child of his Dada year; and in July 1920 he triumphantly notes its conclusion, comparing it, as we have seen, with a magic casket in which an evil spirit has been imprisoned. He did indeed feel liberated in the way he had anticipated in the diary entry of 25 November 1915 (FadZ 70). Prefixing to the completed manuscript a prayer from St. Bernard of Clairvaux,

> O vous, messeigneurs et mes dames,
> Qui contemplez ceste painture,
> Plaise vous prier pour les âmes
> De ceulx qui sont en sepulture,

he put it into his drawer and turned to his investigations into the spirit of Byzantine Christianity.

As might be expected from a book conceived during the Dada rebellion against accepted literary canons, *Tenderenda der Phantast* belies most of the expectations Hugo Ball's contemporaries would have brought to a novel. Characters come and go without explanation; the scene shifts constantly between actual cities and a limbo that may be hell or some astral paradise; real people are mentioned—Huelsenbeck, Ludwig Rubiner, Max Reinhardt, and others who played a part in Ball's life; these jostle characters called Schmidt, Schulze, Meyer, Lilienstein,

Feuerschein, and encounter gods, devils, menacing angels, and vampire-like ghosts along with prophets and visionaries. Some characters and incidents are clearly allegorical:[1] Mulche-Mulche is the spirit of fantasy out of which Dada is born, Musikon the spirit of music and the dance; others, like the couple called Goldkopf in the very last chapter, admit of no simple allegorical 'translation'. There are constant 'jump-cuts' between images and incidents—the chapter which has been principally concerned with attempts to rescue a roundabout-horse (*Karussell-Pferd*) ends with a glimpse of quite different beasts in quite different locations: 'Die Hündin Rosalie lag schwer in den Wochen. Fünf junge Polizeihunde erblickten das Licht der Welt. Auch fing man um diese Zeit in einem Spreekanal zu Berlin einen chinesischen Kraken. Das Tier wurde auf die Polizeiwache gebracht' (TdP 26). The gloss or argument which Ball prefixes to each chapter (in the manner of Boccaccio or eighteenth-century English novelists) pretends to 'explain' such transitions: 'In fernen Ländern begegnet man dem Häuptling Feuerschein, der sich jedoch als Polizeispitzel entpuppt. Daran geknüpft historiologische Bemerkungen über die Niederkunft einer Polizeihündin in Berlin' (TdP 19)— but such ironic explanations only underline the irrationally associational nature of the passage they gloss. The book thus mirrors directly a world in disorder, and an imagination affected by that disorder even while playing with the orts and fragments that it finds. Disorder shows itself from the very first chapter in the transformation of angels into harpies ('kreischende[n] Scharen . . . die wütend den Turm umflogen', TdP 13), in bizarre extensions of ritual ('mit Fasten und Purgativen bereitete sich die Stadt auf eines neuen Gottes Erscheinen vor; die Bitt- und Kaffeeprozessionen', TdP 14), in the annihilation of all difference between great and small (TdP 15), and in the grotesque disasters that befall the shadowy figures peopling the book('Die Glasscherben des zerbrochenen Wunderspiegels aber zerschnitten die Häuser, zerschnitten die Menschen, das Vieh, die Seiltänzereien, die Fördergruben und alle Ungläubigen, so dass sich die Zahl der Verschnittenen mehrte von Tag zu Tag', TdP 18). Yet the allegorical elements already noted; the clear division into three

---

[1] Ball himself, in the glosses, points to the allegorical content of his work; e.g. TdP 121: 'Zärtliche Allegorien in Tiergestalt treten auf.'

Hugo Ball's 'Tenderenda der Phantast' 213

parts, subdivided into self-contained chapters that build up in a way not inaccessible to logical exegesis; the surprisingly 'normal', un-eccentric sentence-structure in which the narrator speaks to his readers throughout; and the many clear-headed, rational comments contained in the arguments or glosses along with ironies and apparent irrelevances—all these counteract the surface anarchy of the book. Ball's keen intellect and powers of rational analysis have not been excluded from *Tenderenda*. They may be suspended for a while, to allow visions to rise from the unconscious without fear of censorship; but they assert themselves in the very shape of the sentences that embody such visions, and are allowed to appear undisguised in such glosses as that on 'Der Untergang des Machetanz' (TdP 27), 'Bulbos Gebet und der gebratene Dichter' (TdP 65), 'Hymnus 2' (TdP 81), and 'Hymnus 3' (TdP 103).

Just as a keenly analytic mind shines through the playful and irrationally creative, so the most fantastic visions cannot hide Ball's constant and deep concern with the realities of the world within which he wrote. 'Das Karussellpferd Johann' belongs to the months immediately preceding the outbreak of war ('Man schreibt den Sommer 1914', TdP 19); 'Satanopolis' suggests the slaughter of the war itself in surreal visions ('Vorbei an den Lampentürmen und Hochöfen, in denen die Leichen der toten Soldaten flammen bei Nacht', TdP 45); while 'Hymnus 3' seems addressed to the very spirit of post-1919 Germany:

> Mit Ersatzscheinen, Blech-, Email-, Papier- und Knopfgeld grüssen wir dich
>
> . . . .
>
> Für eine Mark haben sich hingegeben der tändelnde Dichter, der warme Prolet, der Zeitungsmann und der Priester
>
> . . . .
>
> Unsere alldeutschen Knotenstocke schwingen wir, bemalt mit Runen und Hakenkreuzen. (TdP 83–4.)

Mechanization, levelling of culture, debasement of language through journalism and war propaganda, economic crises, philosophic disorientation—these are as much the 'material' of *Tenderenda der Phantast* as the private fantasies of a sensitive, intelligent, and many-sided artist. And if disorder has, perforce, to be the main theme of the book, its fantastic scenes constantly suggest possibilities of order; suggest meta-natural or metaphysical hierarchies which are usually, it is true, treated with irony. The witches' sabbath of 'Die roten Himmel' is set in the *upper* Inferno and enlivened by 'Tanten aus der siebenten Dimension' (TdP 35); we hear of vergers of the *lower* heavens (TdP 94) and of a place where hell adjoins paradise (TdP 68). The section entitled 'Satanopolis' is said to take place in the lowest ink-hell (TdP 39). 'In der untersten Tintenhölle' is a particularly characteristic and revealing coinage. It suggests a hell as black as ink. It suggests, too, a hell particularly fit for the hero of this particular chapter, a journalist who makes his living by ink-marks on paper and by consigning his enemies to a martyrdom in print that might indeed be called an 'ink-hell'. Last but by no means least, it joins other compound nouns in *Tenderenda*, nouns like 'letter-tree' and 'fable-meadow' (*Buchstabenbaum, Fabelwiese*—TdP 121, 123) in suggesting a world that rises up in the very act of writing and telling a story—a world of fantasy, in fact, that grows out of language itself. Ball shows himself constantly capable of such creation; but he shows himself no less capable of analysing and evaluating his fantasies, and of allowing quite different realities to appear alongside or within them.

Perhaps the most delightful surprise the belated publication of *Tenderenda* has brought is the realization that though it was not completed until 1920, when Ball had turned away from Dada and all its works, it is nevertheless as good a compilation of Dada's literary activities and experiments as one could hope to find between the covers of a single book. The glosses make clear the pride that Ball felt, even after the war, in the splash Dada had been able to make: 'Über keine Rede der Herren Clemenceau und Lloyd George, über keinen Büchsenschuss Ludendorffs regte man sich so auf wie über das schwankende Häuflein dadaistischer Wanderpropheten, die die Kindlichkeit auf ihre Weise verkündeten' (TdP 53).[1] In the gloss on p. 99 he appears in his own person, reading the sound-poem *Karawane* in the costume Janko designed for him. Richard Huelsen-

---

[1] How delighted Hugo Ball could be at Dada's success even after he himself had severed his connection with the movement may be seen in his description of a *Dada-Abend* he attended in Berlin at the end of Apr. 1919 (B 124, letter to Emmy Hennings dated 2 May 1919).

Hugo Ball's 'Tenderenda der Phantast'

beck, holding a flower in his mouth, is exorcised on p. 114; and Mulche-Mulche's first-born ('ein klein Jüdlein, das trug ein klein Krönlein auf purpurnem Haupte und schwang sich sogleich auf die Nabelschnur und begann dort zu turnen', TdP 63) is clearly a caricature of Tristan Tzara. The many grotesque apocalyptic scenes that occur throughout the book remind adverted readers of the close connection between the beginnings of Dada and the visionary, grotesque Expressionism of van Hoddis, Lichtenstein, and Heym:[1]

> Hell brach ein Himmel zusammen. Ein Luftschacht legte sich quer. Über den Himmel hinweg flog eine Kette geflügelter Wöchnerinnen.
>
> Die Gasanstalten, die Bierbrauereien und die Rathauskuppeln gerieten ins Wanken und dröhnten im Paukengeschnatter. Dämonen, bunten Gefieders, beklackerten sein Gehirn, zerzausten und rupften es. Über dem Marktplatz, der in die Sterne versank, ragte mit ungeheurer Sichel der grünliche Rumpf eines Schiffes, das senkrecht auf seiner Spitze stand... (TdP 29.)

Other reminders of Dada's connection with early Expressionism may be found in Ball's emotive use of colour adjectives in *Tenderenda*: '*violetten* Gesichtes' (TdP 14), '*Zitronengelb* stehen die Himmel' (ibid.), 'die *blauen* Katzen' (TdP 37), are only three of many examples that recall Trakl or Marc or Kokoschka. The book allows us to hear something of the *bruitismo* that Dada took over, along with much else, from Italian Futurism, though it put it to rather different use: those dissonant noises, produced by human vocal chords and/or an assortment of drums, rattles, and tin trays, which became a staple of Dada performances. The chapter 'Die roten Himmel' is pervaded, as the gloss explains, by 'ein Konzert heilloser Geräusche, das selbst die Tiere in Erstaunen setzt' (TdP 35); a later chapter presents us with a chorus of ghosts who intone a dirge through cement pipes (TdP 67). Dirges and ritual chants were a speciality of Zürich

---

[1] Cf. J. C. Middleton, 'Dada vs. Expressionism or The Red King's Dream', *German Life and Letters*, N.S. 15 (1961), 44: 'Certainly Dada did canalise the strong absurdist element of early Expressionist poetry into the main stream of modern experiment, which flows into French Surrealism as the idea of a non-literary literature.' I cannot, however, agree with Professor Middleton when he calls the link between Dada and early Expressionism 'dubious'—Hugo Ball's interest in the work of van Hoddis is well attested.

Dada. In *Tenderenda* absurd manifestos are read out, as they were at many a Dada gathering, at the devil's garden restaurant (TdP 45). The novel is full of strange dances, reminding us that *danses nègres* and *kubistische Tänze* frequently featured at Dada soirées. Characters in strange costumes recite nonsense and sing to the accompaniment of protests from the audience: 'Der Teufel trat auf mit Kis de Paris und Ridikül, sprach einiges unwirsches Zeug und sang den Rigoletto. Man rief ihm hinauf, er sei ein gespreizter Einfaltspinsel, er möge die Spässe lassen...' (TdP 42). There are irreverent hoaxes in which *Angst* cannot be dispelled by laughter: 'Als Versuchsballon liessen sie aufsteigen die violettausstrahlende "Kartoffelseele". Auf ihren Leuchtraketen stand: "God save the King" oder "Wir treten zum Beten". Durch ein Schallrohr aber liessen sie auf die Plattform rufen: "Die Angst vor der Gegenwart verzehrt uns"' (TdP 57–8); to which must be added those deliberate provocations that are summed up in the cry of a character named Pimperling: 'Hoch lebe der Skandal!' The book is full of parody and persiflage—the language and situations of the Bible, Goethe's *Faust*, Nietzsche's *Zarathustra* are all imitated, and the reader constantly comes upon fragments of older literature in a deliberately inappropriate context. The *Festprogramm* read out at the last funeral on earth, for instance, contains the opening line of a once popular poem by Gustav Schwab:

> Gott dem Allmächtigen,
> hat es gefallen,
> unsere Urahne, Grossmutter, Mutter und Kind,
> Herrn Gottlieb Zwischenzahn,
> von der Firma Zwischenzahn, Kiefer & Co.,
> Wurst- und Fleischwaren en gros,
> zu sich abzuberufen. (TdP 91.)

The name of the firm which features in this excerpt is one of those schoolboy jokes to which Dada was prone; a deliberate regression that frequently abutted (as it occasionally does in *Tenderenda*) on schoolboy scatology. The passage also demonstrates Dada's obsession with newspaper styles, with the language and method of advertisements and public announcements. The love–hate relationship of Dada and Surrealist painters and poets with modern advertising is a fascinating chapter of history that has yet to be written.

Hugo Ball's 'Tenderenda der Phantast'

Characteristic of Dada, above all, is the nonsense verse, frequently recalling children's rhymes, that is to be found in *Tenderenda*:

> O lalalo lalalo lalalo,
> Der Kopf ist aus Glas und die Hände aus Stroh.
> O lalalo lalalo lalalo!
> Zinnoberzack, Zetter und Mordio!   (TdP 38.)

Zinnoberzack, the word which opens the last line of this, recalls not so much children's verse as the coinages of Hans Arp, whose work Ball admired. Like Arp's poems, *Tenderenda* is pervaded by word-play of every kind. The names of materials or inanimate objects are transmuted into the names of strange creatures: 'Die Beine des Petroleums, das sass an der Ecke und rieb sich den Magen' (TdP 45). Grammatical ambiguities suggest weird visions—is the beleaguered journalist of 'Satanopolis' wearing his pince-nez, or is he using it, in some hardly imaginable way, to keep himself in occupation? The phrase 'das Haus, das Lilienstein mit dem Kneifer besetzt hielt' (TdP 43) leaves both possibilities open. 'High-ups' in the film world (*Filmkanonen*) find themselves transmogrified into 'Kanonen' of a different kind and used in a paramilitary operation (TdP 57). Familiar words grow outcrops that make them strange. Would a *Luftblasenkatarrh* (TdP 33) be less agonizing than a simple *Blasenkatarrh*? And what is a *Flötenbock* (TdP 37, 124), to say nothing of a *sodaseifener Wurm* (TdP 123)? Words are subtly transformed, *Schibboleth* becoming *Schobboleth* in Toto's iron world, *landet* becoming *landelt* (TdP 57, 92). Expressive nonce-words (*sie* zernierten *die Gärten*) are juxtaposed with dialect locutions more familiar to the Swiss than to the German reader: *mit* urchigem *Brüllen*; *gigampfet* (TdP 57, 60, 123). Metaphorical sayings like *das Tanzbein schwingen* are taken literally, with sinister results: 'Lasset uns jeder das Tanzbein schwingen, das er dem andern entrissen hat' (TdP 62). The primitive or pseudo-primitive chants that were a constant feature of early Dada recitals have left their traces in many of the names used in *Tenderenda*: *Koko, der grüne Gott, im Reiche Sambuco, schmutzige Bumbuleute* (pp. 125–6); these names are enshrined in liturgies whose nearest parallel outside the works of Ball himself are Richard Huelsenbeck's *Phantastische Gebete*. Last not least, *Tenderenda* contains several of those poems in invented languages which constitute Ball's most distinctive, certainly his most famous, contribution to Dada literature: *Karawane* (TdP 101), which allows us to recognize weird distortions of such words as 'Elefant', 'Rüssel', 'gross', and 'Holla'; or *baubo sbugi ninga gloffa* (TdP 119), where the words 'Papa' and 'Mama' are transposed into the 'language' of cats and peacocks (*piaûpa, mjama, pâwapa*). It is significant, however, that such sound-poems and linguistic deformations, such absurdities and passages of dreamlogic, are here contained in a novel written, for the most part, in straightforward prose—in sentences which, for all the strangeness of their import, are constructed as regularly as those of any realistic writer of the nineteenth century. Larger sense-units—paragraphs, chapters, sections—are equally present and correct. This gives stylistic expression to another contrast: that between the irrationality and visionary quality of Ball's story-telling on the one hand, and on the other the penetrating psychological analysis contained in such glosses as those on the 'Machetanz' or 'Hymnus 3' chapters (TdP 27, 103). As usual, Ball's diary hits the nail on the head: 'Was nützt es mir, dass ich mich fallen lasse? Ich werde ja doch nicht so sehr den Kopf verlieren, dass ich nicht fallend die Fallgesetze studiere' (FadZ 52). *Tenderenda der Phantast* is the work of a man who can dredge up surreal visions from his unconscious, and then convey and analyse them in measured cadences and balanced prose; who can be both child and adult, visionary and political analyst, mystic and sceptic. These dualisms pervade the novel and make it at once a self-portrait and a self-critique, at once a presentation of Dada and a judgement on it: 'Zweck meines vor zwei Jahren, im Herbst 14 begonnenen "Phantastischen Romans": Zerstörung meiner harten inneren Kontur. Wenn ich ihn beende, werde ich seine Kritik im voraus geschrieben haben' (FadZ 117). Ball wrote these words into his diary in October 1916—they show how he regarded his novel as a means not just of exhibiting, but also of changing himself, and how essential a part self-criticism played in its creation.

Each of the three sections of the novel centres on a figure which reacts to the disorder of the world in its own particular way. In the first section, this figure is 'Machetanz', 'ein Wesen, das Tänze macht und Sensationen liebt' (TdP 27). He is the poet as seismograph, helplessly registering every tremor of the

Hugo Ball's 'Tenderenda der Phantast'

age. The diary describes the chapter devoted to him as 'ein Prosastück, in dem ich eine von allen Schrecken und Furchtbarkeiten untergrabene Existenz darstelle; einen Dichter, der an unerklärlichen und unübersehbaren Tiefen erkrankend, in Nervenkrämpfen und Paralysen zerfällt. Eine hellsüchtige Überempfindlichkeit ist der verfängliche Ausgangspunkt. Er kann sich den Eindrücken weder entziehen noch sie bändigen' (FadZ 79). The novel shows him unable to find true and permanent values, overcome by metaphysical sickness (*ein Würgen am falschen Gott*—TdP 30) until in the end he dissolves himself in an acid bath and dies, cursing, in prison. 'Wir sehen', Ball's gloss explains, 'wie Machetanz Schritt für Schritt der Besessenheit, dann einer tiefen Apathie erliegt. Bis er schliesslich nach fruchtlosen Versuchen, sich ein Alibi zu schaffen, in jene religiös gefärbte Paralyse versinkt, die, mit Exzessen verbunden, seinen völligen physischen und moralischen Ruin besiegelt' (TdP 27). This is clearly one part of what Ball called his own *innere Kontur*—a presentation of possibilities and dangers which his Dada activities made particularly obvious. Machetanz helps to explain why Ball abandoned Dada so soon after assisting in its creation.

The dissolution and death that are the fate of Machetanz in section I threaten Bulbo in section II. Unlike Machetanz, however, Bulbo is able to offer resistance to the forces of the time—standing his ground, in his own epoch and among his own people, he prays for deliverance:

Erlöse uns, o Herr, von der Verzauberung . . .

Ich könnte mich ja in einer anderen Zeit aufhalten. Was nützte es mir, o Herr? Siehe, ich bewurzele mich bewusst in diesem Volke. Als Hungerkünstler nährte ich mich von Askese. Aber die Relativitätstheorie genügt nicht, noch die Philosophie 'als ob'. Unsere Pamphlete verfangen nicht mehr. Die Erscheinungen von expansivem Marasmus mehren sich. Alle sechzig Millionen Seelen meines Volkes quillen aus meinen Poren. Rattenschweiss ist es vor dir, o Herr. Doch erlöse uns, hilf uns, pneumatischer Vater!

(TdP 67–9.)

This grotesque prayer, we are told, pleases the Lord, who delivers Bulbo from the ghouls assembled to devour him, by whirling him away in a dance. In Bulbo's stead the ghouls are thrown a roasted poet (the chapter, indeed, is called 'Bulbos Gebet und der gebratene Dichter'), who is duly eaten to the accompaniment of a mock-heroic funeral oration. The ascetic, the penitent, is saved through prayer, while the poet is sacrificed. What had appeared separately in the central figures of sections I and II—the poet who abandons himself to the influences of his time and the penitent who achieves salvation at the expense of poetry—comes together in Tenderenda himself, the hero of section III. *Laurentius Tenderenda, der Kirchenpoet* is at home in the fantasy world of Machetanz and also in Bulbo's world of prayer. Even the 'roasted poet' of the Bulbo chapter reappears in him: St. Lawrence, from whom his first name derives, is the 'roasted saint' of Christian hagiography. Once again Ball's own gloss is the best possible commentary on the significance of this figure, and its place in the novel that bears his name:

> Der Autor nennt ihn einen Phantasten, er selbst nennt sich in seiner verstiegenen Weise 'Kirchenpoet'. Auch als 'Ritter aus Glanzpapier' bezeichnet er sich, was auf den donquichottischen Aufzug[1] hinweist, in dem Tenderenda bei Lebzeiten sich zu bewegen liebte. Er gesteht, seiner Frölichkeit müde zu sein und erfleht sich den Segen des Himmels.... Da er Chimären in den Stall bringt, könnte man ihn für einen Exorzisten halten. Die Nachstellungen des Teufels, auf die [sein] Segensspruch hinweist, sind jene Phantasmata, über die schon der heilige Ambrosius klagt, und deren Abschwörung ein anderer Heiliger als Bedingung nennt für den Eintritt in den Mönchsstand. Ansonsten ist Tenderendas Situation elegisch und massenscheu. (TdP 109.)

And Hugo Ball adds, in words that have clear autobiographical relevance: 'Die Wortspiele, Wunder und Abenteuer haben ihn mürbe gemacht. Er sehnt sich nach Frieden, Stille und nach lateinischer Abwesenheit' (TdP 109). By making Tenderenda's visions and aspirations embrace those of Machetanz as well as those of Bulbo and by then naming the whole novel after him,

---

[1] Cf. FadZ 118: 'Bouffonnerie und Donquichotterie: beide sind irrational; die eine aus der Tiefe, aus dem Vulgären, die andere aus der Höhe, aus dem Generösen. Man muss nicht Sancho Pansa und Don Quichotte zugleich sein wollen.' The importance of *Don Quixote* for Hugo Ball is well discussed by G. E. Steinke in *The Life and Work of Hugo Ball, Founder of Dadaism*, The Hague 1967, pp. 122 f. For Ball's early fascination by St. Lawrence see Emmy Ball-Hennings, *Hugo Ball. Sein Leben in Briefen und Gedichten*, Berlin 1929, p. 65.

Hugo Ball's 'Tenderenda der Phantast'

Ball suggests that his function is analogous to that of Tiresias in Eliot's *The Waste Land*: 'Tiresias, although a mere spectator and not indeed a 'character', is yet the most important personage in the poem, uniting all the rest. . . . What Tiresias *sees*, in fact, is the substance of the poem.'[1] It is important to realize, however, that Tenderenda not only sees, but is seen: that the narrator of the novel, the man who speaks out in the glosses, 'places' his hero and prevents the reader from identifying the author too readily with his creation.

While we had to take the actual poetry of Machetanz and his roasted colleague for granted, we are allowed to read a *Hymnus* Tenderenda addresses to his own patron saint and says over to himself in hours of depression. We find it full of Dada nonsense, but now no buffoonery can overlay the genuine accent of supplication:

> Du Zymbalum mundi, Koralle des Jenseits, flüssiger Meister,
> Laut weinet die Skala der Menschen und Tiere.
> Laur jammert das Volk der Städte aus Feuer und Rauch.
> Da deine Wunderhörner auftauchten, da du dein
> Tönernes Spielzeug ansahest, da du dein Reich
> Inspiziertest und uns, die Beamten deines Katasters.
> Denn die Schminke brach. Denn die Würfel zersetzten sich.
> Denn nirgends war solche Sünde wie hier.
> (TdP 106–7.)

Yet has Tenderenda found Truth? Who is this God that he addresses? Is he not a creature of a poet's imagination?

> Du Angesicht aus Metaphern gestückt,
> Faschingsgedichtpuppe
> Unserer Angst. Du Duft weissen Papiers! (TdP 107.)

Is this the deity who helped Bulbo to defeat Death, or is he the 'false god' on whom Machetanz was said to choke? What is his relation to 'Koko the Green God' who appears in the book's final chapter, described in the gloss as an 'astral fairy-tale', a 'heavenly puppet-play'? Can he perform what is hoped from Koko?

> Er wird die Verzauberung lösen, die uns besessen hält.
> (TdP 127.)

---

[1] T. S. Eliot, *Collected Poems 1909–1935*, London 1936, p. 80.

No certain answer to such questions is possible. Indeed, the reader is made progressively more aware of the limits of discursive language—a gloss near the end of the second section of *Tenderenda* had declared unequivocally: 'Zu sagen ist nichts mehr. Vielleicht, dass etwas noch gesungen werden kann. "Du magisch Quadrat, jetzt ist es zu spat." So spricht einer, der zu schweigen versteht . . . Eine Hinwendung zur Kirche zeigt sich in Vokabeln und Vokalen' (TdP 75). Tenderenda himself ends in existential uncertainty: 'ich weiss nicht, ob ich zu denen oben oder zu denen unten gehöre' (TdP 113); an uncertainty reflected, as so often in this novel, by verbal ambivalence: 'Die ganze Zeit fällt mir ja ein. Es ist ein grosser Einfall und Hinfall, den ich mit hinfälliger Einfalt festhalten möchte' (TdP 115). *Fällt mir . . . ein, Einfall*: Tenderenda's epoch is present as an idea in his mind, an inspiration, a *trouvaille* that he must try to fix in words—but it is also something outside him, something that falls, or threatens to fall, about his ears. The book therefore seems destined to end on a question-mark, until the narrator ironically offers to help his readers, and himself, in the traditional way of German writers who have run out of ideas of their own: 'Den Kehraus macht, wie es recht und billig ist, ein Vers des Herrn Dichterfürsten Johann von Goethe' (TdP 121). The passage announced with such mock-solemnity must, of course, come from *Faust*, and readers will not be surprised to find it is anything but a straight quotation. Few, however, will be prepared for the terrible dissonance on which it, and the book, ends:

> Das Voll und Ganze wird hier Ereignis.
> Im Totentanze strebt es zum Gleichnis.
> Das Unerhörte — hier tritt es ein.
> In grellem Lichte: Verworfensein.
> (TdP 128.)

The rejection announced by that final word applies to Tenderenda and his world as much as to Machetanz, and it may help to explain why Ball chose to keep unpublished a novel that had occupied him for six years.[1]

---

[1] *In Hugo Balls Weg zu Gott*, Munich 1931, pp. 64–5. Emmy Ball-Hennings describes how carefully Ball worked on this novel: 'Über ein Wortgebilde, über einen einzigen Satz sass er oft Nächte lang.' She tells us that Ball called the work 'kühn bis zur Frechheit, ja bis zur Blasphemie', and suggests that he considered titling or subtitling it *Die Historie von unserer Tage Verwesung*.

Hugo Ball's 'Tenderenda der Phantast'

If there is one image that remains with the reader after he has closed the book, one image which more than any other sums up its spirit, it is the image of the dance. All the central figures—Machetanz, Bulbo, and Tenderenda—are said to be dancers or shown in the act of dancing; and in the second section the traditional dance of Death is countered by the dance of God Himself:

> Da quoll aus Bulbos Mund ein schwarzer Ast, der Tod. Und man warf ihn in der Gespenster Mitte. Und der Tod exerzierte und tanzte auf ihm. Der Herr aber sprach: 'Mea res agitur . . .' . . . Da tanzte Gott mit dem Gerechten gegen den Tod. Drei Erzengel drehten seiner Frisur turmhohes Toupet. Und der Leviathan hing sein Hinterteil über die Himmelsmauer herunter und sah dabei zu. Über der Frisur des Herrn aber schwankte, aus den Gebeten der Israeliter geflochten, die turmhohe Krone. (TdP 69-70.)

The very last lines of the book, as has just been seen, speak of a dance of death, while the last gloss of all calls the parody of Goethe a *Kehraus*, a final dance. Nor could any image be more appropriate. Like a great dancer, Ball showed himself able, in *Tenderenda der Phantast*, to wed tradition with innovation, invention with order, free movement with precision, instinctual grace with understanding—and this, ultimately, explains the deep appeal of what he chose to call, with characteristic modesty, 'der Narrentanz dieses Büchleins' (TdP 103).

Kafka's *Der Bau*, or How to Escape from a Maze

HEINRICH HENEL

FRANZ KAFKA'S *Der Bau* was written in the year before his death and is one of his last works. Like all his stories of any length, it deals with many subjects and touches upon many more, but two major subjects can be identified. The problem of securing one's life is the main concern of the first part of the story, while the question of how to live or to enjoy one's life forms the main concern of the second. The story is told by an animal who has built himself an elaborate burrow.[1] In the first part he wonders just how safe the burrow is, in the second he worries about a noise which disturbs its peace. Both parts begin with contentment and end with perplexity and fear. In the opening sentence the animal, echoing the Lord in Genesis, declares that his creation is good, but he goes on to find one fault after another in his castle and to make—and reject— numerous plans for its improvement. Similarly at the beginning of the second part, when the animal returns from an excursion to the outside world, he greets his burrow with a joyous outburst of almost lyrical intensity, but soon is troubled by a mysterious hissing or whistling whose source he cannot establish. It should be noted, however, that the two parts (which are of almost equal length) are interdependent. The question of happiness is

[1] Heinz Politzer (*Franz Kafka. Parable and Paradox*, Ithaca, New York 1962, p. 329) thinks the animal is a mole, but moles do not eat rats. (See Friedrich Beissner, *Der Schacht von Babel. Aus Kafkas Tagebüchern*, Stuttgart 1963, p. 47 n. 27.) The letter which Kafka wrote twenty years before he wrote the story and which Politzer adduces has nothing to do with *Der Bau*. It is remarkable, though, that the centre of a mole's burrow consists of two concentric tubes and that the animal wishes he had two concentric spheres in the centre of his burrow. The more common assumption (that the animal is a badger) agrees with what we learn about his size and strength, but of course Kafka's vagueness about the species he describes is intentional. As Ralph Freedman ('Kafka's Obscurity: the Illusion of Logic in Narrative', *Modern Fiction Studies*, 8 (1962), 63) remarks, Kafka was precise in the use of realistic detail, but his purpose was not to reproduce nature. His animal is a construct, a symbolic collage of attributes found in real animals—and in men. So it is best to follow the story and to leave the animal nameless.

anticipated in several significant passages of the first, and the question of security is not forgotten in the second half. Thus, for example, only two pages from the beginning of the story the animal comes to realize that the real danger is an unseen foe under the earth and that all his preparations against outside attack are futile—although he continues to make them. Conversely, near the end of the story and long after the animal has decided that his burrow is not primarily a fortress but rather a home, he reproaches himself for having lived in a fool's paradise, wishes he were young and strong enough to improve his defences radically, and even hits upon an entirely new device—provision for landslides to block his tunnels if an intruder appears. Thus, if the progress of the story at first seems to indicate that the animal makes a mistake in trying to be the master of his fate and should concentrate instead on being the captain of his soul, a more careful reading reveals that neither of these goals can be reached exclusive of the other. And since they are both unattainable, nothing is ever settled. The animal himself has flashes of insight in which he admits as much. But he keeps trying.

The disturbing element which undermines both the animal's reliance on his castle and his happiness in it is worry or *Sorge*. It is justified enough, for the world is full of danger. An animal's best weapon against danger is his mind, and Kafka's animal, being unusually intelligent, makes full use of it. An ounce of prevention is worth a pound of cure—that is the principle on which he acts. The trouble with the rational intelligence, however, is that it cannot cope with the contingent. 'Ah,' cries the animal in considering the many threats to his security, 'is there anything that may *not* happen?' And in the second part, when he tries to discover the cause of the hissing, he echoes his exclamation with the rueful sigh: 'The world is complex, and there is never a lack of unpleasant surprises.' Moreover, reasoning is a self-defeating activity because every argument produces a counter-argument. Kafka's sentences are peppered with 'if', 'but', 'yet', 'however', 'indeed', 'to be sure', 'nevertheless', 'on the other hand'. These particles do not negate the preceding observations, they merely qualify them; and since the qualifiers themselves are in turn qualified, the original statements are, at least in part, revalidated. Nothing is totally true or correct, but, on the other hand, nothing is totally false or wrong. What remains is possibilities which, on closer inspection, seem impossible, yet are possibilities after all, for the alternatives seem equally unpromising. This 'but' and 'all the same' style occasionally coagulates into aphorisms such as: 'Some ruses are so subtle that they defeat themselves', and: 'It is precisely caution which, unhappily all too often, demands the risk of one's life.' The grim humour of these comments is so persuasive that one is tempted to search for a similar formula to cover the whole story. Perhaps: 'An animal needs a burrow for his safety, but it is also a trap.' Or: 'A man's home is his castle, but what use is a castle if it is not a home?' Unwittingly almost, the reader who sums up the story in this fashion declares that all the animal does and thinks is paradoxical, and that his paradoxical existence is a parable for man's; and indeed *Parable and Paradox* is the sub-title of one of the best books on the works of Franz Kafka.[1]

But is it really true that peace of mind depends on absolute security? Surely it is possible to withdraw within oneself, to find contentment in one's own company, and to await with equanimity whatever may befall. The Stoics thought so, and there are times when the animal thinks so, too. 'The most beautiful thing about my burrow', he says, 'is the silence.' Repeatedly and emphatically he describes it as quiet and empty. Here he finds peace, here he can play and sleep. The awareness of danger never leaves him, but he does not care; indeed he feels so completely identical with his burrow that he would be willing to be killed here, for his blood would be absorbed by his own soil and would not be lost. If this is so, however, why is he so dreadfully upset by the slight noise which rouses him from sleep and whose cause he tries to find, first in a frenzy of headlong digging, then by putting forth theory after fruitless theory? There are passages where he says that he actually worries more when he is inside the burrow than when he is outside; and there is a sentence—right in the middle of the long passage praising the burrow as a home rather than a mere protective hole—saying that the worries which plague him in his burrow are different, prouder, more weighty, often deeply repressed, but that their destructive effect is perhaps as great as that of the worries caused by life in

[1] The reference is to Politzer's book mentioned in p. 224 n. 1.

the open. What these worries are is never said, but the reader is allowed to guess. They materialize in the mysterious hissing, and since it is heard equally clearly in every part of the burrow it must be in the animal himself. It may be his breath, panting from all the running around and digging, but in a deeper sense it is his fear of the void. If he had made the central cave of his burrow completely proof against attack, so the animal says in strange self-delusion, he could listen there with rapture to the murmur of silence. Well, he does hear it, and his reaction is not rapture, but terror. It has been remarked that he mistakes the inner enemy for an external enemy and that his searching and his theorizing are futile because of this mistake.[1] What has not been noticed is the cause of his blindness and the nature of his enemy. He fails to draw the right conclusion not only from the fact that the noise is audible wherever he goes in his burrow, but also from the fact that it is inaudible when he lies at the entrance, just below the surface and under a thin cover of moss. When he is close to the outside world the hissing stops. Silence and emptiness are what frighten him. This is the worry which he has repressed, this is the knowledge which he must never admit to himself, because it would undermine his whole existence, the pride in his solitude. As a defensive structure, so he said earlier, the burrow simply is not worth the enormous labour that went into its construction. So he must believe, even at the cost of grossest self-deception, that it affords him the life he wants to live. But that life in silence, emptiness, and solitude ultimately drives him to desperation. This is the paradox around which the second part of the story revolves.

We have strayed from what is said in the story to what is not said but is merely implied. We have done so for good reason, but nevertheless prematurely because the emphasis in both parts is on the animal's tremendous effort to solve his problems and on the ironic fact that they become the more insoluble the harder he tries. Rationality is used to dispel fear, but actually makes it worse, for in devising defences against danger the mind constantly discovers new dangers. The impotence of the rational intelligence in the business of practical living is highlighted by a number of passages which refer expressly to scientific method. For example, towards the end of the first part the

[1] Wilhelm Emrich, *Franz Kafka*[2], Frankfurt am Main 1960, p. 179.

animal wants to return to his burrow but is mortally afraid of being caught from behind the moment he uncovers the entrance and descends. So he digs an experimental ditch (*Versuchsgraben*), hides in it, and gathers data about the volume and kind of traffic passing by. He classifies his observations with care, but cannot find 'a universal law or infallible method of descending'. Again in the second part he interrupts his theorizing about the possible cause of the hissing and decides to build a research tunnel (*Forschungsgraben*), listen to the noise every two or three hours, and patiently record his observations. In this way he will find the real cause irrespective of all theory. But he never builds the tunnel. His reasoning back and forth has left him so demoralized that he has no faith in the project. Building the tunnel would merely give him something to do, it would be playing at work—as if to fool a supervisor. The supervisor must be his conscience, his intellectual pride, his conviction that he ought to use his mind. It is a sensible project, he says a little later, which attracts him and attracts him not; but when he reflects how unlikely it is to yield results and how defenceless he will be while carrying it out, he declares that he cannot understand why he ever made the plan and that he cannot find the least bit of sense in what seemed sensible only a short while ago.

Abstract reasoning, experimentation, observation—all are discredited in turn. In searching for improvements of his burrow the animal loses himself in technical considerations and dreams the dream of an absolutely perfect structure. He knows this, and he knows also that while technical achievements are not to be despised, they cannot satisfy all the needs of life. Again, while searching for the cause of the noise, he acknowledges that it is mostly the technological problem which fascinates him. Indeed he goes so far as to say that the technocrat who concentrates on conquering his physical environment undermines his self-assurance and becomes restless and greedy. Yet he pursues his course until he is completely paralysed—not only unable to act, but also unwilling to think, to face reality, and to gain certainty about the noise.

When the animal watches his burrow from the outside he feels as if he were spying on himself in his sleep, as if he had the rare ability to see his dream images, not in the helpless state of the sleeper, but in full possession of consciousness and calm judgement. This is the only place in the story where Kafka goes beyond the form of the animal fable and offers an allegorical interpretation. What the animal is attempting is to psychoanalyse himself. He does not take long to realize that the enterprise is impossible. His experiment, he says, is a half-experiment, indeed a mere one-tenth-experiment: his observations outside the burrow cannot give him a valid impression of the dangers which threaten him inside, because when he is inside his scent attracts his enemies. Translated into the terms of Kafka's allegory, this means that the experiment is vitiated because the animal has split himself into an observing and an observed self.[1] And since the passage forms the transition from the first part of the story to the second, it is clearly intended to explain the animal's inability to discover the source of the noise. To be conscious is to be separated from the unconscious, and this in turn means that the conscious mind can never grasp more than one-half, or perhaps only one-tenth, of one's unconscious knowledge. In the case of the animal, the hidden insight is that he himself is his own true enemy. It is entirely characteristic—and, I believe, psychologically true—that the animal can speak in the abstract of his 'prouder, weightier, often deeply repressed fears', but that he cannot admit their cause to himself when they have come to plague him.

Kafka's primary purpose is to have the reader share the animal's experience, to enmesh him in his dilemma, to make him feel the seriousness of his plight. This is why the story dwells so largely on the animal's anguished search for security and why it explores at such length, and in apparently superfluous repetition, the nine theories which the animal puts forth in trying to track down the troublesome hissing. But Kafka also wants the reader to transcend the dilemma and to resolve the paradoxes. With the cunning peculiar to him, he uses the same device to achieve both purposes. By letting the animal tell the story, not in interior monologue, but in a kind of speech which implies the presence of others,[2] Kafka seems to subject the animal's statements of fact and his thoughts about them to objective verifica-

[1] Walter H. Sokel, *Franz Kafka — Tragik und Ironie*, Munich and Vienna 1964, p. 372.
[2] The distinction between 'interior monologue' and 'expressed thoughts' is made by Hartmut Binder, *Motiv und Gestaltung bei Franz Kafka*, Bonn 1966, pp. 340 f., 345, and nn. 689, 692.

tion. And the animal's credibility is enhanced by his ostentatious self-searching and his apparent eagerness to correct his observations and revise his views. But since in actual fact no interlocutors are present who might challenge him, the animal is allowed to indulge in a number of delusions and contradictions. These are not noticed (and perhaps are not meant to be noticed) on a first reading, but are certainly striking when the story is re-read. It is in them that the voice of the implied author is heard who, gently and almost imperceptibly at first, but then ever more clearly, adds a second perspective to that of the narrator-protagonist.

One such error occurs when the animal plans to build his famous research tunnel. He will build it, he says, in the direction from which the noise comes, but he forgets that he cannot make out the direction because the noise is heard equally clearly in all parts of the burrow. More telling is his confusion about the reason for his sensitivity. The noise was not audible when he first returned to the burrow, he reasons, because he had to feel at home again before he could hear it; perhaps practice in listening has made him quicker of hearing; possibly the years of solitary living have made him hypersensitive, although surely his hearing cannot have improved; it may be the excitement of coming home and the worries of the world which he has not shaken off yet; or is it that owning property has spoilt him and that the vulnerability of his property has rubbed off on the proprietor? These conflicting surmises are widely scattered (they appear over a stretch of thirteen pages, to be exact), their probability is not examined, and none is rejected before the next is made. In planning to strengthen his castle and again in theorizing about the noise the animal weighs the pros and cons and is stultified only because the world is too complex for the mind to figure out all possibilities. But when he turns inward to examine himself he makes wild stabs and neglects to reason.

Still closer to the core of the story is the contrast between the animal's obsessive occupation with his own safety and his naïve brutality towards others. Kafka, who never offends against realism unless he wishes to drop a hint to the reader (the best-known example is the Statue of Liberty holding a sword instead of a torch in *Amerika*), makes the animal store a huge supply of meat in his burrow—as if it could be kept without spoiling—revel in the smell of it, and on occasion gorge himself senselessly.

Small creatures, insects or worms, which blunder into the burrow and disturb its silence 'are quickly put to rest between my teeth', the animal reports. On one occasion he falls asleep with a rat dangling from his teeth. There is a gruesome description of how he pushes his booty through the narrow passages of the maze between the entrance and the burrow proper: there is so much meat and blood that he has to eat and drink some of it and force the rest downward bit by bit. But the most striking illustration of the animal's naïvety is his reflection that the potential intruder might not be an actual enemy, but a person like himself, a connoisseur of fine architecture, a hermit[1]—and a dissolute villain and dirty glutton. In the same passage he rails against innocent little things, loathsome little creatures who might follow him from sheer curiosity and thus betray him to the world. These snarls are hilariously funny because the animal shows an unexpected command of abusive language, but they are also tragic because he curses the harmless and denounces his own kind. They show what a writer of comedy Kafka could have been, had he allowed the ironically detached view of his implied author to prevail over the tragically involved view of his protagonist.

Anyone as wrapped up in himself as the animal must necessarily suffer from a persecution complex. This is suggested repeatedly, perhaps most clearly in the passage in which he wonders whether the hostility of the world against him might not have ceased. He does realize at times that people have their own business and might not even be aware of his existence, but his sense of being threatened by everybody and everything prevails. Finally, the animal's blindness is revealed by his frequent references to his advancing years. He built the burrow as a shelter for his old age, but does not understand that his constant fear is due in part to his failing strength. In a remarkable passage near the end of the story he recalls an experience of his youth when he had just begun to work on the burrow. He heard a noise similar to the noise made by his own digging, but the noise grew weaker and finally disappeared. The experience, he

---

[1] Politzer (p. 328) wrongly translates *Waldbruder* as 'forest brother', and he is mistaken in saying that 'this diatribe sounds more like a personal loss of temper than an integrated part of the story' and that 'it certainly does not contribute to our understanding of the animal's plight or the Burrow's structure and meaning'.

says, should have been a lesson to him, he should have heeded it in planning his burrow. What he does not see, but what the implied author points out by inserting the incident, is that the hissing is different from the noise heard years ago, that he is hearing it only now as he is growing old, and that no modification of his defences against external enemies would have prevented its appearance.[1]

That maze just below the entrance to the burrow was built to trap an invader and to suffocate him. But it was built when the animal was a mere apprentice and not the master builder he has since become, it is the product of youthful playfulness rather than of mature planning, and—so the animal himself tells us—its walls are too thin to withstand serious attack. The metaphor of the maze[2] has often been used to describe Kafka's novels and stories; but should he not also be taken at his word when he says that the maze is a superficial part of the structure, that it is not the work of the master, that the real burrow is infinitely larger and located much farther down, and that escape is possible by breaking through the walls? As long as the reader is hypnotized by the voice of the narrator—and Kafka does much to so hypnotize him—he is aware only of the insoluble conflicts and problems described with such inescapable logic. It is the voice of the implied author which tells the reader to penetrate the wall and to realize that what the animal really fears is himself and the emptiness of his life. This resolution is suggested in the text by the examples of the animal's general blindness in matters of self-knowledge which have been cited, and it is suggested more specifically by his almost perverse obtuseness in failing to see the real fault of his castle and the real cause of the noise. The place of which he is proudest and which makes him happiest is a large central cave where he keeps his

---

[1] Both Politzer (pp. 329 f.) and Sokel (p. 383) fall into Kafka's trap and make the same mistake as the animal: they equate the digging noise heard when the animal was young with the hissing noise heard when he is old. Politzer concludes that the hissing 'represents the spirit of revenge wrought by the Burrow against its inhabitant', and Sokel that the animal could have built an impregnable castle if he had heeded the warning. Politzer's is the kind of allegorical interpretation which can impose almost any meaning on the text, while Sokel—inexplicably—disregards the animal's agonizing about his burrow and his resigned conclusion that a totally perfect structure is a pipe dream.

[2] Lienhard Bergel, 'The Burrow', in *The Kafka Problem*, ed. Angel Flores, New York 1946, p. 205; Freedman, p. 61; Politzer, p. 330.

How to Escape from a Maze

supplies—he calls it his castle yard or keep (*Burgplatz*). His dismay is correspondingly great when he discovers that the noise can be heard even in this supposedly inviolable precinct, and he reproaches himself for not having carried out an old and favourite plan. He should have dug a hollow sphere around the cave (not quite a complete sphere, unfortunately, for of course the wall between the cave and the sphere would have to rest on a pedestal or foundation), lived in the sphere, played there, enjoyed the cave and its treasures without actually seeing them, and above all never have let enemies get near it.[1] A person who could choose between living in the cave and living in the surrounding sphere would certainly prefer the latter. What a most beautiful arrangement that would have been, cries the animal. But surely this is madness. To live all one's life in a hollow around a hollow is the *non plus ultra* of the animal's dreams; and different from all his other dreams of technical perfection, this dream is never questioned, much less revoked. The implied author could hardly have spoken more clearly.

Enough has been said, I think, to explain why the animal does not realize that his nine theories get increasingly implausible and why he does not draw the right conclusion from his observations. A person of his intelligence must know the answer, but he dare not admit it. He must repress the truth: he is living in a void and is his own enemy. In a significant climax he calls the world outside his burrow first 'the strange land' (*die Fremde*), then 'the open' (*das Freie*), and finally, on two occasions, 'the upper world' (*die Oberwelt*). *Das Freie* is one of Kafka's many puns; in everyday language it means 'the open', but it can also be taken literally and would then mean 'the land of freedom'. The implications are clear. When the animal decides to turn his back on 'senseless freedom', he chooses a state of self-imposed unfreedom and becomes the prisoner of his fears, trapped in his castle; and when he decides to leave the upper world, he enters the underworld and makes it his permanent abode. He dwells in a realm akin to the realm of death—silent, mute, empty, and hollow. He has neither wife nor child (in fact he never mentions the possibility of having them), and he takes it for granted that

---

[1] Bergel (p. 200) interprets the image of the concentric spheres correctly. Politzer (p. 326) speaks of two chambers, one above the other, and hence misses the significance of the image.

the hissing indicates the approach of an enemy rather than that of a friendly neighbour. He does indeed at one point consider the advantages of having a trusted person (*Vertrauensmann*—significantly, he does not use the word 'friend'), but decides that while it may be possible to trust a person whom one can watch, and perhaps even a person who is absent, it is impossible to trust someone outside while one lives inside the burrow, in 'a different world'.[1] The animal's naïve brutality, his loneliness, his solipsism, are the psychological and social manifestations of his inner emptiness. Repeatedly he tries to regain his composure by telling himself that the noise is nothing, a mere nothing. This, too, is a pun of Kafka's or the implied author's: the noise is negligible, nothing to worry about, as a signal of external danger, but it is also the sound of nothingness. And when the animal calms his fear of never seeing his burrow again by saying that 'fortunately' this is impossible, he unwittingly makes a macabre joke. I do not have to force myself to climb down, he says, I can just lie here and do nothing, for the burrow and I belong so closely together that nothing can separate us in the long run: I shall most certainly get down there somehow in the end. The only place to which one comes without going there is the grave. So what the animal is saying is that his burrow is a metaphorical underworld, and that even if he does not get back to it, he will certainly get to the real underworld—death. But of course he does not know what he is saying.[2]

The animal has hardly begun to tell his story when he interrupts himself to protest that he is not a coward and that the burrow was not built from cowardice. Who said so? Of course he is not a coward. When he imagines an enemy snooping around his entrance, and again much later, when he visualizes

[1] I am baffled by Politzer's assertion (p. 330) that the burrow is 'a system of communication' and 'the place for an encounter'. To be sure, he means communication and friendly encounter with 'the great opponent, the "Other"', not with external enemies, but this possibility, too, is considered and dismissed by the animal on the last page but one of the text.

[2] Emrich (pp. 177 f.) misses the *double entendre* in *hinabgelangen* and believes that the animal literally does not have to do anything to get back to his burrow. That the animal is in a trance when he finally climbs down indicates to Emrich that he returns to his own world, to self-fulfilment and happiness. The happiness is short-lived, however; self-fulfilment turns into a nightmare of anxiety; and the trance (a state of utter fatigue and semi-consciousness) suggests the deathlike quality of the animal's own world.

the emergence of the beast who makes the noise, he describes the fury with which he would fall upon him and fight him to the death. Then why the protestation? The point is that no enemy ever appears, and that the animal actually wishes he would appear. The negative, as always with Kafka, implies an unspoken positive. The animal is not afraid of the known, but he is afraid of the unknown—his fear is *Angst* rather than *Furcht*. He does not trust his fellow animals, but these fears can be dealt with, at least one can try to deal with them, by building a fortress, by tracking down enemies before they attack, by fighting when the worst comes to the worst. What cannot be dealt with is the unknown, the void, the repressed knowledge that getting old means approaching death and that the animal's death will make an end to a futile life, a life preoccupied with its own preservation and prolongation.

There is one more source of *Angst*. Although it is the most profound source, the story touches upon it only lightly. The animal's existence is deprived not only of the comfort of family, friends, and neighbours, but also of the comfort of faith. As is the case with all his anxieties, he knows it and he knows it not. Quite early in the story he says that there are inner enemies as well as external enemies, that the legends tell about them, but that even legend cannot describe them. These enemies are terrifying because they are not invaders whom one can fight in one's own house. Confronting them, we are not in our house, but in theirs.[1] 'Legend' (*die Sage*) is Kafka's word for Scripture. The ultimate unknown, then, is God, and 'the enemies of the inner earth' are the animal's nagging fears of Him. Throughout the story he acts as if he were autonomous,[2] but on this occasion at least he realizes that God's world is larger than his and that he cannot fight Him on his own ground. He needs the exit of his burrow as an escape-hatch, he says, but knows that it will not save him from the enemies of whom the legend speaks—and he

[1] The same thought crosses the animal's mind when as a young fellow he hears the digging: he must be in somebody else's burrow. Here, however, the thought has social, not religious, significance. The animal realizes for a moment that he, not his neighbour, may be the trespasser. It is an insight as quickly repressed as is his perception that he is in the house of God.
[2] Bergel (p. 200) defines the autarchy which the animal desires merely as independence of reality. Sokel (pp. 380 f.) understands the passage as I do, as referring to religion.

believes firmly in the legend. That threat is easily forgotten, for everyday experience shows much more often that God's mill grinds slow than that it grinds sure. Nevertheless the animal harks back twice to the subject of religion. Admitting that he is too weak to make his fortress impregnable, he has a dim feeling that Providence may have a special interest in saving him, that it will make an exception in his case, and that by an act of grace it will let pass what does not normally pass. If he could trust this feeling, if he had faith, he would indeed be saved; but he mentions the feeling more in self-irony than in earnest and is quick to add that it soon dissipated. Lastly, towards the end of the story the animal wonders why things have gone so well for so long, who guided the paths of his enemies around his burrow all these years, and why he was protected so long only to be so terribly frightened now. He asks these questions when he is sobered by his inability to identify the source of the terrifying noise, but he still does not realize that they include their own answer. At this point the animal is once again quite close to solving the riddle, but the implied author blinds him and does not let him remember what he said earlier about the teaching of the legend. It is left to the reader to put the three passages together and to draw the conclusion.

The observations made so far allow the formulation of three critical principles: Kafka's works are parables, not allegories; their meaning resides in contrasting events and conflicting statements rather than single events or statements which would serve as key passages; and while their subject-matter is usually negative, their substance is positive. There is no common agreement on the distinction between parable and allegory. The distinction I have in mind is that allegories match objects and events from one sphere of experience point for point with those from another, whereas in parables the two spheres touch at only one point, that point being the import of the story as a whole rather than a specific character or incident. Allegories were popular in the Middle Ages. Among the best-known are those describing the battle between feminine virtue and masculine desire as a siege or a hunt, where walls, gates, weapons, or different kinds of game, dogs, and equipment, all have precise metaphorical equivalents. As Ralph Freedman has pointed out, metaphors

How to Escape from a Maze 237

and allegories do occur in Kafka, but none of his novels and stories may be read as a single, consistent allegory.[1] Thus, for example, the allegory which we have noted in *Der Bau* must not be extended to cover the whole story: the thrust of the story is not simply the lesson that self-observation is impossible. Why it is impossible, or at least fruitless, for this particular animal is much more important. For this same reason I reject Heinz Politzer's assertions that 'in an almost allegorical way "The Burrow" is identical with Kafka's own work' and that it 'contains highly significant statements concerning Kafka's own creative paradox: the conflict which existed in his aims as a writer and a human being'. Politzer believes that the labyrinth in *Der Bau*, being beginner's work, is a metaphor for Kafka's early story *Das Urteil*; that the burrow or castle points to the late novel *Das Schloss*; that the animal's passing reference to his guilt invokes the theme of *Der Prozess*; that his playing and somersaulting recall Gregor Samsa's excursions across the walls in *Die Verwandlung*; and that his subterranean corridors 'indicate those parts of Kafka's work which were still unwritten ... and would soon be buried with him'. These identifications (I have arranged them on a descending scale of probability) are so uncertain that Politzer himself wonders whether the labyrinth may not refer to *Das Schloss* rather than to *Das Urteil*. But even if all of them were accepted, we should have discovered nothing more than allusions, metaphorical overtones, that would enrich the passages in which they occur, but would not explain the story. After all, *Der Bau* progresses, it unfolds a situation. If it were the kind of allegory Politzer has in mind, its progress would have to resemble the process of literary production. Since this is not the case, his conception of 'the Burrow as the most appropriate cipher for his [Kafka's] work' turns the story into a mere catalogue of Kafka's output.[2]

To give a final example of the insufficiency of allegorical interpretation, I myself thought upon first reading the story that the labyrinth might be a figure for the convolutions of the brain, and the much larger burrow beneath it a figure for the unconscious.

---

[1] Freedman, pp. 61 f.
[2] Politzer, pp. 319–25. Bergel's study of *Der Bau* is superior to most others not least because he follows the progress of the story, a procedure which makes him see details in their relation to the whole.

Such a reading would go no further than Kafka himself goes in comparing the animal watching his entrance with the conscious mind's attempt to observe the unconscious. But again, if I said that the animal's reliance on the intellect is typical of youth and that experience should have taught him respect for the incommensurable, I should turn an incidental allegory into an all-embracing one and a complex story into a simplistic moral tale.[1]

Concerning the second principle, it is true that Kafka often uses words or phrases which are more emphatic than the occasion demands, and since they are particularly noticeable in a narrative style which is normally level and even subdued, they act like snags on the reader's sensibility and persuade him that he has found the key to the story each time he hits one of them. One such word is 'the destroyer' (*der Verderber*). It occurs only once and in its immediate context is merely an alternative for 'pursuer', 'enemy', 'invader'—words which are used frequently to designate the animal's real or imagined foes. But because of its Biblical overtones it can be connected with the inner enemies known to The Legend and with the reference to Providence and may then lead to the view that The Destroyer is the Devil and that the animal's troubles are due to his godlessness. Now it is undoubtedly true that the Biblical overtones are evoked on purpose and that the animal's plight is remarkably akin to that of the wicked man (*der Gottlose*, says Luther) in the Book of Job 15: 20-5. But to interpret *Der Bau* as an embroidery of the Biblical passage or, more generally, as a religious parable would be a simplification which disregards the multivalence both of Kafka's metaphors and symbols and of his stories as a whole. His mazes are equipped with many signposts, traffic lights, and alarm bells, and while each of them, when properly heeded, yields an important insight, none yields a wholly adequate insight and thus leads out of the maze. What the critic must realize is that there is not one key word or key sentence, but many. Every incident is qualified by a counter-incident,

---

[1] Friedrich Beissner (*Der Erzähler Franz Kafka*, Stuttgart 1952, p. 40) errs in the opposite direction when he maintains that *Der Bau* is simply an animal story describing a sound, unbroken world. He has served Kafka studies well through his polemics against far-fetched allegorical interpretations, but goes too far when he denies that Kafka's fable is what animal fables have always been—parables with a relevance for human readers.

and every assertion by a counter-assertion. The critic must match them, and often he must gather together a whole sheaf of events or statements which are widely scattered in the text, but nevertheless belong together. Walter Sokel's reading of *Der Bau*, for example, relies far too heavily on the passages where the animal describes how he cuddles up in the burrow, rolls over in childlike playfulness, or dozes, dreams, and sleeps. As a result, Sokel accuses the animal of narcissism, says he should have worked harder, and finds that his sense of guilt is due to his carelessness. Work still harder? Was he not actually glad when he bloodied his front pounding down the loose soil in building the central cave? It would be more justifiable to be sorry for the poor brute, for his periods of rest and relaxation are far outweighed by his tireless physical and intellectual toil. Besides, while he does occasionally accuse himself of self-indulgence (although never of self-admiration), his report makes it amply clear that still more work and still more thought would not have made his castle impregnable and would not have solved the riddle of the noise. What the story as a whole teaches is that the animal is incapable of self-examination, not that he is punished for culpable negligence.[1]

[1] Like Sokel, Politzer (p. 322) believes the animal's assertion that he has passed the years of his manhood in childish games, but Politzer's interpretation of the story is not built on self-reproaches so clearly born of desperation. On the other hand, Politzer (p. 332) fastens on the animal's saying 'I can trust only myself and the burrow' as a 'key sentence', although the story makes it abundantly clear that the animal does not trust himself and the burrow. He merely wishes he could. Another lop-sided interpretation is based on the animal's remark that time does not count when he is in his burrow (*immer innerhalb des Baues habe ich endlose Zeit*). Both Emrich (p. 178) and Politzer (p. 323) are misled by this sentence, Emrich asserting that the animal has escaped the torturing consciousness of time, and Politzer asserting that time (as well as space!) has ceased to exist in the burrow and that this timelessness 'corresponds with the suspension of chronological sequences in Kafka's own writings'. Actually, however, the animal's remark is counterbalanced by the many occasions when he acts in haste, regrets his precipitancy, or complains of a lack of time or of having to waste his time (*eiligst, übereilt, in Eile, Übereilung* are the words he uses). When the animal feels safe, he is not conscious of the passage of time; when he feels threatened, he is acutely aware of it. It is only when the two situations are considered together that the true meaning and the sinister implications of the animal's remark are revealed. He has infinite time in the burrow because life in it is a foretaste of death. But as soon as he becomes aware of this, as soon as he hears the hissing, his sense of timelessness is shattered together with his sense of security. His first reaction is frantic scratching and digging in search of the enemy; one of the last reactions is repairing the damage he has done, in case he should die. He acts like a man who puts his affairs in order because he knows that his time is running out—like a man who prepares his own tomb.

Guilt and punishment—these are crucial concepts elsewhere in Kafka, and since the words occur in *Der Bau* they, too, have been seized upon by some critics and treated as key words. 'Punishment' appears twice, and 'guilt' once. The animal finds that having to leave the burrow in order to replenish his supplies by hunting outside is unduly harsh punishment for his occasional binges of needless and immoderate eating. He does not know why he feels the punishment is excessive, and the implied author does not explain it until much later, near the end of the story. Overeating is the result of temporary despair in the earlier passage, and eating as much as he can while he still has the opportunity is the animal's last plan—the only feasible plan when all else has failed. In its second occurrence, the punishment is self-inflicted. The animal tries to force himself to re-enter the burrow, cannot bring himself to do it, and throws himself into a thorn-bush 'to punish myself for a guilt which I do not know'. The unknown guilt is his cowardice, his lack of self-confidence, and these in turn are caused by the repressed knowledge that his life in the burrow is meaningless and not worth the danger of descending. 'Guilt' and 'punishment', then, are indeed keys, but not master keys, not the pillars on which *Der Bau* is erected. Like 'the destroyer', they add a dimension to the story, although its meaning would not be vitally affected if they were absent. They connect it with some of Kafka's other works, but whereas Josef K. in *Der Prozess* does his best not to see what is wrong with himself and his life, the animal tries desperately to find out. The specific problem investigated in *Der Bau* is the impossibility of self-knowledge despite most strenuous effort, and since this failing is involuntary and unconscious, it is 'guilt' only in an extended sense of the word. Put as a general rule, the use of an author's other works for the elucidation of the work under consideration is as hazardous as the use of biographical facts, sources, letters, and diary entries. They may give valuable leads, but they can also lead astray.[1]

[1] For example, Sokel gets off on the wrong foot by opening his chapter on *Der Bau* with a quotation from one of Kafka's letters whose relevance to the story is dubious. The sentence in the letter, 'He is terribly afraid to die because he hasn't lived', does indeed apply to the animal, but Sokel makes much more of the sentence, 'To be able to live, one must renounce self-enjoyment; one must move into the house, not admire and garland it.' The animal *has* moved into his house, and he certainly does not admire and garland it—whatever the meaning of that obscure metaphor may be.

That Kafka's negatives imply unspoken positives is, of course, the main contention of this essay, and some specific examples have already been given. The idea that the whole story, too, is a negative image of a positive thought is not new. It has been developed most resolutely by Wilhelm Emrich,[1] but while I agree with his belief that the animal's intellectual failure points to a moral fault, I disagree with his definition of that fault. Emrich sees little if any difference between the animal and Josef K.: both deny their true selves and both shirk the duty to judge themselves. He quotes in support the passage from the end of *Der Prozess* which says that Josef K. knows not only that he should have judged himself, but also that he should execute the judgement—commit suicide. But in explaining *Der Bau* Emrich asserts that self-judgement, had the animal been able to perform it, would have brought about utopia: the knowledge of good and evil and its acceptance—applying its demands to oneself and only to oneself rather than to others—reconcile the individual with himself and with his fellow creatures. Now this assertion is at variance not only with the text of *Der Bau*, but with all of Kafka's works. No writer was more unwilling to indulge in utopian visions, and none insisted more firmly on the ineluctable problems of man's inner and outer existence. Specifically, the conflict in *Der Bau* is not between the animal's true self and his empirical self, but between his intellect and its objects, an outer world of contingencies which defies rational planning and an inner world so hidden that it eludes self-searching. What refutes Emrich most clearly are the totally different endings of the two stories. Whereas Josef K. realizes at last that he himself, and not the world, is at fault, the animal has no consciousness of guilt (except in the one fleeting moment mentioned), and hence does not feel the need to judge and punish himself. To accommodate the end of *Der Bau* to his interpretation, Emrich says that there is a pessimistic final turn and that the animal perishes of his hostility to himself. The fact is, however, that no enemy appears (not even an enemy who may be understood, as Emrich suggests earlier, as a metaphor for the animal's inner voice) and that the animal does not perish.[2] He just sits there, perplexed

[1] Emrich, pp. 183–6.
[2] Emrich relies on Max Brod's note saying that, according to Dora Dymant, the manuscript of *Der Bau* lacked some pages at the end and that the animal will succumb in a fight with the enemy whose hissing he has heard.

and afraid. Thus, while it is true that both *Der Prozess* and *Der Bau* point to a moral fault which implies an unattained (and, for Kafka's protagonists, unattainable) virtue, Josef K.'s *Angst* is due to his repressed sense of guilt, but the animal's to his repressed sense of futility. Guilt must be punished, but a wasted life is its own punishment. Disagreeing with Emrich, I believe, then, that the two stories present different problems, expose different vices, and are negative images of different virtues. Josef K. lacks self-criticism, the animal lacks self-confidence.[1]

Der Bau is a work of classic perfection.[2] It is like lace: delicately patterned, yet strong. The reader's mind is enmeshed in the logic of the animal's reasoning, but it is also challenged to discover that the logic is inescapable only as long as its premisses are not questioned. If one were asked to pick one of the aphorisms in *Der Bau* as its motto, one might choose 'Worrying when

[1] Bergel's essay takes construction of the burrow as a symbol of man's effort to construct a rational world and defines the story's problem as the conflict between man's dependence on reality and his need to win intellectual independence. The thesis fits the first part of the story, but not the second. For instance, it explains better than other approaches the significance of the burrow's ventilating shafts and of the invigorating effect of life in the open; but it forces Bergel into ambiguity when he explains the cause of the hissing. He takes it as coming from a real animal (in fact as reality attacking the castle of the mind), but also as a projection of the animal's bad conscience. The burrow represents the animal's whole inner existence, not only his *ratio*; and something is wrong with his inner existence itself, not just with its relation to reality. Bergel's conclusion that 'reality wins . . . because it represents the higher value' is too simple. If this were the gist of *Der Bau*, Kafka would have done what Bergel says he did not do and no artist should do—solve problems. Put in my terms, Bergel mistakes Kafka's qualifications for negations (for example, the invigorating effect mentioned is matched by the access of strength which the animal feels when he comes home), and he finds the positive image actually presented in the outcome rather than merely implied in the story as a whole. I gladly acknowledge, however, that Bergel anticipates my emphasis on the intellect's vain struggle with an irrational world, on the animal's solipsism, and on the futility of fears caused by the belief that everybody is watching and pursuing you. And I admire his precise and compact argument for adhering closely to the text—a virtue rarely found in the work of later interpreters, who have taken no notice of him.

[2] Helmut Richter (*Franz Kafka. Werk und Entwurf*, Berlin 1962, pp. 272–6) disagrees. As a socialist realist he takes it for granted that the animal is a mole (see p. 224 n. 1) and complains that *Der Bau* is a 'questionable hotchpotch of animal story and allegory'. The hissing is simply due to the approach of an unknown big animal (realism again!), and the story is easily deciphered: it describes the insecurity of a certain type of artist of the late bourgeois era. Richter would hardly have maintained that the story has 'little artistic value' if—oh well, never mind.

things go well gets you nowhere' (*Unruhe innerhalb des Glücks führt zu nichts*). The motto would not do justice to the profundity and complexity of the story, but it would at least tell what the animal does most of the time—worry. It voices one of the fleeting insights which the animal has and on which he cannot act. He was made to be a worrier, and so was his creator, Franz Kafka. It would be worse than useless, it would be facile to say that they should not have worried so much, and it would be equally facile to contrast them with persons who are by nature sanguine. But it throws light on the story to compare it with the poetry of a man who was haunted by worry, but was able to transcend it—Goethe. Especially in his early manhood, between the ages of twenty-three and thirty, Goethe was profoundly troubled, insecure, at times on the brink of despair. The feeling of guilt, which he knew, had little to do with his crises. When it came it was specific and hence manageable, not all-pervasive and overwhelming as were the guilt feelings of Kafka and of his self-portrait in *Der Prozess*. Rather, it was a sense of futility, doubt in his poetic vocation, fear of a wasted life, which disturbed Goethe and which link him with Kafka and Kafka's other self-portrait, the animal in *Der Bau*. His *Angst* became so intense that, according to his autobiography, there were times when he lay on his bed at night playing with a dagger pointed at his chest. And towards the end of this period, in December 1777, he still was so desperately in need of reassurance, of a sign that Providence would make an exception in his case and would protect him by a special act of grace, that he engaged in an enterprise considered impossibly risky in those days: he climbed the Brocken in mid winter and was jubilant when he returned safely.

The difference between the passage about Providence in *Der Bau* and Goethe's poem, letters, and diary entries about his *Harzreise* explains why Goethe could deal with *Angst* and Kafka could not. Goethe's remedy was deliberate exposure to actual danger, whereas the animal's attempted remedy is anticipation of, and provision against, potential danger. But of course Goethe was young in those years, and Kafka wrote his story near the end of his life. The point is made in *Der Bau* itself, in the section where the animal tells of how in his youth he heard someone digging and approaching him. This was real danger, not an imaginary threat, but the animal stayed and waited for it 'cool and collected'. Indeed, being young, he might not have been displeased if the digger had suddenly emerged from the ground. He does not say that he would have fought him; perhaps he would have greeted him and then, as he says, moved away and built his burrow elsewhere. The passage shows that Kafka was by no means as incapable of projecting himself into persons of temperament different from his own as is sometimes believed. He knew that there is a youthful way of dealing with *Angst*. His trouble was that he never was young.

And now, to conclude, Goethe's poems. The one entitled 'Worry' (*Sorge, c.* 1776) is an incantation asking to be released from worry and doubt and, if this should be impossible, to be granted wisdom instead of happiness:

> Kehre nicht in diesem Kreise
> Neu und immer neu zurück!
> Lass, o lass mir meine Weise,
> Gönn', o gönne mir mein Glück!
> Soll ich fliehen? Soll ich's fassen?
> Nun, gezweifelt ist genug.
> Willst du mich nicht glücklich lassen,
> Sorge, nun so mach' mich klug!

The 'Skating Song' (*Eis-Lebens-Lied*, winter 1775–6) takes skating as a metaphor for life. Skating beyond the point where the boldest have ventured, the speaker encourages himself by saying that even if the ice cracks it will not break, and even if it breaks, it will not break underneath him. Dubious prophecy, but effective medicine. Acting as a psychiatrist treating his own *Angst*, Goethe prescribes seeking out danger and blind trust:

> Sorglos über die Fläche weg,
> Wo vom kühnsten Wager die Bahn
> Dir nicht vorgegraben du siehst,
> Mache dir selber Bahn!
> Stille, Liebchen, mein Herz,
> Kracht's gleich, bricht's doch nicht!
> Bricht's gleich, bricht's nicht mit dir!

If these poems move quickly to the implied positive of Kafka's story, 'Admonition' (*Beherzigung, c.* 1777) dwells more fully on the negative. It actually asks, like *Der Bau*, whether it is better to be a home owner or a vagrant, and decides that, whatever the advantages of ownership may be, security is not one of them. So what shall a man do? There is no universal answer. Let each obey his own nature:

> Ach, was soll der Mensch verlangen?
> Ist es besser, ruhig bleiben?
> Klammernd fest sich anzuhangen?
> Ist es besser, sich zu treiben?
> Soll er sich ein Häuschen bauen?
> Soll er unter Zelten leben?
> Soll er auf die Felsen trauen?
> Selbst die festen Felsen beben.
>
> Eines schickt sich nicht für alle.
> Sehe jeder, wie er's treibe,
> Sehe jeder, wo er bleibe,
> Und wer steht, dass er nicht falle!

Kafka's devotees will object that the animal does obey his nature—and that he wastes his life. But this is the point I am trying to make. Kafka knew how to escape from the maze and he tells his reader how to do it—if he is not Kafka. He lacked hope (Goethe's poems *Hoffnung* and *Einschränkung*), he could not trust blindly, and he always expected the worst. Nor did Goethe find it easy to follow his mother's motto, 'Let's hope for the best'—why else would he have written the gnomes quoted, which are so clearly directed at himself? In a longer, narrative poem of the same period, 'Voyage' (*Seefahrt*, 1776), he uses one of his favourite images to describe the many dangers of life, but also to say that courage and trust (even blind trust in unknown gods) are better helmsmen than worry and fear:

> Und vertrauet, scheiternd oder landend,
> Seinen Göttern.

'Trust whether you founder or land': Goethe's play *Egmont*, whose inception falls in the year 1775, contrasts the Prince of Orange with Egmont, the worrier with the over-confident man, and it is the over-confident who dies. But he dies well, he dies for having lived the way he was made. Faust, on the other hand (his drama, too, was begun early in our period), is deeply infected with Kafka's disease. He doubts the value of all his achievements, he doubts that anything is worth living for, and he is beset by futile worries. Like Kafka, he knows that what one fears rarely comes to pass—

> Du bebst vor allem, was nicht trifft,
> Und was du nie verlierst, das musst du stets beweinen —

but the knowledge does him little good. And when at last, in his old age, he rejects worry, his confidence is as blind as were his fears.[1] *Faust*, subtitled 'A Tragedy', describes the history of a life which, but for some saving grace in his character, might have been Goethe's.

[1] This description refers, of course, to Faust before his pact with Mephistopheles and after his repudiation of it (ll. 11404-9, 11423). He escapes worry with the help of magic, of the magic cloak which he desires and which the devil provides to carry him through the air (ll. 1122 ff., 2065 ff.). There is no such escape for the animal. 'When peace has returned,' he says, 'I shall repair it all thoroughly, and it will be done in a jiffy (*im Fluge*). Ah yes, in fairy-tales everything is done in a jiffy—and I am consoling myself with a fairy-tale.'

Zu Franz Kafkas Erzählung *Elf Söhne*

C. DAVID

'Eilf ist die Sünde.'

SCHILLER (*Wallenstein*)

Elf Söhne wurde von Franz Kafka im Jahre 1919, zusammen mit anderen 'Kleinen Erzählungen', in dem Sammelband *Ein Landarzt* veröffentlicht. Die Literatur über diesen Text ist besonders sparsam. Unter den neueren Interpretationen ist eigentlich nur die von Malcolm Pasley zu erwähnen.[1] Max Brod hatte in seinem Buch über Kafka erzählt, sein Freund habe ihm von dieser Erzählung gesagt: 'Die elf Söhne sind ganz einfach elf Geschichten, an denen ich jetzt gerade arbeite.' J. M. S. Pasley hat nun am Ende des 'sechsten' blauen Oktavhefts, dem wohlbekannten, zusammen mit anderer Prosa aus dem Nachlass nach den *Hochzeitsvorbereitungen auf dem Lande*[2] veröffentlichten Manuskript Kafkas, eine Liste von zwölf Titeln ausfindig gemacht, die diese Behauptung des Dichters zu bestätigen schien. Es handelt sich um eine Zusammenstellung von Titeln der für den *Landarzt* geplanten Sammlung: elf Titel, und als zwölften, eine diese Reihe abschliessende Erzählung, die *Elf Söhne*. J. M. S. Pasley hat nun versucht, die ersten elf Titel, in der Ordnung, in der sie in dem Oktavheft erscheinen, auf die Bilder der elf Söhne zu beziehen, um somit die Anspielungen auf das Werk des Dichters genau zu identifizieren. Dann ist der Versuch auf die Odradek-Erzählung erweitert worden: die Sorge des Hausvaters bezieht sich wieder auf seine Söhne, oder vielmehr auf seinen einzigen Sohn Odradek, der hier für das ganze Werk des Dichters stellvertretend steht.

Diese Interpretation schien seinem Urheber so gesichert, dass er sich kurz nachher auf sie stützte, um darauf eine Datierung der Erzählungen zu fundieren.[3] Und dennoch ist gegen sie viel

[1] 'Two Kafka Enigmas: *Elf Söhne* und *Die Sorge des Hausvaters*', *MLR* 59 (1964), 73–81.
[2] *Hochzeitsvorbereitungen auf dem Lande* und andere Prosa aus dem Nachlass, Frankfurt und New York 1953, S. 447.
[3] M. Pasley und K. Wagenbach, 'Versuch einer Datierung sämtlicher Texte Franz Kafkas', *DVJS* 38 (1964), 149–67.

einzuwenden. Es ist schon am anderen Ort hervorgehoben worden, dass bereits im 'ersten', um einige Monate früheren Oktavheft, eine andere Liste stand, die statt zwölf nur elf, zum Teil verschiedene Titel trug;[1] dass am 7. Juli, wie aus einem Brief an den Verleger Kurt Wolff verlautet, dreizehn Stücke vorgesehen waren,[2] und dass die Landarzt-Sammlung in ihrer endgültigen Fassung nicht zwölf, sondern fünfzehn kleine Erzählungen enthalten sollte. Das ist an sich freilich kein entscheidendes Argument, obwohl man sich fragen muss, warum Kafka den elf Titeln, die einer nur provisorischen Gestaltung des Werkes entsprachen, eine solche Bedeutung beilegte. Vor allem aber: diese elf Söhne mussten in der endgültigen Fassung des *Landarzt* völlig unverständlich werden; um so mehr als Kafka inzwischen die Anordnung der Texte umgeändert hatte. Dies konnte M. Pasley freilich nicht verkennen. Und es blieb ihm keine andere Lösung übrig, als diese Verdunkelung des Sinnes als absichtlich zu bezeichnen: 'this relation was effectively— and, we must suppose, deliberately—obscured.'[3]

Somit wird das Problem aber noch verwickelter. Denn es sieht so aus, als würde Kafka absichtlich seine Leser vor unlösbare Rätsel stellen. Und nicht einmal das Mitteilungsvermögen der Sprache, wie M. Pasley nachher auszuführen versucht, wird somit in Frage gestellt oder exemplifiziert. Denn es würde sich in diesem Fall um eine durchaus mitteilbare Wahrheit handeln, die der Dichter aus irgend einem Grunde zu verheimlichen beschloss: 'the two stories (*Elf Söhne* und *Die Sorge des Hausvaters*) owed their origin to the author's contemplation of other literary objects, whose identity he chose deliberately to withhold.'[4] Warum diese eigentümliche Geheimniskrämerei? M. Pasley gibt zwei Erklärungen, die er beide als möglich hinstellt. Nach der ersten Erklärung spielt sich hier Kafka einmal in die Rolle des allwissenden 'Vaters' hinein und mystifiziert seine Leser, so wie er selbst im Leben so oft mystifiziert worden war: 'the stories are vengeful mystifications.'[5] Die andere Erklärung behauptet dass der Dichter, gleichsam aus pädagogischen Absichten, seine Leser künstlich in die Situation versetzt, in der er

---

[1] *Hochzeitsvorbereitungen*, S. 440.
[2] *Briefe*, 1902–24, Frankfurt und New York 1958, S. 156.
[3] a. a. O., S. 75. [4] a. a. O., S. 78.
[5] a. a. O., S. 90.

sich selbst der Unwegsamkeit und Unmitteilbarkeit der Wahrheit gegenüber befindet; statt der Rache nur ein 'ungewöhnliches Experiment'. In beiden Erklärungsversuchen ist aber die Rätselhaftigkeit nicht mit der Natur der Sache gegeben, sondern absichtlich eingeführt. Man hat es mit einem Werk zu tun, dessen Bedeutung willkürlich verwischt wird, das auf die Beziehung zum Leser prinzipiell verzichtet, das nicht verstanden werden darf. Kafka, dessen leidenschaftliches Anliegen zuerst dahin ging, seine Wahrheit mitzuteilen, wird sich endlich seiner Ohnmacht bewusst und begnügt sich, vielleicht aus Ressentiment, mit einem 'exercise in private virtuosity'.[1]

So hat eine positivistische Interpretation zu dem paradoxen Ergebnis geführt, in *Elf Söhne* eine — wenn auch von Kafka intendierte — Sinnlosigkeit zu statuieren. Um einen äusseren Sinn — die Beziehung auf elf Erzählungen — zu retten, hat man den Text jeder tieferen Bedeutung beraubt. Aber nicht nur das enttäuschende Ergebnis, auch die Methode ist höchst fragwürdig. Es ist ein Rückfall in den Irrtum der frühen Kafka-Exegeten. Denn man befindet sich auf dem Holzweg, sobald man bei Kafka auf reine Virtuosität oder auf Mystifizierung des Lesers schliesst, oder einfach seine Erzählungen als 'Rätsel' auffasst. 'Kafka wrote these stories with definite, secret, references in mind.'[1] Es gibt eine Wahrheit, eine durchaus sagbare Wahrheit; diese ist aber nicht im Text enthalten, sondern irgendwo hinter ihm verborgen. Es ist die alte Auffassung eines metaphorischen, bzw. symbolischen oder allegorischen Kafka, welche die ersten Interpreten zu allen den willkürlichen Deutungen, die so lange gang und gäbe waren, inspiriert hat. Die Wahrheit, wenn es eine gibt, ist im Text immanent als 'offenbares Geheimnis' enthalten. Es gibt dahinter nichts was der Dichter besser wüsste, worauf er indirekt hinwiese oder was er seinem Leser vorenthielte.

Wer diese von allen neueren Kafka-Interpreten anerkannte Wahrheit vergisst, muss in Willkür verfallen. So auch hier. Die Beschreibung des zweiten Sohnes wird zum Beispiel auf die Erzählung *Vor dem Gesetz* bezogen, manchmal auf die allgemeine Bedeutung dieser Erzählung (so ist der zweite Sohn 'schlank und wohlgebaut', weil Kafka mit dieser 'Exegese der Legende' besonders zufrieden war) manchmal auf die Hauptperson (der

[1] a. a. O., S. 81.

zweite Sohn ist klug und welterfahren, wie der arme Mann vom Lande, der vor der Tür des Gesetzes wartet, nachdem er seine Heimat verlassen hat). Hätte man nicht eher diesem armseligen Bauer, der sein Leben erbärmlich vertut, die Welterfahrung absprochen? — Oder der zehnte Sohn, der 'in erstaunlicher, selbstverständlicher und froher Übereinstimmung mit dem Weltganzen' steht, soll mit dem neuen Advokaten, mit dem Streitross Alexanders des Grossen, Bucephalus, identifiziert werden. Dieser kurze Text, der die Reihe der Landarzt-Erzählungen einführt, endet aber gerade mit dem Satz: 'niemand zeigt die Richtung; viele halten Schwerter, aber nur, um mit ihnen zu fuchteln und der Blick, der ihnen folgen will, verwirrt sich.' Dem dritten Sohn wird 'die Schönheit des Sängers' zugesprochen; dies deutet, laut J. M. S. Pasley, auf den lyrischen Charakter der entsprechenden Erzählung, *Eine kaiserliche Botschaft*. Aber gerade diese nüchterne, unpathetische Erzählung entfernt sich mit betonter Absicht vom lyrischen Ton. Solche Beispiele liessen sich beliebig vermehren,[1] und die Identifikationen beliebig umkehren. Die versuchte Beweisführung musste ins Leere laufen. Der Fehler lag in der metaphorischen Interpretation der Texte, als ob Kafka statt eines Dinges ein anderes Ding setzte, als ob jede Zeile entschlüsselt werden müsste, um hinter der oberflächlichen Kruste eine dort verborgene Wirklichkeit zu entdecken: hinter dem 'Sohn' eine Erzählung, hinter dieser Person einen Schakal, hinter jener einen Zirkusartisten. Kafka hat es aber nicht nötig, durch Kunst und 'Virtuosität' die Wahrheit zu verdunkeln; sie ist an sich schon dunkel genug, und nur der unmittelbarsten Darstellung kann es vielleicht gelingen, sie einen Augenblick durchschimmern zu lassen.

Diese Interpretation hat aber auch den anderen Fehler, dass sie Kafkas Verhältnis zu seinem eigenen Werk in ein falsches Licht rückt. Wer seine Zweifel und seine Bedenken kennt, wird schwerlich annehmen, dass er so sorgfältig den Leser auf sein eigenes Werk aufmerksam macht. Selbst wenn er die Fäden derartig durcheinander bringt, dass man ihn nicht mehr verstehen kann, und selbst, wenn er dabei nur der Entfremdung

---

[1] So für den ersten Sohn (*Vor dem Gesetz!*): 'In the phrase "deshalb scheint selbst die heimische Natur vertrauter mit ihm zu sprechen als mit den Daheimgebliebenen" we may find a humorous allusion to the man's attempted conversation with the flees in the doorkeeper's beard!' (a. a. O., S. 74).

Zu Franz Kafkas Erzählung 'Elf Söhne'

seinem eigenen Werk gegenüber Ausdruck geben will. Dies würde Kafka wahrscheinlich als unerlaubte Anmassung empfunden haben. In der Erzählung *Elf Söhne* erkennt Max Brod 'die Wertschätzung der Familie, ja der patriarchalischen Lebensform, wie sie Franz als natürliche Haltung seines Vaters bewunderte, ... das Wunschbild einer Vaterschaft, einer Familiengründung, die dem Vorbild des Vaters etwas Gleichwertiges, das heisst ebenso Patriarchalisch-Grossartiges, in aller Lebensschlichtheit ans Mythische Grenzendes entgegenhalten kann'. Er fügt aber hinzu, dass diese Erklärung der Selbstinterpretation Kafkas, dass die elf Söhne einfach elf Geschichten sind, nicht unbedingt widerspricht. Man muss ihm zustimmen: denn selbst wenn Kafka — was wir nicht glauben — nur elf eigene Erzählungen im Sinne gehabt hat, muss er, sobald er sie als Söhne zu verkleiden beschloss, das Vater – Sohn-Verhältnis ernst genommen haben. Die Beziehung auf das eigene Werk kann höchstens der Ausgangspunkt gewesen sein; in der Ausführung musste das Bild der Sohnschaft überhaupt die Oberhand gewinnen und als solches analysiert werden. Sonst liefe das Ganze auf das eitelste Rätselraten hinaus. Als Stefan George eines seiner Werke den *Siebenten Ring* nannte, wollte er es freilich als seinen siebenten Gedichtband bezeichnen; er verband aber zugleich mit diesem Sinne eine Reihe anderer, halb exoterischer, halb esoterischer Bedeutungen, wie Anspielungen auf die geheime Arithmetik des Werkes, auf Dantes Himmel, auf den, dem Gott Maximin gewidmeten zentralen Ring des Buches. Dabei ist Georges Verhältnis zu seinem Werk, das er bewusst als sein eigenes Denkmal errichtet, von Kafkas höchst fragwürdiger Beziehung zu seinem literarischen Schaffen verschieden. Selbst wenn er einmal dieses Werk als Thema einer Erzählung sollte genommen haben, hätte es Kafka mit anderen Bedeutungen verflochten.

Aber wahrscheinlich ist die Entstehungsgeschichte der Erzählung umgekehrt verlaufen: nicht ein ursprünglich auf das eigene Schaffen bezogene Werk ist nachträglich auf das Vater – Sohn-Motiv erweitert worden, sondern eine zuerst das Vater – Sohn-Verhältnis behandelnde Erzählung ist dann auf das eigene Schaffen übertragen worden. Ein Vater spricht hier von seinen elf Söhnen. Kafka wusste aber, dass er sich nie verheiraten würde, dass er keine anderen Kinder haben würde als seine

Werke. 'Geschichten', schreibt noch Max Brod, 'waren ja seine Kinder, im Schreiben leistete er auf entlegenem Gebiet, aber selbständig etwas, was der Schöpferkraft des Vaters (ich gebe hier Franzens, nicht meine Auffassung wieder) analog war und ihr an die Seite gestellt werden konnte.'[1] Sein zwiespältiges Verhältnis zum eigenen Werk fand Kafka der Beziehung zwischen Vater und Sohn, wie er sie in seiner Erzählung dargestellt hatte, analog. Daher seine zunächst befremdende Erklärung.

Statt also nach zweifelhaften 'Schlüsseln' zu fahnden, wollen wir versuchen, Kafka beim Wort zu nehmen. Er hat es uns aber diesmal nicht leicht gemacht, und scheinbar keinen Anhaltspunkt gegeben. Als Einleitung der blosse Satz: 'Ich habe elf Söhne', als Schluss: 'Dies sind die elf Söhne.' Dazwischen keine Geschichte, sondern eine Reihe von elf Porträts, dessen längstes kaum 30 Zeilen zählt, dessen kürzestes nur sechs Zeilen einnimmt. In diesen Erzählungen aus dem Jahr 1917 hat Kafka auf die pathetische Manier der um 1912–14 entstandenen Texte — wie *Das Urteil, Die Verwandlung, In der Strafkolonie* oder selbst *Der Prozess* — verzichtet. Das 'Peinliche', das er in dem Brief an Kurt Wolff vom 11. Oktober 1916[2] erwähnt, darf künftig in sein Werk keinen Einlass finden. Damit ist alles gemeint, was in diesen frühen Erzählungen die Nerven des Lesers so sehr angriff, die plötzlichen Umschwünge der Handlung, die ekelerregenden Bilder, überhaupt die ganze sadistisch-masochistische Komponente. Die allzu krasse Expressivität wird nun von Kafka als ein zu billiges literarisches Mittel verworfen. Die äusserste Knappheit und Nüchternheit wird nun angestrebt. Die Handlung spielt eine immer geringere Rolle und verschwindet manchmal ganz und gar. Statt des anscheinend realistischen Rahmens werden exotische Landschaften (China, Nordafrika) oder phantastische Motive (*Ein Landarzt, Der Jäger Gracchus*) herangezogen. Die Erzählung nähert sich der Form der Parabel oder des Apologs. Der Stil wird immer kühler, nackter, man würde fast sagen abstrakter, wenn nicht einige äusserst konkrete, mit wenigen Strichen scharf gezeichnete Einzelheiten weiter bestünden, um etwa einen Gesichtszug, eine Attitüde, eine bezeichnende Geste zu veranschaulichen. Wäh-

[1] Max Brod, *Franz Kafka. Eine Biographie*, Berlin und Frankfurt 1954, S. 171.
[2] *Briefe*, S. 150.

rend der erlebte Gehalt in den um 1912–14 verfassten Geschichten kaum verändert immer erkennbar blieb, haben nun die Texte einen allgemeineren, unpersönlicheren, objektiveren Charakter. Anstatt sich wie früher meist mit dem leidenden Helden zu identifizieren, oder wenigstens die Welt aus dessen Augen zu sehen, nimmt nun der Erzähler öfters einen neutralen Standort ein. Diese kühle, gleichsam affektlose Manier wird nun bis zum Ende, bis zu dem *Bau* und zu den *Forschungen eines Hundes* Kafkas Schaffen beherrschen.

In *Elf Söhne* wird diese damals noch wenig erprobte Manier sofort mit Konsequenz durchgeführt: keine Handlung, nichts, was zum Gefühl spricht; ein trockener Bericht, der sich zuerst dem Verständnis zu entziehen scheint. Ein Vater erzählt von seinen elf Söhnen. Das Vater–Sohn-Verhältnis, das im *Urteil* den Mittelpunkt der Erzählung bildete, in der *Verwandlung* einen Teil der Aufmerksamkeit auf sich zog, ist hier wieder das einzige Motiv des Textes. Die Perspektive hat sich aber umgekehrt. Dieses Verhältnis wird nicht mehr vom Standpunkt des Sohnes, des unschuldig-schuldigen Opfers, sondern vom Standpunkt des Vaters beschrieben. Das pathetische Moment wird somit ausgeklammert.

Elf Söhne: eine vielköpfige Familie, aber eine Familie ohne Mädchen. Der endgültige Bruch mit Felice Bauer, der diese erneute Produktivität Kafkas ausgelöst hatte, befreit ihn auch von der Problematik der Ehe und der Beziehung zum anderen Geschlecht, die ihn seit mehreren Jahren fast einzig beschäftigte.

Keiner dieser Söhne wird mit Namen genannt: nicht als Individualität kommen sie in Frage, sondern Bedeutung hat nur ihre Beziehung zum Vater, oder vielmehr die Beziehung des Vaters zu jedem von ihnen. Sie haben also nur einen Funktionswert. Nicht die Geschichte einer Familie wird erzählt; eine besondere Beziehung wird isoliert und für sich analysiert. Dennoch können wir Heinz Politzer nicht zustimmen, wenn er von den elf Söhnen schreibt: 'Der mechanische Fortschritt von Zahl zu Zahl löscht die Unterschiede zwischen einer Figur und der anderen wieder aus', so dass schliesslich 'der Mensch als Dutzendware erscheint'.[1] Denn gerade auf die Verschiedenheit dieser Söhne wird der Nachdruck gelegt. An allen möglichen Typen wird das Vater–Sohn-Verhältnis geprüft und exempli-

[1] H. Politzer, *Franz Kafka, der Künstler*, Frankfurt 1965, S. 152.

fiziert. Es ist auch nicht richtig, wie H. Politzer behauptet, dass Kafkas Absicht darin lag, 'sein eigenes Bild elfmal in Söhnen zu reflektieren, die ihn wie ein Spiegelkabinett umgeben'.[1] Er ist nicht überall; er ist weder der geschickte Fechter (der zweite Sohn) noch der schöne Sänger (der dritte); sicher haben seine Urteile nicht die Unbekümmertheit des vierten Sohnes; der kleine, athletische Körper des achten, der 'für Frauen bestimmte süsse Blick' des neunten wollen wenig zu ihm passen. Kafka spricht hier eben nicht oder nicht nur von sich selbst. Hier in diesen verhältnismässig späten Geschichten gelingt es ihm zum ersten Mal, von sich Abstand zu nehmen; man wird ihn nur zwischen anderen Figuren, die ihm nicht ähnlich sehen, ganz am Ende der Erzählung wiederfinden.

Wie sieht nun dieser Vater seine elf Söhne? Er liebt sie alle, so behauptet er. Aber wie? Er hat sie noch, wenigstens zum Teil, in seiner Gewalt: den dritten zum Beispiel hält er am liebsten im Verborgenen. Und doch sind sie ihm auch teilweise undurchsichtig geworden; er muss sich oft auf die Meinung der anderen verlassen, um sich über seine eigenen Söhne ein Urteil zu bilden; er, als Vater, will zum Beispiel nicht entscheiden, ob oder auf welche Weise der zehnte Sohn ein Heuchler ist. Und doch ist er hellsichtiger und strenger gegen sie als die meisten: niemand wird am zweiten Sohn das 'kleinere Zwinkern des Auges tadelnd bemerken'; er, der Vater, tut es. Er lässt sich nicht bestechen: auch nicht vom süssen Blick des neunten Sohns; weiss er doch, 'dass förmlich ein nasser Schwamm genügt, um allen diesen überirdischen Glanz wegzuwischen'. Er spricht von ihnen wohl mit väterlicher Liebe, vor allem aber mit kühler Objektivität: den siebenten Sohn etwa überschätzt er nicht; er weiss, 'er ist geringfügig genug'.

Das Verhältnis dieses Vaters zu seinen Söhnen ist nicht die patriarchalische Idylle, die Max Brod in dieser Erzählung zu finden meinte. Die Liebe schliesst weder die Distanz noch in manchen Fällen eine gewisse Feindseligkeit aus. Alle diese Söhne sind von ihm entsprossen; sie haben sich aber zu selbständigen Wesen entwickelt, und sich ihm dabei entfremdet. Sie sind 'anders' geworden, und schon dieses Anderssein verurteilt sie.

Die in diesem Text aufgeworfene Frage ist nämlich, wie sich die Söhne vor dem Blick des Vaters bewähren. Gericht wird

[1] a. a. O., S. 151.

über sie gehalten, ein Gericht ohne Nachsicht und Güte; sie werden vom Vater auf ihren Wert geprüft. Nicht alle, aber die meisten, haben, jeder auf seine Weise, eine gewisse Vollkommenheit erreicht; aber es kann geschehen, dass ein kleiner Mangel an ihnen genügt, um diese Vollkommenheit in Frage zu stellen; oder diese Vollkommenheit wird vom Vater gering geachtet, so als wäre sie nicht da. Es gibt kein ideales Bild, nach dem man sich richten könnte. Jeder ist auf die Welt mit seiner eigenen Natur gekommen; jeder ist seinen eigenen Weg gegangen. Am Ende wird keiner ausdrücklich verworfen, keiner aber auch endgültig freigesprochen.

Die Söhne werden so dargestellt, dass sie sich ähnlich sind und doch gleichzeitig miteinander kontrastiert werden. Der erste ist ernsthaft und klug; auch der zweite ist klug, aber dazu welterfahren, gewandt und schön. Der dritte Sohn ist gleichfalls schön; es ist aber eine ganz andere Schönheit. Dieser dritte Sohn fühlt sich fremd in unserer Zeit, der vierte ist im Gegenteil ein wahres Kind seiner Zeit. Der sechste Sohn ist ein Kopfhänger; der zehnte lebt in Übereinstimmung mit dem Weltganzen, 'eine Übereinstimmung, die notwendigerweise den Hals strafft und den Körper erheben lässt'. Alle diese Porträts haben dieselbe Struktur. Sie bestehen aus zwei Teilen: es werden zuerst die Vorzüge genannt, dann im zweiten Teil die Mängel. Diese zwei Teile sind meist durch 'trotzdem' oder 'leider' getrennt. Aber auch innerhalb jedes Satzes werden mit subtiler Kasuistik die guten Eigenschaften und die Fehler abgewogen. Es werden das Gute und das Schlechte auf die Schalen der Waage gelegt, und ein Weniges genügt, um das Gleichgewicht zu stören.

Der erste Sohn wird am schnellsten abgefertigt; er ist ernsthaft und klug, aber unansehnlich und 'zu einfach'. Der Erstgeborene hat kein besonderes Vorrecht.

Der zweite Sohn ist vielleicht derjenige, der von der Natur die grössten Gaben erhalten hat. Er ist klug und schön, kräftig und gewandt; er ist viel gereist, und doch seiner Heimat nicht entfremdet. In ihm scheinen sich die Widersprüche zu versöhnen: wenn er ins Wasser springt, sind seine Bewegungen 'geradezu wild beherrscht'. Nicht jeder verfügt über solche Anmut; er beschämt alle, die ihm seinen Kunstsprung nachmachen wollen. Er hat den Stolz, 'die unnahbare Abgeschlossenheit' des natürlichen Adels. Aber er zwinkert mit dem linken Auge. Niemand, nur dem Vater fällt dieser Fehler auf. Für diesen aber stellt dieser Mangel das ganze Wesen des Sohnes in Frage: er deutet auf tiefere Gebrechen, im Blut oder im Geist. Allerdings ist dieser Fehler der Fehler der ganzen Familie; er müsste eigentlich dem Vater diesen Sohn noch lieber machen. Aber das Gegenteil geschieht: dieser erbliche Makel ist 'überdeutlich'. Wer kennt aber das richtige Mass? Dass dieses richtige Mass leicht verloren geht erblickt man am dritten Sohn. Die unnachahmliche Grazie des älteren Bruders hat sich bei ihm in etwas Unmässiges, Schauspielerhaftes verwandelt. Der Vater möchte ihn am liebsten im Verborgenen halten. Nun ist aber, wie aus dem zweiten Teil des Porträts erhellt, mit dieser Beschreibung das Wahre nicht getroffen. Diese auffällige Schönheit ist nicht die eines Schauspielers; er hat im Gegenteil eine introvertierte Natur, ist mit sich und seiner Zeit unzufrieden. Er drängt sich nicht auf, und diese Bescheidenheit wird von dem Vater auf seine 'Unschuld' zurückgeführt. Aber diese 'Unschuld' wiederum spricht nicht zu seinen Gunsten; es ist die Unschuld desjenigen, der seine Mängel nicht kennt. Sie macht ihn dem Vater nicht lieber, eher im Gegenteil.

Der vierte Sohn ist der genaue Gegensatz des dritten: ein wahres Kind seiner Zeit; unbekümmert, während den anderen nichts aufheitern konnte; jedermann verständlich, wo der andere einsam war und zurückgezogen lebte. Ein extravertierter Mensch, mit etwas Leichtem und Freiem in seinem Gebaren. Aber auch er weiss nicht, Mass zu halten: der dritte krankte an Schwerfälligkeit und Schwermut, dieser 'krankt an allzu grosser Leichtigkeit'. Diesmal verkehrt sich die Liebe des Vaters beinahe in Hass: er weiss, dass dieser bald 'trostlos im öden Staube endet, ein Nichts'.

Über den fünften Sohn ist wenig zu sagen; obwohl von Geburt wenig begabt, hat er es doch zu einigem Ansehen gebracht, und dies durch seine Unschuld. Das einzige, was man ihm vorzuwerfen hätte, ist eben diese Unschuld: er ist 'allzu unschuldig', allzu 'offensichtlich lobenswürdig'. Kann es einen Exzess im Guten geben? Was kann absurder sein als eine übertriebene Unschuld? Man wird aber verstanden haben, dass sich diese paradoxe Theologie jenseits von Sinn und Vernunft entfaltet.

Zu Franz Kafkas Erzählung 'Elf Söhne'

Vor den Augen des Vaters ist Unschuld kein Verdienst: weder Moral noch Natur ist imstande, sein Wohlwollen zu erzwingen.

Der sechste Sohn ist ein Grübler; der Vater behandelt ihn mit noch weniger Liebe, beinahe mit Gereiztheit. Denn er macht es sich leicht mit seinem Denken; ein bequemes Mittel, um sich zu behaupten. Einmal lässt er den Kopf hängen, wenn er es für gut befindet; ein anderes Mal schwätzt er. Man würde ihn für krank halten; dabei ist er gesund und niemals ernstlich in Gefahr: 'braucht keine Hilfe, fällt nicht'. Für diese intellektuelle gefahrlose Akrobatik hat der Vater nicht viel übrig.

Der siebente Sohn müsste dem Herzen des Vaters am nächsten stehen: er gehört ihm vielleicht mehr als alle andern. Er ist der fromme, der gehorsame Sohn, der wohl Unruhe in sich hat, doch nicht genug, um die Überlieferung in Gefahr zu bringen. Das Gesetz ist bei ihm gut aufgehoben. Das Ganze seiner Gesinnung nennt der Vater unanfechtbar, seine Anlage aufmunternd und hoffnungsreich. Aber auch diesen kann der Vater nicht besonders schätzen. Der erste Sohn war 'unansehnlich', der fünfte 'unbedeutend'; dieser ist 'geringfügig genug'. Der Vater fügt sogar mit verbissener Wut hinzu: 'hätte die Welt keinen andern Fehler als den, dass sie ihn nicht zu würdigen weiss, sie wäre noch immer makellos.' Die Selbstzufriedenheit, in der er lebt, kann der Vater wohl begreifen, aber nicht gutheissen. Denn solche schöne Seelen haben keine Zukunft. Dieser Sohn kümmert sich nicht um Mädchen; er wird keine Kinder haben. Von solchen guten, folgsamen Söhnen ist nicht viel zu hoffen. Scheinbar ist ein Gran Bosheit, ein Gran unerlaubter Revolte nötig, um das Geschlecht fortzusetzen, um 'das Rad der Zukunft ins Rollen zu bringen'.

Dieser Gedanke wird im Bild des achten Sohns indirekt bestätigt. Denn dieser ist der Rebell. Er hat alle Verbindungen mit dem Vater abgebrochen. Um dieses Schmerzenskind scheint aber gerade der Vater besorgter zu sein, als um die anderen, die ihm treu geblieben sind. Zum ersten Mal ist etwas wie Zärtlichkeit in den Worten zu spüren, mit denen er ihn beschreibt. Er fühlt sich 'väterlich eng mit ihm verbunden'; früher befiel ihn ein Zittern, wenn er an ihn dachte. Jetzt lässt er ihn gewähren, ohne ihm zu grollen. Das einzige, was er an ihm zu rügen weiss, ist dass er einen Vollbart trägt, was bei einem so kleinen Mann natürlich nicht schön ist.

Der neunte Sohn ist eine künstlerische Natur: ein Verführer und ein Träumer; einer, der 'gedrängt und unanschaulich' zu sprechen weiss. Kein ruchloser Don Juan allerdings: er geht gar nicht auf Verführung aus, und möchte am liebsten immer liegen bleiben und vor sich hin träumen. Der Vater mag diesen Sohn nicht: er lässt sich von diesem angeblich überirdischen Glanz nicht täuschen. Dieser neunte Sohn macht sich anscheinend die Sache zu leicht; und ihn aus seinem sorglosen Schlaf aufzurütteln, wird selbst dem Vater niemals gelingen.

Der zehnte Sohn ist wie ein clergyman (oder wie ein orthodoxer Jude!) gekleidet. Er hat einen feierlichen Gang; er spricht mit Bedacht und Selbstsicherheit. Der zehnte Sohn ist der Zelot. Er gilt als unaufrichtiger Charakter, als grenzenloser Heuchler. Der Vater will die Wahrheit dieses Gerüchtes nicht bestreiten. Einige fühlen sich vom Aussehen dieses Sohnes abgestossen und verfallen doch der Macht oder der Verführung seines Wortes. Andere aber halten gerade sein Wort für heuchlerisch. Und die letzteren sind beachtenswerter als die anderen. Vor dem Blick des Vaters finden die Zeloten wenig Gnade.

Wer aber kann diesem Vater gefallen? Was er will, lässt sich nicht mit Worten sagen. Er selbst wüsste es nicht auszudrücken. An dem einen Sohn rügt er einen Mangel; an einem anderen Sohn den umgekehrten Fehler. Das richtige Mass, das seltene Gleichgewicht, die wunderbare coincidentia oppositorum lässt sich nicht finden, lässt sich kaum als möglich denken. Das Urteil des Vaters scheint zuerst der Laune unterworfen. Es geht aber um mehr als um blosse Laune. Die Liebe des Vaters zu seinen Söhnen macht, dass sie ihm nie genügen können. Aus Liebe muss er sie alle verwerfen.

Es bleibt aber noch ein elfter Sohn, den der Leser mit Neugier erwartet, denn er vermutet, dass diesem Sohn vielleicht eine besondere Rolle zugedacht ist. Dieser ist der schwächste von allen. Selbst wenn er zuweilen kräftig und bestimmt ist, so rührt dies immer noch von seiner Schwäche her. Der Vater gibt zu, dass an dieser Schwäche nichts Beschämendes ist: es ist die Schwäche desjenigen, der sich hienieden nicht wohl fühlt, der fliegen möchte, dem es aber nur gelingt, unbestimmt hin und her zu flattern. Er kann ihn deswegen aber auch nicht lieben. Seine Eigenschaften gehen noch mehr als die des siebenten Sohnes auf Zerstörung der Familie aus. Er ist der Letzte, dem

Zu Franz Kafkas Erzählung 'Elf Söhne'

sich der Vater vertrauen würde. Dieser elfte Sohn wird hier aber nicht ganz wie die anderen behandelt. Er kommt zwar, wie die anderen Brüder, nicht zu Wort. Doch versucht der Vater, die in seinem Blick enthaltene Bitte zu deuten und in Worte zu fassen. Dieser Blick scheint zu sagen: 'Mag ich also wenigstens der Letzte sein.' Ein frommes Wort, ein schüchternes beinahe beschämtes Gebet. In dem elften Sohn, dem schwächsten, unbrauchbarsten von allen, wird man den Dichter Franz Kafka erkannt haben.

Einen zwölften Sohn gibt es nicht. Zwölf wäre die 'Vollzahl' gewesen, in der sich die Widersprüche des Daseins vielleicht gelöst hätten, die heilige Zahl der Apostel oder besser der Stämme Israels. Elf aber ist die Sünde.

Unter allen Erzählungen Kafkas gibt es nur eine, die denselben Aufbau aufweist, wie *Elf Söhne*. Es ist der ungefähr um dieselbe Zeit entstandene *Besuch im Bergwerk*. Da neue Stollen gelegt werden sollen, sind die Ingenieure in die Mine gestiegen, um die ersten Ausmessungen vorzunehmen. Zehn Ingenieure, alle jung und tüchtig, ernst und vital, alle ohne falschen Stolz, ganz bei der Sache, die sie treiben. Aber auch hier tritt eine elfte Person auf, der Kanzleidiener. Er ist unbeschäftigt, geht nur hinter den anderen her. Es ist aber so als hätte sich in ihm der ganze Hochmut, den die anderen längst abgelegt haben, aufgesammelt. Es ist kaum möglich, seine Rolle in der Gesellschaft zu bestimmen; er aber wirft sich in die Brust, erwartet in seiner Livree mit vergoldeten Knöpfen von jedem einen Gruss. Man kann ihn nicht ganz ernst nehmen und lacht hinter seinem Rücken, und doch bleibt er 'als etwas Unverständliches in unserer Achtung'.

In diesem unnützen Glied der Gesellschaft, in diesem eingebildeten Gecken, der eine Achtung beansprucht, die er in nichts verdient, ist wieder der Dichter Franz Kafka zu erkennen. Wie manchmal auf den alten Bildern hat der Meister sein eigenes Bild in einer Ecke dargestellt. Aber nein: der Vergleich will hier nicht passen: denn nur wegen dieser elften Person, wegen dieses armseligen und eingebildeten Kanzleidieners ist diesmal die ganze Geschichte erzählt worden.

Language as the Topic of Modern Fiction

VICTOR LANGE

IT is one of the central assumptions of contemporary criticism that the most dramatic shift of purpose and perspective in modern art has been the change from an effort to represent the concrete world about us to an accounting, both analytical and imaginative, of the process of consciousness by which the virtual world of art is produced. A singularly striking consequence of this shift has been the manner in which language has ceased to be merely the object of conscientious qualitative scrutiny and has become the very topic of poetry and fiction. Indeed, it can be said that the great books of our time, Joyce's *Ulysses*, Mann's *Doktor Faustus*, Musil's *Mann ohne Eigenschaften*, Pound's *Cantos*, or the fictions of Beckett, Borges, or Nabokov, are works about language, about the way in which consciousness, however defined, is constituted and realized in the resources of language.

To speak of this issue with anything like adequacy would require a detailed description of the emergence, within the past century, of an ever-deepening sense of the discrepancy between the substance of the experience to be conveyed and the linguistic conventions available for it; it would presume, no less, an understanding of the views, casual or systematic, that are held at a given time of the function and structure of language itself.

If we consider the concern with the scope of language to be a modern one, we do so only in so far as its implications have in our time become overwhelming and its consequences for the very act of writing radically disturbing. For distrust in the efficacy of speech has been a perennial concern of literature. But it is not until the mid-eighteenth century that a secularized view of language and an increasing doubt in the traditional canon of rules of linguistic behaviour are reflected in the performance of poets and novelists. Sterne, an early and incomparably intelligent critic of conventional forms of perception and communication, is the most brilliant instance of a mercilessly ironic mind who was determined, with infinite ingenuity,

Language as the Topic of Modern Fiction

to turn language into the very theme and form of his fiction. A celebrated passage in *Tristram Shandy* (iii. 12) may serve as a characteristic indication of his attempts at dramatizing an emerging fascination with the problem of linguistic resonance:

> And how did Garrick speak the soliloquy last night?—Oh, against all rule, my Lord,—most ungrammatically! betwixt the substantive and the adjective, which should agree together in number, case, and gender, he made a breach thus,—stopping, as if the point wanted settling;—and betwixt the nominative case, which your lordship knows should govern the verb, he suspended his voice in the epilogue a dozen times three seconds and three fifths by a stop-watch, my Lord, each time.—Admirable grammarian!—But in suspending his voice—was the sense suspended likewise? Did no expression of attitude or countenance fill up the chasm?—Was the eye silent? Did you narrowly look?—I looked only at the stop-watch, my Lord.—Excellent observer!

What matters for Sterne is the articulation of the *expressive energy of art*, a problem that is widely discussed in the aesthetic theory of the eighteenth century: it was a notion that led, in music, to J. J. Rousseau's attacks upon the static form of operatic recitatives and monologues; in choreography to Jean Georges Noverre's conception of a revolutionary form of ballet that was to 'move the heart, stir the soul, convey passions and let genius shine'; and in Garrick's immensely admired performances to a calculated distortion of speech and gesture towards an intensive rendering of emotional and intellectual nuances. If in music, ballet, and theatre the range of expressiveness was to be differentiated and intensified, it was Sterne's intention to narrate in language not so much the intelligible substance of the world as its intractability. Yet while he is forever bent on demonstrating the horrendous difficulties of testifying to the elusive character of reality, he would have thought it absurd to deny to the world a structure of meaning, or to doubt the ultimate capacity of language, however refracted, to communicate the compelling presence of that meaning.

This classical conviction that it should be possible to render through configurations of language the objective substance, the palpable evidence of reality, remains the premiss of all narrative art throughout the eighteenth and nineteenth centuries. It is true that the great realistic novelists, Gogol, Dickens, or Dostoevsky, became increasingly aware of the ambiguity of narrative language and of its more and more oblique and metaphorical function; that, from Jean Paul and Novalis to the symbolist and naturalist writers, new dimensions of speech are drawn into the discourse of fiction, and that an actuality that the reader could no longer fully comprehend in its mysterious complexity is—in the works of Balzac, Stendhal, or E. T. A. Hoffmann—ironically or imaginatively reconstructed in elaborate verbal fictions. Yet, to the end of the nineteenth century it remains an axiom for the masters of epic narrative, for Flaubert, Tolstoy, or Henry James, that in one way or another the world of experienced reality can be encompassed and represented in the shared and intelligible equivalent of language.

The sense of conflict between an increasingly subtle if self-critical consciousness and the linguistic means for its representation was first and most searchingly described by lyrical poets such as Baudelaire or Mallarmé, who were inclined to deny any self-evident relationship between language and actuality, and, later, by H. von Hofmannsthal, whose *Brief des Lord Chandos* (1901) lamented the failure of language to project an existential experience of being. It was deeply felt, though often merely sentimentally proclaimed, by the early German expressionist poets, by Heym and Trakl, and became, in Rilke's *Duineser Elegien*, the recurring preoccupation of a mind desperately isolated in a world in which language had ceased to function objectively.

It was in any case lyrical poetry and not fiction with which the revolutionary proclamations of modernism were customarily concerned: the Italian and Russian Futurist manifestos, as well as Apollinaire's *L'Esprit nouveau et les poètes*, directed their categorical demands for a new radicalism of perception and language at painters, musicians, and poets and not, curiously enough, at the writers of novels. Indeed, Stefan George, Valéry, and Claudel explicitly doubted the continuing validity of the idiom of fiction, André Gide pronounced his negative judgement on Proust's formidable manuscript, and André Breton insisted that the novel, far from illuminating the potential of contemporary consciousness, could do little more than represent its inanity.

Language as the Topic of Modern Fiction

But as early as 1900 it was obvious that the prevailing experience of linguistic inadequacy must be of decisive consequence for the novelist. Such self-conscious narratives as Rilke's *Malte Laurids Brigge* or Musil's *Verwirrungen des Zöglings Törless* explicitly, and by their narrative procedures, raised questions as to what sort of devices of language might be available to a modern analytical narrator whose aesthetic object, beyond any representation of the empirical world, must be the rendering of his own subjective reality. The history of the 'internalization of fiction' and of its consequences for the structure of the contemporary novel is familiar enough: its most tantalizing aspect is the ever-widening distance between the novelist's preoccupation with the character and function of language and the concomitant doubt in the very existence of a reality that can yet be plausibly narrated.

Thomas Mann was perhaps the last among the great architects of modern fiction to assume, in keeping with the epic tradition, the narrator's role as a detached observer and as the commentator upon a manifest, if threatened, universe of culture; with the familiar devices of his art—learned, parodistic, and histrionic—he developed astonishingly subtle variations of the traditional methods of linguistic and rhetorical orchestration, devices comparable to the ironical musical structures adopted at the same time by Richard Strauss or Stravinsky. With an acute though melancholy awareness of his magisterial role as a belated moralist in an obsolescent bourgeois tradition, he acted as the eloquent puppeteer whose figures, however elaborately constructed and however self-conscious, were still marshalled in order to reassure us of the presence of a world in whose objective reality we may discretely share.

In the contemporaneous tradition of the 'lyrical novel', in the work of the early Gide, Hesse, or Virginia Woolf, these narrated figures appear to have lost their recognizable coherence; they are at any rate no longer dependent upon a narrator who reports their symptomatic performance in a setting of familiar characteristics. The inner monologue with its various elements of subjectivity represents, together with Mann's manner of ironic speech, the linguistic mode in which the interplay of speculative and objective reality may still be held in precarious abeyance. Virginia Woolf's sensibility is, even less than Thomas

Mann's, reflected in an intelligible and pragmatic plot; but both offer, in the tradition of European symbolism, designs of suggestive speech, of images and metaphors that function within an essentially conventional syntactical system. Indeed, it is an important aspect of the ironic as well as the lyrical narrative that it develops its strategy largely through an intensification of the word, and that even the later poetics and practices of the expressionist tradition from Ehrenstein and Sternheim to Faulkner or Henry Miller focus primarily upon the affective extension of the lexical unit, particularly of adjectives, adverbs, or verbs.

While the Russian formalists had pointed to the advantages of expanding the potentiality of narrative structures, not merely by intensifying the metaphorical resonances of the word but by a systematic destruction of the conventional syntactical order, few among the experimental novelists were inclined to follow so radical a prescription. Even Alfred Döblin, one of those who were after 1913 eager to develop fresh narrative techniques, and who later produced, in *Berlin Alexanderplatz*, an intricate example of multi-faceted fiction, defended the 'reportorial' character of all epic procedures against their dissolution by radical structural innovations. In an essay entitled 'Der Bau des epischen Werks'[1] he dealt as late as 1929 with the function of language in the 'production of narrative'. Language, he argues there, is an instrument determined by inherent formal characteristics and extendable in its effectiveness only through the capacity to produce a variety of rhetorical 'styles' such as the conversational, the professional, the dialectal, the historical, Lutheran, Goethean, etc. Each of these has its productive energy, but each must be respected as a specific medium with its own coherence: 'Jedem Sprachstil wohnt eine Produktivkraft und ein Zwangscharakter inne.' What Döblin in turn demands is not expressionist metaphors but 'Sprechgesten und Schreibgesten, keine Worte! — wie die Welt ja auch keine einzelnen Gegenstände kennt.' Epic language, he insists, should be neither lyrical nor ironic; no matter how intricate its information, it must, as a medium of accounting, respect the prevailing syntactical order. With such an altogether unbroken regard for the established patterns of language, the novelist should be able to represent the exemplary phenomena of life, 'das Exemplarische des Vor-

[1] Reprinted in *Aufsätze zur Literatur*, Olten and Freiburg i. Br. 1963, pp. 103 f.

Language as the Topic of Modern Fiction

ganges und die Figuren, die geschildert werden und von denen in der Berichtform mitgeteilt wird. Es sind . . . Elementarsituationen des menschlichen Daseins, die herausgearbeitet werden, es sind Elementarhaltungen des Menschen, die in dieser (epischen) Sphäre erscheinen und die, weil sie tausendfach zerlegt wirklich sind, auch so berichtet werden können.'

Döblin's poetics conform to the fundamentally mystical conviction that a transcendent meaning of life can be communicated within the available system of language and within the content-determined structure of the sentence. This is an assumption that is shared by Hermann Broch, an artist profoundly absorbed in questions of language, who deals, in what is perhaps his most important critical study, with the relationship between syntactical and cognitive forms. One of the key sensentences of this essay ('Über syntaktische und kognitive Einheiten')[1] has a direct bearing upon his own narrative practice:

Von der Sprache her wird nichts 'gemeint', vielmehr wird sie, unbeschadet ihrer Autonomie, von einem 'meinenden Akt' der Erkenntnis dirigiert, und ihre Strukturgebilde, also vor allem die Syntax-Einheiten wie der Satz, der Absatz usw. werden bloss dann sinnvoll, und zwar ebensowohl im sprachlichen wie im kognitiven Verstande sinnvoll, wenn als Ergänzung zu ihnen ideale, nicht empirische Kognitiv-Gebilde angenommen werden, mit denen sie in einem Entsprechungs-Verhältnis stehen und deren Ausdruck sie sein sollen . . .

Broch's hypothesis of the epistemological condition of speech leads him to the notion of a specific tension within a sentence, between static and dynamic elements, and subsequently to the suggestion that in the narrative act these diverse features ('satzinterne Begebenheiten') should be conveyed as one simultaneous experience. Broch was well aware that such a paradoxical requirement could hardly be achieved in a conventional linguistic design; indeed—now far removed from Döblin—he came to see that the successive temporal order of syntactical speech might have to be altogether cancelled by some sort of representation of the experience of simultaneity: 'O Ziel aller Dichtung,' he writes, 'wenn sie über alles Beschreiben hinweg sich selbst aufhebt, O Augenblicke der Sprache, in denen sie selber in die Gleichzeitigkeit eintaucht.'

[1] In 'Erkennen und Handeln', *Essays*, vol. ii, Zürich 1955, pp. 151 f.

Long before Broch's own attempt at the end of his *Tod des Vergil* to dissolve the contiguity and consecutiveness of experience in a linguistic fiction of simultaneity, he recognized in the last section of Joyce's *Ulysses* the model of a syntactically differentiated, yet free-flowing and extended text in which the totality of an intricate chain of experiences is rendered as a single unbroken statement. What Joyce attempted to achieve in his novel was clearly a portrayal of contemporary consciousness. But unlike Mann's *Zauberberg*, which represented the available world in familiar and recognizable language, Joyce's *Ulysses* aimed at a more comprehensive effect: it was to transform the substance of the world into language and to make it comprehensible in its linguistic accretions. The extension of Joyce's linguistic technique between *Ulysses* and *Finnegans Wake* anticipates that radically analytical view of the role of language in the making, understanding, and conveying of our experiences that determines the mode of nearly all subsequent major novelists. He proceeded from a conscientious attempt at reproducing available language towards its dismantling and a reconstruction of its ingredients. If in *The Portrait of the Artist* he had given an account of individual growth in terms of the hero's gradual comprehension of language, he dissociated language altogether, in *Finnegans Wake*, from its communicative purposes and, in a web of fragmented and reintegrated linguistic gestures, attempted to 'constitute' consciousness itself. The nature of perception was to become palpable in a model construct that contained virtually the possible experiences of all languages and of all their speakers.

Joyce's Alexandrian project, despite its astonishing ingenuity, reiterates in some measure the classical postulate of the epic tradition that language should be capable, by virtue of its mimetic character, of mirroring the world, however elusive or disjointed it may appear, as a totality of meaning.

This historic—but increasingly dubious and troublesome—faith is in the work of Samuel Beckett turned into its heretical opposite: as the complexity of existence overwhelms our comprehension, our speech can no longer hope to offer an adequate record of representation of it. It can only testify to the continuous diminution of reality under the very scrutiny of language itself.

Language as the Topic of Modern Fiction

If Tolstoy or Henry James or Thomas Mann were masters of a narrative art that encompassed the world in ever more elaborate linguistic figurations, Beckett demonstrates, in a radically laconic, shattered, and self-destroying language, the progressive withdrawal of the world from our grasp. His novels consist of statements that aim at conveying not the effective capacity of discourse of classical fiction, but its approximation to silence. 'I look', Beckett has said, 'for the voice of my silence.' Language, this is to say, cannot describe or identify, it can only provide guesses and hypotheses of a presumed and essentially subjective reality. If words persist in offering themselves, they must not be mistaken for equivalents of discursive memory; they are dubious voices that must not be believed:

> It all boils down [he writes in *The Unnamable*] to a question of words, I must not forget this, I have not forgotten it. But I must have said this before, since I say it now. I have to speak in a certain way, with warmth perhaps, all is possible, first of the creature I am not, as if I were he, and then, as if I were he, of the creature I am. . . . It's a question of voices, of voices to keep going, in the right manner, when they stop, on purpose, to put me to the test, as now the one whose burden is roughly to the effect that I am alive. . . . But what is the right manner, I don't know . . . on the subject of me properly so called, I know what I mean, so far as I know I have received no information up to date. May I speak of a voice, in these conditions? Probably not. And yet I do. The fact is all this business about voices requires to be revised, corrected and then abandoned. Hearing nothing I am nonetheless a prey to communications. And I speak of voices! After all, why not, so long as one knows it's untrue. But there are limits, it appears. Let them come. So nothing about me. That is to say no connected statement.

What Beckett in all his texts narrates is a paralysing experience of language that is no longer capable of communicating substance: words and images lack any telling relationship to objects or beings. If no 'connected statement' is feasible, existence in all its forms can only be experienced in silence and in the voices that reach us in the stillness of that silence.

> No souls, no bodies, neither birth nor life nor death, one must get along without all this, all this has died of words, all this is too much words, they cannot say anything else, they say that there is nothing else, that here there is nothing else, but they will not say it any more,

they will not always say it, they will find something else, no matter what . . . a voice and a silence, a voice of silence, the voice of my silence. (*Textes pour rien.*)

The function of Beckett's texts is not, as that of many of the earlier European documents of the 'crisis of language', to reflect a resigned and melancholy concern with the insufficiency of speech in the face of an overwhelmingly intensified sense of life; it has little to do with the tenor of Hofmannsthal's *Brief* or Rilke's *Malte Laurids Brigge*. The authentic existence which Beckett envisages is in the silence and its story is 'unimaginable, unspeakable'.

He is made of silence . . . he's in the silence, he's the one to be sought, the one to be, the one to be spoken of, the one to speak, but he can't speak . . . his story the story to be told, but he has no story, he hasn't been in story, it's not certain, he's in his own story, unimaginable, unspeakable, that doesn't matter, the attempt must be made, in the old stories incomprehensibly mine, to find his, it must be there somewhere, it must have been mine . . . that's all words, they're all I have, and not many of them, the words fail, the voice fails, so be it.

The burden of performance upon the novelist is thus, paradoxically, one of 'articulating silence', of providing figures of the self-critical imagination, not images of experienced life. It is this belief that, while language cannot convey any given reality, its impact upon experience produces consciousness, which provides the common ground of the most important contemporary fiction. Borges and Nabokov, for instance, each within his distinct view of the purposes of narrative art, share Beckett's conviction that it is not the function of language to offer deceptive reassurances as to the intangible nature of reality. Language, they would agree, freed by the aesthetic and reflective act of all merely empirical relevance, should enable us to construct models of possible configurations of mind and meaning. Beckett's formula 'dire, c'est inventer' may yet imply a metaphysical impulse, it suggests in any case a theory of art shared by all three, in which language provides the theme and topic as well as the medium of fiction.

Beckett's language tends to approximate an ever more indistinct and compulsive murmur of word-bits and quasi-sentences

Language as the Topic of Modern Fiction

with which his figures await the echo signs of that unnameable great silence: 'words can be said without being thought.' Borges, equally uncertain of the efficacy of his speech, nevertheless admits at least a curiosity for a meaning that appears in countless metaphorical refractions and that is represented in an infinite series of interrelated mirror images. In the succession of Mallarmé's theory of language, he establishes in his stories a closed and labyrinthine world of emblematic and mystical symbols such as the spiral, circle, pendulum, or chess-game which in their self-directed monotony and their eternal recurrence point to the nothingness of the universe. To illuminate the indifferent space of creation with narrative and linguistic inventions that are themselves indicative of radical ambiguity, and to meditate on the strategy of such a poetic enterprise, is the object of all of Borges's fiction. With elaborate rhetorical devices and a tantalizing display of pseudo-information, by insinuating at the same time doubt in what is so meticulously asserted, and confidence in the ceremoniously advanced reservations of the narrator, he seems to blur the very design of his stories and to suggest the illusory nature of reality. This inescapable ambiguity of our world we must accept and can only articulate in art; and it is unreality that is its condition: like the invented togography and language of his story, 'Tlön, Ugbar, Orbis Pictus', literature is the 'metaphor of the universe'; it offers us projects of the mind in which space and time can be shown in their ultimate irrelevance.

Nabokov's art, quite different in style and intention from Beckett's or Borges's, categorically denies the aesthetic relevance of questions of meaning or transcendence. It is almost exclusively intent on confining the reader's attention to a scrutiny of surface and structure and—like the form of the detective story with which Nabokov's fiction has much in common—employs language neither in its potential intensity nor as ambient discourse. What matters in Nabokov's work is the capacity of language to serve as the medium of a rigorous exercise in establishing highly artificial and, therefore, ultimately unambiguous relationships between linguistic statements. His language is extraordinarily abstract and synthetic, far more so than Joyce's or Beckett's, which retain a high degree of linguistic concreteness. Nabokov's involuted narratives unfold with the utmost consequence—but also the utmost deviousness—the logic of surface that constitutes the texture of fiction. They do not seem to depend on a distinct, and inevitably subjective, narrator so much as on the inherent tensions of their parts: by his determination to eliminate the vagaries of any external perspective Nabokov is most decisively in the succession of Flaubert.

The devices of his art are wholly self-referential; they function in an entirely hypothetical but meticulously defined space which draws the reader into its maze not so much (as in Borges's stories) to hint at any ultimate ambiguity as rather to insist upon being fully explored and 'realized'. For 'reality', Nabokov has said, 'is a kind of gradual accumulation of information and specialization; it is an infinite succession of levels, levels of perception, of false bottoms, and hence, unquenchable, unattainable'. Reality thus defined can be neither the subject nor the object of art: art creates its own special reality and produces a special sort of 'information'. In fiction, the means of contriving this condition are by necessity linguistic, and to construct in order to induce the explication of such a fabricated linguistic reality without vitiating its logic by extraneous intellectual or moral significances is the purpose of Nabokov's major novels.

Of these, *Pale Fire* is the most elaborate and perhaps the most characteristic. It is composed of several interrelated levels or modes of linguistic behaviour, all, paradoxically, by definition anovelistic: a *Foreword* by an editor whose credibility we must constantly suspect and test by weighing relevant pieces of information offered by him and others; a mock-heroic epic *Poem* in four cantos with curiously elegiac features, composed (by Nabokov) with a view to its eliciting, in the third section, a ponderous *Commentary* by that editor of dubious reliability and uncertain identity; and finally, an *Index* which frequently tests the perspicacity of the reader. The substance of each component is shown, by its oblique illumination through linguistic references in others, to consist of a system of signs which, in itself conclusive, would only serve to demonstrate absurdity, delusion, and madness if it were to be interpreted pragmatically or psychologically, outside the closed orbit of the novel. Nabokov shows his astonishing inventiveness in configuring words and in juggling their twisted ingredients, iridescent vowels, and recurring consonants, puns, and distorted gestures as calculated

Language as the Topic of Modern Fiction

as the compelling puzzle-structure, the crypto-character of his plots. Both combine to create a totally fictitious universe of language that has little to do with existential accounting but that attempts, on the contrary, in the intricate game of art, to transcend the fortuitous character of existence.

Nabokov's—and Borges's—narrative exercises are so far and so deliberately removed from the more traditional moral or spiritual concerns of fiction that they have at times been considered mere self-indulgent exercises of the aesthetic imagination. Yet, in their preoccupation with either the limitations or the generative range of language, they are essentially related to certain other forms of contemporary fiction that proceed from an equally stringent scepticism towards the 'expressive' efficacy of speech. Not only in the works of the *nouveau roman* but particularly in the prose texts of German writers such as H. Heissenbüttel, O. Wiener, and J. Becker, words and gestures of speech, in themselves familiar and commonplace, regain their 'representational' character. But they are here joined or juxtaposed in such a manner that they serve to shock the reader into an acute awareness of their stereotypical vacuity and thus the fundamental social determinacy of speech. H. Heissenbüttel's *Über Literatur* (1966) contains a useful sketch of the effects upon the practices of contemporary prose narrative of this deliberate and exclusive attention to the 'functioning' of language. The often demonstrated dissolution, during the past century, of the single-minded epic intelligence and the concomitant subjective differentiation of language, Heissenbüttel argues, have produced in the reader a more and more radical sense of isolation from the objective social reality. What the novelist (and the poet) must therefore represent in the future is not so much the problematical nature of a subjective consciousness as the external evidence of social behaviour. In language this social functioning becomes unambiguously manifest and there it can be strikingly recorded and in turn made the object of critical reflection. Such anti-subjective postulates draw, of course, for their premises upon the contemporary interest in the various forms of linguistic analysis and particularly in the relationships between linguistics and poetics. Language, whether of poetry or of fiction, has in this perspective ceased to have any expressive or metaphorical justification. What motivates such authors of experimental prose as Mme Sarraute or Francis Ponge, Arno Schmidt, Oswald Wiener or Jürgen Becker, is radically different from the concern of the great novelists from Proust and Mann to Kafka and Beckett with the adequacy of individual, speculative or 'poetic', speech. Fiction, it is now asserted, is no longer capable of offering us a reassuring picture of the world, and corroded by its destructive preoccupation with the fathoming of consciousness it must, for the time being, confine itself to an exploration of the perspectives of the world of language that determine our experience. The narrative act, narrowly qualified in its constituent material, is not, as in the tradition of epic purpose, a symbolizing act but a procedure, appealing and even urgent to an age of finite scruples, of duplicating the world in non-symbolic speech.

A Select List of the Published Writings of E. L. Stahl

Die religiöse und die humanitätsphilosophische Bildungsidee und die Entstehung des deutschen Bildungsromans im 18. Jahrhundert, *Sprache und Dichtung*, 56, Berne 1934.
'The genesis of Schiller's theory of tragedy', in *German studies presented to H. G. Fiedler*, Oxford 1938, pp. 403–23.
'The Duineser Elegien', in *R. M. Rilke. Aspects of his mind and poetry*, ed. W. Rose and B. Craig-Houston, London 1938, pp. 123–71.
Goethe's Die Leiden des jungen Werthers, Blackwell's German Texts, Oxford 1942.
Hölderlin's symbolism. An essay, Oxford 1944.
'The genesis of Symbolist theories in Germany', *MLR* 41 (1946), 306–17.
Heinrich von Kleist's dramas, Oxford 1948; 2nd edn. 1961.
Lessing: Emilia Galotti, Blackwell's German Texts, Oxford 1946.
'Die Wahlverwandschaften', *Publications of the English Goethe Society*, N.S. 15 (1946), 71–95.
'Hölderlin's poetic mission', *GLL* N.S. 2 (1948–9), 45–61.
'Goethe as novelist', in *Essays on Goethe*, ed. W. Rose, London 1949, pp. 46–73.
Goethe's Faust Parts I and II, an abridged version, trans. Louis MacNeice and E. L. Stahl, London 1951; 2nd edn. 1965.
'S. T. Coleridges Theorie der Dichtung im Hinblick auf Goethe', in *Weltliteratur. Festgabe für Fritz Strich zum 70. Geburtstag*, Berne 1952, pp. 101–16.
'Tasso's tragedy and salvation', in *German studies presented to L. A. Willoughby*, Oxford 1952, pp. 191–203.
Friedrich Schiller's drama. Theory and practice, Oxford 1954.
'Darstellung', in *Gestaltprobleme der Dichtung. Festschrift für Günther Müller*, Bonn 1957, pp. 283–98.
'Lessing, *Emilia Galotti*', in *Das deutsche Drama vom Barock bis zur Gegenwart*, ed. B. von Wiese, Düsseldorf 1958, i. 101–12, 481–2.
'Hölderlin's idea of poetry', in *The era of Goethe. Essays presented to James Boyd*, Oxford 1959, pp. 148–62.
'Rilke's letters to Helene', *Oxford Slavonic Papers*, 9 (1959), 129–64.
'Schiller and the composition of Goethe's *Faust*', in *Schiller bicentenary lectures*, ed. F. Norman, London 1960, pp. 24–45.
'Die vier Weltalter', in *Jahrbuch der Schillergesellschaft*, 4 (1960), 301–7.
Creativity. A theme from Faust and the Duino Elegies. An inaugural lecture delivered before the University of Oxford on 2 March 1961, Oxford 1961.
Goethe: Iphigenie auf Tauris, London 1961.
'Schiller on poetry', in *German studies presented to W. H. Bruford*, London 1962, pp. 140–52.

A Select List of E. L. Stahl's Published Writings

Rainer Maria Rilke's Duineser Elegien, Blackwell's German Texts, Oxford 1965.

'Hölderlin's "Friedensfeier" and the structure of mythic poetry', *Oxford German Studies*, 2 (1967), 55-74.

The Oxford Book of German Verse from the 12th to the 15th century, 3rd edn., ed. E. L. Stahl, Oxford 1967.

INDEX

Figures in italics denote references in footnotes

Addison, Joseph, 70
Alberts, Wilhelm, 163
Ampère, André-Marie, *41*
Ampère, Jean-Jacques, *41*
Apollinaire, Henri, 262
Archer, W. G., *185, 187*
Aristotle, 18, 25
Arnold, Armin, *207*
Arnold, Matthew, 70
Arp, Hans, 184, 187, 200, 203, 217
Artaud, Antonin, 184
Aurich, Ursula, *36*
Austen, Jane, *168*
Austin, William W., *190*

Baader, F. von, 160
Ball, Hugo, 184, *186, 187*, 193, *194, 195*, 198, 199, 205–23
Ball-Hennings, Emmy, *214, 220, 222*
Balzac, Honoré de, *186*, 262
Bartók, Béla, 190
St. Basil, 61, 62
Baudelaire, Charles, 262
Bauer, Felice, 253
Bauer, M., *192, 195*
Baumart, Reinhard, 11
Baumgart, Reinhard, *159*
Baumgarth, Christa, *207*
Bäumler, Alfred, 179
Bayer, Konrad, 12
Becker, Jürgen, 12, 13, 271, 272
Beckett, Samuel, 260, 266, 267, 268, 269, 272
Beissner, Friedrich, *225, 238*
Benn, Gottfried, 184, *196*
Bennett, Lerone, *186*
Béranger, Pierre-Jean de, 30
Bergel, Lienhard, *232, 233, 235, 237, 242*
Bergson, Henri, 2
Bergsten, Gunilla, *169*
Bernard of Clairvaux, 211
Bertram, Ernst, *162*, 173, 174
Beutler, Ernst, *36*
Bieber, H., 3
Biedermann, Woldemar Freiherr von, *36, 51*, 175
Bielschowsky, A., 169, 170

Biermann, B., *166*
Binder, Hartmut, 229
Binder, Wolfgang, *92*
Blankenburg, 24
Boccaccio, Giovanni, 212
Böckmann, Paul, 3, 7, 8, *79*
Bode, Wilhelm, 170, 171
Böhme, Jakob, 160
Borchardt, H. H., *129*
Borges, Luis, 260, 268, 269, 270, 271
Brecht, Bertolt, 74, 158, 159, 184
Breton, André, 207, 262
Breuer, Robert, *192*
Brinkmann, R., *199*
Broch, Hermann, 185, 195, 265, 266
Brod, Max, *241*, 247, 251, 252, 254
Browning, Robert, 70
Brüggemann, Fritz, *16*
Brunswick-Wolfenbüttel, Duke of, 17
Büchner, Georg, 74, 183
Burckhardt, Jakob, 1
Burdach, Konrad, 64
Burluik, David, 189
Burney, Fanny, 46, 48
Burton, Sir Richard, 142
Butzmann, H., *21*

Calderón, Pedro, 22
Carlyle, Thomas, 70
Cassian, John, 56–65
Cassirer, Ernst, 168
Cézanne, Paul, 188, *195*
Chadwick, W. O., *56*
Chen, Chuan, *35, 36, 46*
Chlovski, Victor Boris, *201*
St. Chrysostom, *63*
Claudel, Paul, 262
Cleaver, Eldridge, *202*
Coleridge, Samuel Taylor, 70, 73
Corneille, Pierre, 16, 17, 18, 69

Dante Alighieri, 72, 74, 76
Degas, Edgar, 175
Delaunay, 188
Delius, Frederick, 190
Demetz, Peter, 23
Demosthenes, 149

Derain, André, 185
Dickens, Charles, 262
Diderot, Denis, 24, 25
Dilthey, W., 129
Döblin, Alfred, 264, 265
Dostoevsky, F. M., 262
Dryden, John, 72
Dubuffet, Jean, 192
Duncan, Isadora, 188
Dymant, Dora, *241*

Ebert, J. A., 15
Eckermann, Johann Peter, 29, 30, 32, 34, 35, 40, 46, 51, 52, 69, *102*
Ehrenstein, Albert, 264
Eichner, Hans, 180
Einstein, Carl, 192, 193, 194
El Greco, 187
Eliot, George, 70
Eliot, T. S., 67–78, 171, 177, *221*
Emrich, Wilhelm, 227, *234*, *239*, 241, 242
Enders, C., *23*
Engel, J. J., 24
Ephraim, Jan, 191, *199*

Faesi, Robert, 181
Faulkner, William, 264
Feuerbach, Ludwig, 130
Fielding, Henry, 46, 48
Flaubert, Gustave, 262, 270
Forster, E. M., 71
Förster-Nietzsche, E., *147*
Franke, Otto, *36*
Fraser, J. T., *9*
Freedman, Ralph, *224*, *232*, 236, *237*
Friedrich, W.-H., 6
Frobenius, Leo, *193*
Freud, Sigmund, 116, *117*, 118, 119, 120, 121, 124, 127, 192, 195
Furst, Lilian R., *169*

Garrick, David, 261
Gast, Peter, 147
Gauguin, Paul, 184, 186, 187, 188, *189*, *191*
Gebler, J. C., 24
George, Stefan, 71, 251, 262
Gerstenberg, H. W. von, 19
Gibson, Edgar C. S., *56*
Gide, André, 73, 262, 263
Gleim, J. W. L., 22
Glöckner, Ernst, 162

Goethe, Johann Wolfgang, 29–53, 54–66, 67–78, 90, 94, 96, 98, 102, 103, 113, 129, 130, 131, 140, 145, 147, 148, 150, 156, 161, 162, 166, 167, 168, 169, 170, 171, 172, 174, 175, 176, 178, 179, 199, 209, 216, 223, 243, 244, 245, 246
Gogol, Nikolay, 262
Goldwater, Robert J., *185*, *187*, *191*, *192*, *194*
Gottlieb von Murr, Christoph, 36
Gottsched, Johann Christoph, 14, 18, 19, 20
Grillparzer, Franz, 7
Grimm, Jacob, 4, 41
Grimm, Wilhelm, 41
Grosz, Georg, 192
Grünewald, Matthias, 187

Hamburger, Käte, *161*, *181*
Hamm, P., *9*
Hatvani, Paul, *197*
Hebbel, Friedrich, 140
Hein, W., *185*
Heine, Heinrich, 69, 157
Heissenbüttel, H., 271
Heitner, R. R., 16
Heller, Erich, 163, 164
Herder, J. G., 1, 70, 113
Hering, Christoph, 150
Herrenschmidt, J. D., *65*
Heselhaus, Clemens, *80*, *82*, *87*, *91*, *95*, *130*
Hesse, Hermann, 263
Hettner, H., *9*
Heym, Georg, *186*, *192*, 195, *196*, 215, 262
Hitler, Adolf, 178, 179
Hindenburg, Paul von, 178
Hoddis, Jakob van, *196*, 197, 198, 215
Hoerle, Heinrich, *196*
Hofer, W., *2*
Hoffmann, August, 194
Hoffmann, E. T. A., 262
Hofmann, Ludwig von, 167
Hofmannsthal, Hugo von, *175*, 195, 262, 268
Hölderlin, Friedrich, 69, 73
Homer, 152
Howard, Richard C., 29
Hübscher, Arthur, *164*
Huelsenbeck, Richard, *193*, 204, 205, 211, 214, 217

Index

Hugo, Victor, 52
Hulme, T. E., 71
Hume, David, 68, 168
Huyghe, René, *192*

Iffland, A. W., 102

Jacob, Max, 165
Jahnn, Hans Henny, 184
James, Henry, 168, 262, 267
Janko, 214
Jarry, Alfred, 184
Jean Paul, 52, 262
Jenisch, Erich, *36*
Johnson, Samuel, 20
Joyce, James, 71, 169, 260, 266, 269
Jung, C. G., 192

Kafka, Franz, 74, 122, 184, 185, 186, 192, 224–46, 247–59, 272
Kahler, Erich, 202
Kahnweiler, Henri, 185
Kandinsky, W., 183, 184, 187, 188, 190, 191, 193, 195, 197
Kaufmann, Fritz, 159, 160
Kayser, W., *5*
Keats, John, 69, 72
Keller, Gottfried, 129–45, 157
Kerényi, Karl, 137, 172, *180*
Khlebnikov, V. V., 184, 201
Killy, W., *6*
Kirchner, Ernst Ludwig, 187
Klee, Paul, 184, 192, 193, *195*, *197*, 202
Kleist, Heinrich von, 71, 74, 145, 161, 162
Klinger, F. M., 146–57
Klussmann, P. G., *120*
Kohlschmidt, W., *7*
Kokoschka, Oscar, 184, 215
Kommerell, Max, 71, *81*
Korff, Hermann August, 7, 90
Körner, C. G., 103
Kruchenykh, A. E., 184, 201
Krueger, J., *21*
Kulbin, N., 190

La Bruyère, Jean de, 67
Lämmert, Eberhardt, *4*, 5, *163*
Lankheit, Klaus, *189*
La Rochefoucauld, François de, 67, 148, 150, 155
Lasker-Schüler, Else, 196
Lawrence, D. H., 71, 185

St. Lawrence, *220*
Leavis, F. R., 168
Lecain, Mme, *186*
Lehnert, Herbert, *159*, *166*
Leibniz, G. W., 161
Leroux, R., *107*
Le Sage, A. R., 48
Lessing, G. E., 14–28, 70, 171, 182
Lessing, K., *27*
Levin, Harry, *168*
Levinstein, Siegfried, *192*
Lévy-Bruhl, Lucien, *191*
Lewes, George Henry, 70
Lichtenberg, G. C., 148, 150
Lichtenstein, Alfred, 197, 198, 215
Lillo, George, 16, 70
Livshits, Benedict, 201
Longyear, R., 102
Loti, Pierre, *185*
Lucretius, 72
Ludwig, Emil, 174
Luther, Martin, 159, 238

Macke, August, 189, 190
Mahler, Gustav, 167, 190
Maier, R. N., *188*, 194, 200
Mainland, W. F., 99, 100, *104*, 106
Malevich, C., 194
Mallarmé, Stéphane, 262, 269
Malraux, André, 190
Mann, Heinrich, *158*
Mann, Katja, *166*
Mann, Michael, *167*
Mann, Otto, *17*
Mann, Thomas, 24, 74, 153, 158–81, 183, 184, 185, 260, 263, 264, 266, 267, 272
Marc, Franz, *188*, 189, 190, 215
Marcuse, Herbert, 10, 202
Marinetti, F. T., *189*, 199, 207
Markov, V., *189*, *201*
Martens, Wolfgang, 20
Martini, Fritz, 100
Matisse, Henri, 185, 188
May, Kurt, *81*, *82*, *85*, *87*, *89*, *91*, *92*, 95
Meinecke, Friedrich, 2
Meinhof, Carl, *193*, *199*
Meissinger, K. A., *170*
Melville, R., *185*, *187*
Mendelssohn, Moses, 21, 23, 24, 27
Merezhkovsky, D. S., *160*, *169*
Meyer, Herman, 7, *172*
Meyer-Benfey, H., *24*

Index

Michelsen, P., 21
Middleton, J. C., 215
Miller, Henry, 264
Milton, John, 70
Minder, Robert, 8
Molière, 47
Molnard, Ida and William, 186
Montaigne, Michel de, 146, 148, 150
Moore, W. G., 99
Morgenstern, Christian, 184, 192, 195
Mörike, Eduard, 7, 8, 69
Muir, Edwin and Willa, 74
Müller-Seidel, W., 6
Munch, Edvard, 186
Muschg, Walter, 99, *100*
Musil, Robert, 185, 260, 263

Nabokov, Vladimir, 260, 268, 269, 270, 271
Nevinson, C. R. W., 189
Nicholls, R. A., *159*
Nicolai, Friedrich, 17, 20, 21, 24, 25
Nietzsche, Friedrich, 1, 70, 146–57, *160*, *161*, 164, *165*, 172–9, *180*, 183, *188*, 197, 216
Nisbet, R. A., *3*
Nolde, Emil, *191*
Northrop Frye, *167*
Novalis, 114, 121, 126, *180*, 262
Noverre, Jean Georges, 261

Oehlke, W., *23*
Ossian, 70
Ozenfant, A., *194*

Pascal, Blaise, 148
Pasley, J. M. S., *246*, 247, 248, 250
Paulsen, Wolfgang, *94*
Pechstein, Max, *191*
Percy, Bishop, 41, 42
Petsch, R., 20
Pfeil, J. G., 21
Picasso, Pablo, 185, *195*, *196*, 198
Pikulik, Lothar, 19
Pniower, Otto, *170*
Polanyi, Michael, 200
Politzer, Heinz, 224, 226, 231, 232, 233, 234, 237, 239, 253
Ponge, Francis, 272
Pörtner, P., 183
Pound, Ezra, 71, 260
Preisendanz, W., 131
Proust, Marcel, 73, 262, 272

Przybyszewski, Stanislaw, 186

Raabe, Paul, *196*
Rabelais, François, *172*
Racine, Jean, 69
Ranke, Leopold von, 2
Rasch, Wolfdietrich, *145*, *158*, *167*
Reinhardt, Max,
Rempel, Hans, *25*, 26
Rémusat, Abel, *41*, 42, 46, 48, 49, 50, 51, 52, 53
Richter, Helmut, *242*
Richardson, Samuel, 29, 32, 35, 41, 48, 70
Riemer, F. W., 169, 171
Riesmann, D., *3*
Rilke, R. M., 1, 73, 184, 185, *191*, 262, 263, 268
Rilla, Paul, 26
Rimbaud, Arthur, 200
Rödder, Edwin, 109, *110*
Rosenberg, Harold, 183
Rossolo, Luigi, 191
Röthel, H. K., *187*
Rotonchamp, J. de, *189*
Rousseau, Henri, 183, *185*, *186*, 188, 189, 191, *195*, 197
Rousseau, Jean-Jacques, 147, 261
Rubiner, Ludwig, 211
Rychner, Max, 180

Sandberg, Hans-Joachim, *169*, *174*
Sarraute, Nathalie, 272
Sartre, Jean-Paul, 169
Saueressig, Heinz, *167*
Saurin, J. B., 27
Scharfschwerdt, Jürgen, *162*
Scheler, Max, 160
Schelling, F. W. J., 160, 161
Scherrer, Paul, *163*
Schiller, Friedrich, 40, 52, 71, 79–98, 99–112, 131, 143, 144, 145, 148, 160, 161, 169, 170, 173, 247
Schmidt, Arno, 272
Schmidt, Erich, *16*
Schmidtgen, A., *109*
Schopenhauer, Arthur, 148, 150, 151, 156, 163, 164, 165
Schreyer, Lothar, *193*
Schubert, Franz, 103
Schwab, Gustav, 216
Schwitters, Kurt, 196
Scott, Walter, 70

Index

Scriabin, A. N., 190
Seidlin, Oskar, *81*, 85, *86*, *88*, 90, 91, *92*
Seneca, 16, 17, 18
Sengle, Friedrich, *92*
Shakespeare, William, 14, 69, 70, 74, 76, 147
Shattuck, Roger, *186*, *189*, *207*
Shaw, Bernard, 70, 71
Shelley, P B., 67, 72
Silesius, Angelus, 160
Simmel, Georg, 1, 4
Singer, Herbert, *95*
Smollett, Tobias, 48
Sokel, Walter H., *229*, *232*, *235*, 237, *240*, 242
Sommer, Josef, *179*
Spaandonck, Marcel van, *199*
Sprinchorn, Evert, *186*
Stahl, Fritz, *193*
Staiger, Emil, 6, 7, 8, 15, *16*, *91*
Stein, Fritz von, 109
Steinke, G. E., 220
Stendhal, 262
Sterne, Laurence, 52, 260
Sternheim, Carl, 264
Stifter, Adalbert, 148, 162
Stolpe, Sven, *185*
Stramm, August, 193, 194
Strauss, D. F., 155, 156
Strauss, Richard, 263
Stravinsky, Igor, 190, 191, 263
Strich, Fritz, 6, *36*
Strindberg, August, 186, *187*

Thalmann, Marianne, 114, 124, 128
Theocritus, 183
Thiers, Adolphe, 177
Thoms, Peter Perring, 30, 31, 51
Tieck, Ludwig, 113–28
Tolstoy, L. N., 262, 267
Tönnies, F., 3, 4
Trakl, Georg, 195, 197, 215, 262
Troeltsch, Ernst, 6
Trunz, Erich, 63
Tzara, Tristan, 211, 215

Uhde, Wilhelm, 189
Unger, J. F., 40, 41
Urdizil, Johannes, 170

Valéry, Paul, 73, 262
Van Doesburg, *194*
Van Gogh, 187, 188, *195*
Vauvenargues, 67
Virgil, 85
Vlaminck, Maurice, 185
Voltaire, 25, 52, 69, 146, 152
Vortriede, Werner, 121
Voss, J. H., 26, 27
Vulpius, Wolfgang, *36*

Waddell, Helen, *62*
Wagenbach, K., *247*
Wagner, Richard, 70, 148, 151, 152, 156, 157, 165, 180
Walden, Herwarth, 183, *192*
Walden, Nell, *193*
Walter, Jürgen, 197
Walzel, Oskar, 7
Weber, Max, 12
Weigand, Paul, 161
Weisse, C. F., 19
Wenzel, Siegfried, *55*, *59*, *61*
White, Eric Walter, *190*
Wiener, Oswald, 271, 272
Wierlacher, Alois, *25*
Wiese, Benno von, 7, 8, *80*, *85*, *86*, *91*, *97*, 101
Wilde, Oscar, 70
Wilhelm, Richard, *36*
Wilkinson, E. M., *65*, *169*
Wilkinson, James, 41
Wingert, Paul S., *190*
Wirtz, E., *166*
Wittkowski, Wolfgang, 84, *91*
Wolf, Kurt, 248
Wolzogen, Ernst von, 100
Woolf, Virginia, 71, 263
Wordsworth, William, 67, 69, 73
Worringer, Wilhelm, 191, 192, 193, 195
Wyndham Lewis, D. B., 71
Wysling, Hans, *169*, *174*, *175*, *180*

Yeats, W. B., 204
Young, Edward, 70

Zedler, J. H., 65
Zeller, B., *99*
Zervos, Christian, *185*
Zweig, Stefan, *169*, 178

PRINTED IN GREAT BRITAIN
AT THE UNIVERSITY PRESS, OXFORD
BY VIVIAN RIDLER
PRINTER TO THE UNIVERSITY

ABIGAIL E. WEEKS MEMORIAL LIBRARY
UNION COLLEGE
BARBOURVILLE, KENTUCKY

830.9
D611 Discontinuous tradition

FEB 2

FA 343

830.9
D611

Discontinuous tradition